Praise for **Giordano Bruno: Philo**

"A loving and thoughtful accoun
satires and sonnets, dialogues and lesson plans, vagabond days
and star-spangled nights. . . . Ingrid D. Rowland has her reasons
for preferring Bruno to Copernicus, Tycho Brahe, Johannes Kepler,
even Galileo and Leonardo, and they're good ones."

JOHN LEONARD, *Harper's*

"In *Giordano Bruno*, the classicist Ingrid Rowland offers a series of
brilliant vignettes tracing this peripatetic figure from his birth-
place outside Naples, to the Dominican convent in Naples itself
where he studied for the priesthood . . . to Geneva, Toulouse, Paris,
Oxford, London, Wittenberg, Prague, Frankfurt, Zurich and—finally and dangerously—Venice and Rome."

OWEN GINGERICH, *Wall Street Journal*

"*Giordano Bruno: Philosopher/Heretic* gives some support to the view
of Bruno as a visionary of and martyr to science, but Rowland . . .
knows too much about him and his times to accept that simple
picture. Rather, she tells the story of a bright, thin-skinned, rebellious and inquisitive young man from outside Naples who became
a precocious Dominican priest, had some original thoughts, wrote
some interesting treatises and long poems, and pretty quickly got
in trouble with the authorities."

MARC KAUFMAN, *Washington Post Book World*

"In her provocative biography, . . . a marvelous feat of scholarship, Ingrid D. Rowland brings before us today the pieces of an
extraordinary sixteenth-century life. . . . Rowland is a sure-footed
guide on a ground with few tracks. This is intellectual biography
at its best."

PETER N. MILLER, *New Republic*

"Ingrid Rowland's *Giordano Bruno: Philosopher/Heretic* is an excellent starting point for anyone who wants to rediscover the historical figure concealed beneath the cowl on Campo de' Fiori. Her lively and learned biography removes Bruno from myth and polemic, where he has so often resided, and restores him to the time and place that inspired his dual passion for knowledge as well as faith."   PAULA FINDLEN, *Nation*

"Giordano Bruno may justly be described as a maverick. Burned at the stake in Rome on Ash Wednesday in 1600, he seems to have been an unclassifiable mixture of foul-mouthed Neapolitan mountebank, loquacious poet, religious reformer, scholastic philosopher and slightly wacky astronomer."

ANTHONY GOTTLIEB, *New York Times Book Review*

"[Rowland] is . . . a powerful writer, imaginative, resourceful, and eloquent. . . . She helps us see just why this slight, grumpy Neapolitan has posed such problems to everyone who has tried to understand what he believed, what he hoped to fight for, and why he returned, at the peril of his life, to the Italy of the Counter-Reformation. . . .

"Rowland tells this great story in moving, vivid prose, concentrating as much on Bruno's thought as on his life. . . . His restless mind, as she makes clear, not only explored but transformed the heavens."

ANTHONY GRAFTON, *New York Review of Books*

"Whatever else Bruno was, he was wild-minded and extreme, and Rowland communicates this, together with a sense of the excitement that his ideas gave him. . . . It's that feeling for the explosiveness of the period, and [Rowland's] admiration of Bruno for participating in it—indeed, dying for it—that is the central and most cherishable quality of the biography."

JOAN ACOCELLA, *New Yorker*

Giordano Bruno

ALSO BY INGRID D. ROWLAND

The Culture of the High Renaissance
The Scarith of Scornello: A Tale of Renaissance Forgery

Giordano Bruno

PHILOSOPHER/HERETIC

INGRID D. ROWLAND

THE UNIVERSITY OF CHICAGO PRESS

CHICAGO & LONDON

The University of Chicago Press, Chicago 60637
© 2008 by Ingrid D. Rowland
All rights reserved.
Published by arrangement with Farrar, Straus and Giroux, LLC.
Originally published in 2008 by Farrar, Straus and Giroux
University of Chicago Press edition, 2009

Printed in the United States of America

18 17 16 15 14 13 12 11 10 09   1 2 3 4 5

ISBN-13: 978-0-226-73024-0 (paper)
ISBN-10: 0-226-73024-7 (paper)

Library of Congress Cataloging-in-Publication Data

Rowland, Ingrid D. (Ingrid Drake)
Giordano Bruno : philosopher/heretic / Ingrid D. Rowland.
p. cm.
Originally published in 2008 by Farrar, Straus and Giroux.
Includes bibliographical references and index.
ISBN-13: 978-0-226-73024-0 (pbk. : alk. paper)
ISBN-10: 0-226-73024-7 (pbk. : alk. paper) 1. Bruno, Giordano,
1548–1600. 2. Philosophers—Italy—Biography. I. Title.
B783.Z7R595 2009
195—dc22
[B]

2009003360

To Professoressa Hilary Gatti and

Avvocato Dario Guidi Federzoni

Contents

A Note on Translation *ix*

Prologue: The Hooded Friar 3
1. **A Most Solemn Act of Justice** 9
2. **The Nolan Philosopher** 14
3. **"Napoli è tutto il mondo"** 19
4. **"The world is fine as it is"** 25
5. **"I have, in effect, harbored doubts"** 29
6. **"I came into this world to light a fire"** 38
7. **Footprints in the Forest** 45
8. **A Thousand Worlds** 53
9. **Art and Astronomy** 62
10. **Trouble Again** 70
11. **Holy Asininity** 77
12. **The Signs of the Times** 87
13. **A Lonely Sparrow** 96
14. **Thirty** 104
15. **The Gifts of the Magi** 116
16. **The Song of Circe** 132
17. **"Go up to Oxford"** 139
18. **Down Risky Streets** 149
19. **The Art of Magic** 160
20. **Canticles** 173

21. *Squaring the Circle* 188
22. *Consolation and Valediction* 199
23. *Infinities* 214
24. *Return to Italy* 223
25. *The Witness* 244
26. *The Adversary* 251
27. *Gethsemane* 263
28. *Hell's Purgatory* 267
29. *The Sentence* 272
30. *The Field of Flowers* 278
    Epilogue: The Four Rivers 279

    Appendix: Bruno's Sentence 287
    Notes 291
    Bibliography 307
    Acknowledgments 317
    Index 319

A Note on Translation

The translations are all my own. I have rendered vernacular verse in equivalent English iambics, matching Bruno's rhyme scheme wherever possible and also matching his short lines. Latin hexameters are rendered in a rough English equivalent (as in "The Charge of the Light Brigade") that bases meter on stress accent rather than vowel quantity.

Giordano Bruno

Prologue: The Hooded Friar

February 17 marks a peculiarly Roman holiday whose ritual centers on the bronze statue of a hooded friar. Just over life size, clutching a book in manacled hands, he glowers over the marketplace of Campo de' Fiori, the "Field of Flowers" that was also, for many years, one of the city's execution grounds. The statue was meant to point in the opposite direction, facing the sun, but a last-minute decision by the City Council of Rome in 1889 turned it around to face the Vatican, which had complained that the original placement was disrespectful. Because of this change in position, the friar's face is always shadowed, so that he looks more melancholy than defiant. But then, he is a man condemned to die by burning at the stake; he has every reason to be melancholy.

For at least five hundred years, Roman statues have been champions of free speech; three blocks from the Campo de' Fiori, an ancient marble wreck of two torsos and a noseless head named Mastro Pasquino has been papered with acid comments on Roman life ever since the first years of the sixteenth century. From satires of the Borgia pope, Alexander VI, he has moved on to hurling invectives against the current prime minister, and for many years a spray-painted feminist graffito on his base proclaimed him Pasquina.

Down the street in the other direction, a togaed ancient Roman called Abbot Luigi (Abate Luigi) has been talking nearly as long as Pasquino; the removal of his grizzled old head by a thief in the

1970s failed to stop his chatter, and he has long since been recapitated with the portrait of some other stern old senator, one no less pleased to speak his mind without inhibition to latter-day Romans. The friar in the Campo de' Fiori makes a worthy companion to this vocal pair, and to their more distant colleagues Madama Lucrezia and Marforio, both of whom, sadly, have been dumbstruck by modern life: Madama Lucrezia may have begun as the cult image of Isis in ancient Rome's most elaborate Egyptian temple, but she now lords it over a bus stop in Piazza Venezia, while handsome Marforio, a strapping Roman river god, is shut up in the Capitoline Museum, where no one can reach him any longer to give him a paper voice. Instead, Giordano Bruno, the friar of Campo de' Fiori, must now speak for them both. And he does, in letters of bronze on his granite pedestal: "To Bruno, from the generation he foresaw, here, where the pyre burned."

That generation, the first student generation of the newly created Italian state, commissioned the statue in the 1880s from the sculptor Ettore Ferrari, supported by an international subscription campaign. Italy's formation had hinged on seizing political control of Rome and its territories from the governmental dominion of the papacy, and hence the monument to Bruno thumbed its nose at the pope with spectacular impudence by paying tribute to one of the Inquisition's most illustrious victims—and reminded the Vatican just why this new Italy had chosen so eagerly to become a secular state.

The Roman students chose Bruno as their patron martyr not only for his bravery but also for his ideas; more boldly than anyone in his age, including Kepler and Galileo, he had declared that the universe was made of atoms and that it was infinite in size. His violent, public death for those convictions showed the Catholic Church in its most cruelly repressive light, for Bruno had not been a political man, nor had he committed any crime except to speak his mind. For the students of a new Italy and a newly independent Rome, the statue was meant to prove that ideas can and must prevail over the attempt to stifle them.

To this day, then, on the morning of February 17, a contingent from City Hall places a wreath at the bronze Bruno's feet, its laurel leaves draped in red and gold ribbons, the initials "SPQR" embossed in gold letters. By laying a wreath at Bruno's feet, the mayor of Rome continues to assert the modern city's independence from a temporal Church. The process usually displaces an early drinker or two, and as floral offerings pile up around the wreath, together with poems, candles, and invectives, they stay displaced. Late in the afternoon, when the market stalls have been taken down and squirreled away in side streets, the Italian Association of Free Thinkers sets up a microphone at Bruno's feet; meanwhile, the atheists and the pantheists, carefully separated from each other, lay out their tables of books and leaflets on opposite sides of the piazza. In between them, the Free Thinkers guard their microphone jealously, wresting it in turn from the man in the sandwich board who claims to be Giordano Bruno incarnate, from the tipplers who use the statue's base as a convenient perch, from the students, artists, and enthusiasts who think—wrongly, as it turns out—that free thought implies free speech. This microphone is only for organizations, the Free Thinkers declare to all their competitors for the space beneath Giordano's lowering gaze: the Masons, the atheists, and the pantheists, all of whom claim the hooded friar as their very own spiritual leader. Brooding and silent above the fray, steadfast above the dispute between the believers in no god and the believers in all gods, the bronze Giordano Bruno glares at the distant Vatican, which put the real Giordano Bruno to death here in the Campo de' Fiori on February 17, 1600, for obstinate and pertinacious heresy.

By evening, Ettore Ferrari's statue will be covered with offerings, as if Giordano Bruno were a miracle-working saint rather than a condemned heretic.

Since the statue's dedication, Bruno's reputation has undergone several new transformations. If late-nineteenth-century Italians saw him as an apostle of modern science, a pair of mid-twentieth-century scholars at the Warburg Institute in London, Frances Yates and D. P. Walker, recast him as a religious reformer, a mystic, and a practitioner of magic; Giovanni Aquilecchia, their younger contemporary in London, waited years to see Bruno the magician give way to more general acceptance of his own view of Bruno as a philosopher. However diverse their portraits of Bruno, Yates and Aquilecchia were both remarkable writers and teachers who drew a surprisingly wide range of new readers to the Italian heretic. In the mid-1980s, Bruno was still regarded as a marginal figure, and only a handful of books had been dedicated to him since the great burst of interest in the late nineteenth century; a decade later, Giordano had acquired his own periodical, *Bruniana & Campanelliana*, several institutions (including a convent of Dominican nuns in Utrecht) bearing his name, and a remarkable degree of public interest that culminated in widespread commemorations of the four hundredth anniversary of his death—which coincided, by a four-hundred-year-old design, with the great jubilee proclaimed for the Catholic Church by Pope John Paul II. (Bruno's burning had been deliberately set by Pope Clement VIII for the jubilee of 1600.) In recent years, the people who leave flowers on the statue in Campo de' Fiori (and not only on February 17) come from around the world. Their interests in Bruno range as widely as his own writings, from pragmatic observation to rapturous mysticism, from appreciation of his complex prose to uncomplicated admiration for his courage in the defense of free thought.

Ferrari's heroic, imposing Bruno is anything but realistic: Bruno had not worn a Dominican habit for twenty-four years when he was marched off to the stake; indeed, as a final indignity, he was stripped naked before he burned. There are no surviving portraits of the gaunt little man who by that time had spent eight years in inquisitorial prison, only a report of his fierce expression; Ferrari's robust image reflects the man's spirit, not his body. And its placement obeys the laws of urban design rather than historical accuracy: Bruno died in the southwest corner of the piazza, toward Piazza Farnese, not its center, despite the statue's declaration "Here, where the pyre burned." Somber as it is, Ferrari's hooded friar has succeeded so well because he captures the sheer challenge that Bruno posed for his times, a challenge that has lost none of its power since 1600, or 1889. The devout Galileo has been rehabilitated by the church that condemned him to silence in 1633; his offending *Dialogue Concerning the Two Chief World Systems* was reprinted with papal approval as early as 1712, and he was officially pardoned by Pope John Paul II in 1983. But as the anniversary of Bruno's death loomed over the Roman jubilee year of 2000, John Paul declared, through two cardinals, Angelo Sodano and Paul Poupard, that Bruno had deviated too far from Christian doctrine to be granted Christian pardon. The inquisitors who put the philosopher to his gruesome death, the cardinals added, should be judged in the light of their gruesome times. As Sodano noted, in what was obviously a carefully worded document: "It is not our place to express judgments about the conscience of those who were involved in this matter. Objectively, nonetheless, certain aspects of these procedures and in particular their violent result at the hand of civil authority, in this and analogous cases, cannot but constitute a cause for profound regret on the part of the Church."

As a child of those same gruesome times, Giordano Bruno asserted that in the end even the devils would be pardoned and that religious strife, with its human claim to see through God's eyes, was the most misguided strife of all. Despite the optimism of the Roman students who erected his monument in Campo de' Fiori, in many respects the generation he foresaw still belongs to the future.

Bruno poses no less formidable a challenge to historians of science. Working without instrumentation, posing thought problems that reflected both ancient and modern ideas about natural philosophy, he fits uncomfortably into any scheme that aims to trace scientific thought in a neat line from Copernicus through Galileo, Newton, Maxwell, and Einstein. He was, perhaps, more of a poet than an empirical observer. Yet his intellectual contradictions, his blind spots, and his insights serve as a reminder that scientific investigation has always depended on inspiration as well as investigation, on mistakes as well as triumphs.

Above all, Giordano Bruno defies any kind of summary judgment; his life, his ideas, and his personality are as complex as his times are distant from our own. He could be charming or infuriating, charismatic or repellent. For all his faults, however, he was brave and brilliant, and, as these pages aim to show, he was a splendid writer.

CHAPTER ONE

A Most Solemn Act of Justice

CAMPO DE' FIORI, ROME, FEBRUARY 17, 1600

> If you will not accompany [the Nolan] with fifty or a hundred torches—
> which shall certainly not be lacking should he come to die in Roman
> Catholic territory—at least give him one; or, if even this seems too
> much for you, press upon him a lantern with a tallow candle inside.
>   —*The Ash Wednesday Supper*, dialogue 5

For a public execution, it was a strangely rushed affair. In the feeble light of a winter dawn, the parade of officials, inquisitors, and priests could hardly be seen as it pulled away from the prison of Tor di Nona. Not many people were about to see it in any case; shops and market stalls were only beginning to set up for the day. Nothing blocked the procession's brisk progress down the Via Papale to Campo de' Fiori, the "Field of Flowers" that served Rome as both marketplace and execution ground.

As tradition demanded, a mule carried the prisoner. Tradition had its roots in practicality; by the time they had been sentenced to death, many of the condemned could no longer walk on their own. Some, indeed, were already dead, garroted before their bodies were ceremonially burned at the stake. But this prisoner, Giordano Bruno, was physically healthy, and when he reached the Campo de' Fiori, he would be burned alive. There was no other suitable punishment for the heresies he had continued to proclaim during his eight days in Tor di Nona, and for eight previous years in the prisons of the Inquisition. For more than a week, day and night, teams of confessors had tried to change his mind; Dominican, Augustinian, and Franciscan friars succeeded each other in shifts, begging him to save his soul by recanting—because for his body, as they knew, there was no longer any hope. That morning, however, the last team of religious had given up. They handed over their charge once and for all to the black-hooded lay brothers of the Confraternity of Saint John the Beheaded, volunteers who carried out one of their faith's seven works of mercy by providing last-minute companionship for prisoners condemned to death. After offering Bruno the traditional breakfast of almond biscuits dipped in dense brown Marsala wine, the brothers of Saint John prayed over him as the jailers stopped his tongue with a leather gag and set him on his mule. When the procession began to move down the Via Papale, they held high a painting of the crucifix, hoping to catch the gagged man's eye with their gold-framed image of the suffering Christ.

The records for that morning—February 17, 1600—report that Bruno "was led by officers of the law to Campo de' Fiori, and there, stripped naked and tied to a stake, he was burned alive, always accompanied by our company singing the litanies, and the comforters, up to the last, urging him to abandon his obstinacy, with which he finally ended his miserable and unhappy life."

The inquisitors who ordered this strangely ambivalent execution were afraid of what they were doing, and Bruno knew it. Eight days earlier, when they read him his verdict, an eyewitness reported that "he made no other reply than, in a menacing tone, 'You may be more afraid to bring that sentence against me than I am to accept it.'" Sixteen hundred was a jubilee year, when pilgrims from all over the Catholic world came to Rome to earn reprieves from purgatory by visiting seven churches on one day, but not every visitor came to collect the indulgence. Protestant troublemakers had already disrupted services several times this Holy Year, crying "Idolatry!" as the priest held up the Host for consecration, or murmuring and jostling among the congregation until completing the Mass became all but impossible. Bruno himself had spent years in

Protestant countries, almost always moving at the highest levels of society, among kings, ambassadors, dukes, and electors. No one knew what political connections he might still have or who might object to the sight of him burning alive. His execution had already been aborted once, as an agent for the Duke of Urbino had reported earlier in the week:

> Today we thought we would see a most solemn act of justice, and we don't know why it was stopped; it was a Dominican friar from Nola, a most obstinate heretic, whom they sentenced Wednesday in the house of Cardinal Madruzzi as the author of various terrible opinions which he obstinately continued to maintain, and is still maintaining them. Every day theologians visit him. They say that this friar was in Geneva two years, and then he went on to lecture at Toulouse, and afterward at Lyon, and from thence to England, where they say that his opinions were not at all well received. For that reason he went on to Nuremberg, and from there returning to Italy he was captured, and they say that in Germany he disputed with Cardinal Bellarmine on several occasions, and all told, if God doesn't help the wretch, he wants to die obstinate and be burned alive.

The agent's factual information, like most Roman gossip, was not quite correct (Bruno had never met Cardinal Bellarmine in Germany), but he grasped the essentials of the case and the inquisitors' fears: Bruno's ideas terrified them as much as his possible political clout, and they were desperate to find an alternative to public immolation. It was a violent age, and the reigning pope, Clement VIII, had approved some horrific executions in the recent past, like the burning of a Scottish heretic in 1595, dutifully reported to the Duke of Urbino by the same agent who would report on Bruno:

> The execution was carried out in Campo de' Fiori, where to terrify him a huge pile of firewood, charcoal, kindling, and more than ten cartloads of pitch had been prepared, and for the occasion a shirt of pitch was made for him that extended from his waist to his feet, black as coal, and then it was put over his naked flesh so that he would not die as quickly, and his life would be consumed in the fire as painfully as possible. He was con-

ducted to the scaffold with a large escort, and made to sit on an iron chair
next to the fire, which had already been lit. The usual protest was made
on his behalf, as one does for good servants of God, in order to see him
repent: that there was still time to obtain grace, but, as soon as he had
mounted the iron chair, he threw himself with a great hurry into the
burning flames, and buried in them, he died in these earthly flames to
spend an eternity in those other flames of hell.

Giordano Bruno's execution, by contrast, would be quick and
quiet, a pageant to be forgotten. There must have been some fear
that the show would be seen as barbaric, if one of its witnesses, the
Catholic convert Gaspar Schoppe, could rush home to reassure the
Lutheran Conrad Rittershausen, his onetime mentor, that it had all
been perfectly civil:

> This very day prompts me to write, in which Giordano Bruno, because of
> his heresy, was publicly burned in Campo de' Fiori before the Theater of
> Pompey . . . If you were in Rome now, you would hear from many Italians
> that a Lutheran had been burned, and thus you would find no small con-
> firmation for your opinion of our savagery.

The ten cardinals who made up the Roman Inquisition lacked
Schoppe's certainty about what they were doing. Bruno's execution
gave public proof that they had failed in their mission, which was
not to terrify but to "admonish and persuade." The guiding spirit of
the Inquisition's endgame, Cardinal Robert Bellarmine, may have
enjoyed an earthly reputation as the greatest living theologian, but
he had not been able to wield Mother Church's theology with
enough skill to persuade Bruno—himself a trained inquisitor—to
change his mind. Neither could Bellarmine claim to have carried
out the basic mission of his own order, the Society of Jesus, to
"comfort souls." Instead, the cruelties to which the cardinal (and
future saint) had subjected his victims, Bruno included, would
haunt him to the grave. So, perhaps, would the narrowness of his
own Christian vision; Bellarmine, no less than Bruno, had been
fascinated as a young man by the stars and the new astronomy, but
he could not imagine those stars, as Bruno did, set within a heaven

of infinite vastness, governed by a God who, as Bruno insisted, would one day pardon every creature. Yet somehow the heretic's ideas moved the inquisitor, so that when Galileo Galilei began to interest the Inquisition in 1616, Bellarmine used all his authority to warn Galileo away from the conflict.

Even today, Bruno's death still haunts the Catholic Church, which has long since accepted his infinite universe but not his challenge to its own authority. It is not only a matter of Bruno's own conduct and John Paul II's refusal to condone it in the year 2000. To make matters still more complicated, Bruno's inquisitor Cardinal Bellarmine was canonized in 1930; how could an inquiry have gone wrong if guided by a saint? Yet as Robert Bellarmine sensed himself, by proceeding against Giordano Bruno with scrupulous correctness, the Inquisition had made him a martyr.

A martyr to what? That was, and is, the question.

The Nolan Philosopher

NOLA, KINGDOM OF NAPLES, 1548–1562

Bruno never made any secret of his profession; from beginning to end, with unfailing consistency, he called himself a philosopher. Sometimes, more specifically, he described himself as *il Nolano*, "the Nolan," and his philosophy as "the Nolan philosophy," after the small city east of Naples where he spent the first fourteen years of his life.

Bruno's home in fact lay outside the city walls of Nola, in a minuscule settlement beneath the hill that he and his neighbors, with affectionate exaggeration, called Monte Cicala—"Cicada Mountain"—perhaps because its wooded slopes buzzed with the whirr of these insects in the summertime. The hamlet is gone now, although present-day *Nolani* will point out a ruined farmhouse where they boast that Giovanni Bruno and his wife, Fraulissa Savolino, once lived among other members of her family, a clan given to extravagant names: Preziosa, Mercurio, Morgana, Laudomia. Oddest of all was the name Fraulissa; Nola's census takers usually recorded her as "Flaulisa," the only one of her kind.

Giovanni Bruno earned his living as a soldier serving the Spanish crown, for the Kingdom of Naples, since 1503, had been a possession of Spain, ruled by a series of viceroys. Both the Spanish lords and the local nobility competed to exploit the region's agricultural riches, with the help of mercenary soldiers who fought for Spain or the local "barons," or, most often, subdued rebellious peasants (it was to protect against these constant pressures that Spanish-dominated Sicily developed its Mafia and Naples its Camorra). In addition to their salaries, these hired soldiers lived by what they could take from local populations; theirs was not a popular profession, but it paid relatively well. In addition, Giovanni Bruno's position in the military enabled him, if only barely, to claim status as a gentleman. This slight social advantage would prove crucial for his son's future.

When their only child was born in 1548, Giovanni Bruno and Fraulissa Savolino named the boy Filippo, perhaps to honor Bruno's commander in chief, His Most Catholic Majesty Philip II, king of Spain and Naples (Giordano was the younger Bruno's religious name, assumed when he was seventeen). Giovanni Bruno also provided the future Nolan philosopher with his first glimpse of philosophy, at least if we are to credit an anecdote reported by the mature Giordano Bruno in 1585. Here, in a philosophical dialogue, two personalities from Bruno's Nolan childhood, the poet Luigi Tansillo and the soldier Odoardo Cicala, discuss how to live wisely:

TANSILLO: When a certain neighbor of ours said one evening after dinner: "I was never as merry as I am tonight," Giovanni Bruno, the father of the Nolan, replied, "Then you were never as crazy as you are at this moment."

CICALA: Then you mean to say that a gloomy man is a wise man, and a gloomier man is wiser still?

TAN: No, in fact I think that the first one is crazy, and the other one is worse.

CIC: Who, then, would be wise, if the happy man is crazy and the gloomy one is crazy as well?

TAN: The one who is neither happy nor sad.

CIC: Who is that? The one who's asleep? The one who's unconscious? The one who's dead?

TAN: No, rather it's the one who is alive, who sees and understands, and who, taking good and evil into consideration, regards each of them as variable . . . Therefore he neither despairs nor puffs up his spirit, and becomes restrained in his inclinations and temperate in his pleasures—for him pleasure is no pleasure, because its goal is in the present. Likewise, pain for him is no pain, because by force of reasoning he is mindful of its end. Thus . . . I will declare that the wisest man of all is the one who is sometimes able to declare the opposite of what that man said: "I was never less merry than now," or "I was never less unhappy than now."

Bruno never quite managed his father's philosophical detach-ment. He would remember his youth as melancholy; physically small and mentally swift, with an absent father and a lonely mother, he seems to have spent his time, like many a misfit child, watching, reading, and thinking things over. Almost thirty years after he had left Nola forever, he wrote of Monte Cicala as if the mountain had been his confidante:

> Once, when I was a boy, dear hospitable Monte Cicala,
> And in your genial lap you fostered my early affections—
> How you were wreathed around in ivy and branches of olive,
> Branches of cornel and bay, of myrtle, and boughs of rosemary!
> You were girded in chestnut, and oak, poplar, elm, in a happy
> Coupling with grape-bearing vines; it was almost as if you extended
> Your leafy hand, full of grapes, to my tender hand.

Filippo Bruno was also precocious. When a snake crawled into his cradle, at least so he said, he called for help in complete sen-tences, the first words he ever spoke. A few years later, he could still recall the incident with a clarity that unnerved his parents. The story may have been a family anecdote, embellished over time, but the adult Bruno would become famous for his feats of memory. His first experience of school only gave him a lifelong contempt for schoolmasters. Like soldiers, grammar-school teachers clung to meager salaries and the slight social advantage that came with their education. Students traditionally lampooned them as dull, brutal, and raging with lust, but Bruno gave the caricature a bitter insistence that suggests genuine experience.

Before he left Nola at fourteen, he seems to have fallen in love with one of his Savolino cousins—perhaps this was one of the "early affections" he mentioned in verse. He also nurtured an abid-ing passion for his native city and its little mountain. In 1585, twenty-three years after he had left Nola, he described it as if he were still there:

MERCURY: [Jove has] ordered that today at noon two of the melons in Father Franzino's melon patch will be perfectly ripe, but that they won't be picked until three days from now, when they will no longer be considered good to eat. He requests that at the same moment, on the jujube tree at the base of Monte Cicala in the house of Giovanni Bruno, thirty perfect jujubes will be picked, and he says that seven shall fall to earth still green, and that fifteen shall be eaten by worms. That Vasta, wife of Albenzio Savolino, when she means to curl the hair at her temples, shall burn fifty-seven hairs for having let the curling iron get too hot, but she won't burn her scalp and hence shall not swear when she smells the stench, but shall endure it patiently. That from the dung of her ox fifty-two dung beetles shall be born, of which fourteen shall be trampled and killed by Albenzio's foot, twenty-six shall die upside down, twenty-two shall live in a hole, eighty shall make a pilgrim's progress around the yard, forty-two shall retire to live under the stone by the door, sixteen shall roll their ball of dung wherever they please, and the rest shall scurry around at random. Laurenza, when she combs her hair, shall lose seventeen hairs and break thirteen, and of these, ten shall grow back within three days and seven shall never grow back at all. Antonio Savolino's bitch shall conceive five puppies, of which three shall live out their natural lifespan and two shall be thrown away, and of these three the first shall resemble its mother, the second shall be mongrel, and the third shall partly resemble the father and partly resemble Polidoro's dog. In that moment a cuckoo shall be heard from La Starza, cuckooing twelve times, no more and no fewer, whereupon it shall leave and fly to the ruins of Castel Cicala for eleven minutes, and then shall fly off to Scarvaita, and as for what happens next, we'll see to it later. That the skirt Mastro Danese is cutting on his board shall come out crooked. That twelve bedbugs shall leave the slats of Costantino's bed and head toward the pillow: seven large ones, four smaller, and one middle-sized, and as for the one who shall survive until this evening's candlelight, we'll see to it. That fifteen minutes thereafter, because of the movement of her tongue, which she has passed over her palate four times, the old lady of Fiurulo shall lose the third right molar in her lower jaw, and it shall fall without blood and without pain, because that molar has been loose for seventeen months. That Ambrogio on the one hundred twelfth thrust shall finally have driven home his business with his wife, but shall not impregnate her this time, but rather another, using the sperm into which the cooked leek that he has just eaten with millet and wine sauce shall have been converted. Martinello's son is beginning to grow hair on his chest, and his voice is beginning to crack. That Paulino, when he bends over to pick up a broken needle, shall snap the red drawstring of his underpants, and if he should blaspheme for that reason, I mean for him to be punished thus: tonight his soup shall be too salty and taste of smoke, he shall fall and break his wine flask, and should he swear on that occasion, we'll see to it later. That of seven moles who set out four days ago from deep within the earth, taking different paths toward the open air, two shall reach the surface at the same time, one at high noon, and the other fifteen minutes, nineteen seconds later, and one shall emerge three yards, one foot, and half an inch from the other in Anton Favaro's garden. As for the time and place for the other two, we'll see to it later.

Quickly, however, Nola proved too small for Filippo Bruno's talents and Giovanni Bruno's ambitions. Naples lay only thirty miles away, with its universities and the great religious houses where even a struggling gentleman could afford to educate a son superbly. And yet, as Bruno moved in later years from Naples to Paris to London to the Protestant cities of northern Germany, he faithfully called himself "the Nolan" and peopled his writings with characters from Nola. His cousins Laudomia and Giulia Savolino would reappear magically in London as nymphs on the banks of the river Thames; the memory of Luigi Tansillo would guide him toward the life of a heroic poet; and when Giordano Bruno finally embarked on an epic poem about the infinite size of the universe, *On the Immense and the Numberless*, he anchored his transcendent vision by remembering the days when he thought that Nola was the center of the world, and Mount Vesuvius marked its edge.

CHAPTER THREE

"Napoli è tutto il mondo"

NAPLES, 1562–1565

Napoli è tutto il mondo.

Naples is the whole world.

—Giulio Cesare Capaccio, *Il forastiero* (1634)

If Nola somehow anchored the Nolan philosopher's sense of himself, Naples provided his first, indelible glimpse of the rest of the world. Thirty years after the fact, he remembered his journey toward the city in the fall of 1562, a model for all the other journeys he would make to unknown places. He captured the effects of that trip on a boy of fourteen by describing how it transformed his idea of Mount Vesuvius. He had always thought that the volcano marked the end of the world, looming over Nola's southern horizon. Vesuvius had been lying dormant since 1500, but every Nolan knew its history: the burial of Pompeii in ancient Roman times, the airborne columns of ash and pebbles that had branched out like an umbrella pine before molten lava charged down the mountainside like rivers of fire. We can see Vesuvius through the young Bruno's eyes in his poem *On the Immense and the Numberless*, where he is sent off to Naples not by his parents but by his rocky confidante, Monte Cicala:

>   ... It was almost as if you extended
> Your leafy hand, full of grapes, to my tender hand, and you pointed
> With your finger to say to me, "Now take a look southward;
> Look at Vesuvius there, in that direction, my brother—
> My brother mountain who loves you as well as I: Do you hear me?
> Tell me, should I send you off to him? Would you go? For you'll stay there
> Ever after with him." Then turning my crystalline eyes, and
> Gazing upon that formless form, scrutinizing the figure
> Of that amorphous heap, I said, "Who, the crookbacked
> One? Who, the one with the sawtooth hunchback who splits the
> Seamless sky? Who stands back from the whole world isolated,
> Smutty with shadowing smoke, ungenerous in his bounty,
> Not a grape to his name, nor any fruit worth the mention?
> No sweet figs for him; he boasts not one arbor or garden,
> Gloomy, obscure, dour, glowering, miserly, grudging."
> Then you said with a smile, "And yet he's my very own brother,
> Always loving to me; he loves you too. Therefore go now.
> Without scorning his kindness, I know that he shall do nothing
> That might offend you; indeed, you'll only return most unwilling."

And yet, as Bruno then observes, the dreadful mountain became less dreadful as he came closer, and thus, his poem suggests, the strangest things in the world will seem less strange the better we come to know them. Just as he learned to acclimate himself to Mount Vesuvius, and then to Naples, and then to the world, he implicitly urges his readers to dare to acclimate themselves to something as strange as an infinite universe by focusing on its familiar aspects: the sun and stars, and the unfailing presence of God.

Thus, as he discovered, the lower slopes of Vesuvius were covered with grapevines just like those of Monte Cicala, producers of a wine no less famous than Nola's *asprinio*: Lacrima Christi, "Christ's Tears." As in Nola, the volcanic ash that made up the soil of Naples sprouted not only grapevines but lemon, almond, orange, and peach trees, a riot of flowers in the spring and of fruit in the summer. By the time he reached the coast and the flawless curve of the Bay of Naples, Bruno could see that Naples was one of the most beautiful places on earth, basking under what he would one day call a *"benigno cielo,"* using a word, *cielo,* that meant both "sky" and "heaven."

Beneath that benign heaven, however, Bruno found one of the largest cities in the world, 250,000 souls crammed into walls designed to protect an ancient Greek colony with one-tenth of Naples's sixteenth-century population. To make matters worse, huge tracts of land within the crowded city belonged only to the rich: the gardens, courtyards, and cloisters reserved for a privileged few. We know almost nothing of Bruno's first years in Naples, but his later portraits of Neapolitan street life suggest that he spent them in crowded student quarters, a solitary teenager plunged suddenly into urban chaos. Surprisingly, rather than leading him to reject his father's Stoic philosophy of life, his experience of Naples only confirmed it.

In 1562, when Bruno arrived in Naples, only Constantinople, Cairo, Tabriz, and Paris had more inhabitants, and they all lacked the panoramas offered by the long, straight streets, first laid out by the Greeks who settled ancient Neapolis, "the new city," six centuries before the Christian era. From the hill of Saint Elmo down to the port, one endless street split the city in half; its modern nickname, in fact, is Spaccanapoli, "Split Naples." In Bruno's day it was called the Strada del Seggio di Nilo (or Nido), named after the neighborhood (Seggio, or "Seat") where he would eventually make his home.

In the mid-sixteenth century, these ancient streets were lined by high convent walls and the lofty, close-packed palazzi of the nobles, both local barons and transplanted Spanish grandees, who lived in fabulous opulence off the feudal lands they exploited with legendary rapacity. For years the Spanish overlords of Naples had forbidden construction outside the old city walls, and as a result the city's sheer density of buildings and people was almost unparalleled in the rest of Europe. The palazzi in turn were dwarfed by the soaring walls, all fashioned in golden stone, of the city's Gothic churches, at least one for each of the great monastic orders, many of them resting on the ruins of ancient Greek and Roman temples. In the church of San Lorenzo, set atop the agora of ancient Neapolis, the ribald Boccaccio had met his ladylove Fiammetta, and Petrarch had come to worship. San Paolo Maggiore, just across the street, engulfed the ancient temple of Castor and Pollux. A few ancient blocks away, Santa Chiara claimed the tombs of the French kings who had ruled Naples for several centuries before their replacement by kings from Spain. Most powerful of all, San Domenico Maggiore lorded it above the baronial palazzi of the Seggio di Nilo, a huge Gothic barn with a crucifix whose image of Jesus (it was said) had once spoken to Thomas Aquinas.

At the same time, Naples, even the Seggio di Nilo, was packed to bursting with houses and hovels for the working poor: the fishermen, seamstresses, vendors, porters, laundresses, carpenters, sausage makers, blacksmiths, wheelwrights, and water sellers who went barefoot in the mild climate and lived largely on bread and figs (among the urban poor of Europe, Neapolitans enjoyed an unusually healthy diet). Scruffy neighborhoods linked the port of Naples to its chief marketplace, Piazza del Mercato, an open space crammed with eight and more ranks of shopkeepers' stalls and the lean-tos that served as housing for the poorest members of the Neapolitan lower class—beggars, day laborers, cutpurses, prostitutes—when they did not simply live on the street. The gallows in the middle of the square, by contrast, was a sturdy permanent structure, one of three the Spanish viceroys maintained in different areas of the city as symbols of their authority.

In the mid-sixteenth century, Naples, finally squeezed to bursting by its prosperity, had expanded along a new boulevard outside the walls, the Via Toledo, named after the touchy little viceroy who had sponsored its construction, Don Pedro de Toledo. Since 1539, the road had swept from the small market square just beyond San Domenico down to the seashore and the viceregal palace. Straight as the ancient streets but several times as broad, the Via Toledo perfectly set off the opulence of the coaches that had become the latest fashion in transportation for royals, nobles, churchmen, and anyone else who wanted to travel in style. Along its course, behind a showy rank of new Renaissance-style palazzi, new neighborhoods were springing up, most importantly the dense little blocks of apartments that housed the Spanish garrison, a whole community of soldiers poised to sweep down the Via Toledo en masse at any sign of trouble.

Trouble there was, and often: Naples resented its Spanish over-lords for their arrogance and greed, with good reason. The kingdom handed over its wealth of goods and money to the distant Spanish monarchs and received precious little in return; the Via Toledo project was a grand exception. In 1562, just as Bruno arrived, the Spaniards threatened to introduce the Spanish Inquisition, which permitted arrests on the basis of a single accusation rather than the two witnesses required by Roman law. It was the second time Spain had tried to impose Spanish rules; the first attempt, in 1547, had led to street riots and two thousand deaths.

There were other threats to safety as well: the fall of 1562 brought on a year of strange, clammy fogs and an epidemic of the disease Neapolitans called "the influence," *influenza.* On the viceroy's orders, smudge pots burned in the streets night and day to drive off the dangerous air—while creating noxious fumes of their own. In 1563, a band of Turkish pirates took brief control of the suburban area at the foot of the hill called Posillipo—garbled Greek for "Care's End"—a brisk walk down the seaside from the Via Toledo. There were reasons that the city wall of Naples ex-tended straight across its splendid shoreline, blocking the view of Sorrento and Capri for everyone in the lower-lying districts.

The view of Naples we have from Bruno himself is pure hind-sight, although its source, a play from 1582, is one of his earliest surviving works. Like Plato, who had tried his hand at writing tragedy before turning to philosophy, Bruno first tried to communi-cate his ideas about philosophy through drama. But unlike Athens, Naples was no place for tragedy; the city had already begun to develop a form of street theater that would eventually be known as commedia dell'arte. Inevitably, perhaps, the Nolan philosopher introduced his philosophy to the world through a huge, riotous comedy, *Il candelaio* (*The Candlemaker*), written in a pungent Neapolitan vernacular. Bruno took pride in his plain speech, but it was plain speech Italian style—that is, a triumph of rhetoric:

To whom shall I dedicate my *Candlemaker*? To whom (O grand destiny!) would you like me to entitle my handsome groomsman, my excellent chorus leader? To whom shall I send what the heavenly influence of Sir-ius, in these scorching days and torrid hours that we call the dog days, has made the fixed stars precipitate within my brain, the pretty fireflies of the firmament drill into me from on high, the dean of the zodiac blast into my head, and the seven planets whisper in my ears? To whom is it addressed, I say? Toward whom does it look? To His Holiness? No. To His Imperial Majesty? No. To His Serenity? No. To His Highness, His Most Illustrious and Right Reverend Lordship? No, no. By my faith, there is no prince, or cardinal, king, emperor, or pope who will take this candle from my hands in this most solemn offertory.

In keeping with this lowly dedication, the characters of *The Candlemaker* stand barely clear of poverty: they are grammar-school teachers, students, go-betweens, apothecaries, ruffians, thieves, artists, alchemists, soldiers, and loose women. Yet Bruno wrote his riotous black comedy not for these people but for the French royal court. He used *The Candlemaker*'s knowing glimpses into Neapolitan low life to tell these sophisticated readers another story altogether about survival, the city, and himself. As the play's comic figures make their way through the streets of Naples, Bruno's dedication looks far above their heads to an August star shower, those "pretty fireflies of the firmament" that we call the Perseids (and can no longer see within our light-saturated cities). What inspires him to write, at least so he claims, is a vision of the heavens. However chaotic its streets and variegated its people, then, Naples, perhaps precisely because of its hugeness, its beauty, and its brutality, was the crucible in which this young man from Nola, Filippo Bruno, began to forge the life of a philosopher.

CHAPTER FOUR

"The world is fine as it is"

NAPLES, 1562–1565

B runo published his *Candlemaker* twenty years after he arrived in Naples and six years after he had left the city for good, but the play clearly returns to the time when he was a young student scrabbling for a place to live and a place at the university. In other words, he set his philosophical drama in the very time and the very place that had first brought him to philosophy. As he tells his audience, "You should imagine this as the royal city of Naples, somewhere near the Seggio di Nilo," and like the young Bruno himself, his audience must make its way through the noise, crowds, chaos, and bad government to discover the point of it all. As he announces in the play's "Proprologue":

> The comedy will have no prologue and it doesn't matter: its material, its subject, its mode and order and circumstance, I tell you, will appear in proper order, and be put before your eyes in order, which is much better than having them explained to you in order; this is a kind of fabric that has both a warp and a woof; whoever can grasp it, let him grasp it; whoever wants to understand it, let him understand it . . . Note who comes and goes, what is said and what is done, how to understand it, how it can be understood; for certainly depending on how you take these words and actions . . . you will have occasion to laugh or weep mightily.

Precisely because of its hugeness and its confusion, Naples turned Giordano Bruno into a thinker. In its noisy, cruel, complicated heart, he learned to read, study, and train his memory with extraordinary discipline. His philosophy, in turn, would reflect its origins in Europe's most crowded city: he would promise that it fitted citizens for living in the world, even when that world was only a tiny corner of an endless expanse of space.

First, however, Bruno had to find his own way, a slight, ambitious fourteen-year-old confronting the "fabric" of Naples with little more than his wits to help him. That "fabric," in *The Candlemaker*, reflects all the caprice and contradiction of Spanish rule: crime is rife despite the oppressive presence of police attached to "the Court," the dread Spanish tribunal situated in a fortress on the eastern margin of the city. Although it is illegal for a man to kiss a woman in public, the police let the streets swarm with prostitutes, from the streetwalkers who ply their trade alongside the port and the marketplace to the "women of honor," courtesans who receive their wealthy clients so long, one of them muses, as their beauty lasts; the money they make in their teens and early twenties will have to sustain them for a lifetime. Blasphemy is severely punished by law, but every character in the play swears by a pantheon of saints and their relics, as well as the long-suffering Madonna. Greed for money is matched by the scramble for personal advantage; by robbing and tricking rich old men, the women, young men, and ruffians in this profane comedy get by in a harsh, uncompromising world. And yet, as Bruno stresses over and over again through the varying voices of his characters, this world, for all its corruption, is unfolding exactly as it should.

The most eloquent voices in the play, strikingly, are those of the women, who lay bare the cruelty of their society in forthright speeches. It is the courtesan Vittoria who best sums up the comedy's overall meaning: "The world is fine as it is"—"*Il mondo sta bene come sta.*"

> Consider that, like virgins, some of us are called foolish, and others wise; so that among those of us who taste the best fruits the world produces [that is, sex], the crazy ones are the ones who love only for passing pleasure, and don't think about old age stealing up on them so fast that they neither see nor hear it, all the while it's driving our gentlemen friends

away. As old age wrinkles her face, he closes up his wallet; age saps her juices from the inside, his love wilts on the outside, age strikes her at close quarters, he waves goodbye from a distance. So it's important to line things up in time. Whoever waits for time is wasting time. If I wait for time, time won't wait for me. We need to take advantage of their situation when they still think they need us. Grab the prey when it's chasing you, don't wait until it runs away. If you don't know how to keep a bird in a cage, you'll never catch it on the wing. He may have a small brain and a bad back, but he has a fine wallet: as for the first circumstance, too bad for him; as for the second, it's not my problem; as for the third—now, that's something to reckon with. Wise men live for fools, and fools for the wise. If everyone were a lord, they'd be lords no longer: if everyone were wise, no one would be wise, and if they were all fools, none would be fools. The world is fine as it is.

The play's prime mover, Gioan Bernardo, a young painter who ends up bedding both the heroines, is obviously Bruno as he would like to be, a genial, sexy swain, an artist whose greatest work is his own life. His pronouncements have often been read as quick doses of the Nolan philosophy, delivered by the play's most attractive male character, but on the occasions when he appears, Gioan Bernardo is more of a trickster than a philosopher, as slippery as the Don Giovanni of Mozart's opera. Like Don Giovanni, he is almost always playing a part rather than speaking frankly. His most straightforward speech involves the economy of nature:

It is common opinion that things are so ordered that nature never stints on the necessities, and never gives in excess. Oysters have no feet because, no matter where in the sea they find themselves, they have everything they need to sustain them, for they live on water and the heat of the sun (which penetrates into the deep). Moles have no eyes because they live underground, and live on nothing but earth, and can't possibly lose track of it. If someone lacks art, they're not granted tools.

Perhaps, as a creature of wishful thinking as much as out of dramatic necessity, Gioan Bernardo is a little too attractive for his own good. Bruno's real presence in the world, especially when he

first arrived in Naples, was surely more like that of a character who
appears in only one scene of *The Candlemaker*, Ottaviano, a student of the tedious schoolmaster Manfurio, so much brighter than
his teacher that he turns the pedant's rhetoric against him and
walks offstage in triumph. First, however, he butters up the silly old
man with a torrent of sarcastic flattery:

> OTTAVIANO: O gentle master, subtle, eloquent, gallant steward and
> cupbearer of the Muses.
> MANFURIO: O lovely apposition.
> OTT: Patriarch of the Apollonian choir . . .
> MAN: "Apolline" were better.
> OTT: Trumpet of Phoebus, let me kiss your left cheek, for I am unworthy
> to kiss that sweet mouth.
> MAN: I envy not Jove his nectar and ambrosia—

Abruptly, Ottaviano switches from this abject flattery to insult;
by the time Manfurio realizes that Ottaviano has been pulling his
leg, the boy has skipped off, back into the streets where another
student, Filippo Bruno, once scrabbled with the same ingenuity for
survival in a harsh, beautiful, beleaguered city.

Bruno would eventually come to the same philosophical conclusion as Vittoria the courtesan: the world was fine as it was, with
God vitally present in the chaos of everyday reality rather than off
in some transcendent world of Ideas. But that revelation of the
world's essential rightness never kept him from acting to improve
it. His alter ego in *The Candlemaker* is not a prostitute, after all, but
an artist.

Furthermore, Bruno spent his years in Naples at San Domenico
Maggiore, the very center of resistance to Spanish rule. Within its
halls he learned how to link theology with political action.

CHAPTER FIVE

"I have, in effect, harbored doubts"

NAPLES, 1562–1576

In the abstract, Bruno may have eventually come to believe that the world was fine as it was. He spent much of his time, however, trying to change it, beginning, when he was seventeen, with his cell in the convent of San Domenico Maggiore. Bruno's new home was no ordinary convent; its friars came from the most powerful families in the Kingdom of Naples. The novices, therefore, lived like nobles, in vaulted rooms around an immense courtyard.

The Neapolitan barons who sent their younger sons to the convent and their dead to crypts beneath the church also met in the convent's labyrinthine halls to hold learned conversations (eventually enshrined in 1611 as the Accademia degli Oziosi, the "Gentlemen of Leisure") and to plot resistance to the Spaniards, abetted by the friars themselves. Dominicans from San Domenico led the revolt in 1547 against imposing the Spanish Inquisition in Naples; as the city's inquisitors, they would have been responsible for enforcing the harsh Spanish rules. The friars would revolt again in 1599, urged on by their own Fra Tommaso Campanella and a handful of renegade barons. Campanella would spend the next twenty-seven years in prison (and forty hours on a torture seat called the Judas cradle), but the viceroy could not suppress the entire convent, let alone the barons; instead, he kept track of them through the Royal University, still housed on the premises, and by participating in person in the barons' learned gatherings.

In short, the sixty-odd friars of San Domenico were accustomed to exceptional freedom of thought and action, and also to aggressive manipulation of political power. Yet even this loose conventual life proved too strict for many of them. A dozen were convicted of thievery during Bruno's fourteen-year stay, unprepared for the rigors of monastic poverty. Furthermore, it was nearly impossible to separate a sixteenth-century gentleman from his weapons; no matter what religious vows the gentleman may have taken, his arsenal was a matter of basic identity. Steel blades, usually daggers, flashed forth from the friars' white robes with some regularity; in 1571, Fra Teofilo Caracciolo, still an aristocrat to the core, struck another brother with his sword. In an unusually intelligent community, forgery thrived in several media, from bank checks to notarial documents. Novices copied the keys to the outside doors and slipped out into taverns like the notorious Cerriglio, only a few blocks away, or into the taverns' upstairs brothels. The confessional served as another way to meet women; more than one Dominican faced a paternity suit from an outraged neighbor, and one friar barely escaped the man who chased him around Piazza San Domenico with a rake. Punishments for violent infractions, as well as for forgery, were harsh: years of service as a galley slave for the worst offenders, or a lifetime of menial tasks in a distant monastery. In 1580, however, Pope Gregory XIII could still write that he "understood that the inquisitors of the Order of Saint Dominic claim to be entirely immune from obedience to their superiors, and do not want to obey or observe their rule, and leave the convent when they wish without informing anyone where they are going." Religious life within the walls of this singular institution may not have taught Bruno obedience, but it certainly taught him how to move among the ruling class.

And move he did; early in his novitiate, he made a commotion clearing his cell of pictures of the Madonna, Saint Catherine of Siena, and Bishop Antoninus of Florence, leaving himself only a single crucifix. It was the kind of scene that Protestants were making all over Europe, stripping churches of their paintings and statues and calling them pagan idols, but in Naples, with its riotous wealth of religious art, this bid for austerity must have seemed especially odd. San Domenico's novice master, Fra Eugenio Gagliardo, wrote out a formal reprimand, but tore it up later in the day. And he let Filippo da Nola's redecoration stand.

When Bruno made trouble a second time, Fra Eugenio was less accommodating. A novice had been sitting in the courtyard, reading a cheap pamphlet with a devotional poem, *The Seven Joys of the Virgin*, when the little Nolan asked what he was doing with that book and told him to throw it away, and read some other book like the *Lives of the Holy Fathers*. This time, Fra Eugenio reported Filippo da Nola to the Inquisition; he took the incident as more than a case of bad manners, or a demanding scholar's recommendation of sober Latin literature over a vernacular tract. Instead, for a novice who had already banished the Madonna's picture from his cell, criticizing *The Seven Joys* suggested a distinct lack of reverence for the Virgin Mary, an attitude, again, that was particularly surprising in Naples, a city that prided itself on devotion to the Madonna. Reporting this outspoken novice to the Inquisition was only a matter of walking down the hall—the Holy Office, staffed by friars from San Domenico, occupied yet another of the convent's many courtyards—but it was a significant move, one that left Bruno with a permanent record in the Inquisition's archive.

Fra Eugenio recognized that Filippo da Nola, for a Neapolitan Catholic, was behaving suspiciously like a Protestant. In the mountainous regions of northern Italy, native Protestant communities, isolated from big cities, had worshipped in their own way since the late Middle Ages, but Naples, especially under its Spanish overlords, had always adhered staunchly to the Roman Church. Any change in that situation had the potential to upset the city's tense balance of interests among Madrid, the local barons, and Rome, and, equally, the balance among the city's dominant religious orders: the Franciscans, Augustinians, Benedictines, and Dominicans.

Furthermore, the Dominicans of San Domenico Maggiore found themselves in an especially awkward position in the 1560s, caught between pressure from Spain to impose the Spanish Inquisition and pressure from Rome to impose a new set of decrees resulting from the Council of Trent. Convoked unsuccessfully in the

1530s as a response to the Protestant Reformation, seated only in 1545, the council was so riven by conflict among its delegates that it dragged on for nearly two decades, issuing its final decrees only in 1563. Its initial aim, guided by the Venetian cardinal Gasparo Contarini and the Neapolitan Girolamo Seripando, had been to attempt reconciliation with the Protestants by facing up to, and righting, the real problems within the Roman Church. Instead, the council moved toward a fierce defense of the Church's established hierarchies and traditions, especially during the pontificate of Pope Paul IV (reigned 1555–59). The most combative of all the council's traditionalists, Paul, a Neapolitan and the former cardinal Giovanni Pietro Carafa, pinned his own hopes for reforming the Church on a strengthened Inquisition for Catholics, hostility for the Protestants, and ghettos for the Jews. His demands for absolute obedience reflected his upbringing in a grand old baronial family, one of whose chapels stands just to the right of the entrance to the church of San Domenico Maggiore.

Arrogant and cruel, Pope Paul also had his opponents, centered, like the cardinals Contarini and Seripando, in Venice and Naples. Though they may have emerged battered from the Council of Trent, the more conciliatory Catholic reformers continued as a powerful intellectual force, their social status and political weight comparable to those of Carafa and his allies. In Naples, figures like the aristocratic poet Vittoria Colonna (a close friend of Michelangelo's) and a pair of Augustinian cardinals, Giles of Viterbo and Girolamo Seripando, had brought Naples into the reforming currents of the Roman Church, especially Cardinal Seripando, whose personal library in the Augustinian church of San Giovanni a Carbonara had become an important place to read and discuss philosophy and theology.

It is no wonder, under such circumstances, that in San Domenico, Fra Eugenio Gagliardo alerted his colleagues in the Inquisition to Filippo Bruno's strange ideas. If they had come from the young man's own head, the Dominicans faced a simple problem; if, however, they reflected a larger trend in local thought, the problem was more serious—not necessarily for Bruno, but certainly for the Dominican Order in Naples.

In fact, Bruno's private thoughts were far more radical than the novice master knew. After having rid his room of every image except a crucifix, he had begun to wonder seriously about the crucifix as well. When he faced the Inquisition in Venice thirty years later, he claimed that he had begun to doubt the divinity of Jesus at the age of eighteen:

> I have, in effect, harbored doubts about the term ["person"] for the Son and the Holy Spirit, as I have never understood them as persons distinct from the Father . . . I have held this opinion from the time that I was eighteen years old until now, but I have never made a public denial, nor taught or written anything to that effect, but only doubted to myself, as I have said.

But, as Fra Eugenio clearly feared, Bruno's ideas also reflected contacts he had made with other people in Naples. The most important of these people was an Augustinian friar from the convent of San Giovanni a Carbonara, a protégé of Cardinal Seripando's who shared many of his mentor's ways of thinking about God, faith, and the world.

Still, despite his personal doubts about the personhood of Jesus, his studies with a member of another order, and his tendencies toward disobedience, now a matter of record, Filippo da Nola, after a year's novitiate, pronounced his final vows as a friar in the Order of Preachers and began to prepare for his ordination as a priest. The advantages of life at San Domenico Maggiore apparently outweighed the restrictions, and his behavior, though unruly, was not unruly enough for Fra Eugenio to question the young man's fitness for the Order of Preachers. Like several other novices in 1566, Filippo da Nola took the name Fra Giordano in homage to the convent's former prior, Fra Giordano Crispo.

Acceptance into the convent of San Domenico Maggiore and the Dominican Order was only the beginning of Bruno's preparation for the priesthood. His next aim was far more ambitious: admission to the College of San Domenico Maggiore to take a degree in theology. Young men throughout the Kingdom of Naples entered the order by the dozens every year, but the College of San

Domenico had only ten places for what were called "formal students." These ten were the most select and privileged students of any institution in the realm, including the famous Medical School of Salerno, the other Dominican colleges, the other religious colleges, and the Royal University of Naples. The history of the College of San Domenico stretched back to the very beginnings of university education in Europe; only Salerno could make a similar claim.

As for San Domenico's prestige, the faculty had once boasted Thomas Aquinas himself, lured back to Italy from his professorship at the University of Paris. The secular Royal University of Naples rented rooms in the Dominicans' convent, basking in the college's reflected glory.

Formal students were usually admitted to the College of San Domenico, after an extensive period of preparation, as what were called "material students." Material students took private lessons from a variety of teachers; most professors were eager to earn extra money by tutoring on the side. Material students studied without limits on their time or curriculum, but formal students, once admitted to the Dominican college, were required to complete a rigorous course in academic theology within three years. If they did so successfully, they earned the degree of *lector*, "reader." Slower progress meant expulsion. It would take Giordano Bruno eight years to obtain, in 1571, an offer to become a formal student at the Dominican college at Andria, a small city near the Adriatic coast. He passed it up; Andria stood at the opposite end of the kingdom, far from anything Bruno knew and far from the centers of intellectual life, Naples and Rome. He chose instead to continue in Naples as a material student at the College of San Domenico, and his gamble paid off: he was accepted as a formal student in Naples one year later, in May 1572. For all his intelligence, his wide reading, and his phenomenal memory, it had taken him nine years of study to earn admission. He was twenty-four years old.

What we know about Bruno's student days is painfully limited, but the huge church of San Domenico preserves the same general form, despite its remodelings over the centuries. It is fairly easy to imagine the tall, stout aristocrat Aquinas or the burly Calabrian peasant Tommaso Campanella booming out a sermon under San Domenico's lofty vaults, but it must have been a real achievement for little Fra Giordano to project his voice to the very ends of the high, long nave. But project he must have; the Order of Preachers took their mission seriously. The immense church was only the first of many venues where Bruno would make himself heard, learning to carry his ideas not only on his voice but also on the extravagant gestures for which Italian preachers were famous. Here, in silence, students and professors also practiced linking their powers of observation to the development of their memories, scrutinizing every colorful chapel for its statues and paintings, each work of art for its story, saving the whole treasury in their heads for future sermons.

Here the friars must also have spent hours making and listening to music; indeed, as young Bruno grew to adulthood in the convent of San Domenico, one of the era's greatest musicians was growing into his troubled adolescence just next door in the Palazzo Sansevero. Don Carlo Gesualdo, Prince of Venosa, would eventually write piercing love songs in strange, dissonant harmonies, and one of the most sublime of all sacred motets, a setting, for Good Friday, of Lamentations 1:12: "Is it nothing to you, all ye that pass by? behold, and see if there be any sorrow like unto my sorrow." He was no more comfortable than Bruno in his gilded cage, and it is no accident that they both identified themselves with this biblical verse.

Above all, however, Bruno's studies sharpened his appetite for philosophy. Philosophy was a broad field in the sixteenth century, embracing the natural sciences as well as disciplines like logic and metaphysics. Philosophy at the Dominican college, however, hewed to a more narrow definition: it continued diligently in the tradition of its titanic thirteenth-century professor, Thomas Aquinas, whose lecture hall and apartment had become—and still are—carefully preserved shrines. A man as imposing in body as he was in mind (the convent's refectory table had a half-moon cut out of it to accommodate his prominent belly at meals), Thomas was also a great organizer, of people, institutions, and ideas. His lucid, systematic account of Christian theology garnered Bruno's unending respect, as he would emphasize repeatedly to his inquisitors when the time came.

Aquinas himself had drawn inspiration for his system building from Aristotle, whose works on every subject from animal behavior to literary criticism to metaphysics began to appear in Latin translation during the thirteenth century, passed on to the Christian world by Arab merchants. Three hundred years later, Bruno's program of study at San Domenico still included both the ancient Greek sage and his medieval Italian admirer, two prodigiously analytical minds whose writings left virtually no phenomenon of heaven or earth unaccounted for. Their style of argumentation by syllogism and the precise Latin vocabulary that Aquinas and his contemporaries devised for their needs took the name "Scholasticism," and it was as eminently scholarly as any system of thought before or since.

The only drawback with such majestically systematic thinkers as Aristotle and Aquinas was their tendency to dryness; the beauty of their thought lay in its structure rather than in its expression. By Bruno's day, the Dominican program of education and its Scholastic vocabulary had become distinctly old-fashioned; the emphasis on precision and order had been swept away in the fifteenth and early sixteenth centuries by a revival of interest in Plato, the passionate, dramatic prophet of philosophy as a rapture beyond words. Neither Aristotle nor Aquinas spent much time writing descriptions; Plato reveled in them. As a young man, he had hoped to become a writer of tragedy, but when his teacher Socrates was arrested and condemned to death on trumped-up charges, he withdrew from their native Athens, its democracy, and its state-sponsored dramatic festivals to promote his own elaboration of Socrates' philosophy. There is no question that Plato would have been a tragedian of genius; his philosophical dialogues are equally inspired works of literature in an entirely new medium. His skill as a dramatic writer creates vividly real personalities, above all Socrates, and awakens his readers' senses: lingering on the sensation of walking barefoot in soft, shady grass, or lying next to a handsome, tipsy, and decidedly amorous swain, he slyly shifts his focus to ideas, turning philosophy, irresistibly, into the ultimate erotic pursuit. Like the biblical Song of Songs, his dialogues combined torrid reading with uplifting content, and through their echoes in the Gospel of Saint John, the letters of Saint Paul, and the writings of Saint Augustine, they had captured Christian imaginations from the very beginning. In Naples, thanks to Thomas Aquinas, the center for Scholastic education had always been San Domenico Maggiore. For the study of Plato, however, beginning in the fifteenth century, it was the Augustinian convent of San Giovanni a Carbonara, and there Bruno found his own way to Platonic philosophy.

CHAPTER SIX

"I came into this world to light a fire"

NAPLES, BEFORE 1566

> Our Lord says that he inflames his people, where he says in Luke 12: "I
> came into this world to light a fire: what should I want but that it
> burn?" . . . for he who gives love is God.
>
> —Fra Teofilo da Vairano, On the Grace of the New Testament, 163v

From the thirteenth century onward, the most influential members of the Hermits of Saint Augustine had gathered, not at Sant'Agostino in the center of Naples, but at the convent of San Giovanni a Carbonara on the city's eastern edge. Dramatically set into a precipitous volcanic slope along the city wall (which conveniently blocked the sight and smells of the city ditch below it), San Giovanni a Carbonara became the chosen burial place of the last Angevin king, Ladislas II. When the Angevin heirs of Ladislas were expelled by Alfonso of Aragon in 1442, San Giovanni a Carbonara lost the privilege of royal burials to San Domenico Maggiore, and changed its politics from pro-French to pro-Spanish. By the last decades of the fifteenth century, the congregation had also decided to trade its reputation for the love of good food and drink for something more actively spiritual.

In keeping with their self-transformation, these reformed Augustinians introduced a new style of religious oratory. Although they spoke in Latin, they tried to emulate popular preachers like the Franciscan saint Bernardino of Siena, who used humor, empathy, and pithy Tuscan vernacular to reach huge congregations. At the same time, in order to give their own sermons a more sophisticated polish, they studied the principles of ancient rhetoric. Ancient oratory had been a practical art; its primary aim was to teach lawyers how to persuade a jury no matter how weak their case. Hence the ancient rhetorical manuals put supreme emphasis on clarity—and, when clarity was likely to fail, on shamelessly manipulating jurors' emotions. Bernardino was a master of emotional appeals (although he kept his language simple, he had studied ancient rhetoric himself): he brought his congregations to laughter, pity, terror, and, on one occasion, hysterical eagerness, when he promised, with huge fanfare, to give every person present a relic straight from Jesus Christ. (When he crowed, "It's the Gospel!" they all groaned in disappointment.)

The Augustinians found their own version of Saint Bernardino in their prior general, Fra Mariano da Genazzano. Even in Italy, where effusive speech was commonplace, Fra Mariano's sweeping gestures and the dramatic rise and fall of his voice made a striking impression on his listeners. So did the literary quality of his language and the images he conjured up for his hearers to contemplate. Compared with the Franciscans' homespun homilies and the Dominicans' sophisticated logic chopping, his oratory was both elegant and moving; he had cut an unforgettable figure when he preached in San Giovanni a Carbonara. But Fra Mariano's reputation was swiftly eclipsed in the very first years of the sixteenth century by that of his closest protégé, Fra Egidio Antonini da Viterbo (Giles of Viterbo), whose sojourns in Naples were longer and, in the end, still more influential than those of his mentor.

Giles of Viterbo was one of the great preachers of his age. At the beginning of his career, he drew criticism for imitating Fra Mariano too closely, from the austere black robe to the full black beard they both affected, but that line of criticism stopped once the younger man developed a full command of his own powers. Giles was, above all, an enthusiast; this is what captivated most of his listeners still more than the elaborate language and the intricate formal structure of his homilies. His black eyes sparkled and snapped, his hands waved, his voice soared and plummeted as he told stories and shouted exhortations; he drew forth laughter, tears, and battle cries, not to mention money from his hearers' pockets. He made Plato (another brilliant demagogue) seem not only easy to understand but urgently important, an ancient pagan so divinely inspired that he could cast light on Christian doctrine and pressing current events. Furthermore, in an age of rampant anti-Semitism, Giles spoke with deep respect for the Jews. He studied Plato and the Hebrew tradition of Kabbalah as if their mystic doctrines were needed complements to Christian theology, and to his mind they were: he believed that the ancient religions of the world had formed part of a grand divine plan for humanity's gradual and universal enlightenment. Now that we can no longer see or hear him, but only read his writings, Giles's most lasting legacy is a series of word-pictures, images of indelible clarity created to illustrate the abstract reaches of his thought, pictures so clear, in fact, that painters like Michelangelo and Raphael adopted them as their own. When Mariano da Genazzano died in 1506, Giles of Viterbo succeeded him as prior general of their eight-thousand-man order, advancing in 1517 to the position of cardinal protector. He was a strong if unsuccessful candidate for the papacy in 1521 and 1523.

In Naples itself, Giles of Viterbo was known not only as a preacher and reformer but also, and importantly, as a literary figure. He had been a close friend of the city's best writers, Giovanni Gioviano Pontano, who named one of his dialogues after the affable Augustinian (*Aegidius*, 1498), and Jacopo Sannazaro, who undertook his religious epic on the birth of Christ, *On the Virgin's Childbirth* (*De partu Virginis*, 1521), at Giles's explicit suggestion. The friar's influence also extended to less solemn works, like Sannazaro's pastoral novel *Arcadia* (1504) and his book of poems about fishing (*Eclogues*), both of which expressed deep Christian devotion as they entertained. Giles himself wrote at least one vernacular poem, "Love's Beautiful Hunt" ("*La caccia bellissima dell'amore*").

Giles of Viterbo met his closest Neapolitan associate within the walls of San Giovanni a Carbonara. The austere young aristocrat Fra Girolamo Seripando studied closely with Giles during the latter's term as prior general of their order, absorbing his mentor's devotion to Plato and his driving commitment to reforming the Church. He also began to gather a substantial collection of Giles's writings. Eventually Seripando returned to San Giovanni a Carbonara to head the congregation, until, like Giles of Viterbo before him, he became prior general, and then cardinal protector of the Augustinian Order. In those positions of authority, he would follow the interminable efforts toward Catholic reform at the Council of Trent, whose tormented proceedings dragged on for eighteen years from 1545 to 1563, the year of Seripando's own death. During his years at San Giovanni a Carbonara, he shared his splendid personal library with the friars, setting it up in a separate reading room above his family chapel in the church under the care of his brother Antonio; perhaps only San Domenico Maggiore boasted a richer collection in the sixteenth century than these two Augustinian libraries combined. Its visitors included the friar who would become Giordano Bruno's most beloved mentor, Fra Teofilo da Vairano.

The Augustinian library and Seripando's collection were broken up in the nineteenth century. Most of the books were taken to the National Library of Naples, where those that belonged to Seripando still bear the special call numbers of his private library. The only record of Fra Teofilo's own ideas comes from a single manuscript in the Vatican Library, a treatise titled *On the Grace of the New Testament*, written in 1570–71, when the author had just left a chair in metaphysics at the University of Rome to become a private tutor to Prince Ascanio Colonna. This manuscript contains enough evidence to suggest, however, that the friars of San Giovanni a Carbonara had developed a tradition of Platonic studies in Naples as distinctive as the Dominicans' tradition of Scholasticism, and that this tradition exerted a powerful influence on Bruno at the very beginning of his time in Naples.

Like his student, Fra Teofilo was destined for a life of constant movement. Born, like Bruno, in a small town in the Kingdom of Naples, Teofilo da Vairano had been accepted as a student at the Augustinian college at Sant'Agostino in 1558—he was probably ten to fifteen years older than Bruno. By 1562 he had joined the faculty; by 1563 he had earned his baccalaureate degree; and in 1565 he was certified to serve as a professor of metaphysics "on any faculty" in Naples. By May 1566 he had been appointed rector of the Augustinian University of Florence, and moved away from Naples for good; at almost the same time, Filippo da Nola entered the convent of San Domenico Maggiore as a novice.

Given his admiration for Fra Teofilo and his evident affinity for Platonic philosophy, Bruno's decision to join the Dominicans seems somewhat surprising, and the choice, made at a very young age for reasons we do not know, was not an entirely fortunate one. On the other hand, Bruno's mind thrived as much on Scholastic organization as it did on Platonic passion, and in the end his writing showed a personality as divided as his philosophical loyalties. When he wrote in Latin, he wrote with a Dominican's vocabulary and a Dominican's precision. When he wrote in vernacular, he wrote, like Plato, as a dramatist and a philosophical lover.

At the same time, Fra Teofilo's treatise *On the Grace of the New Testament* shows that his own preparation in theology rested on a firm Scholastic base; it displays his mastery of the tightly ordered rules of Scholastic syllogism, and delights in the minute theological arguments that Dominicans, as potential inquisitors, needed to know better than anyone else. He would have been more than adequate as a teacher of logic, an elementary course that prepared young students for the higher realms of metaphysics and theology.

But in a comment to a Parisian bookseller, Bruno called Teofilo da Vairano "his greatest master in philosophy," a description that implies a teacher of an entirely different order. In one section of his treatise, Fra Teofilo describes his own philosophy as "what we have been taught by the Holy Scriptures, the teachings of Augustine, and the great Dionysius the Areopagite, so that the truth shall ever more shine forth," and trains his skill "against some sayings of the Scholastics." He belonged firmly, in other words, to the Platonic tradition that had been developed by the Augustinian Hermits of San Giovanni a Carbonara. In keeping with that tradition, many passages of Fra Teofilo's text show magnificent flights of emotional rhetoric. If Filippo Bruno had never before seen a man driven by ardent love of transcendent ideas, Teofilo da Vairano was certainly such a person. In his work on divine grace, Fra Teofilo described a Church that included the entire human race, whose universal mission was propelled by love. His ecclesiastical name, Teofilo, "beloved of God," could not have been more apt. (Ironically, he dedicated *On the Grace of the New Testament* to Antonio Cardinal Carafa, a nephew of the severe pope Paul IV.)

As it survives today, *On the Grace of the New Testament* is a collection of twelve shorter studies on such subjects as divine grace, infant baptism, original sin, and free will, all matters of urgent debate with the Protestants. Frequently the discussions are cast as dialogues between Fra Teofilo himself and various adversaries, who range over time and space from late-antique dissenters like Pelagius and Donatus, to thirteenth-century luminaries like Thomas Aquinas and the Augustinian Giles of Rome, to near contemporaries: the declared Protestants Luther, Melanchthon, Bucer, and Calvin, and the Catholic reformer Erasmus, who was, like them, consigned to the Inquisition's *Index of Forbidden Books*. From 1559 on, any Catholic who wanted to read Erasmus or the Reformers could do so only by special dispensation, granted by a bishop or the Holy Office; otherwise the reader faced excommunication. Such a dispensation had evidently been granted to Fra Teofilo for some time, permitting him a wide range of readings.

Surprisingly, however, Teofilo da Vairano's position in *On the Grace of the New Testament* diverged significantly from the hard traditional line then prevailing in Spain and Rome. His own view of religion was Catholic in the most trenchantly literal sense of the word; in one paragraph, he reviews the Greek adjective *katholikos* to show that the prefix *kata-* transforms it into a superlative version of *holos*, "whole," "entire." And indeed, to his age of vicious religious strife, Teofilo responded with an ardently universal profession of love for God and for creation. In writing about the passage in the Gospel of Saint Luke where Jesus says, "I came into this world to light a fire: what should I want but that it burn?" Fra Teofilo, unlike many of his contemporaries, saw neither the sacking of cities nor the burning of heretics in the name of religion, but rather a huge blaze of passionate human charity. He declared that the divine favor he called the grace of the New Testament had been available to every human being from Adam and shall be available to everyone, down to the least descendant of humanity on Judgment Day. He included an unusually large number of women in his catalogs of heroic figures from the past. He devoted one essay to

proving that the Hebrew patriarchs were no less aware of full divine truth than Christian saints, fully admitted to "the grace of the
New Testament," and argued elsewhere that Christians were no
less Jewish than the Jews themselves. In Fra Teofilo's work, the
river Jordan repeatedly symbolizes the crossing from ignorance into
awareness, so that the real meaning of the Jews' passage into the
Promised Land is spiritual rather than physical. In his view, their
rebirth is exactly comparable to the baptism of Jesus, and the baptism of every faithful Christian.

When Bruno wrote himself into philosophical dialogues, he
would always take the name Teofilo. As with Fra Teofilo, rivers were
to figure prominently in the imagination of the man who chose for
himself the religious name Giordano, who likened his inspiration
to a great river of eloquence, dreamed of his soul flowing into the
great ocean, and ended his most ambitious dialogue with the baptism of nine blind initiates in the waters of the Thames—the river
Jordan of the Nolan philosophy. He certainly came into the world
to light a fire, and like Fra Teofilo, he saw that fire as an image of
the blazing love that had created both the cosmos and human
hearts. From his cell in the prisons of the Venetian Inquisition, he
would contemplate the stars.

In 1571, shortly after completing On the Grace of the New Testament, Teofilo da Vairano handed his manuscript to the Vatican librarian, Antonio Cardinal Carafa (the book's dedicatee), with a
promise of more to come. The book passed almost immediately to
the pope's Private ("Secret") Archive, where it sat among a series
of volumes that seem to have served as reference texts when the
popes Clement VIII and Paul V ordered hearings on the subjects of
grace and free will, the topics most bitterly contested by Catholics
and Protestants in the late sixteenth and early seventeenth centuries. The fact that the manuscript was never published suggests
that its theology was not easy to digest, especially for those two
stern enforcers. (Nor was Fra Teofilo around to defend himself; he
died in Palermo in April 1588.) It would take another four hundred years for a pope to issue an encyclical that began with the
words "Deus caritas est"—"God is love."

CHAPTER SEVEN

Footprints in the Forest

NAPLES, 1563-1576

Into the woods young Actaeon unleashed
His mastiffs and his hounds, when fateful force
Set him upon the bold incautious course
Of following the track of woodland beasts.
Behold, the sylvan waters now display
The loveliest form that god or man might see;
All alabaster, pearl, and gold is she;
He saw her; and the hunter turned to prey.
The stag who sought to bend
His lightened step toward denser forest depths
His dogs devoured; they caught him in their trap.
The thoughts that I extend
Toward lofty prey recoil and deal me death,
Rending me in their fell and savage snap.

—*The Heroic Frenzies*, I.4

Although there is no way of knowing where Filippo da Nola took his lessons with Fra Teofilo da Vairano, his later writings show explicit echoes of the books gathered in Girolamo Seripando's private library at San Giovanni a Carbonara. These included the indispensable works of Marsilio Ficino, the Florentine physician who first brought Plato to wide attention in

fifteenth-century Italy and urged contemporary philosophical debate from a formal Scholastic question-and-answer toward the
pleasures of literature. His monumental *Platonic Theology* reconciled Plato's philosophy with Christianity, not with historical detachment but with a burning conviction that God had guided the
development of both, "so that the truth shall ever more shine
forth" (to use Fra Teofilo's phrase), and was guiding their reconciliation in the here and now.

Ficino's essay *On Living the Heavenly Life* contained a great deal
of astrological advice, showing how to attract the influence of the
various stars by arranging their favorite stones, colors, and gems;
how to maintain youth by drinking the milk of young mothers; and
how to stave off nearly every bodily ill by eating sugar, marzipan, or
almond cookies. His Neoplatonism was no ascetic's creed, and neither was the Nolan philosophy.

Bruno's work also shows the imprint of less well-known Platonic
authors: the Augustinian cardinal Giles of Viterbo and the Neapolitan poet Marcantonio Epicuro, who committed his own Platonic theology to a verse dialogue called *Blindness* (*Cecaria*). In one
manuscript from the Seripando library, Epicuro's *Cecaria* appears
together with Giles's poem "Love's Beautiful Hunt"; Bruno would
pay homage to both works in his own dialogue *The Heroic Frenzies*.
From Epicuro, he borrowed the image of blindness. From Giles, he
took the image of a forest.

It was an image whose power our deforested era can barely
imagine. Both Giles of Viterbo and Giordano Bruno grew up on
the edge of forests, Giles next to the thick Ciminian wood that
struck such dread into the ancient Romans, and Giordano, of
course, beneath the friendly sylvan slopes of Monte Cicala, "girded
in chestnut, and oak, poplar, elm." The forest is always more than a
metaphor in their writing; they describe it as a vividly experienced
reality; and Giles, at least, was an avid hunter who returned to the
forest whenever he could, to pray and to pursue game. At the same
time, the forest was an old Platonic image, and when Giles of
Viterbo and Giordano Bruno use it, they use it as Plato did, to provide an image of the material world, a place of twisting paths, im-
minent danger, constant growth, and constant decay, bathed in

shifting patterns of light, endlessly fertile and endlessly confusing. Finding a pattern to the forest is as elusive an undertaking as tracking prey.

The very word that Plato used to describe the stuff of nature, *hyle*, was the word that meant "wood"; Latin *materia* would also come to mean either "wood" or "matter." But one translator of Plato's Greek into Latin, a contemporary of Saint Augustine's named Calcidius, employed his own term for *hyle*: *silva*, "woods" or "forest" rather than "wood." And as it happened, Calcidius's peculiar translation of one Platonic dialogue, *Timaeus*, was the single work of Plato's to be read continuously throughout the Middle Ages into the fifteenth century. This translation by Calcidius, *silva* and all, must have provided Giles of Viterbo with his own introduction to Plato, and hence the idea of matter as a forest may have been one of those striking "I used to think" misconceptions developed in youth. Later Giles would read Plato in Marsilio Ficino's infinitely more precise Latin translations, and finally he would read Plato in Greek. But he retained the image of the *silva* as a literal Forest of Matter, and used it to explain a number of Christian truths, as he said, "according to the mind of Plato."

In the first place, the forest was as immediate an image as any for the world's stubborn impenetrability. It could only be seen clearly from the outside, above the treetops, and Giles used this overview to evoke the way the material world must look from the vantage of Plato's higher world of Ideas. On several occasions Plato himself compared the human search for knowledge to hunting game; by the same figure of speech we still "approach," "track down," and "investigate" what we do not know. Marsilio Ficino took the image of the spiritual hunt a step further, as the explicit pursuit of God, an archetypal creator of such brilliance that he was to the sun what the sun is to us: "That hunter is excessively fortunate who has applied himself to pursuing, with all his powers, step by step, the Sun of the sun. He shall have found what he sought, inflamed by its heat, even before he seeks it."

Giles of Viterbo, in his turn, took Plato's brief lines about hunting, together with Ficino's hunt for divinity and the strange image of the Forest of Matter, to spin an extended tale about the human

soul's search for God. From 1506 onward, he set down many of
these ideas in writing from a hermitage in his own Ciminian wood,
as the young Girolamo Seripando studied Plato at his side. One
copy of the resulting book, Seripando's own copy in fact, was eventually lodged in the library at San Giovanni a Carbonara (it is now
in the Biblioteca Nazionale in Naples). This manuscript and other
copies were read eagerly in the sixteenth century, although the
book was never published, because Giles never finished it; he left
off writing it in 1512 to take up other projects.

Giles of Viterbo's influential volume made an attempt to reconcile Christian theology with Platonic philosophy, but he did so in a
curious way. He began with the standard theological textbook of
the day, preserving its chapter headings but entirely rewriting the
contents. The textbook itself had been written in the twelfth century by the Dominican Peter Lombard, who called his work *Sentences*; like the catechism, it made its points by a process of endless
questions and answers, but it did so with encyclopedic, one might
even say plodding, thoroughness: How are the persons of the Holy
Trinity related to one another? What happens when a mouse eats
the Host? (For that question, at least, the answer was lapidary:
"Deus scit"—"God knows.") This intricate apparatus of argument is
what Giles of Viterbo rewrote, using word-pictures, myths, and
metaphors drawn from Plato's dialogues, the poetry of Homer and
Virgil, and classical mythology. To his enterprise, he applied all the
seductive powers of storytelling, imagery, and beautiful erotic language, and called the result *The "Sentences" According to the Mind of
Plato*. He wrote as he and Mariano da Genazzano had trained
themselves to preach: emotionally, rhetorically, in a consciously
classical vein, their new style of Augustinian eloquence set starkly
up against Peter Lombard's Dominican precision.

In Giles of Viterbo's hands, the Forest of Matter transformed
Platonic philosophy into concrete images by taking words like *silva*
and "tracking" literally: matter, *silva*, became the Forest, in which
confused humanity hunted down knowledge of God. He cast the
goddess Diana, the huntress, as a model for the searching human
soul. In the Forest, his Diana sought out tracks or traces, literally
footprints, *vestigia*, of God's divine light. Giles wrote:

Diana is held to be a virgin, because she is herself free from *silva* and matter, and yet she devotes herself to holy hunting in the Forest . . . Diana practices her hunting, that is, she participates in Mind, and spends her time exclusively in hunting and understanding. To these she devotes her efforts, with all her enthusiasm and all her spirit, to exploring and pursuing the light of her homeland.

He urged his readers, in turn, to be like Diana:

[Plato] declares that the soul is happy in heaven, rejoicing not in realities, that is, in created things, but in pure essence, which belongs to God alone. For this reason he teaches that beauty is hunted out from the Forest of Matter, pure beauty, which exists without any mixture or composition . . . But come, let us track the hidden understanding from this Forest with the help that we can find in the human soul as nets and snares.

As with the image of tracking, "footprints" were a common philosophical term already in the ancient and early Christian worlds, to which Peter Lombard's *Sentences* assigned a more specific theological meaning—the Dominican described *vestigia* as traces of divine presence in creation that took less literal form than the "image and likeness" of himself in which God had created Adam. But in transforming Peter Lombard's *"Sentences" According to the Mind of Plato*, Giles of Viterbo worked the same magic on the original abstract formulation of *vestigia* that he had worked on forests and tracking—he took the words literally and conjured them into haunting images:

Sometimes, however, the footprints are so hidden that the power of human intelligence cannot reach them. For this reason we seek help from another source, and bring in experienced dogs so that with their help we may obtain our quarry. Now we are chasing something about God out into the open from its hiding places in Nature, something that we could never succeed in capturing with Nature alone as our guide, not unless we use the demonstrations of dialectic as our dogs and the study of philosophy as our nets. These dogs cannot track hidden quarry except by means of footprints, clear traces of the feet, or odors. Thus in this Forest of Mat-

ter divine footprints lie hidden, but when we take notice of them by
means of reason, and consider them well, we hunt out the hiding places
of the divine light. Plato assents to this in the third book of the *Laws*,
when he teaches that one should track down musical harmonies in the
manner of experienced dogs.

As for the footprints themselves, Giles of Viterbo described
these traces in the Forest of Matter as qualities: beauty, order, number. His Diana was destined to rush about the Forest following the
tracks of beauty and light until they added up to a specific sum.

> God . . . created this external and secondary world according to the di-
> vine archetype, for which reason the whole world itself is a footprint of
> God, and all the things contained in it should be called divine footprints
> . . . we must pursue the tracks by which human hunting brings back the
> Trinity as its prize.

At this point, enraptured, Diana, like the human soul, would
rise above the Forest to become one with the Moon, lifted far
above the Forest of Matter to the realm of Ideas, which Giles as a
good Christian associated with the realm of the angels:

> The nature of intelligent creatures is split in two, for in part it pursues the
> tracks of divinity, but in part, clinging to heaven's palace, it has no desire
> to hunt down sensible things. Thus nature has prepared companions for
> our spirits, heavenly minds, and calls one Diana in the Forest, the other
> the Moon in heaven . . . defined now not in terms of number, or species,
> but by kind. These kinds of minds that are called by the name of the
> Moon have an image that is so superior to our own that they love to im-
> prove ours, and bathe the shadows of our Forests with their limpid rays.
> On Mount Latmos the Moon is said to have loved Endymion, kissing him
> at night when he was asleep, and this story is not without its point.

The point of Giles's story was a radical claim that the classical
gods were nothing more or less than guardian angels: to Endymion
and the Moon he added Ulysses and Minerva, Aeneas and Venus,
treating the ancient heroes as if they had really existed, and the

eros of the gods, as in the case of the Moon and Endymion, was proof that the God of Abraham and Jesus Christ was the same God of love. Thus Giles managed to make both the Forest of Matter and the soul's progress through it compellingly erotic, for he envisioned the world as shot through with a divine love whose joys could best be described for mortal readers in sensual terms. He used the myth of Diana and her lover Endymion to describe the loving care that guardian angels lavished on their human charges. He also returned time and again to the Hebrew love lyrics in the Song of Songs, read in his own day as the romance not only of man and woman but of God and Israel, of Christ and the Church, of Christ and the human soul. His ultimate vision saw the Forest of Matter transformed into a bank of the river Jordan, where pure souls gathered to join forever with Christ the King:

> Those blessed souls drink deep, whom the King caresses like brides with the kisses of his mouth, whom he inundates with the wine that delights human hearts, and the brides, drunk on joyous abundance, sing, as in the nuptial mysteries, "His kisses are sweeter than wine, and more powerful by far."

This was the vision of Giles of Viterbo, less profoundly philosophical than the vision of Marsilio Ficino but also more visually compelling. When Giordano Bruno created his own image of the forest, it would be as vivid as Giles of Viterbo's, and there were few other forests of such ravishing suggestiveness. Furthermore, one of them, the forest of Jacopo Sannazaro's *Arcadia*, was created under Giles's direct influence.

Giles also used the image of Diana in the forest for an allegorical poem, "Love's Beautiful Hunt," in which he contrasted the pursuit of sexual love unfavorably with the pursuit of divinity. Here he resorted to a mythological figure, Actaeon, the hunter who spied a naked Diana bathing in the forest and as punishment was transformed into a stag; his dogs turned on him and tore him to death. The protagonist of Giles's "Beautiful Hunt" has been undone by passion, but because the object of his pursuit is a mere mortal, he, unlike Actaeon, cannot escape his confinement in the Forest of

Matter. He complains about his horned forehead and lacerated flesh:

> I bear what I've become upon my brow
> Depicted better than my pen can say;
> Awareness of my error's been bestowed
> By giving me to my own hounds as prey.
> Torn and destroyed by my own weapons now,
> I taste the fruits of all that I assayed;
> But worst of all the torments that I face,
> I cannot see my way out of this place.
>
> Now some would claim that mine's a lesser grief
> Than Actaeon's, who turned into a stag;
> Yet unlike my misfortune, his was brief,
> Despite the fact that he was torn to rags.
> By suffering at last he gained relief;
> Long as I live, my pain will never flag.
> To my annoyance, Death's rejected me,
> And thus in living I die constantly.

All these images—the forest, the lover, and Actaeon—would appear in Bruno's work, where he connected them, like Giles of Viterbo before him, with the pursuit of God and associated them, like Giles, with the biblical Song of Songs.

A Thousand Worlds

Then Peter opened his mouth, and said, Of a truth I perceive that God is no respecter of persons: But in every nation he that feareth him, and worketh righteousness, is accepted with him.　　—Acts 10:34–35

God is no respecter of persons, for he is prepared to give everyone the same grace, and if he has not given it, it is because you have put up an obstacle.

　—Teofilo da Vairano, *On the Grace of the New Testament,* 106–107r

Officially, the Kingdom of Naples expelled all Jews from its territory in 1563, part of an attempt to keep the city's Spanish overlords from imposing their Inquisition. Many of these people descended from Spanish and Portuguese Sephardim who had been driven from Spain in 1492 or Portugal in 1497 and escaped to Italy. Other families, however, must have been present since ancient Roman times. Rome itself boasted the oldest Jewish community in Europe, and southern Italy had important yeshivas in the fifteenth century, one of which produced the great Jewish convert to Christianity known as Flavius Mithridates. By the sixteenth century, Naples was one of the Italian centers for publication in Hebrew, a fact that implies that the kingdom hosted a substantial reading public.

For the Jews threatened with expulsion, the only alternative was baptism, and this was the choice that many people made, whether as families or as individuals. Expulsion meant automatic confiscation of property; acceptance of baptism might mean the ability to retain most of it, especially in conditions of mass conversion. As a result, despite drastic measures like forced exile and the creation of ghettos by a papal decree in 1555, Italy retained a significant Jewish presence, especially in regions with a policy of tolerance. Most of these refuges were in the north—Venice, Ferrara, Mantua, Pesaro—or along the borders between the Papal States and Tuscany. But even in the Spanish-dominated areas of southern Italy, Jews never disappeared entirely. Some families dispersed into the hinterlands, others took precarious places in a society where the line between Jew and Gentile could never be drawn with total precision. Forced conversions in Spain and Portugal, and then in Italy itself, had created a whole class of "new Christians" who preserved many of their Jewish traditions; compulsory mass baptisms did not make for a secure grounding in the Christian life.

And despite a general climate of hostility, interactions took place between Christians and Jews, especially in the first half of the sixteenth century; the very ubiquity of this contact prompted the Neapolitan pope Paul IV to create ghettos in the first place. For a period in the late fifteenth and early sixteenth centuries, many Christian theologians actively sought out rabbis for enlightenment about their shared biblical texts; Jews attended Christian sermons out of interest rather than coercion.

These were the circumstances in which a series of Christian scholars came into contact with the Hebrew mystic tradition known as Kabbalah, which gave rise to a whole literature of biblical interpretation as well as a discipline that involved using the letters of the Hebrew Bible for purposes of divination. Christian thinkers from Giovanni Pico della Mirandola and Johannes Reuchlin at the end of the fifteenth century to Athanasius Kircher in the seventeenth tried to reconcile the Kabbalah's path toward the knowledge of God with the demands of their own religion, courting controversy as they did so but drawn irresistibly to the kabbalistic literature's powerful imagery of light and darkness, wisdom and ignorance, and unabashed eroticism, a shared legacy from

Plato and his early followers. However vocally sixteenth-century Christians at every social level might denounce their Jewish neighbors, the rejection was never complete, just as many new Christians never entirely abandoned their Jewish past.

The year 1563 was also when the reforming Council of Trent issued its final decrees and disbanded, leaving the Catholic Church in a more intransigent position on a whole series of hotly debated questions than the council's original conveners could ever have imagined, and the rift with the Protestants more drastic than ever. Among the council's harsh new provisions, one of the most startling, in an era of careful textual scholarship, imposed the Vulgate text of the Bible as the definitive version of Scripture. Most of the council's delegates knew perfectly well that Saint Jerome's Latin furnished an imperfect translation of the Bible's original Greek and, especially, Hebrew texts; hence the council's decree knowingly flew in the face of the whole Renaissance scholarly tradition of emphasis on original texts. What adoption of the Latin Bible did, however, was put Scripture and its interpretation firmly in the hands of Rome and Latin Catholic culture, ruling out the authority of the Orthodox Greeks and the rabbis.

The council's decree could not, however, suppress demand for knowledge of Greek and Hebrew; it stood too violently against every standard that humanist scholarship had built up so carefully over the course of the fifteenth and sixteenth centuries. As part of his theological education, Giordano Bruno learned Hebrew at San Domenico and became so proficient that his superiors decided to send him to Rome to perform in that language before Pope Pius V in 1569. He recited Psalm 86, and then, in an early display of his astonishing memory, he recited it backward. During his stay, he also came to know the convert Andrea de Monte, professor of Hebrew at the University of Rome, and noted years later how impressed he had been by de Monte's learning and eloquence.

Ironically, Bruno's performance before the pope came in a period when the Neapolitan branch of the Holy Office, spurred on by this sternly pious pontiff, had prosecuted a large number of converted Jews for alleged reversion to their original faith. When his own turn before the Inquisition came, Bruno, baptized a Catholic, would be subjected to questioning about heresy, not about "Juda-

izing." He did not volunteer information about his readings in Kabbalah, nor was he asked about them, and hence our chief source for
his biography says nothing about how he came into contact with
Jewish wisdom. He surely did so in Naples, however, and one likely
source for such contact would have been his teacher of logic,
Teofilo da Vairano, whose monastic library at San Giovanni a Carbonara included a number of works on Christian Kabbalah collected by the order's former prior general, Giles of Viterbo. Giles,
indeed, ranked as one of the chief exponents in the sixteenth century of Christian Kabbalah as well as Platonic philosophy. He had
corresponded eagerly with Reuchlin, and learned Hebrew and Aramaic well enough to read both and to annotate his collection of
manuscripts in the appropriate language. Through his protégé
Girolamo Seripando, he bequeathed some works on Kabbalah to
the Seripando library alongside his Neoplatonic treatises. And
through Seripando, Giles of Viterbo also gave voice to the ecu-
menical line of Catholic thinking that suffered the most resounding defeat at the Council of Trent.

Despite the hardening doctrinal positions of his own time,
Teofilo da Vairano seems to have shared something of Giles of
Viterbo's ecumenism, at least to judge from his one surviving work,
On the Grace of the New Testament, in which he declared that a
truly Catholic Church was bound by definition to include all hu-
manity without exception because "all are elected by God."

As proof of that universal election, Teofilo incorporated the
Jews into his view of the universal Church by insisting that both
Christians and Jews had been called into the same divine cov-
enant, noting that God's pledges to Abraham and Moses were as
integral a part of the divine plan as the Gospels:

> Let no one think that the people of God who wandered in the desert as
> exiles from Egypt were not the Church of God.
>
> I do not want you to be ignorant, brothers, of the fact that all of our
> fathers were beneath the pillar of cloud, so that all could cross the sea,
> and all were baptized by Moses in the cloud and in the sea, and all of
> them ate the same spiritual food, and all drank the same spiritual drink,
> for they drank from the spiritual rock that contained them—for the rock
> was Christ, the very one.

Conversely, he insisted that Christians could also, and right-fully, be included among what he called "children of the promise," asking Jewish readers rhetorically "to show me a single proof by which you can prove that we are not of the Church and that you are." Although he regarded the Gospels' revelation as the most complete fulfillment of God's plan, Teofilo differs from his contemporaries in his insistence on inclusion of the Jews in that divine plan rather than their division from it, marshaling the testimony of the earliest Church to insist that charity should guide religion above all other principles. If Teofilo da Vairano is the person who encouraged the young Bruno to read Kabbalah, he would have done so from a position of unusual tolerance.

Bruno had already decided in his private thoughts that Jesus of Nazareth could not have been the son of God incarnate in human flesh. When, thirty years later, he told his Venetian inquisitors that he had, "in effect, harbored doubts about the term 'person' for the Son and the Holy Spirit," both he and his inquisitors realized that doubting the validity of the term "person" was an oblique way of expressing doubts about the divinity of Jesus. His examiners then pressed him on that point to see whether he would state it more explicitly. Bruno duly detailed his doubts, but he insisted that these were only doubts in discussing philosophy, not Catholic theology or Christian faith. Still, it must have been clear to these Christian inquisitors that Bruno was no longer defending a Christian position:

> To get to the individual point about which I have been asked concerning the divine persons, that wisdom and that son of the mind whom the philosophers call the intellect and the theologians the Word, if one ought to believe that this took on human flesh, then, philosophically speaking, I have never understood this, but have doubted it and held the belief with inconstant faith.

Pressed further, he continued:

> As for the second person, I declare that in reality I have held it to be one in essence with the first, and likewise the third . . . I have only doubted how this second person could be incarnate, as I have said above, and suf-

fered, but I have never openly denied this or taught it, and if I have said something about this second person, I have done so by referring to the opinions of others.

One of these "others" whom Bruno summoned in support of his arguments was none other than Saint Augustine, one of the four "Fathers" of the Western Church; Bruno said he could not understand the Trinity "if not in the way that I have explained before speaking philosophically, and designating the Father's intellect as the Son and his love as the Holy Spirit, without recognizing the term 'person,' which Saint Augustine says is not an ancient term but a new one of his own time." This command of theological literature and theological argumentation must have been what made Bruno such an extraordinarily difficult defendant; however outrageous his claims may have seemed to Christian orthodoxy, his uncanny ability to put orthodoxy itself into a historical context made the certainties of dogma look uncertain.

In exchange for the dogma he could not accept, Bruno willingly supplied his inquisitors with his own version of the Trinity:

> In the divinity I understand that all the attributes are one and the same thing, together with theologians and the greatest philosophers; I understand three attributes: power, wisdom, and goodness, or mind, intellect, and love.
>
> In my philosophy, moreover, I understand that from this spirit proceed the life and soul of every creature that has a soul and life, which I therefore understand to be immortal, as is also the case with bodies. As for their substance, they are all immortal, for there is no other death but division and congregation, which doctrine, it seems to me, is expressed in Ecclesiastes, where it says, "There is nothing new under the sun: What is? What was. What was? What is," and so on.

In this oral testimony as in his writing, Bruno drew his theology from the Hebrew Bible: the Psalms, the Song of Songs, and Ecclesiastes. Despite his wide-ranging skepticism about so much of received religion, these were passages of Scripture that he never called into question. Nor was he alone in this preference for the oldest parts of the Bible; the Holy Office in Naples heard at least three cases in the late sixteenth century of freethinking Catholics who explicitly identified themselves with Judaism, thus taking a step beyond Bruno's own resolutely independent agenda.

Many of the remarks made about the Jews in Bruno's surviving writings are not complimentary, and they have often been taken as evidence that he shared the anti-Semitic prejudice common to most citizens of Spanish-dominated Naples. These aspersions, how-ever, are cast not by Bruno himself but by his various characters, speaking in character. The most damning of all these denun-ciations comes in his dialogue *Spaccio della bestia trionfante* (*The Expulsion of the Triumphant Beast*), which extols ancient Egyptian religion as it proceeds to redesign the cosmos, arguing that the brawling gods and heroes of ancient Greece are hardly suitable for the glorious order of the heavens. Here the divinity Sophia, whose name is the Greek word for "wisdom," denounces the Jews fero-ciously, along with their Kabbalah:

> Do not infer that the sufficiency of Chaldaean magic comes from Jewish Kabbalah, because the Hebrews have been convicted of being the excre-ment of Egypt, and there has never been anyone who could pretend with any appearance of truth that the Egyptians could have taken any princi-ple, worthy or unworthy, from them. Whence we Greeks recognize Egypt, the great kingdom of literature and nobility, as the parents of our myths, metaphors, and doctrines, and not that generation that never had a palm of land that was its own by nature or civil justice; whence one can con-clude satisfactorily that they are not naturally, nor have they ever been, by long violence of fortune, part of the world.

It is tempting to read this passage as absolute wisdom passing judg-ment on the inferiority of Hebrew tradition to the wisdom of an-cient Egypt, and many of Bruno's readers over the years have succumbed to that temptation. Yet Bruno explicitly makes Sophia speak of herself as Greek, to show that she is specifically Greek wis-dom rather than wisdom absolute, in a dialogue where the Greek model of the heavens is being systematically swept aside for a more elegant design. And indeed Sophia meets an immediate challenge, from a character, Saulino, who bears the name of Bruno's maternal family, the Savolino. If any personage in this dialogue can be taken to represent the author's point of view, it is he—and he will do the same service in the dialogue Bruno wrote shortly after *The Expulsion of the Triumphant Beast*, *The Heroic Frenzies*. Saulino maintains that the Greek wisdom of Sophia is faulty, dictated by the moral shortcomings of the god she serves, that jealous womanizer, Jove, and this faulty wisdom has led her to misunderstand the Jews:

> This, O Sophia, is said by Jove out of envy, because [the Jews] are worthily called and call themselves holy, for being more of a celestial and divine generation than a terrestrial and human one, and not having a worthy part of this world, they have been approved by the angels as heirs to that other one, which is so much more worthy because there is no man, great or small, wise or stupid, who by force of choice or fate can acquire it, and certainly can never have it as his own.

Saulino's reproof is shortly corroborated by the upheaval and renewal of the cosmos, a theme that itself derives from Kabbalah: the great Jubilee in which the universe renews itself every fifty thousand years. Bruno would have known about this great Jubilee from at least two sources: the writings of the fifteenth-century Christian kabbalist Giovanni Pico della Mirandola and the early-sixteenth-century *Dialogues on Love* (*Dialoghi d'amore*) by the Italian Jewish writer Leone Abarbanel, usually known as Leone Ebreo. Both writers mention the most radical version of this doctrine, in which the universe, upon reaching the Jubilee, is re-created from nothingness; the formulations of both also show the profound influence of Marsilio Ficino's philosophy.

In prison in Venice, Bruno spoke to his cellmates about this endlessly renewed and re-created universe. As one of them reported, "He said that God needed the world as much as the world needed God, and that God would be nothing without the world, and for this reason God did nothing but create new worlds."

One of the most important ways in which Bruno himself overturned the conventional cosmos was to make it infinite. He clearly drew his belief in infinite worlds, and a good deal else, from an essay titled *On Learned Ignorance* by the fifteenth-century German philosopher-priest (and eventual cardinal) Nicholas of Cusa. It is also an idea he could have elaborated from Kabbalah, especially from a medieval text that was collected by Giles of Viterbo both in its original and in a garbled translation, part Spanish, part Italian, part Aramaic. There the author describes riding on a cherub "through a thousand worlds":

> He rides upon a cloud, he rides on a cherub and I flew and I fly through a thousand worlds and they ask of that cherub where is the place of highest honor and I ride over a cloud a thousand worlds beyond the world and the cherub flew through ten thousand worlds; eyes have seen nothing but God alone.

In its multiple worlds, its combinations of Hebrew letters, and its interconnections, in addition to its affinities with the Neoplatonic interplay of darkness and light, Kabbalah bore an uncannily close relationship to the way of thinking that Giordano Bruno came to identify as the Nolan philosophy. Bruno's was certainly not a Christian Kabbalah; if anything it was more identifiably Jewish. Neither alternative would find any official approval within the walls of San Domenico. As a student, Bruno restricted his energies to a less dangerous pursuit: the mental exercise known as the art of memory.

CHAPTER NINE

Art and Astronomy

A fool's the only one who would rely
On sense, and not the reasoning behind it.
—*The Heroic Frenzies*, "Second Response of the Heart to the Eyes"

R emembering would become Giordano Bruno's chief profession. In his own day he earned his widest reputation, and often his living, by teaching an ancient technique for the enhancement of memory developed in ancient Greece and called the "artificial memory" by the ancient Romans, who included memory as a basic element in rhetorical training. Bruno first learned to use the artificial memory as a boy in Nola—it formed a standard part of grammar-school education—but in Naples the Dominicans had refined the art of recall to the ultimate degree. The Scriptures, sermons, canon law, and theological tractates they committed to memory provided themes for their preaching and exercise for their minds. Thomas Aquinas had so organized his own thoughts that he could dictate four separate books at once to four different secretaries. And like Thomas Aquinas before him, Giordano Bruno proved to excel at memory, phenomenally so. In 1569, when he was still a material student hoping for admission to the Dominican college, the superiors of San Domenico sent him to Rome to perform feats of recall before Pope Pius V and Scipione Cardinal Rebiba, an honor so unusual that the young friar traveled to Rome by coach, like a nobleman (what he most remembered about the trip was the number of corpses lying along the Appian Way, victims of banditry and malaria). After reciting Psalm 86 forward and backward in Hebrew, he gave the cardinal and the pontiff a brief lesson on the fine points of his art. Apparently, therefore, Bruno had already developed his own version of the artificial memory, one that was both novel and teachable to others. Ten years later, he would compare his own improvements on the ancient system to the difference between publishing books with the printing press and primitive carving on trees. Yet despite his claims that the art of memory could be taught and learned as straightforward technique, he treated it as far more than a clever trick or a preacher's aid. For Giordano Bruno, practicing the art of memory became as deeply symbolic an activity as hunting had been for Giles of Viterbo in the forests of matter and spirit.

The basic principle of the artificial memory was a simple one: to link words with images, and because in fact babies learn to point and speak simultaneously, this association of verbal and visual cues may be deeply rooted in human nature. The ancient Greeks and Romans trained their memories primarily in order to become more persuasive speakers in government and the law courts; we know the details of the artificial memory as they used it from the rhetorical treatises that helped to start ambitious young men on their careers in public service. The advice these treatises impart is mostly practical—speak clearly, organize your thoughts, capture the goodwill of your audience, remember what you mean to say—but ancient rhetoricians used a precise technical vocabulary to pinpoint every trick of persuasion and every moment in a speech. Careful application of the artificial memory enabled ancient orators to deliver speeches of staggering length without a single note on papyrus to interfere with the grace of their gestures or the drape of their togas; good Roman lawyers could hold forth for seven hours of close-packed argumentation in summing up a case. To be sure, some classical orators, of whom Cicero is the most famous, regarded the whole procedure of the artificial memory as too cumbersome to bother with (an opinion Erasmus would share with him fifteen centuries later), but then Cicero must have memorized by simple rote with unusual ease. In the case of people like Giordano Bruno and

Thomas Aquinas, who combined exceptional natural gifts of memory with the rigorous use of artificial discipline, the resulting mental control was incredible to the audiences who watched them perform, and would doubtless seem still more astounding today.

At the end of the thirteenth century, a Catalan mystic named Ramon Llull (1232–1316) introduced his own variant to the classical art of memory, promoting it in many of the 250 books he wrote in the course of his busy life. Ancient orators built up their memories by creating imaginary buildings in their minds and stocking these buildings with people and statues that represented individual ideas or parts of a speech. Llull's "Great Art" (*Ars Magna*), or "combinatory art," replaced these memory buildings with imaginary concentric wheels, each divided into a series of compartments; every spin of a wheel potentially created new ideas with new combinations. At the same time, however, the system's abstract simplicity—all the wheels reduced in the end to one perfect circle—lent a simplicity to the overall structure of Llull's thought, and to Llull's concept of the God who had created such complexity in nature. Llull declared that his Great Art of memory had a higher spiritual purpose:

> We created this Art in order to understand and love God, so that the human intellect can ascend artificially toward the knowledge of God and as a consequence into love, because the intellect can do with artifice what it cannot do without artifice, so long as divine grace and wisdom act as mediators. And because the more God is understood, the more he is loved, therefore this Art brings it about that God is loved as much as possible.

Bruno's art of memory used both Llullian wheels and the classical system's imaginary characters set into imaginary architectures. Despite his own ability to store and recall memories, Bruno always emphasized that his skill was a matter of constant exercise as well as natural ability, and he insisted that his system could be taught to anyone of reasonable intelligence. By 1572, he was a well-drilled friar in the Order of Preachers who knew how to back up his words with gestures and who used pictures, emblems, and diagrams to illustrate his method.

Richly decorated, the church of San Domenico Maggiore was one of the places that supplied the young Bruno with suggestive images. Some of these images recur in his later writings, and they reflect a distinctly sixteenth-century taste. A modern visitor to San Domenico cannot help noticing its splendid thirteenth-century frescoes by the great Roman painter Pietro Cavallini, but Bruno seems to have gravitated instead to Renaissance works done in classical style, with classical gods, allegories, and personified ideals; we can imagine that the architectures he constructed in his head as he cultivated the artificial memory were fashionably modern rather than, like San Domenico, imposingly Gothic.

Within the second chapel on the left of the church, the brand-new tomb of the poet Bernardino Rota, created in 1569–71 while its occupant was still very much alive (he died in 1575), bore beautiful marble reliefs of river gods representing the Tiber and the Arno, an attractively erudite way of calling attention to the fact that Rota composed both in Latin and in vernacular (and specifically the Tuscan vernacular of Dante and Petrarch). Bruno would emulate Rota's versatility, writing Latin hexameter verse and vernacular sonnets, and combine the tomb's river imagery with Teofilo da Vairano's symbolic river Jordan to expound his own Nolan philosophy.

Just to the right of the main portal of San Domenico, inserted into the building as a separate unit in itself, a family chapel had been built by Galeotto Carafa da Sanseverino in 1513 whose arches and columns, in the dark gray volcanic stone called *piperno*, set off a series of marble panels decorated in relief with signs of the zodiac. In the designers' original scheme, the stars and planets served to demonstrate how astrological forces had helped to determine the greatness of the noble Galeotto; his fame was as natural, as inevitable, as the shape of the heavens. The theme was a popular one in an age when astronomy had not yet separated as a discipline from astrology: the stars and planets all had their distinct personalities, their favorite gems, colors, and stones, and their own days of the week, and few people doubted the profound effect of their movements on earthly events.

Bruno learned astronomy as part of his preparation as a material student, using the classic textbook on the subject, *De sphaera* (*On the Sphere*), written about 1230 by a professor at the University of Paris, John of Sacrobosco (who may have been an Englishman). Sacrobosco's clear presentation of spherical geometry provided a solid introduction for anyone who wanted to read the astronomical works of the Alexandrian astronomer Ptolemy and those of his Islamic commentators, and he did this so concisely (the whole work was nine thousand words, not quite forty modern pages), and so effectively, that teachers (including Galileo Galilei) continued to use his textbook until the late seventeenth century, adding their commentaries to his thirteenth-century original.

Sacrobosco's cosmos was a Christian version of the system first presented by Ptolemy in ancient Alexandria: a sphere of fixed stars marked the outer limit of the universe. Nested within it were five more spheres, belonging to Saturn, Jupiter, Mars, Venus, and Mercury, all of them revolving around Earth. Outside the sixth sphere, nothing existed but God. The personalities of the stars and planets still harked back to the ancient gods, goddesses, animals, and heroes whose names they bore, so that charting their movements was an exercise in social dynamics as much as mathematics.

When the Polish mathematician Nicolaus Copernicus proposed a sun-centered universe in his *Little Commentary* (*Commentariolus*) of 1514 and his *De revolutionibus orbium coelestium* (*On the Revolutions of the Heavenly Spheres*) in 1543, his theory had no particular effect on those who regarded the heavens as a place peopled by a set of distinctive characters. If anything, the Copernican cosmos assigned the sun a place more in keeping with its regal nature. Neither did Copernicus conflict significantly with Sacrobosco, for both believed that the universe consisted of spheres in circular motion. As yet there was no prohibition against reading *On the Revolutions of the Heavenly Spheres*, and Bruno certainly read the book, at a moment when his own interests in Plato and Marsilio Ficino made the idea of a universe centered on the sun philosophically appealing.

Bruno's later writings make it clear that he was not an astrologer in any conventional sense; he regarded the personalities ascribed to the heavenly bodies as fictions, and felt perfect freedom to rewrite their stories in one of his dialogues, *The Expulsion of the Triumphant Beast*. In his own day, Plato had invented myths to convey his philosophical truths, and so did Bruno; like Plato, Bruno felt the need to replace the old ribald stories about the feckless classical gods with more uplifting tales. The Neapolitan scholar Eugenio Canone was first to propose that Bruno's initial stimulus for *The Expulsion of the Triumphant Beast* might have come from the astrological reliefs in the Carafa chapel of San Domenico Maggiore. But unlike the pure white marble of those reliefs, the characters and stories that Bruno imagined, both the old and the new, were vibrant with color, ready to be incorporated into his memory as active images, or simply to beguile him as he gazed into the night sky.

At the same time, he could also look at the heavens with the eyes of a natural philosopher in the modern mold. During Bruno's tenure at San Domenico Maggiore, the Calabrian philosopher Bernardino Telesio had been living off and on in the luxurious palazzo of Alfonso Carafa, Duke of Nocera (a short walk away on the stately Via Medina), promoting his view of the world as driven by two mechanical forces, heat and cold. These, Telesio asserted in conversation and in his large, ambitious treatise *On the Nature of Things* (printed in 1586 but written over the course of many years), had been brought into the world by God at the moment of creation as the concentrated bodies of the sun and the earth and had been locked in battle ever since. Bruno would praise Telesio as "most discerning" in one of his dialogues, and eventually adapted many aspects of the elder philosopher's theory of heat and cold to his own view of the universe.

Another view of astronomy met Bruno on his arrival in Rome. By the 1570s, the city had become a center for astronomical studies, especially in the Jesuits' small but ambitious Roman College, housed in temporary quarters until their huge new building was completed near Piazza Venezia. The professor of mathematics, a Portuguese-educated German named Christoph Clavius, had quickly made a name for himself as a superb teacher. In 1570, at the age of thirty-three, Clavius published a thousand copies of his own commentary on Sacrobosco's *On the Sphere* with the Roman publisher Victor Helianus (the first of an eventual six editions).

Shortly after his election in 1572, Pope Gregory XIII would appoint Clavius head of a commission to reform the calendar; the resulting "Gregorian calendar," implemented in 1582, is the same one we use today.

Bruno's house in Rome, the Dominican convent of Santa Maria Sopra Minerva, stood just across the street from the buildings that were razed to make way for the Jesuit college in 1583. He and Clavius were therefore the closest of neighbors, which does not necessarily mean that they met. Institutional relations between the well-established Dominicans and the upstart Jesuits were wary. On the other hand, both men were unusually open-minded, albeit in their own peculiar ways. Clavius would spend the rest of his life revising his *Commentary on the Sphere of Sacrobosco* to keep up with the latest developments in astronomy, from Tycho Brahe's observations of a supernova in 1572 to Galileo's discoveries with the telescope in 1610; he was, in fact, the first person to invite Galileo to lecture in Rome.

For both of them, astronomy was an excitingly unsettled subject in the 1570s. That excitement stemmed as much from new ways of looking at existing data as from the data themselves, which astronomers like the Danish nobleman Tycho Brahe, only two years older than Bruno, were gathering with great precision. As yet, however, there was no real difference between the huge quadrant that Tycho laid out on the wall of his observatory at Uraniborg and the giant instruments that the Arab astronomer Ibn Yunus had used in his Cairo observatory in the tenth century; both made all their measurements with the naked eye. (The telescope was invented in the late sixteenth or early seventeenth century; Galileo began using it in 1610, as noted above, and Campanella at about the same time.) What distinguished Copernicus from Ptolemy in second-century-B.C. Alexandria or Ibn Yunus in tenth-century Cairo was not so much the quality of his data as the form he ascribed to the universe; *On the Revolutions of the Heavenly Spheres* used careful but conventional astronomical measurements to obtain a radically different model of the heavens. The fact that Bruno was more interested in models of the universe than in the gathering of precise observational data does not make him less "scientific" than colleagues like Brahe—science as we know it did not yet exist, and besides, in its present-day form it still depends as vitally on thought problems as on the gathering of data. His ability to treat models of the universe as just that—models—was an ability that modern scientists still recognize as an essential part of their own discipline. It is indicative of Bruno's own training in natural philosophy, however, that he could feel free to rewrite the mythology of the constellations at the same time that he could redraw the geometry of the universe—and did so, as a mature philosopher, in a way that modern scientists find much more valid than the universe of Galileo. His mind, in our terms, was both artistic and scientific. In his terms, both casts of mind were philosophical: one derived from Plato, one from Aristotle.

In the 1570s, however, neither he nor Clavius had any idea how drastically their ideas about the universe would change in succeeding years. They only knew that astronomy was no less exciting for them than it had been for Sacrobosco, galvanized, in his own thirteenth century, by new contact, in Latin translation, with the works of the medieval Arab astronomers.

Bruno's trip to Rome as a master of the art of memory may have marked the high point of his experience as a friar of San Domenico Maggiore. In his closed community, however, this recognition by his superiors may also have marked him out for jealousy and suspicion among his peers.

CHAPTER TEN

Trouble Again

NAPLES AND ROME, 1576

A fter his return from Rome, Fra Giordano's career within San Domenico Maggiore progressed along the usual steps, at the usual pace. He became a subdeacon in 1570, and then a deacon in 1571. For the final step of ordination, the friars of San Domenico Maggiore were normally sent somewhere else in the Kingdom of Naples, to give them a larger view of what it meant to be a priest. Not all of them could expect to stay within the exclusive community of San Domenico Maggiore; most, in fact, would be sent out into a wider and more humble world. For his own ordination, Fra Giordano was assigned to the Dominican convent of San Bartolomeo in Campagna, a beautiful, wealthy little feudal town set among the dramatic volcanic crags behind Salerno. The priors of San Bartolomeo had included some of the most important figures in the Dominican order; as assignments went, his still marked him out for an exceptional future. As Bruno described it, however, Campagna was "far away from Naples." He performed his first Mass in the convent's parish church sometime in the spring of 1572, but by the fall he was back in San Domenico Maggiore, ready to start his first ten-month term as a formal student in the college—after he paid the eleven scudi required to secure his place. His studies would keep him in Naples for the next three academic years.

Bruno passed his three sets of annual examinations without difficulty, and received his license as reader in theology in July 1575, after defending a series of theses, including "Everything that Thomas Aquinas says in the *Summa Against the Gentiles* is right" and "Everything that the Master of the *Sentences* [that is, Peter Lombard] says is right." It was a far cry from Giles of Viterbo's endeavor to rewrite Peter Lombard's *Sentences* "according to the mind of Plato." The course of study prescribed by the Dominican statutes was called "philosophy," but it was philosophy of the most narrowly Scholastic kind, firmly rooted in Aristotle and the Middle Ages, conveyed by endless syllogisms: if A and B, then C. Any potential distraction, like the study of Plato, or Greek, or Hebrew, was strictly excluded. Natural philosophy derived from Aristotle; theology followed the Master of the *Sentences*, stolid, thorough Peter Lombard. The only controversial author in the whole canon of the Order of Preachers was Thomas Aquinas himself. Yet Fra Giordano passed through his three years of theological training at the Dominican college successfully, without a sign of protest.

And then, early in 1576, after nearly ten years of impeccable conformity to the religious life, Fra Giordano was in trouble once again. For some reason, the Dominican provincial of Naples, Fra Domenico Vita, had begun to investigate him in 1575. Fearing a prison sentence, as he later told his Venetian inquisitors, Bruno moved to Rome and the convent of Santa Maria Sopra Minerva, where he may have stayed as long as several months.

Fra Domenico Vita's case against Bruno was based on old information, and may have been based, as Saverio Ricci has suggested, on old rancor. Vita dredged up an incident from 1572, when the convent of San Domenico Maggiore had hosted the Tuscan friar Agostino da Montalcino, a professor of philosophy at the Dominican college in Rome—that is, at Santa Maria Sopra Minerva. On that occasion, Fra Agostino seems to have been holding forth, in classic academic style, about methodology, until Fra Giordano, with his brand-new degree in theology, stopped the harangue in its tracks. As he would tell his Venetian inquisitors:

> Conversing with Fra Montalcino, who said that the heretics were igno-
> rant and lacked the Scholastic terms [for their arguments], I replied that,

although they might not make their points according to Scholastic discipline, still, they stated their intentions effectively, just as the ancient Fathers of the Church had done. I used the heresy of Arius as an example; the Scholastics say that he understood the conception of the Son as an act of nature and not of will, but you can say the same thing in non-Scholastic terms by quoting Saint Augustine, namely that the Son is not of the same substance as the Father, and he proceeds as the creation of his will. At which point that Father jumped up, along with the others present, and said that I was defending the heretics, and I wanted to claim that they were learned.

It was the sort of incident that could have been forgotten with a little forbearance on both sides; in 1572 Bruno was, after all, an eager young scholar measuring himself against an older colleague. His own short description of the episode is enough, however, to reveal both the pomposity of Fra Agostino and the sharp sting of his own wit; he may have been more cutting with his colleague than he meant to be. Had he chosen any other example to prove his point than the divinity of Jesus, the incident might have passed eventually into oblivion. Instead, whether inadvertently or deliberately, he had raised the question that had lodged deep in his private thoughts from his first days as a Dominican, and done so forcefully enough for his provincial to remember the occasion three years later.

His argument with Fra Agostino had arisen over two separate points. The first was a matter of intellectual respect. The elder friar's proclaimed contempt for "the heretics" expressed a prejudice rather than a reasoned response to individual ideas, and on one level Bruno was clearly offended by the sweeping pronouncement that all heretics were ignorant.

It was another matter altogether to defend Arius, the early Christian bishop who denied the divinity of Christ and, according to legend, received a box on the ear from none other than Saint Nicholas for having dared to say so. When Bruno told his Venetian inquisitors that he had "never made a public denial" of the Trinity, "nor taught or written anything to that effect," he may have been sincere; as those records show, he was not the most self-aware of in-

dividuals. But in fact the argument against the personhood and incarnation of Jesus that he presented to his inquisitors in Venice was
substantially the same argument he had presented years before to
Fra Agostino da Montalcino; it was the argument of Arius. Worse
still, on both occasions he brought in Saint Augustine to back up
the Arian position (and with a friar named Augustine!): the term
"person" had been a novelty in the fourth century A.D., and Augustine, at least, was skeptical about its appropriateness to describing the nature of Christ and the Holy Spirit. For a newly minted
theologian who had earned his degree by contending that "everything that the Master of the *Sentences* says is right," the argument
was probably a little too smooth to seem entirely casual. Its point,
furthermore, was to prove the Master of the *Sentences* wrong. Peter
Lombard's "correct" account of the Trinity, its three persons, and
the procession from one to the other simply ignored Saint Augustine's reservations about splitting one God into three persons (not
to mention the Orthodox reservation about the Holy Spirit *proceeding* from both the Father and the Son).

Three years later, as Fra Giordano took in the sights of Rome,
Fra Domenico Vita paid a visit to the Inquisition archives to see
what else the friar from Nola might have asserted over the years.

From the time of Saint Dominic himself, the brothers of his order had been engaged in battling challenges to Christian orthodoxy, initially by investigating individual cases as they arose. These
investigations were called "inquisitions," and initially they involved renegade Christians, like Dominic's chosen enemies, the
Albigensians, or the Catalan mystic Ramon Llull, who claimed to
have visions of the Messiah when he practiced what he called his
Great Art of memory. Within two generations, however, the
growth of Moorish power in Spain and North Africa began to focus
Spanish Christians' attention on a new set of targets: Muslims and
Jews. Educated, wealthy, and adaptable, Spanish Jews coexisted
with the Moors more easily than their crusading Christian neighbors, who massacred them by the thousands in 1391 and converted
the survivors by force, some twenty to twenty-five thousand "new
Christians" created virtually at once. In the mid-fifteenth century,
with Muslim pirates cruising the Mediterranean and the Ottoman

Turks in charge of Constantinople, Spanish Christians once again focused their fears on "Jews and Saracens" (as a papal bull put it in 1451). In 1478, fortified by a bull from Pope Sixtus IV, King Ferdinand of Aragon set up a series of tribunals to be run by Dominican examiners; this was the beginning of the Spanish Inquisition. This new, permanent Inquisition focused relentless attention specifically on converted Jews, charging them with "Judaizing," returning to their old religious ways. In so doing, the Spanish Inquisition obeyed the Spanish crown more than it obeyed the papacy, and Pope Sixtus IV was swift to complain, although with little effect; King Ferdinand the Catholic and his grand inquisitor, Tomás de Torquemada, continued to behave as they wished.

Another kind of external threat, the Protestant Reformation, led Pope Paul III to establish a Roman branch of the Inquisition, the General or Holy Office, in 1542. Its targets reflected these new and different fears: it aimed its investigations at Protestants, deviant Catholics, witches, and the content of printed books. No work of theology could go to press in Catholic cities without preliminary scrutiny by an authorized investigator who would award suitably orthodox manuscripts the order *"Imprimatur"*—"Let it be printed." Some printed books, even if they did not entirely pass muster, could be sold after minor censorship, by crossing out complimentary references to Protestant scholars as "learned" or "erudite" or by removing one or two passages regarded as objectionable by the Inquisition's censors. Some authors were banned altogether—not only such evident troublemakers as John Calvin and Martin Luther, but also staunchly Catholic writers like Erasmus of Rotterdam, guilty of excessive paganism and excessive irreverence in the eyes of Church conservatives.

Public writings were not the only targets of inquisitorial curiosity: the examiners and their informers also probed mercilessly into private life, searching for clues to secret Protestant sympathies, unorthodox beliefs, superstition, or witchcraft. Importantly, however, Rome carried out the Inquisition according to its own protocol, as did the other cities of Italy, Naples included. Despite the best efforts of the Spanish viceroys, the Neapolitan inquisitors continued to take their orders from Rome, where investigators followed ancient Roman law in requiring the independent testimony of two witnesses to obtain a conviction (in Spain, the Inquisition could try and convict on the basis of a single anonymous denunciation). The most recent attempt to impose the Spanish Inquisition, in 1563, had ended, after some street battles and a flurry of pamphlets, with the civic authorities' promise to expel the Jews. For the time being, unless there were two witnesses to each of Fra Giordano's transgressions, he was safe from prosecution. Unfortunately, so far he had always taken his aggressive stands before an audience.

As it turned out, the archives of the Holy Office in San Domenico Maggiore preserved the report of Bruno's attack on *The Seven Joys of the Virgin*. Furthermore, although his novice master had torn up the report of his first offense, a number of friars remembered how the young Bruno had cleared his cell of holy images in 1566. Fra Domenico Vita ordered a search of Bruno's Neapolitan cell without result. But a search of the latrine brought up a copy of the *Commentaries* of Erasmus with Bruno's notes in the margins; he had hidden the book there before going off to Rome.

Neapolitan latrines were not simply holes in the ground, or, as often in Rome, holes in the wall, the balcony, or the stairwell. From ancient Greek times to World War II, Naples was served by a system of interconnecting cisterns carved deep into the city's volcanic bedrock, sometimes extending hundreds of feet below ground level. This underground system collected both water and sewage and was serviced at regular intervals by a squadron of professional cleaners (who had their own exquisite ways of repaying anyone who refused their ministrations). Only the most determined inquisitor would want to riffle through such evidence. Fra Domenico Vita was evidently a man so determined.

The normal penalty for reading forbidden books was excommunication. Although Bruno's later wanderings would show that there were huge gaps in the passage of information from one Dominican house to another, rumors about the developments at San Domenico reached him by letter in Rome. His position at Santa Maria Sopra Minerva seems to have deteriorated as well; as his Venetian host Giovanni Mocenigo would report in 1592: "He told me that he had been arraigned by the Inquisition on 130 counts, and that he fled when his case came up, because he was charged with having thrown his accuser into the Tiber, or at least the person he believed had accused him to the Inquisition."

The Venetian inquisitors did not pursue Mocenigo's insinuation about a murder charge, which suggests that it must have been unfounded. There are no records in Naples or Rome to indicate that Bruno was ever accused of throwing anyone into the Tiber, or arraigned, for that matter, on 130 counts by the Inquisition. On one matter, however, Mocenigo was correct. Bruno did decide to run away. He slipped out of Rome one day in 1576 and headed north.

The ideal refuge for a man of Giordano Bruno's independent opinions would have been Venice or its university town, Padua, both of them proud of their political independence. That independence expressed itself on many levels, including sixteenth-century Italy's closest equivalent to free speech and a free press. But Venice in 1576 was infected with the plague. Bruno chose instead to travel along the coast to the Tuscan cities of Pisa and Livorno, and then on toward Genoa. En route, he abandoned his white Dominican habit, his Dominican name, Giordano, and his clean-shaven face to wander northward as Messer Filippo Bruno, gentleman.

Dominican friars did not change residence without permission from their superiors. Between his forbidden reading and his forbidden travel, Fra Giordano Bruno risked defrocking as well as excommunication. The inquisitors at San Domenico sent his dossier to the Roman Inquisition at Santa Maria Sopra Minerva. This office, in turn, issued a summons ordering him to appear before the office in Rome, but when the scheduled time arrived, he was long gone. The career of Fra Giordano Bruno da Nola, O.P., had lasted exactly ten years.

ƕoly Ƶsininity

GENOA, 1576

He has said that friars . . . are all asses, and that our opinions are the teachings of asses.
>—Giovanni Mocenigo, first letter to the Venetian Inquisition, March 23, 1592

Remarkable that this ass professes himself a doctor.
>—Marginal notation in one of Bruno's books

Traveling north from Rome in the spring of 1576, Bruno stopped off in the port of Genoa. He may well have hoped to find work in that large, important city, and perhaps some time to recuperate; Genoa was an independent state, accustomed to resolving its problems independently of Rome, and he was unlikely to be handed over to any Roman authorities there. Bruno was still present in the city on Palm Sunday, April 15, when the Dominican friars of Santa Maria in Castello displayed their most treasured relic to the public, the tail of the donkey that had carried Jesus into Jerusalem on the first Palm Sunday, wrapped in silk:

I myself saw the friars of Castello in Genoa display the veiled tail for a short time, saying: "Don't touch it, kiss it; this is the holy relic of that blessed ass who was made worthy to carry Our Lord from the Mount of

Olives to Jerusalem. Venerate it, kiss it, give an offering; you will receive a hundred times as much in return, and you will have eternal life."

The scene took the cult of relics to its absurd extreme—Bruno would later note that it was as easy to display the bone of a dog or a hanged man as the bone of a real saint—but there was also a kind of sublime weirdness to the idea that a donkey could provide the key to heaven. His own life had provided evidence enough that asses enjoyed special divine protection: the pedantic ass who had started all his troubles, Fra Agostino da Montalcino, was still pontificating in the bosom of the Order of Preachers, whereas Bruno, for all his wit, had become, almost overnight, a wanderer.

In that fate, the former Fra Giordano was not alone—far from it. Despite the difficulties that travel posed in the sixteenth century, Europe was full of wanderers. Bruno once described the set of vagabonds he had seen in Rome, gathering around the marketplace near his convent:

A mixture of desperate souls, of servants disgraced by their masters, of exiles from storms, of pilgrims, of useless and inert persons, of those who have no other pastime than robbery, of those who have just escaped from prison, of those who have a plan to deceive someone . . . you'll find as many as you like in Rome, in Campo de' Fiori.

In Genoa in 1576, the population of desperate souls also included a large number of refugees from the plague, who brought reports of its spread through the cities of northern Italy. Some brought the plague bacillus as well, traveling along in their rat-infested cargoes. Other travelers were escaping religious persecution. Genoa was a way station for many of the Italian Protestants, would-be Protestants, and dissident Catholics who moved north from the reach of Rome toward what they hoped would be safety, seeking out protection from the Waldensians of Piedmont, the Calvinists of Geneva, the Lutherans of Germany, or the Huguenots of France.

By and large, however, the moving population of Europe observed the same social distinctions as its settled communities. With his degree from the College of San Domenico Maggiore, Bruno belonged at the very top of an intellectual elite, and everything about him—his way of speaking, the way he carried himself, his pale scholar's complexion, and his priest's well-kept hands—identified his place in the world as surely as—for the moment at least—his ragged tonsure and the growing stubble of his scraggly beard. Furthermore, despite their strict conventual rules, individual Dominicans moved from city to city with some regularity, whether they were touring as preachers or advancing their careers as professors or administrators. Making his way as a traveler, not quite resigned to being a fugitive, Bruno continued to depend on the order more than occasionally for lodging and professional connections.

There is little doubt about what he would have done if he had stayed in Rome, or at San Domenico Maggiore, and survived the Inquisition's examination with no more than a reprimand; he had trained, perhaps with the greatest rigor in the Western world, to become a professor of philosophy, and that is surely what he would have become. Wherever he went in his new life of wandering, he always tried first to find a place as a university professor. He worked as a teacher because he actively wanted to teach, just as the greatest philosophers had taught before him: Socrates, the teacher of Plato; Plato, the teacher of Aristotle; Aristotle, the teacher of Alexander the Great; Thomas Aquinas, professor at the University of Paris and the College of San Domenico Maggiore. His writings, like theirs, were teachings (only Socrates refused to write, but he had Plato to do the job for him). Like them, he tried to invent new kinds of writing to convey his philosophical message, experimenting over and over with language, style, and presentation.

Bruno had also developed firm ideas about good and bad teaching. For Fra Teofilo da Vairano, he reserved the word "maestro"—more than a teacher, a master. To most of the rest of the scholarly world he applied the phrase *"asini pedanti"*—"pedant asses"—the grammarians, schoolmasters, and pious bigots who plagued his life from beginning to end, from his grammar-school teachers in Nola to his cellmates in Venice. What he called *asinità*, the defining characteristic of these *asini pedanti*, meant something more than simple "asininity," although it could mean that too. *Asinità*, as he developed his thoughts about it, incorporated both the stubborn stupidity of pure ego and the divine simplicity of pure ignorance. A donkey, after all, is unpredictable, both willfully perverse and admirably patient, with a cry that can only be described as laughable. As Bruno began his wanderings, he had more time than ever before to contemplate the ins and outs of asininity at first hand, and he would eventually make it one of the pillars of the Nolan philosophy. Mules and donkeys were the most usual means of transportation for travelers over long distances in sixteenth-century Europe, and Giordano Bruno, refined but hardly rich enough to afford a horse, must have ridden, when he did not walk, on the back of one of these durable creatures. The furry gray tail he saw reverentially displayed in Genoa would come back to haunt his imagination.

The holy tail also shows up in a popular sixteenth-century ditty, "The Donkey's Testament." With its catchy chorus, "Oh my, oh my, oh my, donkey mine, you're going to die," and its tale about a peasant on the road with his ancient beast, it was the perfect traveler's song, although it also echoed the meter of the terrifying medieval poem about the Last Judgment, *Dies Irae* (Day of Wrath). Before dropping dead and meeting his own Judgment Day, the donkey turns to his master and makes a will:

> Oh my, oh my, oh my,
> donkey mine, you're going to die, oh my . . .
> Let the curia have my cross;
> The cardinals my ears I toss.
> Pass my tail on to the friars
> And my hee-haw to the choirs,
> Preachers get my tongue; instead,
> Let the judges have my head;
> To the porters give my back,
> My feet to peddlers with their pack;
> Give my meat to those who fast;
> Cobblers get my hide at last.
> Give my mane to make a brush,
> Give my bones for dogs to crush,
> Let the vultures have my gut,
> Widows get my you-know-what,
> And—why not?—throw in my nuts.

With his will thus ratified,
Down the donkey lay and died.
As for the remaining bit,
Once the druggist gets his shit
And the doctors get his bladder,
Let the priests dispute the matter.

With its doggerel rhythm and bad jokes, it was the perfect verse to chant on the road. By comparison, Bruno's own "Sonnet in Praise of the Ass," penned in 1584, would rank as great literature, with its careful development of *asinità* in both its senses, as the defining quality of stolid pedants and of holy fools:

SONNET IN PRAISE OF THE ASS
Blest asininity, blest ignorance,
O blest stupidity, pious devotion,
Able alone to set good souls in motion
That human wit and study can't advance;
Nor will the most laborious vigilance
Of art or of invention win promotion
(No more than any philosophic notion)
To heaven, where you build your residence.

What can the value of your study be,
All you who yearn to know how Nature fares,
If stars are made of earth, or fire, or sea?
Blest asininity knows no such cares;
With folded hands it waits on bended knee
For God to parcel out our fated shares,
And nothing perseveres
Except the fruit of infinite repose
That, once the funeral's over, God bestows.

Donkeys also served Europeans as a stereotype of Jews. The Spanish and Italian term for converted Jews may have been *marranos*, Spanish for "pigs," but Jews who persisted in their faith were also compared to stubborn donkeys in the period's more scurrilous literature, down to invidious comparisons between a stereotypical Jewish physiognomy and the long-nosed, big-eared asinine profile. Yet this same imagery could be reversed, as it was by the German writer Cornelius Agrippa of Nettesheim, a great influence on Bruno, who devoted his *Digression in Praise of the Ass* to explaining why Jesus had, in Agrippa's own words, chosen as apostles "idiots from the rude crowd, almost entirely illiterate, ignorant asses":

> Learned Jews explain that the ass is a symbol of extraordinary endurance and strength, of patience and clemency . . . For its qualities are those that are most necessary in a disciple: it lives on little food and is content with whatever it gets; it tolerates poverty, hunger, work, sores, and neglect well, and is patient with every sort of persecution; it is of simple and humble spirit, so that it can hardly distinguish lettuce from thistles, innocent and pure of heart, free from rancor, at peace with all the animals, bearing every burden patiently on its back . . . Did not Christ, through the mouths of his apostles and disciples, those simple, rude idiots and asses, conquer and quash the philosophers of the Gentiles and the lawyers and Pharisees of the Jews?

Asses also had their political aspect, notably for Bruno in a work published in Naples in 1551–52, Giovanni Battista Pino's *Discourse on the Ass*. Pino wrote in the aftermath of the riots that erupted in Naples in 1547 when the viceroy Don Pedro de Toledo tried, for the first time, to impose the Spanish Inquisition. (Pino himself was among the delegates sent by the city to explain the events to the emperor Charles V.) In Pino's *Discourse*, it is the Inquisition's champion, Don Pedro, whose long muzzle and long ears reveal his *asinità*. It is not surprising that the book is now extremely rare—Don Pedro and his successors did their best to suppress it— but in its day it was a great success, passed along eagerly from one Neapolitan reader to the next. As one of the centers of resistance to Spain, San Domenico Maggiore must have had its share of copies.

Just after Pino's *Discourse on the Ass* had begun to circulate in Naples, another book arrived from Spain. In 1554, a Spanish publisher printed the anonymous story of a character named Lazarillo de Tormes, the first of endless editions of what became one of Europe's bestselling books. In Lazarillo's wake there followed a whole series of novels about a type of person called, in Spanish, a *pícaro*. Something about the character struck a chord in Spanish society, and not only there. Naples, as a Spanish dominion, provided its own active public for picaresque novels. By the time the perplexed Neapolitan named Bruno took to the road—Giordano or Filippo?—he was primed to find a world of picaresque adventures around him.

But Naples was not only a creature of Spain; it was a city with a long history of its own, where ancient aristocracies mingled and clashed with the career builders who were sent out from Madrid to make their way in this most unprovincial of provinces. Life offered at least as many picaresque details in Naples as it did in La Mancha. Good birth, good money, and good behavior counted for everything in good society, but no one, in Spain itself, let alone Naples, quite knew how to distinguish good from bad with absolute accuracy. This was the uncertainty that picaresque novels exploited, delighting readers and disconcerting them at the same time. *Pícaros*, bad from birth, shameless by nature, but diabolically clever, confounded civility by climbing up and down the social ladder, starting from nowhere, ending nowhere, and managing to travel everywhere in between. They could be blind idealists like Don Quixote de la Mancha or rogues like Lazarillo de Tormes, but the novels tended to observe a rough rule of social conservatism: although *pícaros* (or female *pícaras*) might be clever enough to get away briefly with a scheme or two, they were never quite clever enough to carry out their deceptions forever. Before they ended back in the underworld that spawned them, however, they took their readers in imagination along a trail of social ups and downs that the readers of picaresque novels, whether they were learned, aristocratic, or middle-class, normally dared not follow in real life.

The Spanish novels tend to ascribe the low birth and the cleverness of Spanish *pícaros* to Jewish ancestry, the obsession of Spaniards ever since the expulsion of the Jews from Spain in 1492. Lazarillo de Tormes, with his properly Hebraic name Lazarus, set the example for a long anti-Semitic tradition (it still shows up in the figure of the *marrano* Leporello in Mozart's *Don Giovanni*, whose librettist, Lorenzo Da Ponte, was a convert from Judaism himself). In Naples, however, where many of Spain's ejected Jews had fled (followed in 1497 by the Jews of Portugal), purity of blood never acquired this same symbolic importance; it was hard to speak of pure ancestry in a city founded by Greeks and settled by Etruscans, Samnites, Oscans, Romans, Arabs, Normans, and French before the Spaniards ever came to town. But Neapolitans certainly warmed to the idea of clever tricksters foiling the rules of society, and created their own version of a *pícaro* in the rogue Pulcinella, the hero of their local form of drama, commedia dell'arte. Pulcinella, in turn, reached England as the Punch of the Punch-and-Judy shows, which were themselves inspired by Neapolitan street drama. *Pícaros* and Pulcinella had begun to appear by the time Filippo Bruno arrived in Naples, and he would eventually encounter Punch and Judy in London. The influence of their broad, brutal comedy shows in his vernacular writing, from the biting farce of *The Candlemaker* to the characters in his philosophical dialogues, most of whom could be played by a troupe of commedia dell'arte actors or, indeed, a set of Punch-and-Judy puppets.

Picaresque adventures were a natural companion to *asinità*, and not just because *pícaros* rode donkeys rather than horses—unless the horse was Don Quixote's broken-down Rocinante. The ups and downs that defined a *pícaro's* life matched popular images of the Wheel of Fortune, shown in contemporary woodcuts and manuscript illuminations as a huge version of a Ferris wheel, with people climbing up its spokes to fame and wealth or plunging down to disgrace. Often, to drive home the point that good luck is random, the human figures riding the wheel have donkeys' heads—especially those on the way up. The Wheel of Fortune was an image that Bruno would evoke again and again as a writer: turning as steadily and as inexorably as the cycles of the heavens, bringing everything and everybody up, down, and back again. He had seen seashells in the soil of Monte Cicala, proof that the dry land around his house had once been underwater. The changeability of his own life applied equally to the ground under his feet, and to the stars overhead with their endlessly shifting patterns. As his father

had said, a wise man "taking good and evil into consideration regards each of them as variable . . . Therefore he neither despairs
nor puffs up his spirit . . . for him pleasure is no pleasure, because its
goal is in the present. Likewise, pain for him is no pain, because by
force of reasoning he is mindful of its end."

In the same vein, Bruno's *Candlemaker* would tell an obscene fable about a lion traveling from Naples in the company of an ass,
the noblest of beasts paired with the most ridiculous:

> Once upon a time the lion and the ass were friends, and when they went
> on a journey together, they promised that when they came to a river each
> would take turns carrying the other across; that is to say, first the ass
> would carry the lion, and the next time the lion would carry the ass. Now
> they had to go to Rome, and because they had neither a boat nor a bridge
> when they arrived at the river Garigliano, the ass took the lion on its
> back, and as he swam to the other side, the lion, for fear of falling, sank
> his claws deeper and deeper into the poor animal's skin until they pene-
> trated almost to the bone. And the poor thing (who, after all, makes a
> profession of his patience) endured it as best he could without making a
> sound; all he did, when they arrived safely out of the water, was shake his
> back a bit and roll over three or four times in the hot sand, and on they
> went. Eight days later, as they made their return, it was time for the lion
> to carry the ass, who, once he had climbed up, in order to keep from
> falling, gripped the lion's neck in his teeth, and because that was not
> enough to keep him in place, he stuck his tool (or as we say, his you-
> know-what), to be blunt, in the space beneath the tail where there is no
> fur, so that the lion felt more pain than a woman in childbirth, and cried,
> "Hey, hey, ow, ow, ow, ouch, hey, traitor!" To which the ass replied with a
> sober countenance and grave tone: "Patience, patience, my brother; you
> see, I have no other claw." And so the lion was compelled to suffer and
> endure until they had crossed the river. That is to say, "Everything
> changes places," and no one is so great an ass that he won't take the op-
> portunity when it comes along.

Life on the road forced Bruno into the virtues of *asinità*: patience, endurance, and, like the ass of his fable, resourcefulness. He
applied all his wits (the best "claws" in his own arsenal) to ensuring

that he would travel as an itinerant professor, a lionlike *virtuoso* rather than an asinine *pícaro*, but the choice was not always his to make. In the beginning, he had no idea which name to use, Filippo or Giordano, whether to wear his habit or cast it off, whether to shave like a Dominican or grow the sparse black beard that was all he could manage. When he eventually settled on an identity, it would be a suitably ambiguous combination of his secular and his Dominican past: he kept the name he had chosen for himself, Giordano, and doffed his friar's habit. But not yet. For the moment, Messer Filippo Bruno was a confused soul for whom the statement "Everything changes places" was a painful, shocking fact rather than a founding principle of the Nolan philosophy.

Bruno did not stay long in Genoa. Ports, with their rat-infested ships coming in and out from every part of the world, had always been prime breeding grounds for plague. When dead rats began to appear in the streets of the city, the rumors began to fly. Filippo of Nola pressed on beyond the Bay of Genoa until he found the remote little seaside town of Noli, politically independent and surrounded on every side by steep mountains. There he stopped, for the first time since he had left Rome.

CHAPTER TWELVE

The Signs of the Times

NOLI AND VENICE, 1576–1577

> When it is evening, ye say, It will be fair weather: for the sky is red. And in the morning, It will be foul weather today: for the sky is red and lowering. O ye hypocrites, ye can discern the face of the sky; but can ye not discern the signs of the times?　　　　　—Matthew 16:2–3

In Noli, as Bruno would tell his Venetian inquisitors, "I stayed four or five months teaching grammar to kids," and again, "I stayed in Noli, as I said, about four months, teaching grammar to children and reading *The Sphere* to certain gentlemen; and afterward I left there and went first to Savona, where I stayed about fifteen days, and from Savona to Turin, and when I couldn't find a situation there to my satisfaction, I came to Venice by the Po."

When Bruno's first chance arose to teach philosophy, then, it was natural philosophy—specifically, astronomy for interested amateurs who must have heard about or seen the new star that appeared in the heavens in 1572. This sudden and evident change in the night sky (it must have been a supernova) threatened to overturn some basic beliefs about the heavens. The stars, in the first place, were supposed to have been fixed to the eighth sphere of the universe, every one of them, ever since the moment of creation. Second, Aristotle claimed that the stars, like the other heavenly bodies and unlike Earth, were made of a special, incorruptible fifth element immune from birth, death, or change. Yet here was a star appearing from one day to the next, to prove that change happened in the heavens after all. The stargazers of Europe rushed to provide an explanation, from Tycho Brahe in the Danish Abbey of Havemark to Christoph Clavius in Rome, not to mention a raft of astrologers in between who tried to explain not only what had happened but also, more importantly, what it meant. In Naples, Bernardino Telesio took the new star as proof that the heavens were made of the same four elements as Earth; the object's sudden appearance was one more episode in the endless battle between heat and cold that kept the universe in motion. From San Domenico Maggiore, Fra Giordano Bruno watched and listened.

Bruno does not say what version or versions of Sacrobosco's *On the Sphere* he used with his adult students in Noli four years later, but Eugenio Canone suggests that it may well have been an Italian vernacular translation by the Servite friar Mauro Fiorentino, whose *Notes on Reading Sacrobosco* of 1550 also contained some of Fra Mauro's own essays and illustrations. The images, the accessible language, and the Platonic slant of *Notes on Reading Sacrobosco* would have appealed both to Bruno and to his gentlemen students, so much so that Bruno would later poach two of the illustrations for his own work.

General books on technical subjects, especially in vernacular, sold well among the growing number of middle-class readers in the sixteenth century. Fra Mauro Fiorentino dedicated the first edition of his Sacrobosco translation, *The Vernacular Sphere* of 1537, to another popular writer, the Spanish mathematician Juan de Ortega, whose *Introduction to Mathematics* (first printed in 1514) dispensed advice about computation in Spanish-accented Italian to aspiring businessmen. The gentlemen of Noli who decided to learn astronomy from a wandering ex-friar stood somewhere between Ortega's potential readers, refreshing their memories about long division, and the natural philosophers who gathered at the house of Bernardino Telesio in Naples to discuss the composition of the universe.

The wandering ex-friar, for his part, devoted a conscious effort to improving on the teaching methods of the *asini pedanti* he hated with such passion. "Teaching *The Sphere*" implied giving an elementary course in astronomy (as he would later do again in Toulouse): showing his gentlemen how to identify constellations, read star charts, and cast elementary horoscopes. We have no way now of knowing whether Bruno took his students stargazing or kept them in the classroom, whether he departed from his textbook, or, if he did depart from it, how bold his departures were. We know only that Sacrobosco's *On the Sphere* was one of the subjects on which sixteenth-century teachers could build reliably as they tried to improve on the ancient methods of their own teachers.

Bruno would certainly have known the edition of Sacrobosco put out in 1570 by his sometime neighbor at the Jesuits' Roman College, Christoph Clavius, and he may not have approved of it. The Society of Jesus encouraged following Thomas Aquinas and Aristotle in all matters of natural philosophy, and indeed in a later edition (1581) of his *Commentary on the Sphere*, Clavius, as an obedient Jesuit, raised vocal doubts about Copernicus:

> Many absurd and erroneous things are contained in the position of Copernicus, namely that the earth is not in the center of the world, and that it is moved by a triple motion . . . and that the sun is situated at the center of the world, and lacks all motion, all of which goes against the common teachings of philosophers and astronomers, and can be seen to contradict those who teach Scripture on several points.

Fame, both for his work on the Gregorian calendar and for his stable of former students scattered from Rome to Beijing, would encourage Clavius to express his own opinions with greater freedom. Later editions of his *Commentary* took careful note of Tycho Brahe's experiments and softened his stance on Copernicus. Years later a fellow Jesuit, Athanasius Kircher, would assert that Clavius's real convictions lay entirely on the side of the Polish astronomer: "Father Malaperti and Father Clavius themselves in no way disapproved the opinion of Copernicus—indeed they would have espoused it openly had they not been pressed and obliged to write according to the premises of Aristotle."

On the other hand, it is not clear what Bruno himself thought about the universe in 1576. Between his time at San Domenico Maggiore and the moment when he published his first surviving books, in 1582, he had changed his mind completely about its structure: in his own words, he gave up a "puerile" Aristotelian worldview for the sun-centered cosmos of Copernicus, and then, more radically still, for an infinite universe without center or limits of any kind. As he moved north from Genoa, he must have been in transit in every possible sense, physical, philosophical, and personal.

After a few months of isolated stability (he may well have stayed longer than he admitted to the inquisitors), Bruno longed for more sophisticated students than the "kids," or even the gentlemen, of Noli. As the threat of plague receded from the Italian Riviera, he set out for Savona, the second-largest port in the region, and then, after a fortnight, for Turin, where the prospects for work and lodging proved equally unpromising. There, too, at the foot of the Alps, Bruno, accustomed to the warm sun of Naples, may also have begun to get his first taste of real cold weather.

Driven by want, he boarded a flat-bottomed boat to float down the river Po toward Venice, where the plague, still endemic, loomed as a less immediate threat than his own lack of a job. He told his Venetian inquisitors: "There I stayed for a month and a half in Frezzaria in a room rented by someone from the Arsenal, whose name I don't know, and while I was there, I published a certain pamphlet called On the Signs of the Times, and had this book printed so that I could gather up a little money to live on. And first I had the Reverend Father Remigio of Florence take a look at it."

To improve potential sales, Bruno wrote On the Signs of the Times in vernacular, aiming at readers like his gentlemen students in Noli. The title is our only surviving clue to the booklet's content. On the face of it, On the Signs of the Times sounds like an almanac or a book of astrological predictions; these issued in cheap editions from Italian presses several times a year, using the position of the stars, monstrous births, and other strange phenomena to make predictions of the weather and of future events. Some were single broadsheets, like the Swiss writer Sebastian Brant's illustrated page dedicated to the fall of the Ensisheim meteorite in 1492. Slightly longer works looked like Gerolamo Cardano's modest pamphlet of predictions, the *Pronostico* (*Prognostication*) of 1534, which offered inside information on the long-term trends of history and detailed reports on forthcoming weather, all based on reading the face of the heavens. "I say in general that men must become worse than they are now, so far as the faith is concerned," he said, while conceding that the Church would begin to improve in 1764; a planetary conjunction in 1564 "denoted the renovation of all the religions, the Christian and the Muslim." According to the *Pronostico*, the emperor Charles V was doomed to perish (instead he thrived) and Francesco Sforza, Duke of Milan, destined to thrive (instead he perished); drought would strike between July 6 and August 9 of 1536, fog and storms on August 25, 1537. Aiming at a popular readership, Cardano wrote his little almanac in Italian vernacular, with enough of an erudite sprinkling of Latin to lend him academic credibility, and he made sure that he acquired clear-cut privileges, the forerunner of copyright, for the work in both Milan and Venice. It was an unassuming start, and it sank virtually without notice. In 1538, however, Cardano, writing in Latin this time, displayed both his grasp of astronomical theory and his practical ability at prediction, in *Two Little Books*. Unlike most of his fellow astrologers, he drew up his own tables of planetary motion from which to produce the data allegedly showing heavenly influences on human character and behavior; at the same time, he performed such eminently astrological operations as tracing the origins of modern religion to the former action of the stars on ancient peoples. Most important for his future, he used the dedication of *Two Little Books* to curry the favor of a well-placed patron, the Milanese-born governor of Rome, while aiming at a patron still more august, the pope.

Other printers published full-fledged works of natural philosophy, like Tycho Brahe's opinion on the new star of 1572, written in Latin, the only language with real international authority, and Copernicus's *On the Revolutions of the Heavenly Spheres*, whose groundbreaking theory lies among page after page of mathematical tables.

Never an author to shy away from new literary forms, Bruno may have used the title of his own booklet to suggest that it would contain a set of predictions—and then offered his readers something completely different. The phrase "the signs of the times" recalled a passage in the Bible where Jesus turns on the scribes and Pharisees: "When it is evening, ye say, It will be fair weather: for the sky is red. And in the morning, It will be foul weather today: for the sky is red and lowering. O ye hypocrites, ye can discern the face of the sky; but can ye not discern the signs of the times?"

Within a few years, Bruno would come to doubt his contemporaries' ability even to "discern the face of the sky," although he may not have said so openly in *The Signs of the Times*. Yet the seeds of that doubt must already have been sown in Noli, as he and his gentlemen went over the centuries-old text of Sacrobosco. Every one of them knew that since Sacrobosco had written about his earth of three continents and his heaven of fixed stars, a Genoese captain named Christopher Columbus had brought Spanish ships to the New World, adding the Americas to the number of continents, and a new star had appeared in the heavens. Were these the signs of the times that Bruno saw around him?

Certainly, *The Signs of the Times*, the published booklet, provided one important signpost for Bruno himself: although he had lost the steady daily rhythms and physical security of the convent, he could still focus his mind on thinking, writing, and maintaining his skill with the artificial memory. The structures he had forged within his own head were strong enough to withstand the pressures of constant travel. As he would write in 1585:

> Above the clouds, upon that lofty site,
> When, in my vagrant thoughts, I flash and flare,
> For my spirit's refreshment and delight
> I build a fiery castle in the air.

In his own description, then, his thoughts were as swift, changeable, and potentially explosive as fire, not only the individual images and sense impressions with which he filled his head, but especially the "castle" of memory in which he filed them all away.

Yet in one of the apparent contradictions that make up his character, Bruno, no matter how novel the signs of the times and how volatile his own thinking, would always claim that there was

THE SIGNS OF THE TIMES

nothing really new under the sun. The biblical verse that he inscribed in several of his books, bought at different times in different places and then discarded along the way, comes from that most world-weary of voices, Ecclesiastes, but as so often with this master of memory, slightly transformed: "What is? What was. What was? What is. There is nothing new under the sun."

For a man trained in Scholastic philosophy and Christian Platonism, old books were still good books. When Bruno taught astronomy again, he continued to use Sacrobosco's *On the Sphere*, just as he continued to read Aquinas, the Bible, and the ancient philosophers. Now that he was free from the convent, he could also devote special attention to Lucretius's great Latin poem *On the Nature of Things*, which had been consigned, along with the works of Luther, Calvin, and Erasmus, to the *Index of Forbidden Books*. In Venice, full of cosmopolitan traders and conveniently set near the borders of Germany, Austria, and Dalmatia, it was easier to find indexed works than anywhere Bruno had ever been. Ever since the invention of printing, the city's economy depended significantly on publishing, and thus the aristocratic clans who ruled the city let the long arm of the Holy Office reach only so far. A copy of Lucretius could surely be found in the bookshop of Aldo Manuzio the Younger, either the edition printed in 1515 by his famous grandfather, Aldo Manuzio, or one of the newer editions printed in Lyon and Paris; Bruno eventually owned a copy edited by Hubertus Grifanius. Bruno made a habit of seeking out bookshops wherever he went; they were good places to exchange news, and places where learned men in need of work might hear about jobs. In Venice, those bookshops were both plentiful and well stocked with merchandise.

Venice may have kept the Holy Office at a distance, but the city nonetheless conformed, at least in name, to all its dictates about publishing. So did Bruno, who submitted his own manuscript, *On the Signs of the Times*, for examination by an eminent Dominican before taking it off to the printer. Fra Remigio Nannini had spent his novitiate and early career at the convent of Santa Maria Novella in Florence. In 1564, his reputation as a scholar and teacher already established, he transferred to the Venetian convent of San Zanipolo ("Saint Johnandpaul," Venetian dialect for Santi

Giovanni e Paolo), a Gothic redoubt whose wealth of doges' tombs proclaimed its authority within the city. So did its location: the church shares its spacious paved *campo* with the marble-encrusted facade of the Scuola Grande di San Marco (once the home of the city's most important confraternity). Between the two buildings, Andrea del Verrocchio's bronze statue of the mercenary captain Bartolomeo Colleoni sits regally astride a powerful, spirited warhorse. Colleoni claimed to have three testicles (*coglioni*); they figure on his coat of arms, and it is no coincidence that the pedestal lofting his statue to the heavens has three pillars. Bruno said nothing about these marvels to his inquisitors (who were Venetians, after all), or about the mosaics of San Marco, the sculpture of the Doge's Palace, Titian's altarpieces, the canals, or the gondolas. But of course he noticed them. His trip in 1577 was only the first time he braved certain danger just to come to Venice. Neither did he reveal to his questioners whether he could afford the city's other delights on this first visit, the seafood and spices and the willing female companionship, although he would soon shock them by asserting that the sins of the flesh were no sin at all.

The Inquisition of Venice was housed not in the aristocratic halls of San Zanipolo but rather in the outlying convent of San Domenico di Castello, surrounded by members of the Venetian working class. Bruno's ability to strike up a relationship with Fra Remigio Nannini, one of the most prominent members of the city's most rarefied Dominican congregation, reveals, once again, how thoroughly the friars of San Domenico Maggiore had prepared him to move within the highest levels of society. He may already have been weighing a return to religious life when he passed his manuscript to a man who might, under other circumstances, have been his colleague.

Venice provided the wanderer with a wealth of other contacts as well. Bruno's landlord worked at the Arsenal, perhaps the most developed industrial organization in the sixteenth-century world. Its technological marvels were a state secret, hidden behind massive walls, but inside, its crews could reportedly build and rig a ship within a single day. Outside marble lions stood guard, many of them looted from ancient Greek sites. One still bears the runic graffiti of Viking visitors. Jews and Protestants, both German and Italian, mixed into the crowd alongside turbaned pashas from Ottoman lands and their veiled consorts, all of them enjoying a rare degree of freedom to associate and to discuss ideas.

Typically, too, the Venetian Inquisition was a milder version of that institution than most. Four years before Bruno's arrival in the city, the painter Paolo Veronese had appeared before them because he had put a dog and two dissolute soldiers into a painting of the Last Supper—for the convent of San Zanipolo. The prior of the convent accused Veronese of sacrilege; the painter defended himself by pleading artistic license:

> We painters take the same license that poets and madmen do, and I made those two halberdiers, the one who is drinking and the one who is eating by the stairs, and put them where they could be handy, and it seemed appropriate to me, because I had been told that the owner of the house was great and rich, and he ought to have that kind of servant.

The inquisitors ordered him to replace the soldiers with something more decorous, but they refused to entertain any charges of sacrilege (instead, Veronese simply changed the title of his painting from *The Last Supper* to *Banquet in the House of Levi*). In his own visits to Fra Remigio, Bruno would have seen the "improved" altarpiece amid San Zanipolo's other artistic treasures (it is now in Venice's Galleria dell'Accademia).

With Fra Remigio's imprimatur in hand, meanwhile, Bruno took his first close look at the craft of publishing, from the details of setting type and cutting the wooden blocks for illustrations to the inside gossip about the Frankfurt book fair, already a twice-yearly European institution. Sadly, the pamphlet *The Signs of the Times* does not survive, nor does the name of its publisher; Bruno carefully omitted giving his inquisitors that information as well.

Once he had consigned his booklet to the press, however, he still needed work. The University of Padua lay on the mainland, just across the lagoon from Venice, and Bruno decided to try his luck there.

CHAPTER THIRTEEN

𝔄 Lonely Sparrow

GENEVA, 1579

Go forth, then: I hope you find
A nobler fate, and have a god to guide you:
The one the sightless dare to say is blind.

Go; and find beside you
Each deity of this masterful design;
And don't return to me unless you're mine.
—From *The Heroic Frenzies*, I.4

As Bruno told the Venetian inquisitors:

When I left here, I went to Padua, where I found some Dominican fathers
I knew, and they convinced me to resume my habit, although I hadn't
wanted to return to religious life, but it seemed to them that it was better
to travel about with the habit than without it, and with this thought I
went to Bergamo. And there I had a cassock made from cheap white
cloth, and over that I put my scapular, which I had kept when I left
Rome, and in this habit I went to Lyon, and when I was in Chambéry,
and went to stay at the convent of the order, and seeing that I was treated
most soberly and discussing this with an Italian father who was living
there, he said, "You'll notice that here you'll get no kindness of any sort,
and the farther ahead you go, the less you'll find." So I turned around and
went to Geneva.

By the fall of 1577, Bruno had spent nearly a year and a half scouring northern Italy in search of work. He was twenty-nine years old, superbly educated, energetic, intelligent, and ambitious, but he might also be facing charges by the Inquisition in Naples, and possibly in Rome. At last, like many Italian fugitives from the Holy Office, he decided to see what the Protestants were all about.

He may have chosen Geneva because it was close, and he may have chosen it for more considered reasons. When John Calvin took over the city, he had dumped its most precious relic, the arm of Saint Anthony, into the river, a far cry from the Genoese who still venerated their silk-wrapped donkey's tail. The various foreign communities in Geneva, like its natives, actively sought out exiles from other places and generally treated them well. Bruno may already have heard about the city's hospitality. Hospitality, however, came only at the price of obedience. Another illustrious exile, Miguel Serveto, had discovered as much in 1553, when he was tried by a Calvinist court and sentenced to burn at the stake.

When Bruno recalled his own experience of Geneva to his Venetian inquisitors, he could hardly bring himself to refer to it by name; he called it "that city," and its brand of Protestantism "the religion of that city." For once he was compelled to stay in an inn, white habit, long black cape, scapular, and all; there were no Dominicans left in Geneva after Calvin and his associates took over. He told his inquisitors:

> Once I arrived there, I went to lodge in the inn, and shortly afterward the Marchese di Vico, a Neapolitan who lived in that city, asked me who I was and whether I had come to stay and profess the religion of that city. After I had given him an account of myself and the reasons for which I had left religious life, I added that I did not intend to profess the religion of that city, because I did not know what religion it was, and that I had come there hoping to live in liberty and safety rather than for any other reason. And persuading myself that in any case it would be better to shed my habit, I took the cloth and had a pair of hose made and other things, and that marchese along with other Italians gave me a sword, a hat, a cape, and all the other things I needed to be properly dressed, and so that I could make a living, they procured me a job as a copy editor. I stayed in that job for two months, and sometimes I went to the sermons, both in

Italian and in French, that they read and preached in that city. Among others, I heard the lectures and sermons of Niccolo Balbani of Lucca, who was reading the letters of Saint Paul and preached on the Gospels. But when I was told that I could not stay any longer unless I decided to accept the religion of that city, and could expect no more help from them, I decided to leave.

The real story had gone somewhat differently, but Bruno was not about to say so to the Inquisition. The news of his arrival in Geneva had spread fast in that well-guarded city, and soon afterward Filippo Giordano Bruno, as he called himself just then, received a visit from the de facto leader of the Italian exiles in Geneva, a Neapolitan count, Gian Galeazzo Caracciolo, Marchese di Vico. A former page of the emperor Charles V, married to a grandniece of Pope Paul IV, Caracciolo had been forced to flee Naples after his conversion to Calvinism, leaving his wife, his family, and his properties behind. In Geneva, he established the city's first Italian evangelical congregation. For this pioneering service and for his exalted social origins, he became the natural spokesman for an Italian community that numbered in the hundreds. In keeping with his role, Caracciolo introduced Bruno to their other compatriots, an unusually cultured, accomplished group of refugees. Most had arrived with nothing, after a dangerous passage out of Italy, but once they settled in Geneva, they prospered. Their own experiences taught them to be generous with new arrivals: Bruno's gifts of hat, cape, sword, and job were typical. Besides, with five or six Italian presses operating in Geneva, there was a real need for good copy editors. Up to this point, Bruno's tale to his inquisitors rings true. However, when Bruno's hosts pressed him to convert, he made no effort to leave Geneva. He obliged.

As he admitted to his inquisitors, Bruno had attended Calvinist services in Italian and French. Protestant reformers were virtually unanimous in calling for vernacular liturgy and vernacular translations of the Bible, so that, as the English reformer Thomas Cranmer put it, "the Word of God should be in a language understood of the people." Furthermore, they encouraged all members of the congregation to read the Bible for themselves. The Council of

Trent, on the other hand, had responded to these same demands by establishing the Latin Vulgate as the only acceptable biblical text, preserving Latin Mass, and insisting that the task of reading and interpreting Scripture be entrusted to priests. Outside the Church, in universities and learned academies, Latin was still the universal language of educated people, enabling Bruno to lecture in England and Germany as well as in Italy, Francophone Switzerland, and France. But the Reformers' decision to adopt vernacular liturgy would gradually erode the influence of Latin in other spheres. Bruno, responding to this change, would write his philosophical works both in Latin and in Italian vernacular. In the meantime, he began learning French by attending French sermons.

The Italian preacher Niccolo Balbani, whose sermons Bruno mentioned to the inquisitors, went well beyond a simple call for vernacular liturgy. One of his pamphlets, from 1564, bears the title *Responses . . . in Which, with the Word of God, It Is Shown That the Sacrifice of the Mass Is a Human Invention and a Horrible Idolatry.* The problem, as Balbani saw it, was the Catholic contention that the bread and wine of the Eucharist were truly transformed into the body and blood of Christ. To the most adamant Reformers, the Host was a symbol of the bread passed at the Last Supper, but it did not at any time contain the "real presence" of Christ. Hence venerating a crucifix or elevating the Host during the Mass was no different from the Hebrews' bowing down before the golden calf; all of these objects were the works of human hands, not of God, and hence all of them counted as the "graven images" whose worship was prohibited by the first commandment. Relics of the saints were scarcely different. The most militant Protestants stripped churches of their ornament, smashed statues, and dumped relics into the nearest river.

The Giordano Bruno who entered the stripped churches of Geneva was not the same Filippo Bruno who had emptied his elaborate cell at San Domenico Maggiore of its holy images. He had spent all but a few months of his life in Italy, surrounded everywhere by works of art, stocking his own memory with figures, emblems, and imagery that spill over into his writing. Even a stripped cell at San Domenico was a work of sophisticated, ornamental ar-

chitecture. He had never before seen what Protestant severity really meant for a sensitive eye. He saw it now.

On May 29, 1579, Bruno enrolled in the University of Geneva
as "Philippus Brunus Nolanus, professor of sacred theology." Although true, the qualification was an odd one to stress at a university that had been entirely turned over to John Calvin's version of
the Reformation; indeed, so long as he lived, Calvin himself took
the chair of philosophy at the University of Geneva. But it was important to Bruno here, as everywhere in his travels, to assert his
status as a learned man and a gentleman. The fact that the Italians
of Geneva gave him a sword, hat, and cape means that they recognized him as a person of rank.

Unfortunately for Bruno and for the University of Geneva, he
arrived when the course in philosophy had passed to an acolyte of
Calvin's successor, Theodor Beza: Antoine de La Faye. Ambitious,
vain, and greedy, La Faye collected as many salaries and official res-
idences as he could: acting principal of the college, professor of
philosophy, and, eventually, professor of theology, rector of the university, pastor of the city, and principal minister of Geneva. His
competence in his various jobs was another matter: he had nearly
been fired from the chair in philosophy in 1577.

Debate did not feature in the classrooms of the University of
Geneva; the professor read from his lectern and his audience listened. Beza had already decreed that lecturers should not "turn away
even the slightest bit from the opinions of Aristotle." For Philippus
Brunus Nolanus, professor of sacred theology, sitting as a captive of
Antoine de La Faye and pretending to be a student again proved
unbearable. Forbidden to challenge his professor in class, he resorted instead to the press. In August 1579, the printer Jean Berjon
issued a broadsheet in which Bruno listed twenty mistakes that La
Faye had made in a single lecture, "treating exclusively questions of
knowledge, with nothing about God or the magistrates."

La Faye, of course, had nearly lost his job two years before. It is
not surprising that he reacted badly to such public criticism of
his competence, and because he could count on the support of
Theodor Beza, he took the case before the Consistory, Geneva's
equivalent of the Inquisition. There he charged Bruno with slan-

der, making it known all the while that his authoritative position could justify turning the charge from slander to sacrilege, and the penalty from jail to death.

On August 6, 1579, Bruno and the printer Berjon were both arrested and thrown into prison. Berjon was released after an overnight stay and fined fifty florins. Bruno stood trial before the Consistory, which admonished him to "follow the true doctrine" and excommunicated him until he should make a proper confession. After two and a half weeks in jail, he capitulated, apologizing on his knees to La Faye and to the Consistory for having wrongly slandered them (although he had not slandered the Consistory in his broadsheet, he had talked back to them during his hearings with his usual lack of tact) and watching as all the known copies of his broadsheet were fed to the flames.

Two roads led out of Geneva. One pointed toward Germany, and one toward France. Despite the Dominican friar's warning in Chambéry that French hospitality grew colder with every step farther into the country, Bruno took the road back to Lyon. If nothing else, he could understand French, and presumably speak it as well. His excommunication as a Calvinist followed him, but this, at least, was an excommunication he was happy to accept.

One of the images that Bruno would invoke repeatedly in his writing was that of the "solitary sparrow," a brilliant blue bird whose English name, blue rock thrush, evokes its form, color, and habitat, but not its behavior. The ancient Hebrews and Romans, on the other hand, like modern Italians, had been more struck by its social habits; unlike most sparrows, the little bird sings alone rather than wheeling around in a flock.

The "solitary sparrow" appears in a despondent psalm (Vulgate 101; King James 102) that figures in the lectionary for Ash Wednesday and recurred several times in Bruno's own work, an image of the loneliness that must have accompanied him through the Alps and the limestone crags of Provence, on his way to Lyon:

Hear my prayer, O Lord, and let my cry come unto thee.
Hide not thy face from me in the time of my trouble; incline thine ear
   unto me; hear me when I call, and that right soon.

For my days pass away like smoke: I waste away because I cannot eat my
   bread.
I groan aloud and am weary; my bones cleave fast to my skin.
I am become like an owl in the wilderness: yea, even like an owl among
   the ruins.
I am solitary, and lie sleepless because of my groaning, like a sparrow
   that sitteth alone on the housetop.
Mine enemies revile me all the day long, and they that are enraged
   against me conspire to do me hurt.
Surely I have eaten ashes as if they were bread, and mingled my drink
   with weeping,
Because of thy indignation and wrath: for thou hast taken me up and
   cast me away.
My days are gone like a shadow: and I am withered like grass.

In a sonnet by Bruno, the sparrow pushes onward, a free soul for
whom "the world is fine as it is." These days of 1578 and 1579 were
when Bruno's philosophical thoughts at last began to gather into a
coherent shape. The hardship of his physical life did nothing to
dim his faith that the world was governed by a transcendent love to
which philosophy, the love of wisdom, made answer. The "I" of his
poem sends the "lonely sparrow" off to find its way, just as a mother
releases her grown child (another image Bruno uses in the same set
of poems), knowing all the while that the sparrow will probably
never return; in some sense, he suggests in a Platonic vein, the soul
never truly belongs to the person it inhabits. By the time he wrote
this sonnet, Bruno knew that he would surely never see his parents
again, or Nola, or Naples, and that sense of loss, coupled with optimism and undying affection, suffuses its verse:

> My lonely sparrow, in those lofty parts
> That cast their shade and burden down my will,
> Soon build your nest, confirm your every skill;
> There lavish all your industry and art.
>
> Be born again, and there bring up your flock
> Of pretty fledglings, now that all the force

Of hostile fate has run its final course
Against the quest to which it posed a block.

Go forth, then: I hope you find
A nobler fate, and have a god to guide you:
The one the sightless dare to say is blind.

Go; and find beside you
Each deity of this masterful design;
And don't return to me unless you're mine.

Once again, Giordano Bruno, like his lonely sparrow, went forth.

Thirty

LYON AND TOULOUSE, 1579-1581

Against Love's blows I built a strong redoubt;
When his assaults struck, countless, everywhere,
Pounding my heart within its diamond lair—
Still, over his my own desires won out.

At last (as was the heavens' plan throughout)
I chanced one day upon a holy pair
Of lights, and through my own lights, then and there
They found an entry to my heart laid out.
—From *The Heroic Frenzies*, 2.1

From Geneva, as Bruno told the Venetian inquisitors,

I went to Lyon, where I stayed for a month, and as I could not find any way
to earn enough to live on and to meet my needs, from there I went to
Toulouse, where there is a famous university, and having made the ac-
quaintance of intelligent persons there, I was invited to lecture on the
Sphere to various scholars, and I lectured along with other lessons on philosophy for maybe six months. Meanwhile, the post of reader of philosophy came vacant in that city, which is filled by competition, and I decided
to take a higher degree, which I did, as Master of Arts. And so I entered
the competition and was admitted and approved, and for two years after

that I lectured on the text of Aristotle's *On the Soul* and other lessons in philosophy. And then, because of the civil wars, I left and went to Paris.

As the site of a book fair nearly as important as that of Frankfurt, and a major point of exchange between Italy and France, Lyon should have been a promising place for Bruno to find work. France, however, was a battleground, and its economy was in a shambles. The worst of the massacres had occurred on Saint Bartholomew's Day, August 24, 1572, when French Catholics led by King Charles IX, his wife, Catherine de Médicis, the cardinal of Lorraine, and the duc de Guise slaughtered thousands of Protestant Huguenots in Paris, Toulouse, Lyon, Bourges, Rouen, and Orléans. With a series of bad harvests adding to the misery, Lyon was paralyzed, religiously, politically, and economically.

Bruno moved northward, penniless but remarkably resilient. His education represented its own kind of wealth. So did his philosophy—both his father's Stoic creed and his own increasingly lucid thoughts. He arrived in Toulouse not as a vagabond but as a scholar, with a scholar's hopes of finding a position in the university. And in Toulouse, for the first time since his flight from Rome, he settled into a stable position, first as a private tutor, studying at the same time for his master's degree, and then, at last, as professor of philosophy at the University of Toulouse. The list of courses he provided to his Venetian interrogators serves as a reminder that what he knew as philosophy was a broad range of disciplines (we can see a remnant of that range in the number of disciplines that grant Ph.D. degrees, which are still literally doctorates "of philosophy"). Teaching Sacrobosco's *Sphere* implied teaching natural philosophy, especially astronomy; Aristotle's *On the Soul* was the standard text for metaphysics. Thus Bruno was teaching both the makeup of the physical world and—an assumption that could be taken for granted in his century—the divine principles that governed it.

Accepted at last, in the company of "intelligent persons," with students to sharpen his ideas, Bruno later believed that his philosophy transformed in a crucial way during this period. He would always say that the revelation happened when he was thirty, the

same age as Dante in *The Divine Comedy*, "in the middle of our
life's journey." Perhaps the number thirty was more an approximation than a precise reality, but he was certainly close to that age
when, like Dante, he saw the universe open up to him: inferno,
purgatory, and paradise.

The universe in which Dante played out *The Divine Comedy* was
that of Sacrobosco, a nest of eight crystalline spheres rotating
around the earth, with the fixed stars set in the outermost sphere,
where God had placed them at the moment of creation. When
Dante spoke of "the world," he might mean secular society, the
three continents of Earth, or the whole eight-sphered cosmos. The
stars and planets had distinct personalities, and so did numbers;
the disciplines of astrology and numerology focused on interpreting
these celestial and numerical personalities and their interactions.
The most complex mathematical operation that Dante knew was
long division. Hindu-Arabic numerals had been in use in Italy
for only a century, introduced in 1202 by the Tuscan merchant
Leonardo Fibonacci of Pisa.

For Bruno and his contemporaries, a *Divine Comedy* was much
harder to write. Dante's certainties about natural philosophy were
no longer certain. Astronomy had begun to split away from astrology, substituting a mechanical system of stars and planets for a system tied to the gods of Olympus. Mathematicians like Copernicus
could track their movements with the help of complex equations,
an activity as absorbing, in the end, as tracking their personalities
had been in times past. In a whole series of applications, from cosmology to mechanics to geometry, algebra promised more exciting
discoveries than numerology. At the end of the fifteenth century,
Leonardo da Vinci had already confided in one of his notebooks
that mathematics, combined with experimentation, provided the
secret to all knowledge:

> No human investigation can be called real knowledge if it does not pass
> through mathematical demonstrations; and if you say that the kinds of
> knowledge that begin and end in the mind have any value as truth, this
> cannot be conceded, but rather must be denied for many reasons, and first
> of all because in such mental discussions there is no experimentation,
> without which nothing provides certainty of itself.

Leonardo thus anticipated, by more than a century, Galileo's famous statement about mathematics in *The Assayer*, his 1623 attack on the Jesuit scientist Orazio Grassi:

> Philosophy is written in this great book that stands ever open before our eyes (I mean the universe), but it cannot be understood without first learning to understand the language and recognize the characters in which it is written. It is written in mathematical language, and the characters are triangles, circles, and other geometric figures; without these tools it is impossible for a human being to understand a word; [to be] without them is to wander aimlessly through a dark labyrinth.

Bruno's scrutiny of the universe reflected a different kind of mind from Galileo's. Astronomers like Copernicus, Tycho Brahe, and Galileo all had the mental habit of counting everything they saw. They could happily spend night after night watching the stars, measuring and tallying, until their individual observations added up to a larger theory. Bruno's mind ran, more spectacularly than most, to visual imagery (although his minute account of the puppies and bedbugs of Nola suggests that he might have been a compulsive counter, too). Geometry intrigued him in a way that calculation did not. Yet he, too, was attracted by the idea of a universe run by mechanical principles: when he looked out at the stars, he saw Bernardino Telesio's battle between heat and cold creating pinpoints of light in a vast sea of darkness.

At the same time, with another part of his imagination, he could still look at the stars in their old role, as mythological figures, but here, too, he did so in a new way, using the stars, and their characters, to create new myths. Bruno's versatility—part poet, part artist, part natural philosopher, part moralist, part theologian— makes him hard to fit into contemporary ideas of science, but this is not a problem unique to him: many of the best scientists today face it as well.

There was nothing like teaching Aristotle to remind Bruno how much he resented the grand old Greek. No other thinker, not even Plato, could simply be called "the Philosopher," but then no one else had earned such a position of authority on so many topics. In one sense, of course, the Philosopher was an ancient sage, but in another sense, as Bruno would point out, Aristotle's thinking was younger, more immature, than that of the philosophers who came after him. In Bruno's dialogue *The Ash Wednesday Supper*, the pedant Prudenzio praises the wisdom of the ancients until Bruno's alter ego, Teofilo, turns an old proverb on its head:

PRUDENZIO: Have it as you like, but I don't like to depart from the opinion of the ancients, for, as the proverb says, "Wisdom lies in antiquity."

TEOFILO: And adds, "And prudence lies in great age." If you really understood what you were saying, you would see that your statement implies the opposite of what you think: I mean that we are more ancient and greater in age than our predecessors; at least regarding some of the opinions we have been discussing. The judgment of [Aristotle's student] Eudoxus (who lived just after the rebirth of astronomy, if he was not that rebirth himself) cannot have been as mature as that of Callippus, who lived 30 years after the death of Alexander the Great, for just as he added years upon years, he also added observations to observations. Hipparchus, for the same reasons, had to have known more than Callipus, because he saw the changes that had occurred up to 196 years after the death of Alexander. Menelaus Romanus the geometer understood more than Hipparchus for the simple fact that he saw what had been set in motion 432 years after the death of Alexander. Mahomet of Arak [an Arab astronomer] had to have seen still more 1,202 years afterward. Copernicus saw still more, because he lived almost up to our own time, 1,849 years after [Alexander's death]. And if those closer to us in time have been no wiser than those who went before them, and most people today have no extra wit, it is because (what's worse) they have lived their lives as if they were dead.

Bruno saw no reason to cling to Aristotle's ideas simply because Aristotle had been a great man and had lived a long time ago. Where data contradicted the Philosopher's conjectures, he accepted the data. But he also reserved the right to conjecture as freely as the Philosopher had before him, confident that humanity had learned something in its nineteen added centuries of existence—and confident, like many an academic before and since, that his own native abilities were a good match for those of the Philosopher in any case.

Copernicus did not invent the idea that the Earth might revolve around the sun; a Greek astronomer living in Samos, Aristarchus, had already made the proposal in the third century B.C. The behavior of the stars and planets fit the Earth-centered and sun-centered schemes just about equally, that is, well but not perfectly, especially because everyone from ancient Greece up to Bruno's time took it for granted that the heavenly bodies orbited in perfect circles. The slight differences in measurement on which Copernicus based his argument were not as interesting to Bruno as the idea that all these measurements produced at best an approximation of a larger reality; in the old Platonic sense, they were as "real" as footprints in a forest. What interested Bruno was the forest itself.

The Arab astronomers, like the Greeks, recognized that their measurements produced only approximate proof that the universe was a set of nested spheres surrounded by a realm of fixed stars and the enigmatic Milky Way. In tenth-century Cairo, the Egyptian court astronomer Ibn Yunus used extremely large instruments in hopes of making more accurate readings of heavenly motions that occurred on a gigantic scale. A fifteenth-century German cardinal, Nicholas of Cusa (in Latin, Nicolaus Cusanus), proposed the idea that the universe might be infinitely large, and that each of the fixed stars might loom as large as the sun, if only we were to come close enough. Cusanus, in addition to his temporal and religious duties, was a philosopher who loved paradoxes of all sorts; his treatise On the None Other declared, "The None Other is none other than the None Other." In his greatest work of paradox, On Learned Ignorance, an obvious inspiration for Bruno's preoccupation with holy asininity, Cusanus suggested that perhaps only an infinitely large universe did proper justice to God, who, as Saint Augustine had insisted, was "the measure beyond measure."

For his fellow cardinals of less ample imagination, Cusanus's universe posed an immediate problem for their own role in the world: What, exactly, was the place of the human race, put on earth at the creation in order to be saved some four thousand years later by Jesus Christ, whose Church continued his work of salvation through his vicar the pope, and themselves? Fortunately for the cardinal, the Inquisition had not yet become a permanent institution, and his speculations were punished only by indifference. As for the place of Jesus Christ within an expanded cosmos, Cusanus himself simply marveled at the full scope of divine Providence.

So did the Jewish mystics who wrote about riding on cherubs "over a cloud a thousand worlds beyond the world" with eyes that "have seen nothing but God alone." At around the age of thirty, Giordano Bruno began to cast his own imagination a thousand worlds beyond the world and find that the universe he had been teaching looked pitifully inadequate. More and more, he found himself agreeing with Cusanus.

The change of mind might have come initially as a flash of insight (and Bruno's writings suggest that it did), but it would take him years to work out its details. Among the tools he applied to the task of understanding very large numbers, almost from the beginning, was his magnificent trained memory. Within his head, the artificial memory constituted its own kind of infinite universe. Already at Toulouse he had begun to work on a book about the art of recollection that he would call *Clavis magna* (*The Great Key*). Somehow, he believed that a strictly disciplined mind would provide the necessary guidance for people who finally realized the full complexity of creation. As it did to Cusanus, the prospect of an opening, massively expanding universe seems to have filled him with awe rather than terror, "fear of God" in its most positive sense.

Bruno described his revelation, however, as falling in love. In Greek, *philosophia* means "love of wisdom," and Plato, the most voluptuous of writers, had long ago used the language of erotic love to suggest that the pleasures of philosophical love were similar, but incomparably more intense. The Platonic philosophy of Marsilio Ficino and Giles of Viterbo reconciled this eroticism with Christian faith; Giles in particular connected the most sensuous passages of Plato with the erotic poetry of the biblical Song of Songs, a book he and his contemporaries read as a series of allegorical love songs between God and the human soul, or Christ and the Church. Fi-

cino, like Plato's Socrates, focused both his erotic and his philosophical desire on young men, whereas Giles, by introducing the
Song of Songs, transformed both divine and philosophical love
into the love of male and female, variously conceived as the love of
God and the soul (*anima*), Christ and the Church, or the philosopher and Wisdom (a feminine noun in Greek, Latin, and Hebrew).

Bruno described his illumination in a sonnet, where the "twin
lights" of truth and goodness enter through his eyes into his heart
and transform him into their passionate lover:

> Against Love's blows I built a strong redoubt;
> When his assaults struck, countless, everywhere,
> Pounding my heart within its diamond lair—
> Still, over his my own desires won out.
>
> At last (as was the heavens' plan throughout)
> I chanced one day upon a holy pair
> Of lights, and through my own lights, then and there
> They found an entry to my heart laid out.
>
> Toward me then a double arrow sailed,
> Shot by a hand that held a warrior's rage
> Who'd fought for thirty years and always failed.
>
> But now he'd marked the spot and pressed the siege;
> Planting his trophy right where he prevailed,
> And forced my wayward wings into his cage.
>
> On a more solemn stage
> The angers of my sweetest enemy
> Will never cease to strike my heart, and me.

As a proper successor not only to Plato but also to Plato's student the Philosopher, Bruno saw that his ideas would have spiritual
and ethical repercussions as well as mathematical. Bernardino
Telesio had already argued that the whole universe was composed
of the same elements without distinction; Bruno agreed, and thus

could envision the whole expanse of the stars as hot "suns" surrounded by cold, lightless "earths" invisible to the human eye.

In an infinite expanse of space, the motions of these "suns" and "earths," like those of the sun, moon, Earth, and planets, became a matter not of one body revolving around another but of motions within an infinite continuum. The cosmic systems of Aristotle, Ptolemy, and Copernicus were all relative—schematic expressions of one tiny part of an immeasurably larger set of motions.

The nested wheels he had borrowed from Ramon Llull's art of memory now served Bruno as a useful model for analyzing large numbers; each successive wheel created an exponential increase in the system's number of possible combinations and allowed him to arrive mentally, at least, at nearly limitless magnitudes. He began to think about what kind of a mathematics could deal with infinite numbers: extremes not only of immensity but also of tininess. Arithmetic and geometry as he knew them were not enough.

Bruno's was the century in which European merchants and scholars definitively abandoned Roman numerals and their traditional ancient tools of abacus and counting stick for Hindu-Arabic numerals. The Arabic numerals came along with a related discipline that bore an Arabic name, algebra, and opened out the range of subjects that mathematicians could investigate—long division no longer represented the peak of their sophistication. Just before Bruno's birth, therefore, Gerolamo Cardano provided a mathematical account of probability in his *Book on Games of Chance*. Even Fortune had her rational side.

Through the development of complex equations, made possible by Hindu-Arabic notation, arithmetic could keep up at last with geometry. At the same time, however, mathematicians faced the insoluble mysteries of irrational numbers, the geometric quantities that could be drawn easily but never be calculated with arithmetical precision: square roots and the golden section, both having to do with the ratio between the side of a rectangle and its diagonals; and pi, the ratio between a circle's radius and its circumference. Bruno's writings reveal his own eagerness to confront one of the places where geometry and arithmetic collide most insistently with each other: the mathematics of motion. He had begun, in other words, to ask the questions to which only calculus would provide answers. Working a century before Newton and Leibniz and without their deeply arithmetical feel for numbers—as his writings show, to the end of his career he was still a numerologist at heart—Bruno simply lacked the mathematical means to answer his own questions himself.

Often, like his contemporaries, Bruno uses the word *mathematici* to mean astronomers, and *mathematici* of the 1590s stood on the verge of revolution. Bruno heaped praise on the observational data of Tycho Brahe and the theoretical insight of Copernicus, but the real empirical breakthroughs in astronomy would come after Bruno's death, with the invention of the telescope in 1609. In 1610, Galileo would train his own telescope on the heavens, and publish the discoveries in his *Starry Messenger* that same year: the moons of Jupiter, the seas and craters on the moon's surface, and the remarkable number of the Pleiades. Bruno, by contrast, had arrived at his own idea of the infinite universe with nothing more than the naked eye. Furthermore, in one of his philosophy's most sophisticated developments, he understood that such a universe must involve a mathematics of infinite quantities and infinitesimal quantities, numbers so inconceivably large that they were all equal and so inconceivably tiny that they were equal again.

At the same time that the heavens began to open for the Nolan philosophy, one of Bruno's colleagues at the University of Toulouse was exploring his own paradoxes in the spirit of Cusanus and *On Learned Ignorance*. The faculty's other professor of philosophy, Francisco Sánchez, published his best-known work, *Why Nothing Is Known*, in Lyon in 1581. He gave Bruno a copy, which he inscribed "To the most illustrious Giordano Bruno, Keen-Witted Doctor of Philosophy, in friendship and esteem." Bruno added his own inscription in the margin of the title page, alongside the last word in the byline, "Franciscus Sánchez, Philosopher and Physician, Doctor": "Remarkable that this ass professes himself a doctor." On the first page of Sánchez's text, Bruno added another note: "Remarkable that he presumes to teach"—a barb at the teacher's insistence, at such length, that "nothing is known." Bruno's keen wits were never tempered by charity toward his weaker colleagues. Other

asses might be redeemed by their patience and their ability to endure, but he seemed to exempt pedant asses from any such hope of
salvation.

In Toulouse, with the rest of his life settling into place, Bruno
pondered returning to the Church, and to his order. In the secrecy
of a confessional, he confided his whole situation to a Jesuit priest,
for Jesuits had the authority to grant absolution to repentant
heretics without involving the Inquisition. There were other advantages to consulting a Jesuit as well. Gossip traveled fast from
one Dominican house to the next; that was how Bruno learned
that he had been excommunicated in absentia and defrocked by
the Dominican provincial of Naples, Fra Domenico Vita. Any in-
quiries he made among the Dominicans, however discreet, were
likely to be passed back to Italy, and fast. Of the other orders, the
Jesuits were among the least likely to divulge any information to
the Dominicans: the two orders, one old, one new, were archrivals,
for papal favor, for the best minds in the Church, and for the reputation as Catholicism's intellectual vanguard. Some years later, that
old rivalry still instinctive, Bruno would tell a Parisian bookseller
that "he despised . . . all the philosophy of the Jesuits, which is
nothing but questions about the text and intelligence of Aristotle."
Yet when Bruno entered a confessional in Lyon for the first time in
years, he must have hoped to find a receptive hearing. For all its famous rigor, its spiritual exercises, and its vows of obedience, the Society of Jesus had bred some remarkably independent and flexible
minds: Christoph Clavius was only one example, but an example
any professor of astronomy—as Bruno was—knew as well as Sacrobosco's *On the Sphere*.

The Jesuit listened, but he could do no more than listen. As he
explained through the confessional screen, he lacked the authority
to perform absolution on an excommunicate—that is, to forgive the sins just confessed—unless, or until, Bruno rejoined the
Church. Rejoining the Church, in turn, would require, at the very
least, the approval of a bishop. In the meantime, the priest warned
against participating in the Mass; to do so under excommunication
was a grave sin. It was no sin, however, to pray privately, and prayer
was perfectly permissible within a church at any time. The confes-

sor could do little else to fulfill his order's mission "to comfort souls," and Bruno carefully respected his counsel, avoiding Mass and especially Communion, but listening to sermons and vesper services, and continuing, at least for the moment, to pray for private absolution every time he sinned. The conversation in the confessional cannot have been easy for either party.

Reconciliation was no less impossible in the world outside between French Catholics, loyal to King Henri III, and Protestant Huguenots, who had found a champion in Henri IV, king of Navarre. In the spring of 1581, the city of Toulouse imprisoned emissaries sent from the Catholics of southern Provence to negotiate with Henri IV. When the city council refused to release the Provençal delegates, Henri III, from Paris, threatened to send in his army.

Shortly thereafter, Giordano Bruno, the new professor of philosophy at the University of Toulouse, set out for Paris, intent on obtaining a place at the Sorbonne. Ever since his arrival in Geneva, if not long before, he had hoped to find a place to live in "liberty and safety." With Toulouse threatening to explode, he seems to have hoped that such a refuge might be waiting for him in the only other European city to rival Naples for size, complexity, and political turmoil.

CHAPTER FIFTEEN

The Gifts of the Magi

PARIS, 1581–1583

There was a certain rich man, which was clothed in purple and fine linen, and fared sumptuously every day; And there was a certain beggar named Lazarus, which was laid at his gate, full of sores . . . And it came to pass, that the beggar died, and was carried by the angels into Abraham's bosom: the rich man also died, and was buried; And in hell he lift up his eyes, being in torments, and seeth Abraham afar off, and Lazarus in his bosom. And he cried and said, Father Abraham, have mercy on me, and send Lazarus, that he may dip the tip of his finger in water, and cool my tongue; for I am tormented in this flame. But Abraham said, Son, remember that thou in thy lifetime receivedst thy good things, and likewise Lazarus evil things; but now he is comforted, and thou art tormented. And beside all this, between us and you there is a great gulf fixed: so that they which would pass from hence to you cannot; neither can they pass to us, that would come from thence. Then he said, I pray thee therefore, Father, that thou wouldest send him to my Father's house; For I have five brethren; that he may testify unto them, lest they also come into this place of torment. Abraham saith unto him, They have Moses and the prophets; let them hear them. And he said, Nay, Father Abraham: but if one went unto them from the dead, they will repent. And he said unto him, If they hear not Moses and the prophets, neither will they be persuaded, though one rose from the dead.

—Luke 16:19–31

By the time he arrived in Paris, in the summer of 1581, Giordano Bruno had been moving across Italy and France for six years, and if we are to believe his description of himself, the strain had begun to show:

> If you knew the Author, you would say that he has the look of a lost soul; he seems always to be contemplating the punishments of hell, he seems to be pressed flat as a beret, someone who laughs only to fit in; for the most part you'll see him irritated, recalcitrant, and strange, content with nothing, stubborn as an old man of eighty, skittish as a dog that has been whipped a thousand times, a weepy onion eater.

Whipped and skittish he may have felt, but he continued to move with the aristocratic confidence of a friar from San Domenico Maggiore. For when Giordano Bruno reached the French capital, he headed straight for the Sorbonne and the court of King Henri III, offering to earn his keep by teaching king, courtiers, and professors the art of memory. At the same time, he also hinted at a certain expertise in magic, though Bruno's idea of magic, as individual as the rest of his thought, had more to do with ancient wisdom than with either superstition or conjuring tricks. The three Magi who brought their gifts of gold, frankincense, and myrrh to the Christ Child were the kinds of magicians with whom Bruno felt a kinship, not the charlatans and mountebanks who performed stunts from the backs of their carts and sold miraculous unguents in the marketplace. Real Magi were wise men, not tricksters, and their art derived its power from understanding how the world worked.

Like most people of his time and place, however, Giordano Bruno did believe in demons. As a child in Nola, he had known them as evanescent creatures who threw stones and snatched cloaks in the night, especially in the forest near his house. They continued throughout his life to play practical jokes, misplacing things more for the sheer mischief of it than out of real malevolence. When he described them in On the Immense and the Numberless, his great sober poem about the structure of the cosmos, he did so with his best efforts at philosophical rigor:

Certainly in the interior regions of this [earth] there are living creatures of more subtle body, lively, not terribly rational, that have little in common with us; and [in the night air] there are daemons, neither terribly friendly to human beings nor terribly unfriendly, but nonetheless mockers and liars. They may have no more wit than we, but they excel in this: because their bodies are as ductile as the bodies of clouds, they can fuse and contract themselves into various shapes, and enter into our dreams, and announce things to us that they have seen more rapidly than we. Hence they are thought to see the future, when in fact they are a good deal less discerning than we.

Like Jesus and his apostles, experts at casting out spirits, the Church maintained a corps of exorcists to keep control over the demonic population. As inquisitors, some of Bruno's fellow Dominicans kept special watch on the sorcerers and witches who tried to use demons rather than drive them away. The difference between sorcery and witchcraft was largely a difference in the social standing of their practitioners. Witches were poor and unlettered people, vagabonds, local eccentrics, or purveyors of home remedies. Their "magic" involved the occult business of casting or lifting the evil eye, mixing love potions, or predicting the future. This was the magic for desperate people, the magic to call upon when medicines failed, lovers strayed, enemies prospered, children died. It was practiced disproportionately by people on the margins of society: by women, especially old women, by traveling sages, foreigners, Muslim slaves; surprisingly, the people who seemed to have power over the unseen world were conspicuously powerless in the world of everyday, as powerless as the customers who turned to them as a last resort. The roots of their folk magic ran deep. Many of its rituals were already common among the ancient Greeks who colonized southern Italy. Like their Greek forebears, Italian women in Bruno's day told fortunes by "throwing the beans": casting dried fava beans and other objects in order to read the future from the way they fell. In other ancient rituals, they floated drops of oil on a dish of water to test for the evil eye, read palms, and prepared love philters.

Sorcerers and magicians stood at the other end of the social spectrum; their education in the magic arts came from books, most of them in Latin. Their clients were often more curious than desperate. Rather than solving individual problems, this magic looked for general principles to explain the workings of the world. In many ways, the discipline that Bruno and his contemporaries called "natural magic" was just another branch of natural philosophy: a discipline that focused its attention on nature's many and baffling shortcuts. Phenomena like magnetism, meteors, phosphorescence, and gunpowder were surpassingly strange, but they behaved with a certain consistency, and natural magic aimed to understand them as well as control them. In a sense, every kind of magic tried to turn nature's powers to personal advantage, but natural magic tried to do so more systematically than its folk counterpart: superstitious sixteenth-century lovers wore magnets to become more magnetically attractive, but sixteenth-century magicians might also want to know what magnetism was.

All magic, whatever its level of sophistication, worked on the principle of analogy. The analogies at the base of popular magic were literal-minded—wearing magnets to become irresistibly attractive, sticking pins into wax dolls to harm an enemy, or more elaborate rituals, like this cure performed on a seventeenth-century Knight of Malta (typically, the healers were foreigners): "A Greek who healed spleens . . . made me put my left foot on a prickly-pear leaf, and then cut it around my foot as his wife said 'what are you doing?' and he replied 'I'm cutting Fra Paolo's spleen,' and they repeated these words three times."

The ideas behind natural magic could be equally literal, as in the fifteenth-century Florentine philosopher and physician Marsilio Ficino's regimen outlined in On Living the Heavenly Life (De vita coelitus comparanda), with its recommendations to drink the milk of young women or eat sweets to preserve youth, and carefully place stones, gems, and colors associated with each planet in strategic places around the house to focus their benevolent influence and scatter the bad.

Although Bruno readily acknowledged Ficino's influence on the Nolan philosophy, his own version of natural magic seems to have borne little resemblance to the Florentine's sweet life. For one thing, Bruno had been constantly on the move; in temporary quarters it was harder to place stones, find the right food, and persuade young mothers to give up their milk to middle-aged men. Appropriately to his situation, his magic had become more abstract, more intellectual, more portable; rather than arranging external objects around him, he arranged ideas inside his head and held them there fast.

The ancient Greeks and Romans often described magical operations as capturing, binding, or chaining their object—"fascination," the Roman word for the evil eye, was another word for "binding," derived from *fascia*, a strip of cloth. Bruno preferred the image of chains or bonds; one of his magical treatises would eventually be called *On Bonds in General*. The fundamental key to Bruno's natural magic, however, was neither strips nor chains but the art of memory; by storing and manipulating the knowledge within his own mind, he declared, he could gain power over the entire universe. This was what he seems, at least implicitly, to have promised to teach to the king of France.

What could the art of memory do for a king like Henri III? For a monarch, more than for most people, memory really was a source of power, especially if the monarch were directly involved in government, as Henri certainly was. If he could remember what he had to do, what he meant to do, what he had already done, it was obvious that he would govern his state more efficiently. Bureaucratic records were kept in large paper books, and however well these might be organized (usually they were organized very well indeed), the best way to search them quickly was to know, and to remember, what they contained. If Bruno professed a particularly powerful art of memory, and his public performances certainly suggest that he did, a king could make use of those same talents to do much more than astonish the learned. To an extent not permitted to most of his contemporaries, Henri really could control the world around him.

Bruno told his inquisitors how he first attracted the king's attention:

> I gave a course as adjunct professor to make myself known and show what
> I was about. I gave thirty lectures, taking thirty attributes of divinity from

the first book of Saint Thomas; and then I stayed on, because I was asked to give a regular course, but I did not want to accept it, because the public professors in that city ordinarily go to Mass and the other services. And I have always avoided doing this, knowing that I had been excommunicated for having left religious life. And by lecturing as an adjunct professor, I acquired such a reputation that King Henri III summoned me one day, examining me to find out whether the memory I used and taught was natural or a magical art. I gave him satisfaction, and from what I told him and had him try on his own, he understood that it worked not by magic arts but by knowledge. After this I published a book on memory under the title *On the Shadows of Ideas*, which I dedicated to His Majesty, and on that occasion he made me an adjunct professor with a living.

Bruno's initial series of lectures (the ones by which he made himself known in Paris) must have concerned logic and metaphysics. They were drawn from the first book of Thomas Aquinas's masterwork, the *Summa theologiae*; the first book was sometimes treated as a treatise in its own right, *On the One God*. Bruno cannot have been unaware that he was lecturing in the same city where Aquinas had been a student, and where the great Dominican, a Neapolitan nobleman, had first established his own reputation. The Nolan philosopher's choice of subject, then, was peculiarly appropriate to his situation. Alongside Aquinas, Bruno probably used Aristotle's *Metaphysics* as a textbook, just as he had in Toulouse. Ten years later, when he lectured on the same subjects in Zurich, he devoted special attention to the vocabulary associated with this branch of philosophy and how it might connect to the study of natural philosophy; it seems likely that he did the same in Paris. As his ideas about the structure of the universe developed, they spurred him to think about how this infinitely expanded physical world might affect his concept of God, and of the significance of human life.

For the first time, we also have a report from one of Bruno's students about his success as a teacher. Johann von Nostitz, writing in 1615, would recall: "It was thirty-one years ago in Paris that I first heard Jordano Bruno make a magnificent presentation of himself in the arts of Ramon Llull and mnemonology or memory, attracting many private students and auditors." Through those auditors Bruno came to the attention of King Henri III. Three years younger than Bruno, with an Italian mother, Catherine de Médicis, Henri was Catholic, but not militantly so; he did his best to mend the tensions between Catholics and Huguenots rather than suppress the Protestants altogether. Furthermore, as the Spanish ambassador to France informed his king, Philip II, Henri spent "three long hours a day listening to philosophy." He was a monarch after Bruno's own heart.

Henri, in turn, was impressed enough by the Nolan philosopher to appoint him a *lecteur royale*, or royal reader, part of a group of professors that met outside the Sorbonne at the Collège de Cambrai. The appointment was temporary, but illustrious. Bruno's plan to "make [him]self known" had worked to perfection; as von Nostitz reveals, the Nolan had cleverly used a standard course on logic and metaphysics as an opportunity to introduce his art of memory. He made equally shrewd use of the printing press to spread his reputation.

The earliest of Bruno's printed memory manuals, *The Great Key*, has been lost. We do not know where or when he wrote it. He published the next three in Paris in a single year, 1582, dedicating them to Henri III and two members of the royal court. These three works, *On the Shadows of Ideas* (*De umbris idearum*), *The Song of Circe* (*Cantus Circaeus*), and *On the Compendious Architecture and Complement to the Art of Ramon Llull* (*De compendiosa architectura et complemento artis Lullii*), prove how emphatically Bruno regarded his version of the artificial memory as an art, which in the sixteenth century implied a divinely inspired creation. Like the paintings of the "divine" Raphael or the sculpture of the "divine" Michelangelo, Bruno's art of memory brought heaven down to earth by capturing sublime ideas in physical form. Although he often compared his art to painting and writing, he called it architecture, an internal mental architecture where the imagination, rather than painter's brush or writer's pen, acted as the tool: "Just as painting and sculpture use tools to shape their material, so, too, this art has no lack of tools to make its pictures."

Bruno's first surviving work on the art of memory, *On the Shadows of Ideas*, is in fact the first of his works on any subject to survive

to the present day. It was printed in Paris by a distinguished publisher, Gilles Gourbin, who may have regretted his association with
the volatile Italian from the first moment type met paper. Bruno
was an inveterate corrector, and he stood next to Gourbin's press
through the whole run: correcting, revising, changing his mind so
often that the hundred-odd surviving copies of *On the Shadows of
Ideas* differ significantly from one another—and every single one
bears penned corrections in Bruno's own hand. Dedicated to
Henri III in person, and addressed to readers already armed with a
copy of *The Great Key*, *On the Shadows of Ideas* sets out to liberate
the art of memory from every gloom of misunderstanding that has
clouded it since ancient times—little Bruno never thought small.

In this first book, he describes the practice of artificial memory
as "clever application of thought" to "presenting, modeling, noting,
or indicating in the likeness of painting or writing, in order to express or signify." In other words, the art of memory isolated individual sense perceptions from the stream of consciousness and
endowed these perceptions with special characteristics that transformed them into thoughts; the thoughts thus singled out for attention could then be put into what Bruno called "a distilled and
developed order of conceivable species, arranged as statues, or a
microcosm, or some other kind of architecture . . . by focusing
the chaos of imagination." Like files, these statue collections or
architectures of imagination were designed to store thoughts in a
way that made them easily accessible, easy to recall. The stored
thoughts could be recalled because they were in themselves memo-
rable, first, because of their vivid individual detail and, second, because of the rigorous order in which they were kept within their
architectures of memory.

Bruno himself ordered all manner of thoughts and perceptions
by means of these mental architectures. He describes one system in
detail for the king, which works by storing words as their individual
component syllables: the first syllable as an "agent" who is a mythological figure (the Egyptian Apis bull, Apollo, the witch Circe); the
second syllable as an action (sailing, on the carpet, broken); the
third syllable as an adjective (ignored, blind, at leisure); the fourth
as an associated object (shell, serpent, fetters); the fifth as a "cir-

cumstance" (a woman dressed in pearls, a man riding a sea monster). Hence the "NU" in "NUMERO"—"number"—is the Apis
bull, "ME" is "on the carpet," "RO" is "neglected." "NUMERATI"
is "the Apis bull (NU) on the carpet (ME), lamented (RA rather
than RO 'neglected'), with a snake (TI)." Bruno, clearly influenced
by Ramon Llull, advises envisioning these stored sets of syllables
and their imagery on concentric wheels, each with thirty compartments corresponding to the various combinations of letters. The
outermost wheel in the system stores the agents (or first syllables of
words), the second wheel stores the actions (or second syllables),
the third wheel stores adjectives (or third syllables), and so on in-
ward to the fifth wheel. A single sentence thus becomes a pageant
of mythological characters set in strange places, engaged in strange
actions in strange company. A speech stored in this way could contain the population of a small city.

On the Shadows of Ideas also supplies several other brief descriptions of model memory architectures, these also formed on Llullian
wheels. Bruno's own mental structures must have been far more
complex, and must surely have included real architectures like the
vast Gothic interior of San Domenico as well as the whirling circles of Ramon Llull.

Bruno realized that even the simplest of these systems might
sound excessively complicated to a reader, and preemptively lam-
poons a detractor in the book's prologue:

> Pharfacon, Doctor of Civil and Canon Law, Philosopher and Man of Let-
> ters, believes that this art weighs down its practitioners rather than light-
> ening their burden, because whereas without the art there are only things
> to recollect, with the art we are obliged to recollect things, places, and
> images, lots of them, by which no one will doubt that natural memory is
> only further confused and baffled.

Bruno's immediate reply to the pedantic Pharfacon drips sar-
casm: "Wit that sharp ought to be carded with an iron comb." But
the criticism was a real one, and Bruno addressed it later in the
book by arguing that the artificial memory worked more efficiently
than rote memory because it exploited the actual physical process

of recollection (in essence we use the same argument today, but now we speak of human development rather than the physiology of the soul). Bruno lodged the process of recollection in the immortal soul he called *anima*, and called the art itself "a habit of the reasoning soul"—artificial not in the modern sense of something false, but in the sense of something created by discipline, a skill, like holding a pen, or an exercise as primal as walking upright. Hence he saw the art itself as an integral part of the human mind: "a technical extension or ordered reserve in the imaginative faculty, consisting in species of receptacles that flow in from the windows of the soul, divided into different parts, to receive all things seen and heard and retain them according to the pleasure of the soul."

The real point of the artificial memory, Bruno argued, was to order sense perceptions, imagination, and, ultimately, understanding to reflect the basic harmony of the world itself. The very rightness of the process is what made it easier to carry out than the Pharfacons of the world would suspect:

> Just as a hand joined to an arm, a foot to a leg, or an eye to a head is more recognizable than when it is separated, likewise with parts and whole species, let nothing be set aside and out of order (which is utterly simple, perfect, and beyond number in the primal mind) if we intend to connect them with each other and unite them: What then can we not understand, remember, and do?

Memory, then, served as the prelude to action, by organizing experience in a usable way. On the most basic level, this is how a child learns; in the same way, Aristotle claimed that adult actions also responded to previous sense perceptions. Bruno claims in addition that adult actions proceed most usefully from organized knowledge, from a world that makes sense. *On the Shadows of Ideas* goes on to declare that the organizing impulses expressed in the art of memory begin at nature's most minute level of organization, the "seeds of those first principles" that were his name for atoms:

> This art can be called nothing else but a faculty of nature inborn with reason, together with the seeds of those first principles in which there is

the power, when they are attracted outside themselves by different objects as by so many charms, and are illuminated by the active intellect as if by a radiant sun, and receive influences from the eternal Ideas as if from the course of the stars, when they have been fertilized by the supreme being, to order all things in actuality and pursue their own end to the full extent of their strength.

In *On the Shadows of Ideas*, the first of all his surviving works, Bruno writes as a philosopher and as a poet, mixing dense analytical language from his Scholastic training with the vibrant imagery of Plato and his followers. Its title deliberately evokes the symbolic shadows and forests of his early Platonic readings. In the first decade of the sixteenth century, Giles of Viterbo had already used the phrase "shadow of idea" to explain what he meant by his image of footprints in the Forest of Matter: "A footprint is not an idea . . . it is something that lies outside idea, or is a shadow of idea."

Giles goes on to call this shadow of idea a "medium," both the "mean" between darkness and light and the "means" by which human thought leaves the state of unknowing that Plato described as a cave, and the poet Virgil as a "blind prison." Bruno, echoing Giles of Viterbo, describes his own "shadows of ideas" as footprints: "Shadow is not of darkness, but rather the footprint of darkness in light, or the footprint of light in darkness, or participant in light and darkness." Like Giles, he describes those shadows of ideas as a medium between the darkness of ignorance and the light of wisdom: "Nor does Nature suffer an immediate progression from one extreme to the other, but only through mediating shadows . . ."

Like his "shadows of ideas" themselves, Bruno's book proposed to act as a medium for the king's own progress from shadowy knowledge to expertise in the art of memory. Bruno tried to keep its language simple and its concepts clear, but without giving his whole technique away. Without Bruno present to explain his art in person, *On the Shadows of Ideas* is still something of a mystery. But we can see the sense of power it must have promised to the king and his courtiers. When Bruno's art brought forth even the most concrete event or ordinary object into the light, this effort at recollection was a revelation as much as a mechanical act. For among the patterns written into the primordial seeds of nature was the history of the soul itself. In a famous image, Plato's dialogue *Phaedrus* recounted how every human soul (*anima*) had fallen from a primeval grace into the prison of the physical body. In occasional flashes of insight, at the sight of a beautiful object, or rapt in contemplation, a soul will grow wings and fly upward to glimpse what Plato called ultimate reality. Marsilio Ficino and Giles of Viterbo called it *patria lux*, "light of the homeland," a radiance that made the sun dull by comparison, a brightness whose glory made nothing on earth so desirable as returning back. Every good deed, every search for God, responded to that primordial memory of sheer joy in the divine presence experienced as pure light. Disciplined memory, as a form of contemplation, prepared the soul to revisit this heavenly homeland. Bruno (like Plato, Ficino, and Giles of Viterbo before him) described the feeling of this homecoming as the sensation of emerging from shadow to bask in the light of the sun.

Always, therefore, Bruno's art of memory focused on these ancient soul-memories as well as the immediate world of sights, sounds, thoughts, and words, and the more powerful the soul-memories, the more powerful the art of recalling them: "A clearer soul, more exposed to divine Ideas, will take up the forms of objects with greater concentration, just as those who have sharper vision are able to discern what they see more easily and correctly."

The syllables Bruno describes in such detail in the second section of *On the Shadows of Ideas*, stored on their five concentric wheels, are only a preliminary, small-scale exercise in what should become the soul's grandest enterprise, its emergence, as he says himself, from the Forest of Matter:

> The light—life, understanding, the primal unity—contains all species, perfections, truths, and degrees of phenomena. Whereas those things that occur in Nature are different from one another, contrary, and diverse, in [the light] they are like, harmonious, and single. Try, therefore, if you are able with your powers, to identify, harmonize, and unite the phenomena you perceive, and you shall not exhaust your faculties, you shall not upset your mind, and you shall not confound your memory.

For Bruno, importantly, the world itself was neither entirely dark nor entirely evil. The practitioner of Giordano Bruno's art of memory, at least as proposed in *On the Shadows of Ideas*, will eventually see beyond those shadows of ideas to pure idea; it is the same progress envisioned by Plato, with the difference that Bruno puts idea not in a world beyond but in the world as it is:

> We decided that this art languished beneath the shadows of ideas, until it would either spur on sluggish Nature by going ahead of her, or direct and guide her if she is deviant and exorbitant, or strengthen and support her if she is exhausted, or correct her if she goes astray, or follow her if she is perfect, and emulate her industry.

His pamphlets on memory, written in academic Latin, could express only part of that world for Giordano Bruno. As a writer, and probably as a thinker as well, he was split from the beginning into three personalities: one had a Dominican's philosophical rigor, one a Platonist's poetic exaltation, and one a dark wit born in his parents' little house on the slopes of Monte Cicala and stiletto-sharpened on the streets of Naples. The caricatured detractors who mutter their imprecations in the prologue to *On the Shadows of Ideas* provide a foretaste of the characters who populate another of his works from 1582. Again, the terrain is that shadow land of the Forest of Matter, but the medium is comedy, for this was also the year in which Giordano Bruno published his sprawling play, *The Candlemaker*.

In its dedication to a mysterious "Signora Morgana B.," ostensibly a woman of Naples (or perhaps Nola), Bruno describes his philosophy as hovering on the margins between day and night:

> Time takes away all and grants all, everything changes, nothing is destroyed; only one thing cannot change, one, alone and eternal, and only one can abide eternally, consistent and identical. With this philosophy my spirit grows large, and my intellect is magnified. Thus, whatever the point should be of this coming evening, if the change is real, I who am in the night await the day, and those who are in the day await the night; everything that is, is either here or there, near or far, now or later, sooner or later. Rejoice, then, and if you can, be well, and love the one who loves you.

His audience receives a less solicitous plea, a sonnet in which we are to imagine the author, naked as a baby, wheedling some rich, learned man to honor his farce with a dedicatory poem and himself with a tip:

> O you who suckle at the Muses' tit,
> And in their creamy broth prefer to swim,
> Lips foremost, Sir, now listen to my whim:
> If you by faith and charity are lit,
> I wheedle, ask, and beg of you a bit
> Of epigram, encomium, ode, or hymn,
> To flutter from my vessel's prow or stem
> For Mom and Dad's especial benefit.
>
> Alas, I'd love to go about in style;
> Alas, I'm barer than an ancient seer;
> And worse: I may be forced, as I'm so vile,
> To show the ladylove whom I revere
> My prick and ass, like Adam all the while
> He went about his cloister unaware;
>   And as I beg a pair
> Of breeches, in the meantime from the valley
> I see a cavalcade of pedants sally.

Yet in his letter of dedication to Signora Morgana B., Bruno also explains, in tones more passionate and serious than the rest of his riotous text, that his comedy is a work about the art of memory. Addressing a woman who by that time existed for him only in memory, he writes: "You, cultivator of the field of my heart, with divine water that springs from the fountain of your spirit, you slaked the thirst of my intellect . . . What is offered to you through this *Candlemaker* may clarify certain *Shadows of Ideas* that scare off the wild animals or, like the devils in Dante, keep the donkeys at bay."

Whether Morgana B. was a real woman or an imaginative ideal, we learn in Bruno's letter to her that he has drawn his portrait of Naples along its broad lines for a precise reason. His characters, with their stock personalities, their pranks, and their disguises, work on the stage as the memory images from *On the Shadows of Ideas* work within the mind, crying for individual attention, then receding, combining with other images, and all the while playing out the picaresque enterprise of survival in the real world. The plot of *The Candlemaker* revolves around three well-off older men, each a victim in his own way of misplaced passion, who for their sins of deranged desire are deceived, cuckolded, robbed, and beaten by the other characters: Bonifacio, an epicene maker of candles (whose phallic symbolism Bruno exploits relentlessly), loves Vittoria the courtesan and neglects his young, beautiful wife, Carubina. Bartolomeo, the alchemist, loves gold and silver and neglects a wife, Marta, who is elderly and wise. Manfurio, the schoolteacher, has never married; he loves young boys and tries to woo them with pitiful displays of his own pedantry. Meanwhile, the artist Gioan Bernardo creates paintings, devises plots, and jumps merrily into bed with Vittoria and Carubina without invoking love; Bruno himself would later describe sex with similar practicality as "serving nature."

At a running time of over five hours, *The Candlemaker* may never have been intended for production, but Bruno shows a deep familiarity with theater nonetheless, and upsets the conventions of sixteenth-century staged drama with comic abandon. *The Candlemaker* has no prologue; instead, it begins with an antiprologue, followed by a proprologue, which is interrupted by a talkative janitor, who is revealed as the deliverer of the prologue only after the action starts. Many of *The Candlemaker*'s readers have taken the play as a work of pure philosophy rather than staged drama, a text meant, like Plato's dialogues, for intimate, individual reading rather than public performance. Yet Plato himself had begun as an aspiring tragedian, and dialogues like the *Symposium* make for superb drama when they are acted out. Bruno's philosophical drama can also be staged successfully.

The Candlemaker's letter of dedication and its choice of setting suggest that Bruno also wrote the play as a kind of autobiography, rearranging the memories of his own life in an act of creation. He turns his mind back to Morgana B. as a confirmed exile, evoking the biblical parable of the rich man and Lazarus the pauper, who once begged at his doorstep; when both have died, the rich man burns in hell for his greed as he watches the pauper Lazarus rest in the bosom of Abraham. As Abraham tells the rich man, their fates have been reversed, and between them there now "lies a great gulf fixed": the impassable border between heaven and hell. If Signora Morgana B. is also resting in the bosom of Abraham, she may be dead, and the great gulf that separates her from Bruno is not the distance between Paris and Naples, but rather the distance between death and life:

> Back when we could still touch hands, I first addressed "My joyous thoughts" to you, and then "The stem of living water." Now that between you, who rest in the bosom of Abraham, and myself, who desperately burns to ash, without expectation of that succor of yours that used to refresh my tongue, there lies a great gulf fixed . . . In the meantime, be well and become fatter than you are, because for my part I hope to recover my lard where I lost my green youth, if not under one guise, then under another; if not in this life, then in another.

With his absent lady and his vivid picture of a city he had not seen for six years and in fact would never see again, Bruno seems to suggest that there is a special kind of reality attached to the Naples he holds in his memory, huge, cruel, and chaotic as it may have been. By 1582, in an equally huge, chaotic Paris, as a royal reader at the Collège de Cambrai and private tutor to the king of France, the whipped dog, "irritated, recalcitrant, and strange, content with nothing, stubborn as an old man of eighty," had risen about as high in the world as a philosopher could rise.

And then Fortune turned the wheel.

The Song of Circe

PARIS, 1582–LONDON, 1583

MOERIS: Lady Circe, will you please explain to me: What are those lights glowing in the night? What could lie concealed beneath their surface?

CIRCE: Those are the learned, the wise, and the illustrious, in among the idiots, the asses, and the obscure.

—*The Song of Circe*, 1582

By 1582, Giordano Bruno had attained a certain degree of worldly success. At the same time, exiled and excommunicated, he felt as much like an outsider as ever. The title page of his *Candlemaker* describes him not as a royal reader or a courtier of King Henri III but as "Bruno the Nolan, the Academic of no Academy; nicknamed the exasperated." A motto follows the title: "*In tristitia hilaris, in hilaritate tristis*"—"Cheerful in gloom, gloomy in cheer"—that same philosophy of even-tempered detachment that Bruno first heard expressed by his father. For a man whose nickname was "the exasperated," detachment must have been more an ideal than a reality. Both Bruno's writings and the reports of his contemporaries describe him as a man more passionate than tranquil, an effusive lecturer who held his listeners spellbound more often than not. His students would prove uncommonly loyal. One of them, Raphael Eglin, described what his lectures were like:

"Off-the-cuff, see how well you can follow along with your pen, talk and think at the same time; that's how quick his wits were, and that was the power of his mind!"

Literally, "lecture" meant "reading," and many sixteenth-century professors did precisely that, standing at their lecterns with a copy of Aristotle, or Aquinas, or Peter Lombard, and droning away. The Parisians who practiced this ancient style of teaching looked on the little Italian with suspicion, about his accent, his enthusiasm, his popularity, and the ideas that sometimes departed so radically from the texts on which his "readings" were ostensibly based.

Bruno also provided his own texts on occasion. *The Song of Circe*, published, like *On the Shadows of Ideas* and *The Candlemaker*, in Paris in 1582, was obviously meant to accompany his lectures; there is even an advertisement for his course in the middle of the text: "There is only one difficulty: no one can learn this art on his own. He learns it all from the teacher." The little book's letter of dedication, addressed to the important statesman Henri d'Angoulême by his secretary Jean Regnault, notes that Bruno's art of memory is both effective and economical:

> This art requires much less work, industry, and practice than all the others you might read about, so that within three or four months it offers an easier, more certain method for those who choose it than those who follow other methods will attain in three or four years . . . As for remembering things and phrases, it is plain enough that once anyone has heard the basic teachings of this art, he can use it to the best of his abilities, and no reasonable person can be excluded from competence in it.

The Nolan himself strikes a more sober tone than his friend Regnault. Only a truly dedicated student will succeed, and only with constant practice:

> ALBERICUS: I hear that you are skilled in the art, one of Giordano's inventions, that is described in *On the Shadows of Ideas*, an art that is not mere playacting, as some accuse, but that many say is extremely difficult, and almost impossible to study on one's own.

BORISTA: If many learned people do not understand it on their own, it
is not for their ignorance, nor a confusion in the art itself . . . It is because
they are occupied with other concerns, and read about the art with scant
attention.

The Song of Circe presents a series of systems for storing memories, together with brief explanations and examples; it could have
served as an exercise book, but Bruno provides only sketchy in-
structions about how to use those exercises—like any good adver-
tiser, he whetted his customers' appetite without satisfying it. On
the Shadows of Ideas provides some added clues to what The Song of
Circe may be about. Yet a lecture from Bruno would make it all so
much clearer, and the whole series of lectures would make The Song
of Circe clearer still.

For Parisians, Circe was the enchantress of Homer's Odyssey
who turns Odysseus's henchmen into animals, as wily Odysseus,
protected by Athena, foils the sorceress and spends the night with
her in human form, in a human bed, hearing her secrets. For a
Neapolitan like Giordano Bruno, however, Circe was more than a
literary figure; she was a neighbor whose abode on the promontory
of San Felice Circeo he had passed at least three times on the road
to and from Rome. Naples abounded in such mysterious, legendary
places: the Sirens, whose song lured sailors to their deaths, had
given their name to Sorrento, the spit of land that rounded out the
Bay of Naples. North of the city, the mouth of hell was said to open
into the still, dark waters of Lake Avernus (a volcanic crater);
nearby, the Sibyl of Cumae had predicted the coming of Christ
from a cave carved into the volcanic rock. In 1499, Giles of
Viterbo, the Augustinian friar and future cardinal, had stopped in
Cumae and Avernus to commune with the pagan spirits and declared afterward that he was no less pious a Christian for having
done so; after all, the classical deities were nothing other than
guardian angels. Bruno's deities were no less rooted in the same real
places. And like Giles of Viterbo, Bruno reserved each of these
same gods a place in the heavens.

Bruno begins his book by having Circe call upon the gods; as he
will explain later, her invocations run through a whole series of

categories that can be used to store information. When she summons Apollo, Jupiter, and their companions, she is also summoning
the physical bodies of the sun, moon, and planets, listing their
names, their attributes, their local titles, their special animals and
birds, lining them up in careful categories. Element by element,
then, in rigorous sequence, Circe calls the whole universe to order,
beginning with the sun:

> Sun, who alone bathes all things in light. Apollo, author of poetry, quiver
> bearer, bowman, of the powerful arrows, Pythian, laurel-crowned, pro-
> phetic, shepherd, seer, priest, and physician. Brilliant, rosy, long-haired,
> beautiful-locked, blond, bright, placid, bard, singer, teller of truth. Titan-
> ian, Milesian, Palatine, Cyrrhaean, Timbraean, Delian, Delphic, Leuca-
> dian, Tegean, Capitoline, Smintheus, Ismenian, and Latin. Who imparts
> to the elements their marvelous natures: by whose dispensation the seas
> swell and are calmed, the air and sky are troubled and soothed, the lively
> strength and power of fire is roused and repressed. By whose ministry the
> mechanism of this universe thrives, so that the many qualities of herbs and
> the other plants and of stones are able to draw the universal spirit to them-
> selves. Appear by the prayers of your daughter Circe . . .
>
> Again I stretch out my hands to you, O Sun. I am here for you, all
> yours. Reveal, I pray, your lions, your lynxes, goats, baboons, seagulls,
> calves, snakes, elephants, and the other kinds of animals that belong to
> you. Halcyons, swallows, partridges, ravens, crows, sandpipers, cicadas,
> and scarabs, and all your other flying creatures. The turtle, butterfish,
> tuna, ray, whale, and all your other creatures of that kind. You who are
> Ubius, Alexikakos, Phanes, Horus, Apollo by day, Dionysus by night, and
> called the Day Father. Whose power is administered in your place by
> gold, hyacinth, ruby, and carbuncle. Worthy of reverence in the center of
> the planetary system, clearing and showing the way for all: drawing forth,
> producing, and ripening all things, lord of rulers and counselors, illustri-
> ous in your blazing rays. You are the prince of the universe, the eye of
> heaven, the mirror of nature, the architecture of the soul of the world,
> and the seal of the Most High Architect.

In his lectures, as in his conversations with the king, Bruno
would have made it clear that Homer's Circe may have been a sor-

ceress but his own Circe is simply using orderly thought to align the powers already inherent in nature. He had anticipated possible accusations of magic in *On the Shadows of Ideas* and dealt with them there in no uncertain terms:

> LOGIFER: What will you reply to Mr. Ad Hoc, who thinks that those people who perform memory operations before the crowd are magicians or possessed or some other similar species of man? (You can see how senile he has gone by studying.)
>
> PHILOTHIMUS: I do not doubt that he is the nephew of that ass who was booked on Noah's Ark to preserve the species.

So, too, Jean Regnault writes in the preface to *The Song of Circe* that Bruno's art of memory looks impressive, and is impressive, but it is entirely natural. Designed specifically to exploit a chain of mental associations, it enables a diligent student to master the whole technique in a remarkably short time. There is nothing diabolical or unnatural about it.

There were, however, some controversial aspects to the song of the enchantress. Circe's invocation implicitly sets the sun within a Copernican cosmos, where it, not the earth, stands at the center of the universe. A central sun, in fact, only enhanced the imagery of divine light that pervades Plato, the Gospel of Saint John, and Saint Augustine, and through them thinkers like Marsilio Ficino and Giles of Viterbo. *The Song of Circe* is not a book about cosmology, however; it is a book about how anyone can increase the power of memory with the help of imagination, concentration, and diligent practice.

Despite its magical overtones, Bruno's art of memory was not so far removed from the contemporary efforts of natural philosophers to create schemes by which they could classify plants, animals, minerals, chemicals, peoples, languages, and all the other bewilderingly varied phenomena of nature and culture. All of them, Bruno along with a chemist like Paracelsus or a naturalist like Conrad Gesner (and, two centuries later, a taxonomist like Linnaeus), believed that by organizing the world, they could increase their abilities to understand it, perhaps to control it, and certainly to control their own relationship with it. They were hardly the first to think so: Cicero had noted, as the ancient Roman Republic degenerated into chaos, that the idea of grouping phenomena into kinds and disciplines had marked the beginning of civilization.

By applying his art of memory, Bruno may have been able to call the whole world to attention within his head. Perhaps Henri III could do so, too. But in the troubled Europe of the late sixteenth century, mental mastery of the world did not translate into real mastery. In France, Catholic and Huguenot no more put down their weapons than lions, lynxes, and tuna fish snapped to attention on some Parisian street beneath the benevolent sun. Henri had signed a truce in December 1580 that allowed him to rule over a peaceful France for two years, 1581 and 1582. He kept both sides calm by continuing to make concessions, to the Huguenots and to the powerful Catholic dynasties of de Guise and Lorraine. By 1583, however, the fragile truce had begun to come apart, and no song of Circe could put it right again.

Henri responded to the tensions by asserting his own Catholicism more and more aggressively. On March 28, 1583, the English ambassador to Paris, Henry Cobham, reported to Queen Elizabeth's "principal secretary," Francis Walsingham, that tolerance of English Catholics had suddenly increased in France, whereas English Protestants had reason to be concerned:

> If her Highness endure the evil treatment of her subjects in Italy, she may have in short time the like used in France . . . Besides, the English papists are allowed to make sermons in Paris; I think heretofore this was not permitted . . .

Later the same day, Cobham added:

> I hear the king is sending M. de San Martin to the King of Navarre, upon the sundry bruits which are spread that those of the Religion were preparing for their defence, being threatened with the publishing of the Council of Trent, and the Inquisition.

Cobham's first letter also mentioned that two Jesuit priests had just arrived in England from Rome, and that "Il Signor Doctor Jordano Bruno, Nolano, professor in philosophy, intends to pass into

England." Bruno, it would soon transpire, had cast his eye on London and Oxford. Although the "Academic of no Academy" had actually amassed a whole series of excellent academic connections
(and evidently aimed at forging yet another one), in matters of religion he truly did belong to no one. For the first time, he must
have recognized that his choices in 1576 had determined the rest
of his life. Aware, perhaps for the first time, that he was well and
truly excluded from the Roman Church, with rumors flying about
the Inquisition coming to France, and with his old Neapolitan
street sense still as active as ever, the Nolan philosopher looked for
a way out, and decided on England, where Queen Elizabeth had
earned a reputation for her culture and her tolerance.

Bruno said nothing specific to the Venetian Inquisition about
the "tumults that broke out" before he left Paris (or, for that matter, what kind of violence he might have seen in Toulouse, or in
Spanish-dominated Naples). Like his hatred of pedophile teachers,
his aversion to religious war was strong enough to suggest that his
magnificent memory contained images he would rather have forgotten.

CHAPTER SEVENTEEN

"Go up to Oxford"

And if you don't believe it, go up to Oxford, and have them tell you the things that happened to the Nolan when he disputed in public with those doctors of theology in the presence of Prince Alasco, the Pole, and other English nobles. Let them tell you how ably he responded to the arguments; how by means of fifteen syllogisms that poor doctor whom they put forward as leader of the Academy's comic chorus was left on fifteen occasions like a chick in the chaff. Let them tell you about the churlish discourtesy with which that pig proceeded, and about the patience and humanity of the Nolan, who showed himself to be a real Neapolitan, born and raised under a more benign heaven.

—*The Ash Wednesday Supper*, dialogue 4

In April 1583, Giordano Bruno touched down in Dover. He describes the experience of crossing the Channel for what it revealed to him about the curvature of the earth, one of the only references to travel that we find in the writings of this unusually well-traveled man. His arrival did not come unannounced. Shortly before, the English ambassador to Paris, Henry Cobham, had written Francis Walsingham, Queen Elizabeth's ruthless head of secret services, to forewarn him, "Il Signor Doctor Jordano Bruno, Nolano, professor in philosophy, intends to pass into England, whose religion I cannot commend."

From Walsingham's standpoint, Bruno could have been suspect either by association with the Catholic king and the Catholic government of France, by his troubled relationship with Geneva, or because he harbored more peculiar beliefs. But Walsingham was prepared for the Italian's arrival no matter what the circumstances: he already had a spy installed in the French embassy to keep him abreast of the household's activities.

From Bruno's standpoint, England and Germany were the two most logical places to go from France, but England, from the outside, may have had special attractions. Queen Elizabeth's version of Protestant reform aimed, as best it could, to subdue tension on all sides. It was a task she undertook with Machiavellian practicality, flanked by her secretary, Walsingham, and his network of informers. Still, her willingness to listen to both sides of the Reformation led some of her radically Protestant subjects to suspect her of Catholic sympathies. Despite her occasionally brutal tactics and the virtual cult by which she preserved her own personal power, on the European stage she seemed to be setting out a deliberately moderate middle ground between Calvin, Luther, and the papacy, and in the long term a balance among these branches of Christianity is precisely what she hewed out for the Anglican Church.

On a more personal front, Bruno exchanged a publicly funded position as royal reader for a position under private patronage, as "gentleman of the household." His sponsor in London, Michel de Castelnau, Lord of Mauvissière, had served for nearly eight years as Henri III's ambassador to the Court of St. James's. Like any aristocrat of worth from Paris to Constantinople—or for that matter, like an ancient Roman paterfamilias—Castelnau assembled a court around him that could provide him with entertainment, enlightenment, or reputation according to his tastes. Some contemporaries, like the Gonzaga of Mantua, loaded their palazzi with dwarfs, freaks, and dogs (perhaps to distract attention from the Gonzaga's hereditary hunchback, just as the dwarfs at the Spanish court took attention away from the Habsburg jaw: as Diego Velázquez was to show more incisively than anyone in his paintings of the Spanish court, monarchs were sports of nature as extraordinary as any of their subjects). Michel de Castelnau collected conversationalists, a skill at which at least one of Bruno's companions, John Florio, said the Nolan excelled.

The ambassador maintained his residence on Butcher Row, a narrow lane that ran from Fleet Street to the banks of the Thames, set between the imposing Gothic convents of the Dominican Blackfriars and the Carmelite Whitefriars. Both the City of London to the east and the royal palace at Whitehall could be reached by road or ferry. High walls protected all these compounds from London lowlife; Castelnau also had to fear disturbances from Protestants, rich and poor, who resented the presence of a French papist living so openly, and so lavishly, on English soil. The Great Fire of 1666, the Victorian world empire, and Hitler's Blitz have long since destroyed any real trace of Bruno's London neighborhood except the Inns of Court, whose Gothic windows still grasp after every bit of light from the northern sky, a sky Bruno would come to regard as harsh by comparison with the skies of Naples. But the streets have all been paved now, and their sewage flows underground. The buildings are mostly modern colossi. Electric lights and closed-circuit cameras now dispel the darkness so effectively that the color of the night sky has changed from starry black to foggy brown; in Bruno's day, the only lights on the street were the torches or lanterns that passersby brought themselves. The pyramidal spire of Charing Cross, a monument from 1290 that once signaled the junction between Fleet Street and the road to the royal palace at Whitehall, survives in a Victorian reproduction. Bridges span the Thames where in Bruno's day there were only ferries; London Bridge provided the single fixed crossing. Rather than the noise of internal combustion engines and rubber on asphalt, Bruno heard hooves on mud, vendors' cries, creaking wooden wheels, and night watchmen enforcing the curfew. The smells that reached his nostrils indoors and outdoors were organic smells, from the garbage and slops that sluiced down the streets to the seldom-changed clothing, seldom-washed bodies, sweat, and foul breath that prevailed inside. The climate of Naples meant that people could live outdoors; London winters made that impossible.

Yet life within the household on Butcher Row must have been entertaining, to judge from the liveliness of the books that were produced in its midst. One of Bruno's table companions, the Anglo-Italian John Florio, became a close friend. Born in England of Italian Protestant parents from Siena, Florio had grown up in Switzerland; he had moved to England in the 1570s. He and Bruno shared a sense of humor and a sense of rootlessness. Most of all, they shared a passion for language. Florio now provides one of the most penetrating portraits of their contemporary English culture through his Italian-English dictionary, A Worlde of Wordes, in its own way as provocative and opinionated as Dr. Johnson's Dictionary, produced only a few hundred yards (and two centuries) away. Four hundred years after its printing, A Worlde of Wordes now provides an indispensable key not only to Bruno's Italian but also to the Falstaffian richness of English, the English that a young, ambitious actor named William Shakespeare was beginning to bring to London's theater in precisely those years. The words in Florio's dictionary, which he describes as an exuberant tumult rather than a sober intellectual enterprise—"no brain-babe Minerva, but a bouncing boie, Bacchus-like, all names"—literally do create a world. The pleasures of the body dominate its lexicon, from the rich vocabulary of "bellie-cheere" to the congress between men and women that could be described, in addition to our surviving terms, as japing, swiving, sarding, sporting, and occupying. Earringed men who wept openly, kissed each other on the mouth, and sniffed at roses (a matter of olfactory self-defense in those days) plied words as deftly as they did their rapiers. Florio himself was no amateur at verbal swordsmanship:

> As for critiks I accompt of them as crickets; no goodly bird if a man marke them, no sweete note if a man heare them, no good luck if a man have them: they lurke in corners, but catch cold if they look out; they lie in sight of the furnace that tryes others, but will not come neare the flame that should purifie themselves: they are bred of filth, and fed with filth, what vermine to call them I know not, or wormes, or flyes, or what worse? . . . Demonstrative rethorique is their studies, and the doggs letter they can snarle alreadie.

At the French embassy, Florio served as official tutor to Castelnau's eight-year-old daughter, but Bruno's own fondness for the little girl suggests that he may have taught her a thing or two himself, perhaps a bit of On the Sphere or tricks of memory. In some sense, Giordano Bruno seems to have felt before he left Paris for London that Elizabethan England was the best place for him to develop his Nolan philosophy. He ultimately hoped, however, to leave the ambassador's patronage and return to a university.

His opportunity to "make [him]self known and show what [he] was about" at Oxford came in June, about a month after his arrival in England, when the Polish prince Albert Laski made a state visit, escorted by the university's chancellor, Robert Dudley, Earl of Leicester, and Dudley's refined nephew, Sir Philip Sidney. The occasion demanded speeches and debates, from Oxford professors and from the visitors, and, perhaps through Castelnau's intercession, Bruno obtained a place on the program, engaging in a staged debate with the theologian John Underhill, rector of Lincoln College. With his varied experience as a teacher and professor, he had every hope of success; he had, after all, taught the art of memory to Pope Pius V, won an open competition for the chair of philosophy at Toulouse, and, most recently, caught the attention of the court and the king of France. He must have expected a similar reception in Oxford when he debated on theology, the field in which he held formal qualifications from two of Europe's most prestigious universities.

Yet nothing in all his travels had prepared him for the reaction he received. The English laughed at him. They made fun of his accent, his gestures, his passionate energy, and his tiny stature. They would have found his Latin difficult to understand; the dons pronounced the ancient language as if it were written in English, so that the blessing "benedicite" that began their opening prayers became "bene-dice-itee." Bruno pronounced Latin as if it were Italian, and said "bene-dee-chee-tay." His audience listened to how he spoke rather than to what he said, and smirked as they listened.

Any teacher looks out to see whether students understand; Bruno could not have missed the looks passing among the people he had most hoped to impress. His growing sense of bewilderment, and then humiliation, made him more frantic, more Italian, and still funnier to his audience. Elizabethan England was not a place that took much pity on suffering: one of London's chief attractions on the south shore of the Thames, just down the road from the George Inn Theatre and the future site of the Globe, was a bear pit, where captive bears were chained to a stake and attacked by savage dogs. Bruno's presentation at Oxford began to offer some of the same sadistic pleasures as watching a bear "at the stake," and when, like the bears, he grew angry and agitated, he only added to the public's glee. By the time he had finished, he was furious, and it is unlikely that anyone had listened to what he said except to imitate him later.

It was not a good time to be an Italian professor in England. In London, Queen Elizabeth and her court might speak and read Italian, Sir Philip Sidney and his friends might try their hand at combining Italian sonnet form with English iambic pentameter, and Italian bankers might dominate Lombard Street, but to a don tucked away at Oxford or Cambridge, teaching theology for future clerics in the Church of England, an Italian was a papist, stuffed full of wrong ideas and likely to be a subversive, and his strange-sounding Latin was a terrible effort to understand; needless to say, in England, English pronunciation, no matter how far removed it might be from the way the ancient Romans had spoken their own language, was by definition correct. Several other recent Italian and Spanish visitors to Oxford had been subjected to the same mockery as Bruno simply because of their nationality. The island nation could close in on itself with hermetic complacency as well as open out to the world.

Furthermore, English wit permitted (and still permits) a level of personal attack unthinkable in Spain or Italy. John Florio's *Worlde of Wordes* describes how hearers would shout their disapproval "when one is about to tell a thing & knows not what it is":

> or that a scholer would faine read his lesson and cannot, and that we by some signe or voice will let him knowe that he is out, wide, and saies he wots not what. [In Italian] we use to say Boccata, as in English, yea in my other hose, or iump as Germins lips, you are as wise as Walthams calfe, and such other phrases.

The Italian insult *boccata* is studiously abstract; it means "a mouthful," or—as may be most relevant here—a "breath" of fresh air. The

English jibes, however, are all intimately personal, and "iump as Germins lips" shows that papists were not the only butts of English nationalist invective. After only a month in Britain, Bruno could not yet come back to his adversaries on the spot with a pungent "swive thou" or "beef-witted clotpole"; he could only store up his rancor—and retell the story of his experience at Oxford, when the time came, in his own magnificently abusive Italian.

One onlooker, George Abbot, compared him as he spoke to an industrious little waterbird, the little grebe, dabchick, or didapper (*Tachybaptus ruficollis*), which bobs up and down on English ponds and rivers in search of fish:

> When that Italian Didapper, who intituled himselfe Philotheus Iordanus Brunus Nolanus, magis elaboratae Theologiae Doctor etc. with a name longer than his body, had in the traine of Alasco the Polish Duke, seene our University in the yeare 1583, his hart was on fire, to make himselfe by some worthy exploite to become famous in that celebrious place.

As Abbot makes clear, "our University," "that celebrious place," swiftly closed ranks against the little man with "his hart . . . on fire."

Shortly thereafter, Bruno petitioned the rector for a teaching position, in terms that fit in perfectly with Neapolitan street rhetoric and less well, perhaps, with British academic etiquette:

> Philotheus Jordanus Brunus Nolanus, doctor of a more sophisticated theology, professor of a more pure and innocent wisdom, known to the best academies of Europe, a proven and honored philosopher, a stranger only among barbarians and knaves, the awakener of sleeping spirits, the tamer of presumptuous and stubborn ignorance, who professes a general love of humanity in all his actions, who prefers as company neither Briton nor Italian, male nor female, bishop nor king, robe nor armor, friar nor layman, but only those whose conversation is more peaceable, more civil, more faithful, and more valuable, who respects not the anointed head, the signed forehead, the washed hands, or the circumcised penis, but rather the spirit and culture of mind (which can be read in the face of a real person); whom the propagators of stupidity and the small-time hypocrites detest, whom the sober and studious love, and whom the most no-

ble minds acclaim, to the most excellent and illustrious vice-chancellor
of the University of Oxford, many greetings.

The letter ended no less graphically:

> In the meantime, I would not want it to come to pass, as in the days of
> the Flood, when the asses' dung said to the golden apples, "We [road] ap-
> ples can swim too," that now, too, any stupid ass might obtrude upon our
> station, here or anywhere else, or in any other way; but if there be anyone
> whose claims to stature and qualification will not be held for any reason
> as unworthy of our company, and to whom we can respond without any
> detriment to our condition, he shall find me a man prompt and prepared,
> for whom it may be worthwhile to try the weight of my mettle. Farewell.

Yet the letter achieved its purpose. Bruno arrived in Oxford
again in August, lecturing this time on the cosmos, aiming to show
his audience how the Copernican system provided more effective
reinforcement for Marsilio Ficino's Platonic theology than the traditional Earth-centered universe. His choice of subject should have
harmonized well with Oxford's emphasis on modern humanistic
studies, for which Ficino's philosophy had played a fundamental
role. In Oxford, moreover, Bruno could openly share his admiration for Erasmus rather than hide the great man's works in the latrine for fear of the Inquisition. Unfortunately, for once in his life
he took the term "lecture" too literally; his citations from Ficino's
On Living the Heavenly Life were so exact (thanks to Bruno's well-
trained memory) that one of the dons suspected him of plagiarism.
Again, George Abbot was there:

> Not long after returning againe, when he had more boldly than wisely,
> got up into the highest place of our best and most renowned schoole,
> stripping up his sleeves like some Iugler, and telling us much of *chentrum*
> and *chirculus* and *cirumferenchia* (after the pronunciation of his Country
> language) he undertooke among very many other matters to set on foote
> the opinion of Copernicus, that the earth did goe round, and the heavens
> did stand still; whereas in truth it was his owne head which rather did run
> round, and his braines did not stand stil.

When he had read his first Lecture, a grave man, and both then and now of good place in that University, seemed to himselfe, some where to have read those things which the Doctor propounded; but silencing his conceit till he heard him the second time, remembered himselfe then, and repayring to his study, found both the former and later Lecture, taken almost verbatim out of the worke of Marsilius Ficinus. Wherewith when he had acquainted that rare and excellent Ornament of our land, the Reverend Bishop of Durham that now is, but then Deane of Christs-Church, it was at the first thought fit, to notifie to the Illustrious Reader, so much as they had discovered. But afterward hee who gave the first light, did most wisely intreate, that once more they might make trial of him; and if he persevered to abuse himselfe, and that Auditory the thirde time, they shoulde then do their pleasure. After which, *Iordanus* continuing to be *idem* [the same] *Iordanus*, thay caused some to make knowne unto him their former patience, and the paines which he had taken with them, and so with great honesty of the little man's part, there was an end of that matter.

The "end of that matter" also meant the end of Bruno's hopes for an academic career in England. He returned to London, where he would have found a sympathetic listener in John Florio, who, despite his English birth and with impeccable Protestant credentials, had also found it difficult to adjust to England after growing up in Switzerland. It was Florio who would later warn:

> Be circumspect how you offend schollers, for knowe,
> A serpents tooth bites not so ill,
> As dooth a schollers angrie quill.

With his tongue virtually stopped, Giordano Bruno took up his "angrie quill" to prove that the Nolan philosophy was anything but plagiarized Ficino. He began by continuing his aborted lectures on Ficino and cosmology, but now he gave up Latin for his native Neapolitan vernacular, explicitly addressing his work not to English academe but to members of the English court.

His first words on the matter were an invective addressed "To the Malcontent":

If you've been worried in a cynic's bite,
You brought it on yourself, you barbarous cur,
In showing me your weaponry you err
Unless you're careful not to rouse my spite.

The frontal charge you made was hardly right;
I'll shred your hide and pull out all your fur,
And if I hit the ground, you'll still concur:
Like diamond, I repel the taunts you write.

Don't rob a hive of honey in the nude;
Don't bite unless you know it's stone or bread;
Don't scatter thorns unless you're wearing shoes.

On spiderwebs a fly should not intrude;
A rat that follows frogs is good as dead;
Hens and their brood all foxes should refuse.

And trust the Gospel verse
That tells you, kind and terse:
For him who sows a field with errors and lies,
A harvest of regret shall be the prize.

For the next two years, Giordano Bruno would write six Italian vernacular dialogues in what he would call a fit of heroic frenzy. Rather than run away from his conflict with English academe, he did his best to stand his ground, and in the process he matured immeasurably as a writer and as a philosopher, and perhaps also as a man. Eventually his life would depend on what he learned in London.

Down Risky Streets

LONDON, 1583

> "But now," said the Nolan, "let us set out, and pray that God will guide
> us in this dark evening, on so long a journey, down such risky streets."
> —*The Ash Wednesday Supper*, dialogue 2

Bruno's failure at Oxford was a devastating blow. From their ridicule of his personal manner to their accusations of plagiarism, the dons had stripped him of every kind of dignity, as a man, as a citizen of the world, and as a philosopher. Silenced as a lecturer, he wrote instead, from the shelter of the French embassy and the company of people who did appreciate what he had to say. Two thousand years before, another bitterly disappointed philosopher, Plato, had turned to writing in the isolated grove of Academus when politics and human fickleness betrayed his own ambitious hopes. It may be no surprise that Bruno turned to Plato's medium, the dialogue, and to his own Neapolitan vernacular; under attack, he fell back on what was most essential to him: the world of philosophy, Neapolitan and Platonic, he had discovered in the company of Fra Teofilo da Vairano. Bruno dedicated his first of what would be six Italian dialogues to Castelnau, his host, published it with a local printer, John Charlewood (who gave the book a Venice imprint to lend it an air of Continental sophistication), and called it *The Ash Wednesday Supper*. He was surely thinking of Plato's *Symposium*, the dramatically flawless dialogue, set after a dinner party, that describes philosophy, literally, the "love of wisdom," as the highest form of human passion. Astutely, Plato leavens the profound discussions with fits of hiccups, droning bores, a bravura performance by the comedian Aristophanes, and an intrusive drunk. The dialogue is as funny as it is achingly beautiful. Bruno must first have known the *Symposium* from its Latin translation, made in the fifteenth century by that very Marsilio Ficino he was said to have plagiarized at Oxford.

Plato's dialogue is set during a holiday, the Dionysia, Athens's great dramatic festival. Bruno set his own at the beginning of Lent, and like Plato, he plunges right into a conversation, in his case between the Englishman Smitho and Teofilo, "beloved of God," the character who represents Bruno:

SMITHO: Did they speak good Latin?

TEOFILO: Yes.

S: Gentlemen?

T: Yes.

S: Of good reputation?

T: Yes.

S: Learned?

T: Most competently.

S: Well-bred, courteous, civil?

T: Not enough.

S: Doctors?

T: Yes, sir, yes, Father, yes, ma'am, yes indeed; from Oxford, I believe.

S: Qualified?

T: Of course. Leading men, of flowing robes, dressed in velvet; one of whom had two shiny gold chains around his neck, the other, by God! with that precious hand (that contained twelve rings on two fingers) he looked like a rich jeweler; your eyes and heart popped out just looking at it.

S: Were they steeped in Greek?

T: And in beer, too, forsooth.

The gentlemen, as it turns out, had been guests, along with the Nolan, at a dinner party in Whitehall, hosted by Sir Fulke Greville, a close friend of Sir Philip Sidney's. Greville had earlier met Bruno near Fleet Street and invited him to discuss his views about cosmology: "Next Wednesday, eight days from now, which will be Ash Wednesday, you will be invited to a banquet with many gentlemen and learned persons, so that after eating we may hold a discussion of many fine things."

The Nolan had accepted the invitation, but only with reservations: "But, I pray you, do not bring ignoble persons before me, ill educated and ill versed in similar speculations." The trauma of Oxford cut deep, so that "not knowing the extent to which he would be understood, he feared doing as those people do who say their piece to statues and go off to converse with the dead."

The dialogue continues by dashing each one of Bruno's high expectations, beginning with the schedule. Banqueting in Italy meant an invitation for midday, but by lunchtime on Ash Wednesday Bruno had heard nothing and went off with some Italian friends. He returned at dusk to find his housemate John Florio and their physician friend Matthew Gwinne at the embassy door, impatient to collect him for supper. The Nolan urged them to calm themselves:

> "Up to now only one thing has gone wrong for me: that I had hoped to conduct this business in the light of day, and I see that the debate will happen by candlelight . . . But now," said the Nolan, "let us set out, and pray that God will guide us in this dark evening, on so long a journey, down such risky streets."

The streets of sixteenth-century London were as rough as anything Bruno would have seen in Naples or Paris, where at least he could speak the language. The trip from Butcher Row to Whitehall is a phantasmagoric pilgrimage, first in a ferryboat that seems to be plying the river Styx rather than the Thames, and then on foot, through a pelting British rain, knee-deep in mud, and jostled by Cockneys; to one, Bruno tries out his English and replies, "Tanchi, maester"—"Thankee, Master!" Teofilo rants on the Nolan's behalf about the rudeness of Londoners, and their hatred of anything foreign:

England can brag of having a populace that is second to none that the earth nurtures in her bosom for being disrespectful, uncivil, rough, rustic, savage, and badly brought up . . . When they see a foreigner, they look, by God, like so many wolves, so many bears who have that expression on their faces that a pig has when its meal is being taken away . . . and, recognizing that you are some kind of foreigner, [they] look down their noses, laugh at you, smirk at you, fart at you with their lips, and call you, in their language, a dog, a traitor, a stranger—for this among them is an insult . . . Now, if you should have the misfortune to touch one of them, or put your hand to your weapon, behold, in an instant you'll be in the midst of a horde of rustics, popping up quicker than legend says the dragon's teeth sowed by Jason turned into armed men; it seems as if they emerge from the earth, but they are certainly coming out of their workshops, and they make an honor guard of staves, rods, halberds, javelins, and rusty pitchforks . . . and so you'll see them set upon you with rustic fury, each one venting the scorn they have for foreigners . . . as happened a few months ago to poor Messer Alessandro Citolino, who, to the delight and laughter of the whole crowd, had his arm smashed and broken . . . So if you want to go out, don't think you can simply take a walk about the city. Cross yourself, arm yourself with a breastplate of patience—bulletproof—and bear with what's not so bad for fear that you'll suffer worse.

The gentlemen, as it turns out, are scarcely better. By arriving late for the Ash Wednesday meal, Bruno and his company have missed the ritual passing of the "loving-cup," which Teofilo counts as an advantage. The idea of sharing a goblet with his fellow diners revolted the fastidiously neat Bruno, who dwells in horrified detail on the way that the men of England gather scraps of food in their beards and neglect to wipe their mouths before drinking.

Against this shadowy background of men gathered in a dark, wood-paneled dining room to exchange their barbarous ceremonies in the last dank vestiges of English winter, the Nolan philosophy and its proponent are intended to blaze like the sun, and they do. At the same time, the unworthiness of Greville's two donnish guests forces Bruno, in effect, to talk to statues and converse with the living dead. When he begins to speak about Copernicus, they spout adages from Erasmus and shout, "Ad rem, ad rem"—"Get to the point"—with Bruno yelling back, "This IS the point!"

The dialogue's endless play between dark, light, and shadow broadly emphasizes the Nolan's ability to shed light everywhere, in order to discern reality from its image, in human nature, in religion, and in the infinite reaches of the heavens. Armed with his philosophy, he strikes a sure path through a world of oscillating appearances. His struggles on the streets of London and the waters of the Thames are a symbol, like the dark, dangerous Naples of *The Candlemaker*, of maneuvering through a world he had once thought was "fine as it is." That world had since shown him much more of its cruelty, and he aimed his praise of it more at the stars in heaven than at the maelstrom on the ground. He also directed a good measure of praise to himself. To all those who had missed his message in Oxford, Bruno drives home the originality of his ideas, in the words of his character Teofilo. (It is worth remembering that extravagant self-promotion, like extravagant flattery, was frequent among sixteenth-century men, from Benvenuto Cellini, whose biography is a masterpiece of inflated exploits, to Theophrastus Aureolus Bombastus von Hohenheim, alias Paracelsus, who gave the world the adjective "bombastic.")

> Now, what shall I say of the Nolan? Perhaps, when he is as close to me as I am to myself, it is inappropriate for me to praise him? Certainly, there is no reasonable man who would reprove me for that, for on this occasion it is not only appropriate but also necessary.

He goes on, remarkably, to make a stinging condemnation of European colonialism, before contrasting the effects of the Nolan philosophy with the effects of capitalist greed. At the time, England had only begun its colonial explorations; Bruno was writing primarily about Spain and Portugal. He must have read the denunciations of Spanish cruelty in Mexico made by the Dominican Bartolomé de Las Casas—most probably in Naples, where the Dominicans knew a thing or two about Spanish oppression themselves.

> Now, in order for you to understand the present business and its importance, I set for you the premise to a conclusion that will be easily proven shortly: namely, that if Tiphys is praised for having invented the first ships

and crossed the sea with the Argonauts, if Columbus is acclaimed in our own time for being "the Tiphys who uncovered new worlds," what is to be done with him who has discovered the way to climb the heavens, traverse the circumference of the stars, and leave the convex surface of the firmament at his back? The Tiphyses of this world have found the way to disturb the peace of others, violate the ancestral spirits of the regions, muddle what nature had kept distinct, and for the sake of commerce redouble the defects, and add further vice to the vices of each party, violently propagating new follies and planting unheard-of madness where it had never been before, concluding at last that the stronger are also the wiser, displaying new sciences, instruments, and arts by which to tyrannize and murder one another, so that the time will come, thanks to those actions, that by the oscillation of all things, those who have thus far endured to their misfortune will learn, and be able to give back to us, the worst fruits of such pernicious invention.

The Nolan, to cause entirely contrary effects, has released the human spirit and intellect, which were confined in the narrow prison of the turbulent atmosphere; whence they scarcely had the capacity to look, as through certain holes, upon the distant stars, and whose wings were clipped, so that they could not fly through the veil of these clouds and see what is really to be found above . . . Now behold him, who has crossed the air, penetrated the heavens, wandered among the stars, and passed beyond the margins of this world, made to vanish the imaginary walls of the first, eighth, ninth, tenth, and as many other spheres as you would like to add, according to the reports of vain astronomers and the blind visions of vulgar philosophers; [who] thus, in the presence of all sense and reason, with the key of clever investigation has opened those cloisters of the truth, that can be opened by us, stripped naked the covered and veiled truth, given eyes to moles, enlightened the blind who could not focus their eyes to admire their own image in these many mirrors appearing on every side, loosened the tongue of the mute who could not and dared not express their innermost feelings, healed the lame who could not make that progress with their spirits that our ignoble and dissolute flesh cannot make, and makes them no less present than if they were dwellers on the Sun, the Moon, and the other known stars . . . These flaming bodies are the ambassadors who proclaim the glory and majesty of God. Thus we are moved to discover the infinite effect of the infinite cause, the true and living footprint of the infinite vigor, and we have a teaching that tells us not to seek divinity outside ourselves, but within, more deeply inside us than we are ourselves.

From footprints in the Forest of Matter—explicitly evoked in the sentence above—the Nolan philosophy has moved to footprints among the stars. Bruno sets all the uncertainties of the physical world, with its oscillation from one extreme to the other, its changing fortunes, and its evils, against the steady presence of God, both in the infinite space of the universe and deep within the individual spirit. Rather than defending the Copernican system, Bruno's *Ash Wednesday Supper* sets Copernicus within a much larger vision of the universe, where solar systems are as plentiful as the stars in the sky. The recognition that this is our true position in the world, Bruno promises, will be good for everyone's mental and spiritual health. Certainly, the Nolan philosophy prepared its misanthropic creator, the Academic of no Academy, nicknamed "the exasperated," to love every creature from here to outer space, a realm, possibly inhabited, that is suddenly given a distinct identity in this section of *The Ash Wednesday Supper*. Nor is outer space Bruno's only innovation in these pages: they also mark one of the first times that a natural philosopher describes the earth together with its atmosphere. Behind all the dialogue's heated Neapolitan rhetoric, professions of grandeur, and Platonic spirituality, *The Ash Wednesday Supper* contains serious ideas about natural philosophy. Some readers, at least, recognized those serious ideas; in many ways, Galileo Galilei's *Dialogue Concerning the Two Chief World Systems* (1632) is a direct response to Bruno's maddening, scintillating *Ash Wednesday Supper*.

Bruno knew that he had produced a work that fitted poorly into any category except, perhaps, that of Plato's *Symposium*. He called it a banquet to emphasize the variety of its offerings, and, as with *The Candlemaker*, he simply trusted his readers to make sense of it all. Bruno used his own systematic prose for his art of memory. His Italian dialogues, on the other hand, are discourses on philosophy, but they are also dramas, with poems attached. It was impossible for Bruno to separate the poet in him from the natural philosopher, the natural philosopher from the priest—and in his own day these distinctions did not yet matter as much as they would a century later. Galileo himself was a poet and musician as well as a natural philosopher and mathematician—that is, astronomer.

To his many personalities in *The Ash Wednesday Supper*, Bruno was compelled to add one more: the courtier. He had exchanged a post as royal reader in a Catholic absolute monarchy for a Protestant monarchy that had included a strong parliamentary system since 1215. Repelled as he was by Londoners, Bruno could not bring himself to imagine a system of government that would include such people rather than simply rule them, but he appreciated the way in which Elizabeth managed to maneuver between Catholic and Protestant, monarchy and parliament. As for the explosion of inventiveness in art, literature, and music she inspired, he joined right in.

> Spread your wings, Teofilo, and get yourself in order, and recognize that at the moment it is no time to speak about the highest things in the world. You have not the material here to speak of that earthly divinity, that singular and rare Lady, who from this chill sky near the Arctic Circle sheds such clear light on the whole terrestrial globe; Elizabeth, I say, who in title and royal station is inferior to no king in this world; for judgment, sagacity, counsel, and government she cannot easily come second to any who bears a scepter on this earth, in knowledge of the arts, awareness of the sciences, intelligence, and fluency in all the languages that common people and scholars may speak in Europe, I let the whole world judge what rank she holds among all the other princes. To be sure, if the empire of Fortune corresponded to and equaled the empire of her generous spirit and wit, this great Queen of the Sea, this Amphitrite, would needs open her borders and expand her circumference, so that just as she commands Britannia and Ireland, she would be given an entire globe, equal in size to our own, so that with fuller meaning her powerful hand would hold the orb of a general and universal monarchy.

In the meantime, Bruno's attacks on English rudeness hit back harder than he may have anticipated. If he had found a trip through the streets of London a risky enterprise before, it was worse after *The Ash Wednesday Supper* appeared in John Charlewood's bookstall. Bruno had already finished a second dialogue, *Cause, Principle, and Unity*, when *The Ash Wednesday Supper* caused its furor. He added a section to the new work in which he tried to explain himself, complaining that he could barely leave the French embassy for fear of being accosted. Writing as Filoteo, he suggests to his English friends Elitropio and Armesso that his English readers have been oversensitive:

FILOTEO: Now what customs have I named that cannot be found—similar, worse, or much stranger in kind, species, and number—in parts of the most excellent parts and provinces of the world? Would you call me an ungrateful slanderer of my homeland if I were to say that criminal customs like these, and worse, are to be found in Italy, in Naples, in Nola? Will I for that reason disparage that region, delightful to heaven, set from time to time at the head and right hand of this globe as the governor and ruler of all other peoples, ever esteemed by ourselves and others as the mistress, nurse, and mother of all the virtues, disciplines, humanities, modesties, and courtesies? Do we exaggerate what the poets have said about her—those same poets who have also called her the mistress of every vice, deception, greed, and cruelty? . . . Tell me the truth.

ARMESSO: It pains me, Teofilo [*sic*], that in our genteel country you should have come upon such experiences as gave you the occasion to complain in an ashy supper, when there have been many, many others who have shown you that however separated our country may be from the rest of the world, it is still devoted to the pursuit of good literature, of arms, chivalry, humanity, and courtesy.

Yet Bruno must have circulated in London society more than his rhetoric suggests: he had made a new friend, Alexander Dicson, a Scotsman who shared his interest in the art of memory and who appears as a character in the four original sections of *Cause, Principle, and Unity*. There Dicson understands the Nolan philosophy well enough to expound it in tandem with Teofilo. Neither does the controversy surrounding *The Ash Wednesday Supper* seem to have hurt its sales; John Charlewood continued to publish the

Nolan's dialogues as fast as he could write them. They were the young printer's first venture into publishing Italian, but far from being his last; in London, at least, Italian books found a good market.

Cause, Principle, and Unity develops the Nolan philosophy by taking familiar philosophical terms from the Scholastic tradition and redefining them to fit an infinite universe pervaded by life. Once Bruno has vented his spleen against Englishmen and pedant asses in its first section, he gets down, amid some comic interludes, to a dense philosophical discussion about matter, form, nature, idea, and, not least, women. This second dialogue's reigning pedant, Poliinnio, finds confirmation for his own misogyny in Aristotle:

> As I was studying in my little sanctuary of the Muses, I came upon that passage in Aristotle, at the beginning of the *Physics*, in which, when he wishes to expound upon what the primal matter may be, he takes as its mirror the feminine sex, that sex, I say, which is wayward, fragile, inconstant, soft, feeble, unlucky, ignoble, vile, abject, despicable, unworthy, reprobate, sinister, detestable, frigid, deformed, empty, vain, indiscreet, insane, perfidious, sluggish, affected, filthy, ungrateful, lacking, maimed, imperfect, inchoate, insufficient, cut short, attenuated, that rust, that caterpillar, that chaff, plague, disease, death.
>
> > Among us placed by nature at God's will
> > To be a burden and a bitter pill.

Gervasio, the comic character, blames Poliinnio's outburst on his preference for boys:

> You humanists, who call yourselves professors of good literature, when you grow so full of your great ideas that you can't contain yourselves anymore, you have nothing better to do than dump them on the poor women, just as, when another kind of frenzy takes you, you vent it on the first of your wretched students who passes by.

Teofilo and Dicson, on the other hand, mount a spirited defense of women, introducing the example not only of Elizabeth but also of Bruno's hostess, Madame de Castelnau, and her young daughter,

John Florio's pupil Catherine-Marie. Bruno's letter to the vice-chancellor of Oxford had claimed that he "[preferred] as company neither Briton nor Italian, male nor female, bishop nor king," and this equality was surely his ideal. In the real world, his escape from the convent also meant an escape from the vows of chastity and obedience, and he pursued women with Falstaffian matter-of-factness rather than poetic pining.

For the moment, however, he concentrated most of his energies on presenting the Nolan philosophy, so that no one who read *The Ash Wednesday Supper*, *Cause, Principle, and Unity*, or his next dialogue, *On the Infinite Universe and Worlds*, could think for a moment that Giordano Bruno was only a plagiarist of Marsilio Ficino and an apologist for Copernicus. In these later dialogues, the fury that seethed in *The Ash Wednesday Supper* subsides, overwhelmed by Bruno's enthusiasm for his real concern: to show how the realization that we inhabit an infinite universe will transform every aspect of our lives. It is also clear from these dialogues that Bruno was able, in the end, to make constructive use of his experience at Oxford. Shattering as it had been to his pride, the setback also shocked him into sharpening his ideas. He used his dialogues to vent his anger, but he used them still more importantly to refine his arguments.

CHAPTER NINETEEN

The Art of Magic

It is said that the art of magic is so important that against nature it makes the rivers run backward, stops the sea, makes the mountains moo, the abyss groan, restrains the sun, detaches the moon, uproots the stars, removes day, and holds back the night; hence the Academic of no Academy said, in that odious title and lost poem:

> It makes the rivers rush in upward flight,
> Displaces stars from heaven's lofty space,
> Turns night to day and turns the day to night,
> Uproots the moon from her own orbit's trace,
> Switches her crescent's left horn to the right,
> Swells ocean waves, and freezes them in place.
> It alters earth and water, air and fire,
> And molts the plumes of all human desire.
> —*The Candlemaker*, act I, scene 2

However new and radical the Nolan philosophy must have seemed in Elizabethan England, its inventor insisted that there was really nothing new about it. His dialogues on the structure of the universe, *Cause, Principle, and Unity* and *On the Infinite Universe and Worlds*, refer back insistently to the ancient philosophers who preceded Plato and Aristotle, and in *The Ash*

Wednesday Supper he explicitly describes his own enterprise as re-newing "the ancient philosophy":

> The point on which we should fix our mind's eye is this: Do we abide in
> the daytime with the light of truth above our horizon, or are we in the re-
> gions of our adversaries, our antipodes? Do we stand in the shadows, or
> rather they? Do we, in conclusion, who begin to renew the ancient phi-
> losophy, stand in the morning to put an end to the night, or in the
> evening to put an end to the day?

For Giordano Bruno, as for the ancient Greeks, there was no civilization older than that of Egypt. For fourteen years, he had lived in Naples alongside a battered statue of the river Nile that stood just off Piazza San Domenico; it gave its name to his district, the Seggio di Nilo. Perhaps for its nudity, the image was called the *Corpo di Napoli*—the *Body of Naples*—but it might well have begun life as a "Body of Alexandria." Ancient Neapolis had maintained an active colony of merchants from Alexandria in Egypt, for whom this little statue must once have stood as a reminder of home. Along with their trade, their expertise, and their ancient culture, the Alexandrians also brought their cult of the goddess Isis, which took its first firm hold in the region of Naples a little more than a century before another religion, Christianity, began to make its own appearance. For three centuries, the worship of Isis continued to make converts in waves of devotional enthusiasm that shook the Roman Empire, until Christian priests finally stamped it out; by then, however, important aspects of her cult had been transferred to worship of the Virgin Mary, another loving mother, devoted mourner, and patient consoler of souls. In Naples, the little statue of the Nile must have remained aboveground well into the Christian era if it was still mentioned in thirteenth-century chronicles; shortly afterward, however, it was buried, and rediscovered in 1446.

Medieval Neapolitans had lost any idea of what the weathered marble figure might have portrayed; they guessed that it might have been a reclining woman with children. By the fifteenth century, however, the statue's new neighbors, who included scholars like Lorenzo Valla, Antonio Panormita, and the young Giovanni

Gioviano Pontano, could pick out lion's paws on the "child" and the traces of a pharaoh's *nemes* headdress on its shoulders, which allowed them to identify it correctly as an Egyptian sphinx. The reclining figure that used the sphinx as an armrest, they knew, must then be the river god who evoked the idea of Egypt; Valla, especially, who had lived in Rome, knew that there were other, grander examples of these Nile statues on display there.

Twenty years later, in 1466, the philosopher and physician Marsilio Ficino acquired a manuscript in Florence that brought back memories of Egypt as forcefully as the *Corpo di Napoli*. Under the name of Hermes Trismegistus—"Thrice-Great Hermes"—it contained a series of texts written in Greek and set in ancient Egypt (where Greek had served as the diplomatic language under both the Ptolemys and the Roman Empire). These Hermetic books, most of them in the form of dialogues, described the process of divine interaction with the material world and a program for human enlightenment that strikingly paralleled some of the formulations of Plato and his followers, of Hebrew mystics, and to a certain extent of Christianity. The dialogues spoke of Egyptian hieroglyphs, Egyptian wisdom, and Egyptian ways of attracting the powers of God and the spirits to bring long life, good health, and spiritual enlightenment. Ficino and his contemporaries read the ancient books with amazement, debating whether Hermes Trismegistus came before or after Moses; some scholars suggested that Hermes might be the master from whom Moses had first learned the secret wisdom of Egypt. The more they read, the more Ficino and his friends became convinced that the texts of Hermes Trismegistus must rank among the most influential works of all time.

In 1614, the Protestant scholar Isaac Casaubon would demolish the reputation of Hermes Trismegistus by suggesting that these supposedly primeval documents had been drafted in the same environment that produced the statue of the Nile in Naples: the cosmopolitan world of Alexandria, where Greeks, Jews, Romans, Persians, and merchants of the whole Mediterranean met, exchanged ideas, and came up with new, sophisticated syntheses. By Casaubon's reading, the Hermetic texts sounded like so many different religious traditions not because they had served those traditions as a single primordial source, but because they were written at a time of lively and liberal intercultural borrowing. In Giordano Bruno's day, however, the writings of Hermes Trismegistus still exerted all their Egyptian allure, exotic and yet familiar. The Nolan read them as eagerly as the rest of his contemporaries.

The most famous passage in the Hermetic writings is an apocalyptic prediction of Egypt's eclipse, attractive to Renaissance readers for its clear reference to hieroglyphs, the "letters in stone" that recall the Egyptians' "pious deeds." This "lament for Egypt" gained an added poignancy for Hermes' readers in 1519, when Cairo fell to the Ottoman Turks; European scholars had come to identify the Hermetic texts as so essential a component of their own Christian tradition that an assault on Egypt was an assault on themselves. As the century progressed, and Italians engaged in an ongoing battle with Turkish marauders on their own shores, the Hermetic prediction of Egypt's conquest by "Scythians and Indians, or other savages" continued to have a menacing immediacy: after the brief Turkish invasion of Naples in 1562 came the terrible siege of Malta in 1565, narrowly won by the Christian Knights of Saint John with their international garrison. Even the Italian naval victory at Lepanto in 1571 could not entirely stave off fear that Naples or Malta might end up like Constantinople and Cairo before them, paying homage to the sultan. In such dangerous times, the Hermetic "lament for Egypt" could read as a potential lament for European civilization:

> Do you not know . . . that Egypt is the image of heaven, and to state it more clearly, the colony of all things that are governed and exercised in heaven? To tell the truth, our land is the temple of the world. But, alas, the time will come when Egypt will seem to have been the pious worshipper of divinity all in vain, for divinity, returning to heaven, will leave Egypt deserted, and this throne of divinity will become widowed of all religion, piety, law, and creed. O Egypt, Egypt, of your religions only the tales will remain, unbelievable to future generations, and they will have no one to tell of your pious deeds except the letters carved in stone, which will not speak to gods and men (for the latter will be dead, and deity transmigrated to heaven), but to Scythians and Indians, or other sav-

ages. Darkness shall prevail over light, death shall be judged more useful than life, the religious person shall be judged insane, the impious prudent, the madman strong, the worst man good.

Giordano Bruno must have come to Hermes Trismegistus through his readings of Marsilio Ficino, not only through Ficino's translation of the Hermetic dialogues themselves, but also his manual titled On Living the Heavenly Life, in which the Florentine philosopher invokes the example of the ancient Egyptians to explain how he has learned to attract beneficial influences from the stars, using gems, colors, and, importantly for Bruno, images, by which Ficino meant both statues and images held in the mind.

Ficino himself associated images not only with an internal system of symbolism but also with the external workings of the cosmos. They brought God to a human level, but also raised human souls toward God. But Ficino's cosmos, like that of Hermes Trismegistus, was the old system of crystalline spheres and fixed stars. Bruno, who had already used geometric diagrams and philosophical terms to present an infinite universe, now wrote a dialogue in which he transformed the cosmos by transforming its imagery. He called it The Expulsion of the Triumphant Beast, a phrase that brought to mind the book of Revelation: "And the devil that deceived them was cast into the lake of fire and brimstone, where the beast and the false prophet are, and shall be tormented day and night for ever and ever . . . And I saw a new heaven and a new earth: for the first heaven and the first earth were passed away."

Bruno begins, however, not with a Christian vision but with Jupiter, king of the gods, fretting about the signs of old age; the ancient womanizer no longer has the energy to change into bulls, lightning, or showers of gold in pursuit of nubile young women. After a long and none too distinguished career as rulers of the universe, the gods of Olympus, he recognizes, are on their way out of power. But perhaps, Jove muses, he can stave off retirement by reforming the heavens. Too many of the constellations enshrine monsters, cruel kings, and degenerate princesses, not to mention a large, timid rabbit. By promising to reform the cosmos—and doing so on his own terms—the father of the gods hopes to buy more time for himself and his regime.

Bruno addressed this dialogue to Sir Philip Sidney, aiming, therefore, at a powerful patron within English society, as well as a reader and writer of exceptional refinement. As he explains to Sidney at length, Jupiter, fickle, weak-willed, and fallible, represents both the material world and human nature. The triumphant beast is "the vices that dominate and trample the divine part" of our spirit; by expelling that triumphant beast, "the spirit is purged of error and comes to be clothed in virtue."

Bruno flanks his Jupiter with the figures of Momus, the mocker of the gods (who, as he tells Sidney, represents conscience); the Egyptian Isis; Sophia, the image of Greek wisdom; and Saulino, whose name echoes that of his own maternal family, the Savolino, but has also been read as a Hebrew name. The characters represent, then, entire cultures as well as individuals.

Unlike most of his contemporaries, who gave the universe about six thousand years of existence since creation, the Nolan philosopher had already proclaimed that it was infinitely old; in *The Expulsion of the Triumphant Beast*, he insists that the universe holds cultures and memories that have come and gone and will come and go again. He could look back to Plato for confirmation and, most of all, to ancient Egypt. Plato's dialogues *Timaeus* and *Critias* tell of an Egyptian wise man who informs the Greek statesman Solon that he knows nothing of history: nine thousand years ago, the Egyptian notes, Athens was under siege by the people of Atlantis. Now, he tells Solon with a sigh, all is forgotten.

Ancient philosophy proved to Bruno that some ideas about humanity and its place in the cosmos were as old as human memory, although the expressions of those ideas might change as languages or scripts or cultures changed. Hence the essential truths of Egyptian religion as he understood them were not so different from the Nolan philosophy. This is not to say that Bruno intended to revive Egyptian religion, far from it. He regarded his own philosophy as vastly superior to ancient Egyptian religion, and vastly more suited to his own time and place. But as he wrote from the bloody soil of France and Britain, he pointed up the virtues of Egyptian idolatry to provide an example of extreme tolerance in his violently intolerant world.

As Bruno has Isis explain to the rest of the gods, the Egyptians had made sense of their world, using their "irrational" worship of animals and idols to eminently rational ends:

> The stupid, insensitive idolaters had no reason to laugh at the magic and divine religion of the Egyptians, who in every cause and every effect, according to the principles appropriate to each, contemplated divinity, and knew how to obtain the benefits of Nature by means of the species that are in her womb: just as she gives fish from sea and river, wild animals from the desert, metals from mines, fruits from trees, so from certain parts, certain animals, certain beasts, certain plants, there are offered certain destinies, powers, fortunes, and impressions. Hence the divinity in the sea was called Neptune, in the sun, Apollo, in the earth, Ceres, in the desert, Diana, and so differently in the other species, all of which refer back to a god of gods and wellspring of all ideas that exists above Nature. That god, being absolute, has nothing to do with us, but inasmuch as he is communicated through the effects of Nature and is more intimate to them than Nature herself, if he is not Nature per se, certainly he is the nature of Nature and is the soul of the soul of the world, if not its soul per se: hence those who wanted to receive his help had to present themselves by the order of species, adjusting themselves to particular principles, just as whoever wants bread goes to the baker, whoever wants wine goes to the winemaker, whoever wants fruit goes to the gardener, whoever wants learning goes to the teacher, and so it goes for all the other things: so that one goodness, one joy, one absolute origin for all richness and good, contracted to different principles, pours out the gifts according to particular needs. From this you can infer how the wisdom of the Egyptians, which is now lost, worshipped crocodiles, lizards, snakes, onions, not just the earth, the moon, the sun, and other stars in the heavens—and this magic and divine rite (by which divinity was so conveniently transmitted to men) were lamented by the Thrice-Great Hermes.

In its own way, in its own time, then, Bruno argues, Egyptian religion presented the same essential truths as the Nolan philosophy; thus Isis uses a phrase from *Cause, Principle, and Unity*, "the soul of the soul of the world," to describe the transcendent God who underpins all the minor gods of Egypt, but also Bruno's own transcendent God. Sophia, Greek wisdom, presents the same story as Egyptian Isis, proving that all the civilizations of antiquity had developed their own foreshadowings of the Nolan philosophy, and like Isis, she uses the term "magic" in connection with those insights:

> You can see, then, how a simple divinity that is found in all things, a fertile nature, preserving mother of the universe, shines forth in different subjects according to the different ways in which she is communicated and takes on different names. You see how it is necessary to ascend to that one [nature] in different ways through participation in different gifts; otherwise, you try to enclose water with nets and go fishing with a shovel. Therefore [the ancients] understood the two sovereign bodies near our globe and mother goddess, that is, the sun and the moon, as the life force that informs things according to the two sovereign principles. Next, they understood her [Nature] according to seven other principles, distributing them among the seven lights called wanderers [planets]; tracing the differences among species of every kind to those [seven] as if to their first beginning and fertile cause; saying of plants, animals, stones, influences, and such, these are Saturn's, these belong to Jove, these to Mars, this and that to this planet and that one. So, too, [are] the parts, the members, the colors, the seals, the characters, the signs, the images distributed among the seven species. But it does not mean that because of this [the ancients] failed to understand that a single divinity is to be found in all things, which pours forth and communicates itself in numberless ways, and hence it has numberless names, and it can be sought out by numberless paths, with distinct principles and appropriate to each: at the same time it is honored and worshipped by numberless rites, because we seek to request numberless kinds of favors from it. But in this there is a need for that wisdom and judgment, that art, industry, and use of intellectual enlightenment that is revealed, sometimes greatly, sometimes scarcely, by the intelligible sun to the world, more in certain times than in others. This habit is called magic: and when it involves itself in supernatural principles, it is divine, when it turns to the contemplation of Nature and the close scrutiny of her secrets, it is natural, and it is called intermediary

and mathematical when it considers the principles and activities of the soul, which stands at the border between body and spirit, spirit and intellect.

Here Sophia sounds like wisdom absolute, and yet, for all her rationality and her resounding name, "wisdom," Bruno shows that she, too, is limited by her own time and place.

For Bruno, indeed, the infinite stretches of time and space bred, at least ideally, an infinite tolerance for the various ways that people have sought God and wisdom (although he never quite found the patience to tolerate Calvinists or pedant asses). Sometimes, as in speeches of Isis and Sophia, he used the word "magic" to refer to this long tradition of human wisdom. This association of magic with ancient wisdom fitted equally well with the biblical Magi: the three kings' knowledge of ancient traditions had led them to expect the coming of the Messiah, just as their expertise in astronomy reassured them that following a star would be as good as following a map to reach the rock-cut stables of Bethlehem in Judaea. The Magi were also clever, attentive to political conditions in the states through which they traveled. As the Gospel notes, after handing over their gifts of gold, frankincense, and myrrh to the Christ Child, they slipped out of Judaea by a back road to elude the Roman puppet King Herod and his praetorian guard. Like the wisdom of the Magi, what Bruno calls "magic" sometimes looks like plain common sense. Part of the ancient wisdom was simple skill at survival.

The supreme magic in the reformed heavens of *The Expulsion of the Triumphant Beast* is no different from the supreme revelation expounded in Bruno's other dialogues: the most urgent task for modern philosophy in all these works is to comprehend the infinite extent of the universe, space, time, and God. From his courtesan Vittoria, for whom "the world is fine as it is," his Italian dialogues come nearer in tone to the book of Genesis: "And God saw everything that He had made, and behold, it was very good." Indeed, the more Bruno became convinced of the world's grand immensity, the more he insisted on its goodness.

Savagely comic in much of its text, *The Expulsion of the Tri-*

umphant Beast inspired Bruno to write a still more savage coda, a dialogue he called *The Kabbalah of the Horse Pegasus* and dedicated not to a potential sponsor but rather to a pedantic Neapolitan cleric from his past, "Don Sapatino," who was probably a relative from Nola, Don Sabatino Savolino. The "Sonnet in Praise of the Ass" that he places at the beginning of the dialogue (see Chapter 11) reveals the true nature of the horse Pegasus.

Pedant asses and holy asses, as the sonnet makes clear, have no need for the Nolan philosophy and its questions about the structure of the cosmos. But Bruno could see close parallels between the Jewish tradition of Kabbalah, which used the letters of the Hebrew alphabet to call down the ten emanations of God, and his own art of memory, which used Hebrew as well as Roman letters to fix the world's complexity on orderly wheels. Furthermore, Hebrew mystics were the ones who had envisioned traversing a thousand worlds, riding on cherubs, long before the Nolan could write that he had "discovered the way to climb the heavens, traverse the circumference of the stars, and leave the convex surface of the firmament at his back."

Both Bruno's Dominican training and his early experience with the Augustinians in Naples required him to devote close attention to the Hebrew tradition as well as the ancient wisdom of Egypt, Greece, and Rome, to recognize Kabbalah as another means to live the heavenly life. Like Isis and Sophia, the Hebrew personifications of divine wisdom—Hochmah and Shekinah—were female; philosophers like Ficino's pupils Giovanni Pico della Mirandola and Giles of Viterbo had already applied the techniques of Kabbalah to Christian spirituality. *The Kabbalah of the Horse Pegasus*, with its mixture of Hebrew mysticism and Greek mythology, also spun off its own brief appendix, *The Cyllenian Ass*, that is, *The Ass of Hermes*.

Like Virgil escorting Dante through the inferno, these wise ancients helped to guide both Bruno and his readers in their first steps through the infinite universe, but in the end all their philosophies and religions, however worthy, could present only the shadows of that universe rather than reality itself. Bruno's real project was to find a language that could adequately describe infinity. He sensed that there were several possibilities, none of them simple. His dialogues *Cause, Principle, and Unity* and *On the Infinite Universe and Worlds* outline what might be required of mathematics, beginning with the ability to account for infinities and infinitesimals. *The Expulsion of the Triumphant Beast* explores adapting the ancient art of memory—multiplying images as the heavens multiply worlds. In his sixth Italian dialogue, *The Heroic Frenzies*, he turned, at last, to words. It was no coincidence that he did so in England; the peculiarities of its politics and culture had created a fever of excitement about language in the late fifteenth century.

When Giordano Bruno arrived in London, Spain was already beginning to gather its Invincible Armada to fling against the Protestants, but there were many Londoners who already knew Spanish well. The city was one of the poles of the international cloth trade, the chief outlet for prized Cotswold wool, traded in a chain of connections that finally led, through Venice and Constantinople, down the Silk Road to China. As a result, English merchants had long maintained close contacts with merchants in Flanders and the Netherlands, which were beginning to rebel in the late sixteenth century against decades of Spanish control. Spanish dominion had nearly spread to England itself when Elizabeth's predecessor, the Catholic queen Mary Tudor, married Philip II of Spain; now, married to a Habsburg cousin who was also his niece, Philip still yearned after the British Isles.

Elizabeth fought back the Spanish threat by building up her own fleet, led by dashing warlords like Sir Francis Drake and Sir Walter Raleigh, half merchants, half pirates, but she also fought back through culture; she had read her Thucydides and her Machiavelli well enough to apply their wisdom to her own circumstances. Learned in Greek and Latin, she spoke Spanish, French, and Italian well enough to negotiate in these languages, but above all, she had at her disposal an English that had begun to grow and change so radically that it seemed as new as the New World itself. Its basis both in Anglo-Saxon and in Norman French gave it a host of synonyms, as well as a structure that absorbed new coinages from Latin and Italian as if they were natural. Elizabethan poets, inspired by Italian models, were beginning to discover the potential of English to express the same vagaries of love as the sonnets of Petrarch and his followers. They adopted the discipline of sonnet form, even though Italian was far easier to rhyme than English, adapting a rhythm created for and by long, inflected words to Anglo-Saxon's monosyllabic punch:

How can my Muse want subject to invent
While thou dost breathe, that pour'st into my verse
Thine own sweet argument, too excellent
For every vulgar paper to rehearse?
O, give thyself the thanks if aught in me
Worthy perusal stand against thy sight;
For who's so dumb that cannot write to thee,
When thou thouself dost give invention light?
Be thou the tenth Muse, ten times more in words
Than those old nine which rhymers invocate,
And he that calls on thee, let him bring forth
Eternal numbers to outlive long date.
    If my slight Muse do please these curious days,
    The pain be mine, but thine shall be the praise.

As William Shakespeare began to test the powers of English to express the full range of human behavior, Giordano Bruno made his own test of language: to see whether Neapolitan vernacular could sing the praises of philosophy. To counterbalance the unruly crowd of gods, animals, and personifications who populate *The Expulsion of the Triumphant Beast*, he claims to have resorted to plain, simple language, but for anyone born north of Rome, the plain, simple language of Naples sounded more like a torrent of oratory:

Here Giordano speaks the common language, he names names freely . . . he calls bread bread, wine wine, a head a head, a foot a foot, and other parts by their proper name, he calls eating eating, sleeping sleeping, drinking drinking . . . He holds miracles as miracles, prodigies and marvels as prodigies and marvels, truth as truth, doctrine as doctrine, goodness and virtue as goodness and virtue, impostures as impostures, deceptions as deceptions, knife and fire as knife and fire, words and dreams

as words and dreams, peace as peace, love as love. He regards philosophers as philosophers, pedants as pedants, monks as monks, ministers as
ministers, preachers as preachers, bloodsuckers as bloodsuckers, ne'er-do-
wells, mountebanks, charlatans, triflers, barterers, actors, parrots as that
which they are called, show themselves to be, are; workers, benefactors,
sages, and heroes as themselves.

It was perhaps inevitable that when Bruno came to describe the
actions of those workers, benefactors, sages, and heroes, he turned
to a different kind of language entirely: the poetry of love.

CHAPTER TWENTY

Canticles

LONDON, 1584–1585

Thus, great with childe to speak, and helplesse in my throwes,
Biting my trewand pen, beating myselfe for spite,
Fool, said my Muse to me, looke in thy heart, and write.
—Sir Philip Sidney, *Astrophel and Stella*, Sonnet I

The sheer variety of Giordano Bruno's writings shows how difficult he found it to convey his ideas about the universe. Leonardo and Galileo might write that the language of nature was mathematics, but sixteenth-century mathematics could barely be distinguished from arithmetic and geometry. These disciplines worked reasonably well for charting the movements of the stars and planets as seen from the earth, but they had yet to provide a good account for something as simple as the flight of a ball, let alone a bird. Bruno understood enough about the universe, and about contemporary mathematics, to realize that all the planetary systems propounded in his day, no matter whether they centered on the earth or on the sun, were only models; the real movements of the heavens took place on a much larger scale where, in the ancient formula of Hermes Trismegistus, repeated by Augustine and Cusanus, "the center was everywhere and the circumference nowhere."

Bruno tried to convey his philosophy through pictures, both

geometric diagrams and the mental images of the artificial memory. For the diagrams, there were always insurmountable limitations imposed by the size of a printed page and his own skill as an engraver—he seems to have made all his own illustrations for his books. For the artificial memory, he could only suggest images and how to combine them; the final result was always hidden away within the heads of his hearers and readers. As a writer, he used every kind of language at his disposal, poetry and prose, Italian and Latin, high rhetoric, expository prose, ribald vulgarity.

He faced a second problem because he believed that his findings about the universe should have consequences for human behavior. He began to outline those consequences first in his comedy, *The Candlemaker*, and then in his Italian dialogues. Living out the Nolan philosophy meant accepting the world as it was, which in turn implied accepting a much larger definition of life in which the earth, stars, and planets were also living things, infused with divinity. At the same time, Bruno still believed that the universe demanded moral behavior: no matter how huge and abstract its movements might seem, the world's pervasive goodness demanded a matching goodness from all its creatures. The cosmos was not simply a huge mechanical system but something that he could only describe in emotional metaphors: a mother, a nursemaid, a wellspring, light, love, a creation truly worthy of an omnipotent God.

He did not describe any part of this creation as radically evil; he spent much more time denouncing pedant asses and rude Englishmen than he ever did inveighing against Satan. Although he had seen his share, and perhaps more than his share, of poverty, disease, bad government, cruelty, prejudice, intrigue, and religious hatred, he ascribed most of these calamities to the changeability inherent in the structure of the cosmos rather than to any immanent principle of evil. Many of our problems, he maintained, were as self-inflicted as the agonies of lovers. Returning, like Plato before him, to the ancient analogy between human love and the love of wisdom, Bruno created the longest and most complex of his Italian dialogues. He dedicated it to Sir Philip Sidney in 1585.

Like Plato's *Symposium*, *De gli heroici furori* (*The Heroic Frenzies*) presents love from a series of viewpoints, from the most physical to the most sublimely spiritual. He regarded that spiritual love as so disruptive of normal human existence that he called it raving madness, *furore*, Ficino's translation for *mania*, the word Plato used to describe the divine possession that affects prophets, poets, healers, and lovers, especially lovers of wisdom—philosophers. By insisting in his title that he will discuss "heroic" divine possession, Bruno prepares his readers for a dialogue that, like Plato's *Symposium*, will take them closer and closer to understanding the joys of philosophical love. Nothing in the restrained, elegant Plato can compare, however, with the bitter impetus of Bruno's opening charge to Sir Philip Sidney:

It is truly, O most generous Sir, the work of a low, filthy animal nature to have made oneself the constant admirer, and to have fixed a solicitous attachment upon or around the beauty of a woman's body. Good God! What more vile and ignoble vision can present itself to a clear-sighted eye than a man, brooding, afflicted, tormented, sorry, melancholy; who waxes now cold, now hot, now boiling, now trembling, now pale, now blushing, now in a pose of perplexity, now in the act of decisiveness, a man who spends the best season and the choicest fruits of his life distilling the elixir of his brain toward putting into thought and writ and sealing in public monuments those endless tortures, those grave torments, those reasoned arguments, those laborious thoughts and those bitter desires addressed to the tyranny of an unworthy, imbecilic, foolish and sordid smut?

What tragicomedy, what act, I say, more deserving of pity and laughter could be produced in this theater of the world, on this stage of our perceptions, than these many subjugated men, rendered pensive, contemplative, constant, steadfast, faithful, lovers, devotees, adorers, and slaves of a thing without faith, bereft of all constancy, destitute of intelligence, empty of all merit, void of any acknowledgment or gratitude, where no more sense, intellect, or goodness is to be obtained than might be found in a statue or a painting on a wall? And where there abound more disdain, arrogance, effrontery, vainglory, rage, scorn, perfidy, lust, greed, ingratitude, and other mortal vices than the poisons and instruments of death that could have issued forth from Pandora's box, all to have, alas, such expansive accommodation within the brain of such a monster? Be-

hold, inscribed on paper, enclosed in books, set before the eyes, and in-
toned in the ears, a noise, a commotion, a clash of devices, of emblems, of
mottoes, of epistles, of sonnets, of epigrams, of books, of chattering scrib-
bles, of terminal sweats, of lives consumed, of cries that deafen the stars,
laments that make hell's caverns reverberate, aches that strike the living
dumb, sights that exhaust the pity of the gods, for those eyes, for those
cheeks, for that bosom, for that white, for that crimson, for that tongue,
for that tooth, for that lip, for that hair, that dress, that mantle, that
glove, that slipper, that high heel, that avarice, that giggle, that scorn,
that empty window, that eclipse of the sun, that throbbing, that disgust,
that stench, that sepulchre, that cesspit, that menstruation, that carrion,
that malaria, that uttermost insult and lapse of nature, that with a surface, a shadow, a phantasm, a dream, an enchantment of Circe plied in
the service of reproduction, should deceive in the matter of beauty;
which simultaneously comes and goes, issues and dies, flowers and rots,
and is somewhat beautiful on the outside, but truly and fixedly contains
within a shipyard, a workshop, a customhouse, a marketplace of every
foulness, toxin, and poison that our stepmother Nature has managed to
produce: and once the seed she requires has been paid out, she often re-
pays it with a morass, a remorse, a sadness, a flaccidity, a headache, a las-
situde, this and that distemper that are known to all the world, so that
every place aches bitterly where it itched so sweetly before.

The invective launched by Bruno's misogynist Poliinnio in
Cause, Principle, and Unity pales by comparison. In that dialogue,
moreover, the other characters rush to refute him by praising the
virtues of women. Bruno's letter to Sidney produces no such counterbalance; instead, the argument proceeds to sidestep women altogether: poetry, the Nolan insists at resonant length, should be
devoted to philosophical rather than physical love.

Bruno's vehemence may have reflected events in his own life, or
perhaps in Sidney's. Sidney had been betrothed for several years to
Penelope Devereux, daughter of the Earl of Essex, but in 1581 the
beautiful eighteen-year-old had been married instead, against her
own objections, to Robert Rich, Earl of Warwick. In the following
year, Sidney began to circulate, in manuscript, a sequence of sonnets and songs, *Astrophel and Stella*, that told the story of his love

and its inevitable frustration (Astrophel means "star lover" in Greek, and Stella is "star" in Latin). By 1583, Sidney himself had married Frances Walsingham, daughter of Sir Francis, Queen Elizabeth's head of secret services, but *Astrophel and Stella* continued to circulate among his friends.

To a Sir Philip Sidney newly (and by all accounts happily) married, *The Heroic Frenzies* argues that the love of God is the only love worth pursuing to the point of extreme self-denial; sexual love can and should be fulfilled physically. The dialogue is much more than a dialogue; it is also a veritable anthology of love poetry: a massive collection of sonnets, emblems, versicles, and songs, some of them borrowed from other writers, most of them Bruno's own. Their widely differing tones and qualities suggest that he must have been writing poetry most of his life.

Any writer of Italian vernacular sonnets looked back to only one master, the virtual inventor of the form, Francesco Petrarca, known to his English admirers, like Sidney, Florio, and Matthew Gwinne, as Petrarch. Bruno's admiration for Petrarch's verse, and his liberal borrowings from it, did not prevent his harsh disapproval of the fact that these poems were inspired by their author's obsessive, unrequited love for the woman he called Laura. As the preface to *The Heroic Frenzies* declared to Sidney, such self-denying "courtly" love was an absurd waste of time:

I mean for the world to be certain of one thing: namely, that the purpose for which I agitate myself in this prefatory outline, where I speak individually to you, excellent Lord, and in the Dialogues created around the following articles, sonnets, and verses, is that I want everyone to know that I would hold myself as most unworthy and beastly if with great expenditure of thought, desire, and labor I would ever have been satisfied with imitating (as they say) Orpheus in the worship of a living woman, and after death, if it were possible, retrieving her from hell . . . And by my faith, if I mean to equip myself to defend as noble the spirit of that Tuscan poet who showed himself so distraught along the banks of the Sorgue for a lady of Vaucluse, and do not mean to say that he was fit to be tied, I would give myself over to believing and force myself to persuade others that he studiously nourished that melancholy for lack of a talent equal to higher matters, to lavish his own gifts on such stuff, by spelling out the affections of an obstinate love that was vulgar, animal, and bestial.

Bruno's dialogue begins in Nola, with two friends of his father's, the poet Luigi Tansillo and the officer Odoardo Cicala (called "Cicada" in the text), discussing a series of sonnets, four of them Tansillo's own. Indeed, Tansillo must have exerted a great influence on the young Bruno, who echoes his work repeatedly. There is nothing in the poet's flowing, polished occasional verse to indicate that his love sonnets are any different from Petrarch's; like Petrarch's *Songbook* (*Canzoniere*), they seem to tell a biographical tale, in Tansillo's case about his love for Laura Monforte, his travels abroad, his break with her, and his eventual marriage to Luisa Puccio. But Bruno presents Tansillo without hesitation as a writer of allegory, whose love poetry is really, like Bruno's, poetry about the love of wisdom.

The four sonnets that Bruno chooses from Tansillo certainly fit well with an allegorical interpretation. In them, God is light and warmth, inflaming the soul with desire for wisdom; vice, stupidity, laziness, and ignorance are dark, heavy, and cold:

> With pretty blazes and with noble ties,
> Beauty ignites me, honest virtue binds me;
> In flames and servitude my pleasure finds me,
> In flight from liberty and fear of ice.
>
> The inferno rages; I endure the heat;
> The world and I alike admire my noose.
> Fear cannot chill me, nor pain set me loose;
> The ardor's peaceful, and the bondage sweet.
>
> Above I see the light that draws me higher,
> The cord spun out from such a sumptuous thread
> As makes my thoughts arise, desires fall dead.
>
> Within my heart there shines so fair a fire,
> So sweet a shackle's closed around my will,
> My shade's enslaved, my embers smolder still.

Like any good Neapolitan, Tansillo can also sling invective
with gusto:

> Felonious child of Love and Rivalry,
> Who turns her father's raptures to distress,
> Alert to evil, blind to happiness,
> The Minister of Torture, Jealousy.
>
> Hell's Fury, fetid Harpy, born to swindle
> And poison other people's sweet delight.
> Cruel gale from the south, before whose blight
> My hope's most lovely flower is bound to dwindle.
>
> Brute hateful to yourself, fell bird of fate,
> With omens of distress your only screed,
> You find a thousand ways to penetrate
>
> The heart; but were you driven from the gate
> Love's kingdom would be lovelier indeed,
> Sweet as a world released from death and hate.

Thus, as Bruno alerts his readers, the love poems of *The Heroic
Frenzies*—including Tansillo's—only seem to form a collection of
conventional love poetry. In fact, as he notes to Sidney in his letter
of dedication, they are arranged to convey the same divine message
as the erotic poetry of the biblical Song of Songs, however great
their differences of form or content:

> Finally, I mean to say that these heroic frenzies achieve a heroic subject
> and object, and for that reason they can no more be reduced to consider-
> ation as common and natural loves than dolphins can be seen in the trees
> of the forest, or wild boars beneath the sea cliffs. Therefore, in order to
> liberate them all from such a suspicion, I first thought of giving this book
> a title similar to that of Solomon, who under the cover of ordinary love
> and emotion contains similar divine and heroic passions, as the mystical
> and kabbalistic doctors interpret them. I wanted, that is to say, to call it
> *Canticles*. But for several reasons I resisted in the end, of which I will note
> only two. First of all, because of the fear that I have conceived of the rig-

orous disapproval of certain Pharisees, who would regard me as profane for usurping sacred and supernatural titles for my natural and physical discourse, whereas they, criminals and ministers of every ribaldry, usurp more profoundly than one can say the titles of holy men, of saints, of divine orators, of sons of God, of priests, of kings; while we await that divine judgment that will make plain their malign ignorance and the learning of others, our simple liberty and their malicious rules, censures, and institutions. Second, for the great difference one can see between this work and that, however identical the mystery and substance of soul that are contained beneath the shadow of the one and the other. Now, in the one case, no one doubts that the basic intention of the Wise Man was to represent divine matters rather than anything else; for there the images are openly and manifestly images, and the metaphorical sense is so well-known that it cannot be denied as a metaphor: where you hear those dove's eyes, that neck like a tower, that tongue of milk, that fragrance of frankincense, those teeth that are like flocks of sheep come up from the washing, that hair like the goats who appear from Mount Gilead.

In other words, the Italian vernacular verse of *The Heroic Frenzies* introduces, for Bruno's own place and time, the same truths that Solomon expounded in his Song, and Plato in dialogues like *Symposium* and *Phaedrus*. His Neapolitan vernacular *Canticles*, like the Hebrew verse of Solomon's Song and the dramatic dialogue of Plato's *Symposium*, lays out the human soul's path to understanding divinity through language that does not reveal itself immediately except to the worthy and the initiated. All three works are thus the equivalent, in their way, of Egyptian hieroglyphs. As so often in Bruno, what is most new about the Nolan philosophy is as old as the universe that philosophy reveals, old beyond the creation narrative of the Bible, old as Egyptian chronicles and the geological record of nature. Tansillo, in his allegorical poetry, thus acts as a kind of Copernicus to the Nolan's more radical allegories about a more curious universe. But that universe has existed all along, and wise men all along have seen it, though not quite with the Nolan's same penetration.

But in fact, evoking the Song of Songs chiefly served his readers notice that for Giordano Bruno, no less than for Petrarch, poetry was the language in which he most appropriately expressed his greatest love. The word "philosophy" itself, by its very etymology, declared its love of wisdom; the term was said to have been invented by Pythagoras. Bruno's own love of philosophy drove him to nearly the same levels of literary productivity as Petrarch himself, and unlike Petrarch's expressed willingness to lay down his life for love, which brought him a life of fame and leisure, Bruno's love for philosophy was repeatedly put to the test. His prefatory letter to Sir Philip Sidney presses the point insistently; it is not unrequited love for a woman that drives him, but the love of a higher idea:

In this poetry, however, you will not discern a face that so vividly urges you to seek after hidden and occult sentiment, as its ordinary manner of speech and its comparisons, which are more attuned to the common images that lovers use and which the usual poets put in verse and rhyme, resemble the feelings of those who spoke to Cythereis, or Lycoris, to Doris, to Cynthia, to Lesbia, to Corinna, to Laura, and the like. For which reason it would be easy to think that my first and basic intention had been directed by an ordinary love that inspired me to such conceits, and then by dint of rejection had taken wings and become heroic, just as it is possible to convert any ballad, romance, dream, and prophetic riddle and transfer it by the power of metaphor and the pretext of allegory to signify whatever might please those who are better able to press their emotions into creating anything out of anything, just as the wise Anaxagoras said, "All is in all." But let any of them think what he likes and pleases, because in the end, like it or not, in all fairness everyone should understand and define it as I understand and define it, and not as they would understand or define it. Because just as the passions of that wise Jew have their own style, order, and title, which no one could understand or better explain than he himself, were he present, so, too, these canticles have their own proper title, order, and style, which no one can explain and understand better than I myself, if I am not absent.

The order and style that Bruno has imposed on his *Heroic Frenzies* relegate the figure of Luigi Tansillo, graceful poet of love, to the first half of the work. He is thus a dominant but not definitive figure, a figure who marks the initial stages in the heroic lover's passage from passionate raving to calm enlightenment.

Indeed, the dramatic two-part structure of *The Heroic Frenzies* carefully divides the five conversations of Tansillo and Cicada from the more profound conversations in part 2 of Cesarino, Maricondo, Liberio, Laodomio, Severino, Minutolo, and, in the last section, two young ladies of Nola, Laodomia and Giulia—probably, again, members of the Savolino clan and Bruno's cousins. Miguel Angel Granada has identified the dividing line of the dialogue as the moment when the lover leaves off belief in the immortality of the individual soul. But Bruno himself more evidently denotes the break between the first and the second parts of his work by a change of setting: part 1 concentrates on the lover's interior development; part 2 thrusts him into the surrounding world. In a general sense, then, Tansillo, like Plato's Socrates, serves as the teacher who begins to nurture a philosophical spirit but must inevitably then send that spirit on its way.

In effect, *The Heroic Frenzies*, despite profound differences of structure and content, are to Bruno's Nolan philosophy what the *Symposium* was to the philosophy of Plato, an initiation into philosophy through the imagery of love, in which Luigi Tansillo, like Socrates, provides a father figure who eventually steps aside to admit a higher wisdom. Remarkably, this higher wisdom is revealed, in both dialogues, by women. Bruno's description of his female characters, Laodomia and Giulia, says a good deal about his own reading of Plato's Diotima, the prophetess of the *Symposium*, who must be one of the most misunderstood figures in Western literature. Bruno writes:

> because two women are introduced, for whom (according to the custom of my country) it is inappropriate to comment, argue, decipher, know much, and act as professors as if to usurp a man's prerogative to teach, establish guidelines, rules, and teaching, but they may, on the other hand, divine and prophesy whenever the spirit moves their bodies. Let it suffice, therefore, to make them only the players of the allegory, leaving the ideas and the business of declaring the meaning to some masculine wit.

Plato, on the other hand, flouting the custom of his country, has his prophetess Diotima tell Socrates the deepest truths about philosophy, including matters she doubts that he shall be able to understand completely:

These are the lesser mysteries of love, into which even you, Socrates, may enter; to the greater and more hidden ones which are the crown of these, and to which, if you pursue them in a right spirit, they will lead, I know not whether you will be able to attain. But I will do my utmost to inform you, and do you follow if you can.

And yet the final revelation of *The Heroic Frenzies* will also re-volve around a woman who is as capable and enlightened as Dio-tima. The last section of *The Heroic Frenzies* is taken up with nine young men, all of them blinded by love, who have stumbled along together from Naples to arrive at the banks of the Thames, carrying a jar of water given to them by the goddess Circe. If they can open it, the enchantress has told them, they will be cured of their blind-ness. Laodomia and Giulia, standing at the riverside, help them to open the jar, and at that moment the nine blind men see the "twin lights" of an English nymph's eyes, and are cured of their inability to see.

The blind men are a direct borrowing from the Neapolitan poet Marcantonio Epicuro's poem *Cecaria* (*Blindness*), published in 1543, but also available in Girolamo Seripando's library in manu-script, bound together with Giles of Viterbo's "Love's Beautiful Hunt." Although the swains are nine in number, they parallel, in their travels and their experience, another, single, man who once left Circe's lair as a blind lover, only to find full enlightenment in England: Bruno himself. The nymph whose eyes restore the blind man's power of sight is naturally to be understood as Elizabeth, a fine courtly tribute to the queen, but the symbolism does not end there. The fact that there are two eyes, two "lights," two "win-dows," suggests that there is always more than one path to philoso-phy's transcendent vision: Bruno describes these two guiding beacons elsewhere in the dialogue as "the lights of the twin splen-dor of divine goodness and beauty." If two can become one, so can infinity.

Like Plato's *Symposium*, *The Heroic Frenzies* is more than a liter-ary tour de force: it is a call to action, an encouragement for Philip Sidney to turn his own poetic talents away from glorifying an indi-vidual woman, Penelope Rich née Devereux, to glorifying God, creating not another version of Petrarch's *Songbook*, but rather the

sacred love poetry of Solomon's Song of Songs, just as Bruno himself has done at impressive length.

Although *The Heroic Frenzies* emphasizes the Nolan's connections to ancient philosophy, the dialogue also points out the novelty
of his own convictions. Like hieroglyphs in Egypt, like the Song of
Songs in Israel, like Plato's *Symposium* in Greece, the dialogue
has been written in a combination of visual imagery with contemporary language, so that the Nolan can share his experience as a
philosopher-lover with those, like Sidney, who can understand it,
but without divulging his insights wholesale to everyone. The Nolan
philosophy requires proclamation to the wise as well as hiding from
the ignorant, so that eventually it can redeem the world, a world of
almost inconceivable immensity. For the wise few, the very shape
of the heavens has changed: not simply purified, as in *The Expulsion
of the Triumphant Beast*, but revealed in its full, boundless majesty.
The Nolan and humanity are on the threshold of something new:

> But here contemplate the harmony and consonance of all the spheres, in-
> telligences, muses, and instruments together, where heaven, the move-
> ment of the worlds, the works of nature, the discourses of intellect, the
> mind's contemplation, the decrees of divine Providence, all celebrate
> with one accord the lofty and magnificent oscillation that equals the
> lower waters with the higher, exchanges night for day, and day for night,
> so that divinity is in all things, so that everything is capable of every-
> thing, and the infinite goodness communicates itself without end accord-
> ing to the full capacity of all things.

For Bruno himself, this enlightenment came through physical
displacement as well as expenditure of time, study, and passionate
devotion. The journey that began in Nola in the house of Giovanni Bruno ends on the banks of the Thames, as it does, too, for
the blind men, who sing:

> As day and night grant mutual release
> When night's star-spangled mantle steals away
> The color from the chariot of day,
> Our ruler thus secures

His law that e'er endures:
The lofty fall, the humble shall increase.

The lofty fall, the humble shall increase
By law of him who keeps the great machine
That, spinning quickly, slowly, in between,
Has power to dispense
Throughout the world immense
What's hidden and what everybody sees.

What's hidden and what everybody sees:
Deny it not, nor claim that it prevails
Over the peerless end to our travails
Through mountain, countryside,
Pond, river, ocean wide;
Through crags and gorges, thorns and rocks and trees.

The dialogue's closing vision shows Elizabeth as ruler of the
heavens and the oceans alike, a goddess on a par with Jove and
Neptune, because, as we already know from *The Expulsion of the
Triumphant Beast*, she is wiser by far than either of these two ancient gods, and here again, two become one:

"O Jove, I envy not your firmament,"
Said Father Ocean, with his haughty glance,
"For I am well content
With such delights as my own empire grants."

"What arrogance is this?" Great Jove replied;
"What added to the riches that you know?
God of the raging tide,
Why does your crazy daring overflow?"

"You have," the briny god said, "in your hands
The flaming heaven, where the zodiac
Bears on its burning back
The chorus of the planets in their dance;

"The Sun earns universal admiration
Among them, but I tell you that it pales
Before her who regales
Me with the brightest light in all creation.

"And I within my vasty breast contain
That land among all others where the source
Is found of Thames's glad course,
Whose lovely nymphs gambol in pleasant train.

"And one among them beams with such a light
As ought to make you, Thunderer on high,
Love sea better than sky;
Your sun can't so outshine the starry night."

Jove answered: "God who rules the bounding sea,
My happiness can never be exceeded,
For so Fate has decreed it,
But we may share our riches equally.

"Among your nymphs the Sun shall take the station
She held, and by the laws that regulate
Our kingdoms alternate
She'll shed her glow among my constellations."

From the invectives against women in his opening letter, Bruno
has moved by the end of his dialogue to a vision in which a woman
wields power equal to that of any man; like Plato and Saint Paul,
he occasionally stated, and must have believed on some level, that
male and female made no real difference to the potential of an individual soul. Society, however, was another matter.

Giordano Bruno may have found his illumination on the banks
of the Thames, but his host, Michel de Castelnau, was bound to
follow more worldly orders. The ambassador had fallen from royal
favor already in 1584, although his family's desperate financial situation had earned him a year's extension of his position in London.
In October 1585, the household left for Paris. No other sponsor

had made a bid to sustain Bruno in England, and hence the Nolan philosopher had no choice but to return with Castelnau's entourage; only John Florio stayed behind. The trip was disastrous; thieves robbed the family of everything they owned, and they arrived in Paris looking, as Castelnau himself described it, "like those Irish exiles who walk around the city with their children in hand, begging." Fortunately for Bruno, the thieves were not literate thieves; he was able to salvage a manuscript he had begun in London: the first three books of his long Latin poem *On the Immense and the Numberless*.

Without his official position abroad, Castelnau could no longer keep gentlemen in his house. Once again, therefore, Giordano Bruno set out on his own. In Paris, at least, he could make his own living.

CHAPTER TWENTY-ONE

Squaring the Circle

PARIS, 1585–1586

I think he'll be stoned by this university. But he's heading soon for
Germany.
—Jacopo Corbinelli

The Paris to which Michel de Castelnau and Giordano Bruno
returned in October 1585 was a menacing, unstable place.
In the two and a half years since Bruno's departure, the
Catholic faction led by the duc de Guise had become ever more
powerful and ever more impatient with Henri III's tolerance of the
Huguenots; de Guise, after all, had struck the first blow in the
Saint Bartholomew's Day Massacre. In 1584, when Bruno had already left for England, the king, under pressure, rescinded the edict
that had granted a degree of recognition to French Protestants
since 1576.

In this militant Paris, Bruno had every reason to fear for his
safety. He tried again to reconcile with the Church. Again, too, he
went to a Jesuit to present his case. If the Society hoped to attract
Protestants back into the Catholic fold, perhaps he could hope to
be received as well. As he told his inquisitors: "[I presented myself
to a confessor] another time in Paris, to another Jesuit, while I was
negotiating a return to religious life through Monsignor the bishop
of Bergamo, who was then nuncio in Paris, and Don Bernardin de
Mendoza, with the intention of making my confession." Once

again, the Jesuit had to tell the renegade Dominican that only a higher authority could handle his case. Bruno knew Mendoza from London; as a native of Nola and a resident of Naples, the Nolan was still officially a subject of the Spanish king, Philip II (the same Philip after whom he had been named by his parents). Mendoza had been serving in London as Spain's ambassador to the Court of St. James's, where he gained a reputation as a ruthless intriguer at the very time when Spain was beginning to build up its Invincible Armada. Not surprisingly, Francis Walsingham expelled him in 1585, and he moved on to Paris to serve Philip II at the court of Henri III. On Bruno's behalf, Mendoza, in turn, contacted the papal nuncio, Girolamo Ragazzoni, whose office treated all the problems that would have fallen to the Inquisition in Spain or Italy. This time Bruno asked specifically to have his excommunication lifted, but also to be released from his obligation to live in a convent. The ambassador and the nuncio agreed that under such conditions, only the pope could make the final decision.

Popes did in fact lift bans of excommunication, and normally the nuncio would simply have written to Rome to endorse Bruno's request. But Girolamo Ragazzoni had no pull with Pope Sixtus V; he had been appointed nuncio by the previous pope, Gregory XIII, and, like many of Gregory's appointments, had already been officially replaced. He was only waiting in Paris for that replacement to arrive.

Sixtus V is best known now for his obsession with ancient Egyptian obelisks, four of which he would eventually place in strategic piazzas around Rome as signposts to pilgrims and monuments to the victory of Christianity; each obelisk had been carefully baptized, exorcised, and topped with a cross. Sixtus was as implacable about religion as he was about city planning, and much less imaginative. He encouraged the Huguenots to convert en masse, but he was unlikely to lend a receptive ear to a lapsed Dominican who had traveled and lived among the infidels, and was now proclaiming a new philosophy of heaven and earth. It was enough that his predecessor, Gregory XIII, had changed the calendar.

Any return to the Church would have required severe acts of

penitence. The Bible's stories of redemption all happen to people who have lost everything: Job, whose tribulations are sent as a test by Satan, and who, after crying out his protest, hears God's response and replies: "Then I abhor myself, and repent in dust and ashes." The prodigal son of the parable has squandered everything he owns, and returns to his father's house as a total surrender of his personal pride.

Saint Peter, after denying that he knew Jesus, "went out and wept bitterly" (Matthew 26:75). In the sixteenth century, repentance often followed on a crisis of faith, like the spiritual crisis that transformed Ignatius of Loyola from a terribly wounded mercenary soldier into the founder of a new religious order built on the idea of intellectual militancy.

But Giordano Bruno's faith in God had never been so strong; everything he had discovered about the immensity of the universe only strengthened his awe at creation and his joy at coming closer to its source. His attention was fixed not on what he had done wrong in his life but on what he had learned in its course, and he was consumed with eagerness to communicate those discoveries. Furthermore, he observed repeatedly that in deepening his knowledge of the universe, he had also deepened his communion with religion's most basic truths. He quoted Psalm 19 in support of his philosophy: "The heavens declare the glory of God, and the firmament sheweth his handiwork." And if Bruno maintained that Solomon and Pythagoras had both understood that there was "nothing new under the sun," he also believed that the universe and the individual experienced unending renewal. Like Mendoza and Ragazzoni (and as a former friar of San Domenico Maggiore, that most political of convents), he understood perfectly well that religion had its political side. He was anything but a dogmatic Catholic, but in many respects Catholic ideas and Catholic disciplines continued to regulate his life. So long as Sixtus V was pope, however, he could abandon any hope of being restored to participating in the sacraments. With his old Neapolitan survival instincts as active as ever, the Nolan philosopher knew that he could not stay in Paris. He wrote ahead to several German universities to ask whether there were any positions open.

In Paris, meanwhile, Bruno had returned to the Collège de Cambrai to live, but thought better of asking Henri for a reappointment as royal reader. The deteriorating political climate, his isolation in England, and his disastrous reception at Oxford had turned him into a more guarded soul than he had been two and a half years before. He did, however, renew two important friendships from his previous stay: those with Jacopo Corbinelli, the Florentine secretary of Queen Mother Catherine de Médicis, and Piero Del Bene, abbot of Belleville, almoner to Henri III. It is Corbinelli who reveals why Bruno, despite his prickly character, continued to make so many friends in high places, for the Florentine calls him "a delightful companion at the table, much given to the Epicurean life," and we can certainly see that side of Bruno, with his sense of humor and his quicksilver wit, in his Italian works. The Nolan also began to spend time reading in the magnificent library of the abbey of Saint Victor, as well as talking to the librarian, Guillaume Cotin, whose diary of those years gives us another of our rare pictures of Bruno as others saw him. Cotin's picture is less happy than Corbinelli's. When he first met the French librarian, Bruno reported that "he had just been in England with the king's ambassador, and lectured at Oxford," putting the best face on his recent past. As he got to know Cotin better, however, the Nolan's bitterness began to emerge. So did his devastating loneliness:

December 7: Jordanus came back again. He told me that the cathedral of Nola is dedicated to Saint Felix. He was born in 1548; he is thirty-seven years old. He has been a fugitive from Italy for eight years, both for a murder committed by one of his [Dominican] brothers, for which he is hated and fears for his life, and to avoid the slander of the inquisitors, who are ignorant, and if they understood his philosophy, would condemn it as heretical. He said that in an hour he knows how to demonstrate the artificial memory . . . and he can make a child understand it. He says that his principal master in philosophy was [Fra Teofilo da Vairano], an Augustinian, who is deceased. He is a doctor of theology, received in Rome . . . He prizes Saint Thomas . . . he condemns the subtleties of the Scholastics, the sacraments, and also the Eucharist, which he says Saint Peter and Saint Paul knew nothing about; all they knew was "This is my body." He says that all the troubles about religion will be removed when these debates are removed, and he says that he expects the end to come soon. But most of all he detests the heretics of France and England, because they disdain good works and prefer the certainty of their own faith and their justification [by it]. He disdains Cajetan and Pico della Mirandola, and all the philosophy of the Jesuits, which is nothing but debates about the text and intelligence of Aristotle.

In what must have been Bruno's tirade to his new friend, we can pick out his impatience with the arguments that divided Catholic from Protestant, Calvinist from Anglican: the number of the sacraments, how to take Communion, the relative importance of faith or good works to living the good Christian life. He observed these debates, moreover, as a person banned, by what he himself may have seen as technicalities, from taking Communion altogether. Like many of the Reformers, he reread the Gospels to discover how much of current Christian practice, on both sides of the Reformation, drew from traditions not stated in the Bible. He also recognized, at the same time, that religious tradition was often instrumental in creating orderly societies, as well as tearing them apart (in *The Ash Wednesday Supper*, anticipating Galileo, he argued that the Bible was better used for moral guidance than for mapping the heavens). The twentieth-century cosmologist Harold Urey, who fully accepted an infinitely large universe governed by quantum principles, would also say, "Fundamentally, I am a Catholic." In 1586, Giordano Bruno was saying much the same thing, but the times were drastically different, and that "fundamentally" did not count as much as adherence to a particular side in the debates about sacraments, good works, and free will.

On February 2, 1586, Cotin's diary reports a new arrival in the city: "Jordanus told me that Fabrizio Mordente is here in Paris, sixty years old, the god of geometers, and in that field he surpasses everyone who has gone before and everyone today, even though he knows no Latin; Jordanus will have his works printed in Latin."

Mordente came originally from Salerno in the Kingdom of Naples, where he had served as a soldier alongside Giovanni Bruno, Giordano's father, who was now living in retirement in

Nola. In 1554, Mordente had invented an instrument called the reduction compass, a compass whose two arms were both of adjustable length. Over the years he continued to publish essays on his invention and offer them to well-placed sponsors, including the Holy Roman emperor Maximilian II and his son King Rudolf II of Bohemia. In 1584, Mordente published yet another account of his compass, this time with the editor Christophe Plantin in Antwerp, and then, in 1585, in Paris, where he was encouraged by Abbot Piero Del Bene. With the help of this device, Mordente claimed to have solved one of the great geometric problems of all time, squaring the circle, that is, creating a circle and a square with perimeters of equal length. Solving the problem was perfectly easy with a loop of string; all it took was rearranging the shape of the loop. Making the same transformation with the geometer's tools of compass, straightedge, and pen was another matter entirely. Not one of the ancient Greek geometers or their medieval successors had ever found a solution, nor had any modern mathematician, at least until Mordente trumpeted his own success with the help of modern technology.

From Mordente's point of view, squaring the circle was a pretext for showing off the excellence of his compass. For Bruno, on the other hand, squaring the circle was important for its theoretical implications, and it was these that made him praise Mordente as "the god of geometers."

The Nolan philosopher was hardly unique in his time for thinking that mathematics had to change if it were to have any value for natural philosophy. Arithmetic, geometry, and algebra had found no satisfactory way to account for phenomena like motion, gravity, or the behavior of liquids, or to calculate the area of curved shapes. In the next century, that same dissatisfaction would inspire the simultaneous invention of calculus in two different places, Cambridge and Hannover, by two different people, Isaac Newton and Gottfried Wilhelm Leibniz, who arrived at the discovery by two different paths. The questions that drove them, however, were essentially the same, and common to the whole community of natural philosophers, including, in the late sixteenth century, Johannes Kepler, Galileo Galilei, and Giordano Bruno.

Bruno hoped to find mathematical formulas for motion, but more than any of his contemporaries he sought formulas that would work on a huge scale, throughout the infinite expanse of the universe, and also, as he was beginning to realize, on a scale of infinite smallness. In other words, he was moving toward the calculus himself, and could already outline what would become some of its fundamental ideas in theory, if he could not yet express them in usable equations.

There were two stages in Bruno's life when he wrote specifically on mathematical subjects. His encounter with Fabrizio Mordente and the reduction compass gave him his first impetus to do so. For Bruno, squaring the circle made an important step toward solving one of the outstanding problems posed by the Nolan philosophy: finding the mathematical means to analyze a shift from linear motion to circular motion, which would enable him to link the motion of individual objects on the earth, and by implication on other planets, with the motion of the heavenly bodies. When he offered to translate Mordente's work into Latin, he was thinking at the same time of developing it further on his own. Mordente, absorbed in his own researches, never suspected that the Nolan's interest in him might also involve self-interest. Besides, Bruno took an uncomplicated delight in making the contact with a fellow Neapolitan, and especially with a Neapolitan who had known the father he never expected to see again.

Well traveled as they were, both Mordente and Bruno believed fervently in the importance of translation, an interest on Bruno's part that had been further stimulated by his friendship with John Florio, who would turn into a superb translator of Montaigne. In the first section of *Cause, Principle, and Unity*, Armesso regrets the fact that Bruno's dialogues have not been translated: "I'd gladly have them translated into our [English] language, so that they could serve as a lesson."

In collaboration with Mordente, Bruno transformed that philosophical impetus into two publications in Latin: *Mordente* and *On Mordente's Compass*, both published in Paris in the spring of 1586, not long after Bruno's conversation with the librarian Cotin.

For these two works, Bruno used the word "translation" (*transla-*

tio) in another sense: to describe the changeover from circular to linear motion and vice versa (for translation from one language to another, he actually used the Latin word *traductio*). This kind of translation was the goal toward which he directed all his own involvement with the reduction compass, which for him was really an involvement with geometry. He used Mordente's instrument to divide arcs and chords of a circle into fractions, and then divided the fractions into fractions until he reached the level of infinitesimal units; this was the place where "translation" occurred. To effect that translation, however, the reduction compass proved useless; he needed—and lacked—not an instrument but a set of ideas: the approximations by which calculus transformed infinitesimals into workable mathematical formulas. The last part of Bruno's *On Mordente's Compass* is an appendix called "A Dream," in which, as himself, he writes:

> Is it not then possible to measure in turn both the motion and the thing that moves? Should it not follow that the definite law of what rotates in a connected continuum around a definite center apply to every other definite point directed toward that center? Should not the translation of one part of a continuum be followed by the translation of the whole?

The answer would eventually prove to be yes, but in order for that "yes" to have more than a purely abstract significance, mathematicians would have to make yet another translation: from words into numbers. It was a translation that Bruno himself was unable to make, and among his contemporaries only Kepler came close.

As Mordente read (or had read to him) Bruno's "translations" of his work, he realized that they were not translations at all: however effusive their praise of "the god of geometers" and his divine compass, their real subject was the Nolan philosophy, and their real hero came not from Salerno but from Nola. In *On Mordente's Compass*, Mordente is made to demonstrate his instrument to a character named Botero (surely the philosopher Giovanni Botero, then on a mission abroad in Paris for the Duke of Savoy), while remarking how grateful he is that his own "puerile" literary style and confused ideas have been so wonderfully improved by his translator.

Mordente began to complain to anyone who would listen about Bruno's "ingratitude." Stung, and probably well aware by that time that the reduction compass did not actually square the circle, Bruno turned from translating Mordente to attacking him. Although Mordente's name meant "biting," the real biter was Bruno's pen, which subjected "the god of geometers" to an expulsion worthy of the Triumphant Beast. Rather than simply gossiping, Bruno published a pamphlet called *The Triumphant Idiot*, a dialogue that begins with this blistering exchange between the characters Philotheus and Savolinus:

> PHILOTHEUS: Why don't you think it right (O Savolinus) for our Mordentius to call himself nearly divine, the instrument and image of nature at work, the parent of mechanical inventions, the restorer of fallen arts, the finder of what has been lost, the discoverer of new things, to whom a hundred gods owe a hundred sacrifices, to whom previous geometers must give way, and who alone shall be lofted to heaven by his successors?
> SAVOLINUS: Because I regard him as an idiot, a mere mechanic, uncouth and infantile in his speech, inexperienced in all the other arts that serve the truth of the art he professes, and bereft of any outstanding power of reason.

Without explicitly saying so—he had learned that much about strategy from his libel suit in Geneva—Bruno went on to insinuate that the real ideas in *Mordente* and *On Mordente's Compass* had been not Mordente's but his own. As Savolinus remarks at the end of *The Triumphant Idiot*:

> This man who mentions such mighty matters, yet who does not even know how to explain them competently: I can hardly believe that he was the inventor of this technique, but rather that he accepted help from some other, unknown man, whose name has been suppressed, a man who had wandered these regions for a long time; for many others think as I do, and take it as obvious enough.

Philotheus quickly suggests that it is better to err on the side of generosity, but the accusation has been voiced all the same.

After *The Triumphant Idiot*, Bruno followed with another pamphlet, *On the Interpretation of Dreams*, in which he continued the discussion he began in his "Dream" from *On Mordente's Compass*. Explicitly now, rather than implicitly, he takes credit, and perhaps justifiably so, for all the mathematical developments of Mordente's geometries.

Fabrizio Mordente may not have known Latin, but he was as experienced a courtier as Bruno, and knew how to defend himself with a courtier's cunning. Turning their argument from a mathematical into a political problem, he denounced the Nolan to the duc de Guise.

At the same time, unfortunately, Bruno had been courting notoriety on another front. Taking advantage of the Collège de Cambrai's independence from the Sorbonne and its Scholastic heritage, he presented a lecture in 1586 in which he promised to refute 120 errors of Aristotle. Shortly before, he had convinced his student Jean Hennequin, a young French nobleman, to publish, under his own name, Bruno's *One Hundred and Twenty Articles on Nature and the World Against the Aristotelians* and dedicate it to Henri III. At the end of his lecture, the Nolan stepped down from the podium and let Hennequin take his place to field the questions that were bound to arise from such a bold attack on the Philosopher. Indeed, a brash young French lawyer, Raoul Callier, arose to defend Aristotle, and did so forcefully enough to confound poor Hennequin, who naturally turned to Bruno for help—the offending lecture, after all, had been Bruno's, not his. But Bruno simply complained that it was late in the afternoon and tried to leave as Hennequin and his other students pulled on his sleeves and begged him to respond. At last, he agreed to return on the following day to debate Callier.

The reports of that debate are sketchy and evenly divided in handing the victory to Callier or to Bruno. They all agree, however, on the discussion's vitriolic tone. Corbinelli saw little hope for Bruno and his campaign against Aristotle: "I think he'll be stoned by this university. But he's heading soon for Germany."

As Corbinelli predicted, Bruno left Paris shortly afterward. He stopped first along the Rhine, at Mainz. Founded as a Roman military camp, the city still preserved some of its Roman ruins, as well as a beautiful Gothic cathedral in rust-red stone. But he failed to find a job, and moved on to Wiesbaden, and then to Marburg. There, he signed the register of the university on July 25, 1586, as "Iordanus Neapolitanus, Doctor of Roman Theology." This "Roman" qualification did not sit well with the university's Protestant rector, Petrus Nigidius, who forbade Bruno to lecture in public. The Nolan exploded, and as Nigidius reported: "He went so far as to insult me in my home as if I had acted against the public interest, the custom of all the universities of Germany, and the good of knowledge." The rector erased Bruno's name from the university register, noting in the margin that the erasure had been done "with the unanimous consensus of the faculty in philosophy." One of those faculty members, in turn, erased the rector's note; apparently the faculty was not so unanimous after all, nor the rector so universally popular. By then, however, the doctor of Roman theology was on his way to Wittenberg, the very town where, in 1517, Martin Luther had posted his Ninety-five Theses and ushered in the Reformation.

On August 20, 1586, "Iordanus Brunus Nolanus, Italian doctor" inscribed himself in the register of the University of Wittenberg, ready to see what the Lutheran version of the Reform might offer.

CHAPTER TWENTY-TWO

Consolation and Valediction

WITTENBERG, PRAGUE, AND HELMSTEDT, 1586–1589

It is immoral to hold an opinion in order to curry another's favor; mercenary, servile, and against the dignity of human liberty to yield and submit. —*One Hundred and Twenty Articles Against Mathematicians and Philosophers*

The bracing weather and northern light of Upper Saxony could not have made a stronger contrast with the "benign heaven" of Giordano Bruno's youth. The landscape around Naples had been shaped by subterranean fires, a chain of volcanic cones and craters, most of them eroded into jagged, precipitous crags. Germany was shaped by water, by rivers and streams snaking through gently rolling hills. Sprawling, neat half-timbered houses, barns, brooks, and fields emerged from the dense German woods that in their time had swallowed up whole Roman legions. The slopes above the Rhine near Mainz and Wiesbaden may have been famous for their vineyards, but Wittenberg was so far north that it could brew only beer. And, as always, there was an Italian in place, someone afflicted by the same wanderlust as Marco Polo, Christopher Columbus, Amerigo Vespucci, and Father Matteo Ricci, the Italian Jesuit who had just arrived in those days in China and would end his days as a mandarin in Beijing. In Wittenberg, the wandering Italian was a Protestant lawyer named Alberico Gentili.

Exiled from Italy because of his beliefs, Gentili had come to Oxford in 1580, where, with the help of a recommendation from the
Earl of Leicester, the university's chancellor, he secured a position
lecturing in civil law at St. John's College. He had heard Bruno's
lectures and was unimpressed: "I happen to have heard the most
false, absurd, and ridiculous things from the greatest of men . . . of
a moon that is a world with many cities and mountains, that the
earth moves, that other elements stand still, and countless similar
things." Despite his high connections in Elizabeth's court, Gentili
could tell his own tales of Oxford's hostility; in 1585, when he
mentioned his hopes to succeed to the highest position on the law
faculty, Regius Professor, his English colleagues (who were also his
rivals for the post) accused him of "Italian levity." Gentili then
threatened to leave England altogether, at least until Francis Walsingham secured him a temporary mission as secretary to the
queen's ambassador to Saxony, Giorgio Pallavicino—the plan was
to remove Gentili for a time until the situation at Oxford had settled. In Pallavicino's entourage, Gentili had arrived in Wittenberg
in the summer of 1586, not long before Bruno. It was long enough,
however, for the famous Italian jurist to use his influence on
Bruno's behalf, a sign that he had changed his mind about the
Nolan since their last encounter in 1583—the six Italian dialogues
and three new Latin works that Bruno had written in the ensuing
three years may have improved his opinion about the little philosopher. Gentili's own story had a happy ending: he would return to
Oxford the following year as Regius Professor of Civil Law, his am-
bition fulfilled.

Bruno's story had taken a happier turn as well. He responded to
his German colleagues and their hospitality with unusual warmth.
His admiration for German philosophers began with Nicolaus Cusanus and continued with Copernicus (whom he considered a German rather than a Pole), but he was no less impressed by the
openness of his colleagues at Wittenberg. His lectures at the university concentrated, in standard fashion, on readings from Aristotle. For the first time in his career, apparently, he presented a
course on rhetoric. Rhetoric provided Bruno with a perfect pretext
to introduce the art of memory but also to acquaint his Protestant

students with the refinements of public speaking that he had learned himself as a Dominican preacher in Naples. His own research concentrated on natural philosophy, and in the process he conceived a wary respect for the Swiss doctor and alchemist Paracelsus. He also gathered a coterie of students, many of whom would become serious professional scholars, including the physician Hieronymus Besler.

Bruno's gratitude to his new colleagues suffuses the preface to his next book, *The Llullian Combinatory Lamp*, printed in Wittenberg in 1587. He planned the work as the first of a series of *Lamps*, each one meant to shed light on a different aspect of the Nolan philosophy, and as he often did, he began with the secure terrain of his own art of memory. Despite his love for wild Neapolitan rhetoric, the tone he adopted to address his German colleagues was unusually positive and unusually sober. The professors of Wittenberg must have provided a striking—and welcome—contrast to the xenophobic mockery he had met in England, and he thanked them with rare humility:

> On behalf of such a university, the foremost in spacious, august, powerful Germany, the highest praises should be raised, where free and welcome access and residence is open, not only to students, but also, according to their talents, to professors from all of Europe (which is the sole mother and preserver of all the disciplines). Certainly in my own case, you received me from the beginning with such humanity, and kept me for a year with such hospitality, and have with such benevolence included me as your friend and colleague, so that anything could happen except that I should feel myself a stranger in your house . . . You took me in, accepted me, and have treated me kindly up to this very day, a man of no reputation among you for fame or worth, a refugee from the French wars, supported by no prince's recommendation, distinguished by no exterior signs (such as the crowd is wont to demand) . . . Thus (as is only right for the Athens of Germany), let me recognize what is truly a university.

After *The Llullian Combinatory Lamp* came a commentary on Aristotle, *On the Progress and Hunter's Lamp of the Logicians*, and *The Lamp of Thirty Statues*, a work on memory that he decided not to publish for the time being. (Preserved in two contemporary manuscript copies, one with Bruno's own notes, it was finally published for the first time in the nineteenth century.) If the Nolan philosopher seemed to be moving back to the subjects that had first captured his interest as a young scholar, he was doing so with the maturity of an experienced professor, a maturity that showed up both in his relentless emphasis on ever clearer methods of presentation and in genuine, if not entirely successful, attempts to tone down his combative personality, both in public and in print.

Bruno's idyll in Wittenberg lasted almost two years, and then, once again, the Wheel of Fortune began to move. Like most of the tiny states that made up Germany, Wittenberg was governed by a duke, whose privileges included electing the Holy Roman emperor (although generations of electors had simply chosen successive members of the Habsburg family). The city's moderate Lutheran politics had long reflected the convictions of Duke Augustus I, whose policies had made the University of Wittenberg into the "Athens of Germany," as Bruno described it. Augustus, however, died in 1586, shortly after Bruno's arrival. His son, Christian I, lacked his father's political skill; more ominously for the university's faculty, he preferred Calvin to Luther, and strictness to leniency. He began to pressure the Lutheran professors to change their creed. In 1587, Polycarp Leyser, one of the university's most illustrious professors, left the University of Wittenberg to head the Lutheran church of Braunschweig, complaining of persecution for his beliefs. Soon many of Bruno's closest colleagues admitted to feeling the same pressures as Leyser. As a diplomat of the English embassy, Alberico Gentili was relatively secure, but he soon returned to Anglican Oxford and his long-awaited Regius professorship.

Bruno knew that it was only a matter of time before someone unearthed his own history with the Calvinists, and so he decided to act on a tip. A friend, Nicodemus Frischlin, had passed through Wittenberg in 1587, bragging about earning a salary of three hundred talers a year in Prague, paid out by the king of Bohemia, Rudolf II. The Habsburg ruler of Austria, Hungary, Bohemia, and, nominally, parts of Germany, Rudolf nurtured passionate interests in astrology, magic, alchemy, and the arts, and had gathered a remarkable group of scholars and artists around him. He would eventually lure Tycho Brahe and Johannes Kepler to serve as his court mathematicians, but he had already attracted Tycho's sister Sophie, a superb mathematician in her own right, and her alchemist husband, Erik Lange. Rudolf's galleries included works by the fanciful Italian painter Giuseppe Arcimboldo, who painted strange images of people made from assemblages of fruit, grain, or fish, and the German Bartolomäus Spranger, whose erotic mythological allegories drew from Albrecht Dürer and from the stylish Florentines who had dominated Italian art since the mid-sixteenth century.

Educated as a strict Catholic in the Spanish court of his greatuncle Philip II, Rudolf tried with indifferent success to impose a Catholic regime in Prague, hindered by a largely Calvinist aristocracy in Bohemia and Lutherans in Germany and parts of Austria, as well as the city's fifteen thousand Jews, the second-largest Jewish community in Europe (after Salonica). His own antipathy to the Jesuits further hampered his efforts to create a Catholic state; as a result, the twice-excommunicated Bruno could hope, like Prague's other scholars, to work relatively undisturbed.

Before he left Wittenberg, on March 8, 1588, Bruno delivered a heartfelt farewell speech to his colleagues, the *Valedictory Oration*. It was both an expression of thanks and a forceful plea in favor of the society that Duke Augustus and his moderate Lutheran creed had managed to create. Bruno used the ancient Greek myth of the Judgment of Paris to describe the pursuit of philosophy that had led him to the north of Germany. The story began with the goddess Strife throwing a golden apple among the gods of Olympus, with the inscription "To the Fairest." Predictably, an argument erupted, with Juno, Venus, and Minerva each claiming her right to the apple. Finally the gods decided to appeal to a mortal judge, Paris, the handsome prince of Troy. Each goddess offered the young man a bribe for his vote: Juno promised power, Minerva wisdom, and Venus the most beautiful woman in the world. Never distinguished for his intellect, Paris chose Venus, and was soon packing off for Sparta to abduct that most beautiful woman, Helen of Sparta, and turn her into Helen of Troy—at least until her husband and an expedition of a thousand Greek ships set sail to take her back.

Bruno had already used the myth of the Judgment of Paris before, in his *Heroic Frenzies*, to show that philosophy participated in all three kinds of beauty and granted all three gifts:

> Venus, third heaven's goddess and the mother
> Of the blind archer, tamer of every heart,
> And she who had the Jovial head as father,
> And haughty Juno, Jupiter's counterpart,
> Call forth the Trojan shepherd to advise
> Which beauty should receive the golden prize.
> And yet if my own goddess were so tested
> Then Venus, Pallas, Juno would be bested.
>
> For pretty limbs the measure
> Is Cypria; Minerva for the mind;
> For Saturn's daughter, beauty's in the shine
>
> Of lofty rank, the Thunderer's chief pleasure.
> But she wins for all three:
> Beauty, intelligence, and majesty.

In Wittenberg, however, Bruno's oration moved swiftly from classical myth to Scripture. He quoted the Bible to show all the reasons for which he, unlike Paris, had chosen Minerva and wisdom as the fairest of goddesses. Ironically, he chose a biblical book, the Wisdom of Solomon, that most Protestants had rejected as apocryphal:

Hear Solomon: *And I preferred her before kingdoms and thrones, and esteemed riches nothing in comparison of her. Neither did I compare unto her any precious stone: for all gold in comparison of her, is as a little sand, and silver in respect to her shall be counted as clay. I loved her above health and beauty, and chose to have her instead of light: for her light cannot be put out . . . Her have I loved, and have sought her out from my youth, and have desired to take for my spouse, and I became a lover of her beauty.*

Bruno himself extended the biblical image to describe the University of Wittenberg as a house of wisdom, enumerating each of the liberal arts taught under its aegis, and then describing his own journey toward Saxony as a pilgrimage:

> I came myself among many others to see this house of wisdom, burning with ardor to see this Minerva, for whom I was not ashamed to suffer poverty, envy, and the hatred of my own people, curses, ingratitude of those I wanted to benefit, and benefited, the effects of extreme barbarism and sordid greed; from those who owed me love, service, and honor, accusations, slanders, insults, even infamy . . . but for her it has been no shame to suffer labor, pain, exile, because in laboring I improved, in suffering I became experienced, in exile I learned, for I found daily rest in brief labor, immense joy in slight pain, and a broad homeland in my narrow exile.

Soon afterward, the broad homeland of his narrow exile had expanded its horizons into the hills of Bohemia. After the imposing but spare Gothic architecture of Saxony, Prague was a blaze of ornament, with its forests of Gothic spires and gold leaf gleaming in the sunlight, and its great ornate cathedral dedicated to Saint Vitus, a figure familiar to Bruno from his youth in the Kingdom of Naples, where the saint's famous dance preserved the remnants of an ancient Greek orgiastic cult. But Bruno soon discovered that his friend Frischlin had exaggerated the amount of easy money to be earned in "golden Prague." Not all the emperor's choices for intellectual companionship were as inspired as Kepler, Tycho, and Arcimboldo; Rudolf had a weakness for charlatans and showmen as well as philosophers and artists. To be sure, he had turned a skeptical eye on the English scholar John Dee and his oleaginous assistant Edward Kelley, who had arrived at the end of a long journey from England in 1587. (Dee may have seen Bruno debate with John Underhill at Oxford in 1583 during the visit of the Polish prince Albert Laski.) Like Bruno, Dee was interested in mathematics, but he had become still more interested in probing the secrets of the universe by making direct contact with the supernatural world. Unable to make those contacts himself, he had hired a series of scryers, or crystal gazers, to act as his mediums. Of these characters, Kelley was by far the most gifted; he had introduced Dee to a series of angels, from the archangels Uriel and Michael to a mischievous imp named Madimi, who had revealed the course of current political events and dictated the elements of their angelic language. The two had followed Laski to Poland in 1583, proceeding on to Prague, with wives and children in tow, so that Dee could bring the emperor Rudolf an angelic command to repent of his sins. By the time Bruno arrived in the city, Dee and Kelley had been banished to the countryside, where they were quarreling fiercely: Kelley had convinced Dee that the angels were commanding them to share their wives.

Rudolf was not always so suspicious, but then most of the alchemists, kabbalists, and astrologers who flocked to his court were more circumspect than Dee had been. Often the emperor withdrew from his state responsibilities into conclaves with scholars and magicians. He hoped to construct an obelisk that would call down the power of the stars, and would shortly collaborate with a local rabbi to summon a golem, a spirit—which seems to have had mechanical components as well. Rudolf liked the concreteness of alchemical alembics, the traditional astronomical paraphernalia of astrolabes and sextants, and the giant instruments that Tycho Brahe was building on his island observatory in the Danish strait. In fact, Rudolf liked objects of every kind, and collected them with princely avidity: marvels of nature, monstrous creatures, gems, stone inlays, minerals, and lathe-turned ivory pinnacles (he would eventually be tutored himself in this art by the Nuremberg turner Peter Zick). In 1606, Rudolf's siblings would finally have him declared a madman and pass control of the Holy Roman Empire to his younger brother Matthias.

Bruno made his approach to the eccentric emperor through the Spanish ambassador, Don Guillén de Haro de San Clemente. Still, after all these years, Bruno counted as a citizen of Naples, for whom San Clemente was his official representative in Bohemia. As a calling card, he dedicated a short book to the diplomat, *On the Scrutiny of Species and the Combinatory Lamp of Ramon Llull*. It was another in his series of *Lamps*—in fact, he recycled literal pages, and most of the title, of one of his Wittenberg *Lamps*, *The Llullian Combinatory Lamp*, for this new publication. His letter of dedication made certain to emphasize the Catalan heritage that San Clemente shared with Llull, and the tribute worked well enough to obtain the Nolan philosopher an audience with Rudolf. Bruno must have hoped to impress the emperor on that occasion with his more intense recent interests, which included climate, the atmosphere, the microstructure of the universe, and the way that profound study of these subjects would require a new kind of mathematics. He dedicated his next book to Rudolf, with a polemical title: *One Hundred and Twenty Articles Against Mathematicians and Philosophers*. The letter of dedication was a striking document in itself, with its bleak account of the wreck that religious war had made of Europe, Bruno's expressed hopes that the Holy Roman emperor could help to set the turmoil right, and his profession of a religion beyond controversy:

> It happens that, against every reason, state, and nature, human law and consequently the true order of Almighty God instilled in all things, the bonds of nature lie unbound, and by the suggestion of misanthropic spirits and the ministry of hell's Furies (who fan the flames among nations rather than bringing peace, and insert the sword of dissent between those who are most closely joined, selling themselves as Mercurys descended from heaven among their tricks and their many pretenses), it has come to the point that humanity quarrels most of all with itself, and is more contested by itself than by any other living creature, and that law of love that is spread far and wide lies everywhere neglected, which derives not from some evil demon but certainly from God the father of all things, so that it is in harmony with all nature, and teaches a general philanthropy by which we love even our enemies, lest we become like brutes and barbarians, and are transformed into his image who makes his sun rise over good and bad, and pours out a rain of grace upon the just and the unjust. This is the religion that I observe, which is without controversy and beyond all dispute, whether of the spirit's inclination or the principle of ancestral or national custom.

As the *One Hundred and Twenty Articles* left the press in Prague, a sudden storm off the coast of France descended on Philip II's fleet, the Invincible Armada, launched to strike a mortal blow against Queen Elizabeth and her Protestant regime. Instead, it was the Catholic fleet that sank, opening the world to the British naval power, British colonialism, and British trade.

For his book, in the meantime, Rudolf paid Giordano Bruno three hundred talers. It was exactly the amount he had offered to Bruno's friend Nicodemus Frischlin, but in Frischlin's case the talers represented a salary; for the Nolan philosopher they were a onetime payment with no promise of any further support, and they were a terrible disappointment. On the other hand, he had offered the emperor a work that was singularly difficult to interpret. It began by presenting the elements of geometry and ended with a series of enigmatic woodcuts, most of them geometric designs with strange names like "The Ray of Thoth," "Mirror of Magicians," some pictures of objects—a snake labeled "Prometheus," a lute called "Mother of Life"—and many illustrations with no label at all. Bruno was still trying to find a way to analyze the infinite universe. The art of memory gave him a way to obtain very large numbers; geometry gave him a way to describe infinitesimals. He needed both infinitely large numbers and infinitely small intervals to describe the actions of the universe, and the *One Hundred and Twenty Articles* tried to link all these ideas into a single coherent system. The effort was only partially successful, but on another front Bruno expressed himself with unprecedented clarity.

His letter of dedication to the emperor Rudolf links the liberal arts to "the dignity of human liberty," a reminder that the root underlying both words is *liber*, the Latin word for "free":

> As for the liberal arts, may I be spared habits of belief and the traditions of teachers or parents, along with that common sense that (in my judgment) convinces us, many times and in many ways, to deceive and circle around the point, so that I shall never make any philosophical pronouncement that is bold or unreasoned . . . It is immoral to hold an opinion in order to curry another's favor; mercenary, servile, and against the dignity of human liberty to yield and submit; supremely stupid to believe as a matter of habit; irrational to decide according to the majority opinion, as if the number of sages exceeded the infinite number of fools . . . Endowed with the eyes of sense and intelligence by the bounty of Almighty God, and therefore confirmed as judge and jury in the matter, I would be ungrateful and insane, unworthy of that participation in light, if I were to act as agent and champion for someone else, seeing, perceiving, and judging by another's lights.

It was a remarkable set of assertions to make to an emperor. Machiavelli's *Prince* may have advised princes to shun flatterers, but few monarchs have ever followed Machiavelli's advice, including the Holy Roman emperor Rudolf II. As the autumn leaves began to turn, marking the start of another academic year, Bruno packed his trunk and headed back to Germany, to Tübingen, a beautiful little city set within the forests of the Swabian Alps. By November 17, 1588, he had been inscribed in the University of Tübingen's books as "some Italian" (*Italus quidam*), forbidden to give public lectures, granted permission to lecture privately, and told that if he simply moved on altogether he would be given a bit of money "for humanitarian purposes." Four days later, Martin Crusius, the school's professor of rhetoric, recalled: "On November 21, Signor Giordano Bruno, Italian of Nola (who was teaching privately at Wittenberg), told me that because Frischlin bragged about having received three hundred talers a year from the emperor, he had believed him, and gone to Prague in hopes of receiving the same treatment from the emperor, but to no avail."

By January 1589, the "Italian of Nola" had returned to Saxony, this time to the Lutheran city of Helmstedt, whose ruler, Julius, Duke of Braunschweig and Lüneburg, had lent his name and his Lutheran leanings to the local university, the Academia Julia (unfortunately for Bruno, the Academia's beautifully airy sixteenth-century lecture hall was built just after he left). Helmstedt is not far from Wittenberg, and soon Bruno's student Hieronymus Besler came to join him. Besler's own interest in magic prompted Bruno to draw up outlines for several courses on the subject, as we can see from a manuscript (made up of several different works bound together at a later date) now preserved in the National Library of Moscow. Most of these texts are in Besler's handwriting, with marginal comments and some brief passages by Bruno and several pages by another, unknown, copyist. The papers, their arrangement, and their meaning are not easy to sort out, for they show Bruno's thought, never simple, as it has been filtered through Besler, a scholar with his own share of complex ideas. They may be lecture notes, they may be the prospectus for a book, they may be both. It is equally difficult to assess their importance as a record of Bruno's thought, although the fact that they were never published may indicate that Bruno regarded his other works in progress as more urgent.

The very meaning of magic itself is not easy to define in these papers. On Mathematical Magic sets out a general outline of the principles on which magic depends:

> God flows into the angels, the angels into the heavenly bodies, the heavenly bodies into the elements, the elements into compounds, compounds into the senses, the senses into the spirit, the spirit into the living creature [Bruno uses the word "animal"]; the living creature ascends through the spirit to sense, through sense to compounds, through compounds to elements, through elements to the heavens, through them into the demons and angels, through them to God or into divine operations. Thus the descent of God or from God is through the world to the living creature; the living creature's ascent is through the world to God.

The next paragraphs of On Mathematical Magic explicitly mention both Plato and the Hebrew Kabbalah as ways to understand this transit back and forth between God and the world, both God's descent into living creatures and living creatures' ascent toward God. Bruno had already described the experience of the philosopher-lovers in The Heroic Frenzies as a similar meeting between divine emanation and human aspiration.

> I, for the exaltation of my goal
> Though once the least of men, reach godly height . . .
> And I (with thanks to Love)
> Change from inferior form to a god above.

The first paragraph of On Mathematical Magic is one of the only places that Bruno mentions angels. His heavens are usually filled to bursting instead with stars and suns and earths, those great animals of the firmament, far greater than the demons and messengers of traditional Christian theology. This is one of many clues that On Mathematical Magic is meant to lay out a conventional course of study rather than marking a new, magical stage in the Nolan philosophy. Magic had always been a part of his "natural and physical discourse," but that discourse was, pointedly, natural and physical, and it depended absolutely on adjusting to the realities of the infinite universe. As a result, Bruno's definition of magic brought him closer to Tycho Brahe's observatory than to John Dee's conversations with angels. When we read another of his magical works, *On Bonds in General*, it is important to remember that modern chemists use this same term to describe the pull of one atom on another within a molecule.

At the same time that Hieronymus Besler was drafting the magical works that would interest him for the rest of his own career, another student of Bruno's was at work on reading Paracelsus. That unnamed student's marginal notes are still preserved in a copy of Paracelsus in the library at Wolfenbüttel, where many of the books from the Academia Julia of Helmstedt eventually ended up, and on occasion they sound remarkably like his teacher:

> Whoever comes across this book should prepare his mind for understanding; nor should he defame perversely and furiously by bold, hasty judgment what cannot be grasped by a first look. Let him imitate the alchemists who finally in their seventh operation obtain gold or gems. For here, too, on the seventh reading the reader will soberly perceive the author's intentions and praise them, just as assayers of goods let the needle of their judgment waver until it finds its balance . . . There is nothing absurd, nothing obscure, nothing impious in this book, except to mules and asses . . . For in this book the true and certain wisdom is described . . . And there is nothing doubtful. Whoever arrogantly and disdainfully spurns this deep philosophy knows little or nothing, or else maliciously and willfully fights the truth . . .
>
> Don't miss the preface, reader.

Many of the magical operations that Bruno describes, especially those that fall under the category of "Natural Magic," come closer to scientific experiments than they do to the scrying and incantations by which John Dee's assistants called up angels. Bruno did retain a magician's attachment to signs and seals, but he associated these images with using his art of memory, which, in an age before computers, was the most massive and reliable device available for storing information. But he must also have regarded his memory as capable of greater feats than the simple retrieval of facts. In one enigmatic passage of *On Mathematical Magic*, he claims that the signs and seals of that art can be used to act "against nature":

> The things that seem appropriate to this art are such that they can be seen in action in natural actions; that is, signs, notes, characters, and seals, in which it is possible, as seems appropriate, to act outside nature, above nature, and, if the business requires it, against nature.

He spent most of his time, however, trying to convince the rest of the world that nature itself was larger and more complex than they had ever imagined.

In May, Duke Julius died, and Bruno offered a funeral oration in his honor as a way of making himself known to a larger public in Helmstedt; to guarantee its effect, he published the text of this *Consolatory Oration* with a local printer. Again, the theme of wandering and exile is prominent:

> This supreme concern and anxious care trouble me; I greatly fear that someone . . . will misinterpret what an obscure foreigner, whose purpose among you is unclear, should of my own volition, recognized by no one (as it seems) or encouraged to intrude on your mourning . . .

Yet intrude he must, Bruno insists, for he could not be called a lover of the arts if he did not praise Julius and the Academia Julia, where no lover of wisdom is made to feel unwelcome.

As an added flourish for his German audience, Bruno added a frontal attack on the Catholic Church, taking up the imagery of a redesigned heaven from his *Expulsion of the Triumphant Beast* to depict a firmament inscribed with the virtues of Duke Julius. This time, however, the Triumphant Beast is not some generic embodiment of vice but the pope in person, Sixtus V incarnate as the head of the Gorgon Medusa:

> That severed head of the Gorgon, in which snakes are implanted in place of hair, is the manifestation of the perverse tyranny of the pope, whose

blasphemous tongues, more numerous than the hairs of her head, assist and administer, every one of them, against God, Nature, and humanity, who infect the world for the worst with their poison of ignorance and depravity, which we see cut off and weeded out by your virtue in these regions. That diamond-hard sword, red with the slaughter of the monster, is the constancy of an invincible mind, by which you slew that horrible beast.

The speech apparently pleased the new duke, Heinrich Julius, who continued to support Bruno just as his father had done. But in other ways, history in Saxony began to repeat itself. After his father's death, Heinrich Julius proved powerless against the wranglings for power of Helmstedt's head Lutheran pastor, Gilbert Voët, who took a hard line against dissent of any kind, and against Bruno in particular. For reasons that are no longer entirely clear (and seem to have included intense personal dislike), Voët subjected the Nolan to a public writ of excommunication—remarkably, he charged Bruno with harboring Calvinist beliefs.

To counteract the harsh judgments of his head pastor, Duke Heinrich Julius received Bruno and Besler at his riverside palace in Wolfenbüttel, a stately little classical building whose rows of wooden columns quaintly mimic ancient marble. The visit was more than symbolic; on the same occasion, Heinrich Julius also gave Bruno a gift of forty florins, obviously aware that the Nolan was planning to resume his travels. Bruno and Besler discussed a transfer to Magdeburg, where they could stay with Besler's uncle, but from Bruno's own standpoint the most promising destination seemed to be Frankfurt, with its book fair, its publishers, and its staunch independence of any imposed creed—the printers and the fair thrived on Frankfurt's policy of tolerance. For once, Bruno felt a stronger need to be near a publisher than a university; since his days in England, he had been writing a large work on the structure of the universe, and he was nearly ready to see it through the press. The Frankfurt book fairs provided an incomparable market for any writer, but especially for one who needed money. To Frankfurt he went at last, in the spring of 1589.

CHAPTER TWENTY-THREE

Infinities

FRANKFURT AND ZURICH, 1589–1591

Love hides in molecular structures.   —Jim Morrison

A t the same time that he wrote his Italian dialogues in England, Bruno began putting his thoughts on the universe into Latin verse. His model was the ancient Roman philosopher Lucretius, who had also chosen to cast his ideas into Latin poetry, and not just any poetry. Lucretius's *On the Nature of Things* (*De rerum natura*) is written in dactylic hexameter, the meter that Greeks and Romans used for epic. In ancient Rome, especially among the ambitious patricians of the late Roman Republic and early empire, poetry was particularly popular if it had an educational slant. Most people could only read aloud, and they especially enjoyed reading in company, taking turns with reading and listening. For wealthy Romans, learning astronomy, philosophy, or gardening through a poetic text promised to combine business with pleasure—though not perhaps to the point of trying to build a plow from the poetic directions that Virgil gave in his *Georgics*. It was no easy task to press Latin into a set of poetic meters originally invented for Greek, a language with a different repertory of sounds and a host of one-syllable words, but Lucretius acquitted himself remarkably well, especially in view of his intractable subject matter: atomic theory and the Epicurean philosophy of calm detachment from the world and its folly.

Unlike Lucretius, Bruno could never quite make his Latin lyrical; whenever he seems to have succeeded, the melodious phrase turns out to have been borrowed from Virgil, or Horace, or Lucretius himself. He must have recognized that much of his own poetry was impossibly obscure, for he supplied almost every passage of his Latin poems with a prose explanation of what it was he had just tried to say in verse. Yet for all their obscurities, his poems, three of them in all, were not only published, in Frankfurt in 1591, but also read, by Germans in particular, including Kepler, Leibniz, and the Jesuit scholar Athanasius Kircher. By this unusual means, some of Bruno's most radical ideas were transmitted to generations of readers in their most developed form.

Like most early modern writers, for whom paper was expensive and printing even more so, Bruno did not edit himself much by modern standards. He may have corrected individual proof sheets with fanatical care, but he still printed a good deal of what he wrote without cutting or rewriting, leaving a trail of clues both to his physical wanderings and to the steady development (and occasional meandering) of his ideas. Thus traces of local color and earlier ideas in the last of his poems to be published, *On the Immense and the Numberless*, show that it must also have been the first one he started to write, perhaps already in Paris in 1582, and certainly by the time he arrived in England. In fact, he published it before he had managed to complete all its lines of verse—but then, Virgil's great epic, *The Aeneid*, also unfinished, has some of the same tantalizing gaps.

On the Immense traced a biography of the universe, but also, at the same time, of Bruno himself. He recalls his childhood in Nola, when he believed that the world ended beyond Mount Vesuvius, and repeatedly describes the philosophy of Aristotle as "puerile," because he himself was a boy when he learned it and marked his manhood by the moment when he rejected it. The change that Giordano Bruno underwent at age thirty may well have referred to the moment when he exchanged a conventional "puerile" idea of the cosmos for a vision of infinity. In *On the Immense*, he admits that he spent his youth believing what he was taught in school, and credits the fifteenth-century German cardinal Nicolaus Cusanus with finally opening his eyes to the realities of the cosmos. But Bruno's vision of an infinite universe went far beyond anything

Cusanus suggested, not least because Bruno saw that such an idea would have cataclysmic implications for the understanding of mathematics in his own day.

As an adult, he had put away childish beliefs, but in *On the Immense* he no longer refers to a moment of sudden revelation. He had lived with his infinite universe too long to be galvanized anymore by its novelty; it had simply become his way of seeing, and he seems more preoccupied by what its mathematics will be than by its effects on his personal life. If he followed his philosophy to its ultimate implications, the man Giordano Bruno was only a temporary conglomeration of atoms in the great sea of the world-soul.

Atoms were the last piece of the Nolan philosophy to fall into place, the minimum particles that composed his boundless universe, and they only appear as a fully developed aspect of the Nolan philosophy in 1591. Bruno may have begun *On the Immense* first among his three Latin poems, but the one he was so eager to publish in Frankfurt was his discussion of atoms, *On the Triple Minimum*, because it was in this poem that he finally managed to put atomic theory at the heart of his cosmic system.

Many of Bruno's most revolutionary ideas had already been ventured by ancient Greek philosophers. Aristarchus of Samos had proposed a solar system (appropriately, in Hellenistic Egypt, the land of the sun god). The Greek philosopher Democritus of Abdera had been the first person to use the term *atoma*, "things uncut," to denote the smallest particles of matter, but the Roman Lucretius was atomic theory's most eloquent ancient spokesman.

But the ancients had confronted nature by using a mathematics that relied on geometry and numerology, contemplating the individual characters of numbers rather than subjecting them to arithmetical, and especially algebraic, operations. Bruno himself never had a mathematician's instinct for calculation, but he did have a sense of what calculation might do. Lacking algebraic formulas for those operations, he resorted instead to diagrams that were meant to illustrate the ways of nature to those readers erudite enough to penetrate poetry, prose, and graphics. *On the Triple Minimum* uses precisely this combination to show how the infinite universe is built, throughout its entire vast extent, of tiny particles floating within a field of energy that he describes variously as a soul, as love, as an ocean.

The Nolan philosopher had never written for a large public (how could he, writing Italian vernacular in France and Britain?), but his Frankfurt poems aimed at a still more restricted readership. "I write for other than the crowd," he declared in *On the Immense*, echoing the Roman poet Horace's declaration "I hate the profane crowd and shun it." In Frankfurt, he took up lodgings in a Dominican convent, but as a lay boarder rather than a friar, and spent his time with printers and booksellers. As always, the book fair attracted a large number of Italians, who brought him news of the death of Pope Sixtus V and of the conclave that eventually elected Clement VIII, the former Cardinal Aldobrandini. They all nourished high expectations for the new pope.

Bruno continued to refine his "natural and physical discourse" in a second poem, *On the Monad*, published shortly after *On the Triple Minimum*, and finally in *On the Immense*. "Monad" means "unit of one"; it was a term also used by John Dee in his book *The Hieroglyphic Monad* of 1564, in which the English magician combined all the planetary symbols in one (and would be used again by Leibniz in the following century). Bruno had already discussed the oneness of the world's creator in his Italian dialogue *Cause, Principle, and Unity*, but now he linked his ideas to atomic theory, adding further points to the contrast between the unity of God and the universe and the incalculable variety of the particles and creatures within that universe. *On the Monad* then proceeded to list the qualities and virtues of two, three, four, five, six, seven, eight, nine, and ten. Like Pythagoras, Bruno saw mathematics primarily through geometry and numerology. It was not yet easy to see how to combine geometry with calculation, but that combination would prove to unlock more secrets of the infinite universe than any other— and also of its infinitesimal counterpart.

Democritus and Lucretius had called atoms "seeds of things," and Bruno borrowed the same term (*semina rerum*) from the Latin poet. These seeds mixed and matched in an eternally oscillating exchange of forms and compounds that Bruno called "vicissitude" (but has been translated in this book as "oscillation"). The only stable feature of this shifting universe was God, an all-pervading world-soul that Bruno likened to the ocean and sometimes personified in the sea queen Amphitrite, an image he once used for Queen Elizabeth, but had transformed long since into a cosmic principle. At the end of *On the Immense*, he calls this innermost property of all things

> Principle of existence, wellspring of every species,
> Mind, God, Being, One, Truth, Destiny, Reason, Order.

The four elements, whose atoms, charged by heat or sluggish from cold (a legacy from Bernardino Telesio), mingled together in various, ever-changing compounds throughout the infinite reaches of space. As *On the Immense* put it, in Lucretian dactylic hexameters:

> Never shall you see the face of immense and starry Olympus
> Come to an end, rather space fills what it continues conceiving
> Stars without number, indeed, whole worlds of these wandering bodies
> Nor can you think that of these a single one is less fertile
> Than earth, for all are compacted of the identical elements.
> Of such does measureless space shine by the splendor of starlight.

Following Telesio, Bruno divided the cosmos into two types of heavenly bodies, hot stars—suns—orbited by colder planets, which Bruno called "earths" in *On the Immense*:

> Sun and Earth are the primal animals, first among species
> Of things, and from the primal elements they have been fashioned;
> They in themselves contain the archetype of every compound,
> Whence all the dry parts conjoin with all the parts that are humid,
> And in amid them thereafter, when air has been interjected,
> Then they create great caverns, of ever burgeoning vastness.
> Thus what lies latent in small scale can be observed when it's larger;
> What may be hidden in parts may be revealed in its wholeness.

The fixed stars were only fixed, Bruno declared, from our own point of view, so distantly removed from them that their motions were imperceptible. It was absurd to think that such a massive system would make a complete rotation about the earth every twenty-four hours. *On the Immense* asks:

> Isn't it the mother of all follies
> That this infinite space, with no observable limits,
> Laid out in numberless worlds (stars is how we define them),
> Large enough of themselves to be fully self-sufficient . . .
> Should be creating but one single continuous orbit
> Around this point, rotating in such measureless circles
> In such a short span of time?

In addition to infinite space, Bruno touched upon the concept of infinite time, although he seems not to have made much of it. In one of the prose explanations that accompany the verse of *On the Immense*, he says: "Now, if you please, ask me: Where is place, space, vacuum, time, body? In the universe. Where is the universe? In every place, space, time, body. Is there anything outside the universe? No. Why? Because there is no place nor space nor motion nor body."

In this last exchange, in effect, time becomes subsumed in motion and disappears from his account. As for the fullness of time and God's eternity, these, of course, are both standard features of Christian doctrine. But it is difficult to see Bruno, who loved reversals of time, place, and substance, failing to face the prospect of an infinite time past, whether infinite in our own eyes or infinite absolutely. Once again, *On the Immense* tantalizes:

> Past time or present, whichever you happen to choose, or the future:
> All are a single present, before God an unending oneness.
> Hence contradictory things can never persist at the same time . . .
> Everything, when it is, because it is, must exist, then.
> God chooses what he wants, he grants it, he knows it, creates it;
> He cannot change himself, nor can he deny his own judgment:
> What he wills always is one; his will is one with his power.
> Nothing can ever be done without his willing its doing,
> For he is fate itself; he is the divine will in person.

This "unending oneness" does not sound like a universe created only six thousand years earlier, as strict interpretation of the Bible had encouraged most contemporary Christians to believe. Nor was Bruno the only thinker to wonder about the age of the earth. It was risky, however, to express any such doubts openly in either Catholic or Protestant circles. Even Bruno seems to avoid raising the problem explicitly.

It was equally risky to suggest, as Bruno did in one of the passages already cited, that this unending universe carried the seeds of its own propagation everywhere, as the atoms that were the "seeds of things" tumbled through the world-soul that gave their compounds the spark of life. Like Lucretius before him and Athanasius Kircher afterward, Bruno beheld a world that, because of these seeds and the loving world-soul that surrounded them, was not only infinitely immense but infinitely sexual:

> Bacchus and Ceres are thus; the Sun and the Earth, too: as neighbors
> Hidden from our senses' reach, they clinch in amazing embraces.
> These are the beautiful seeds of God; these the excellent prime source
> Of offspring up to the present tally of each of the species,
> Everywhere that they touch the fecund thighs of the mother
> With their dew . . .

He continues:

> Now, this sex among gods is of a condition far better
> Than our own: as for us, the gentle power of pleasure
> Lasts a short while; moreover, the mounting force of our ardor
> Breaks forth at once, in only one part of ourselves, whereas Earth can
> Revel in every part, can revel in pleasure forever,
> Ceaselessly, as her rotation affords her a thousand positions.

The idea of a universal divine fertility argued against the basic principle of Christianity: that God had become incarnate only once, at the birth of Jesus Christ; in Bruno's world, God was everywhere and everywhere incarnate, although Bruno also seems to have thought, like Pythagoras, that souls, once embodied, were immortal, destined to endless reincarnation. Another central Christian mystery, transubstantiation, the transformation of the Host into the body of Christ, in Bruno's cosmos was not a miracle that occurred only at Mass through the agency of an officiating priest. As a practicing Dominican priest, he had certainly effected that transformation repeatedly, but in his developed philosophy change of substance was the constant order of nature, and there was no reason to single out some specific moment in God's boundless continuum. Neither did Bruno any longer see the need for the singular incarnation of God in Jesus Christ during the early years of the Roman Empire in order to save humanity from primal sin: God was present in everything, everywhere, always. So was heaven. Humanity needed to be saved less from primal sin than from primal stupidity, to recognize the divinity within itself and in the whole world outside. Bruno thinks of his soul as flying free through the "ethereal country" of the universe, no longer hampered by the fear of death or any other evil. It is the same journey the philosopher-lover made in *The Heroic Frenzies*, but carried, if anything, to a further degree:

> Hence, as I make my journey, secure and sufficiently happy,
> Suddenly I am raised aloft by primordial passion;
> I become Leader, Law, Light, Prophet, Father, Author, and Journey,
> Rising above this world to the others that shine in their splendor.
> I wander through every part of that ethereal country;
> Then, far away, as they gape at the marvel, I leave them behind me.

Bruno's cosmology brought other repercussions as well. Although the preface to *On the Immense* effusively praises the Duke of Braunschweig-Anhalt, the poem itself suggests that Bruno is looking elsewhere for the true "example of civilization and love of virtue" that he claims to identify in Heinrich Julius.

For Bruno's universe is a republic of stars, not a monarchy, in which all stars are created equal, all circled by equal "earths"— Bruno insists vehemently on their sameness, going so far as to deny that the retrograde motion of Mercury and Venus proves their closer proximity to the sun.

It may have been that state of mind that took him to Zurich, on

the German-speaking side of Switzerland, far from French-speaking
Geneva and its Calvinists. At the Frankfurt book fair in the fall of
1590, he had met two noblemen from that city who invited him to
teach a series of courses. His stay in Zurich lasted for five months;
one of the two noblemen, Raphael Eglin, would eventually publish
the notes from one of those courses as the *Summary of Metaphysical
Terms*. Bruno then returned to Frankfurt to publish two more
works: *On Bonds in General* and *On the Composition of Images*, his
last foray into the art of memory. His position in the German-
speaking world looked promising, both in Frankfurt and in Zurich.
And yet, in 1591, he made an entirely unexpected move: he returned to Italy.

Return to Italy

PADUA AND VENICE, 1591

O God, I could be bounded in a nutshell and count myself a king of
infinite space—were it not that I have bad dreams.

—*Hamlet*, 2.2.254–56

B runo's first destination in Italy was Padua, whose university
had been famous as a haven for free thought since its foundation, in 1222, by a group of students determined to break
away from the University of Bologna. In their new setting, the students chartered their own institution, independent of kings, popes,
or bishops, and because Padua lay just across the lagoon from the
equally independent Venetian Republic, the University of Padua
soon became the de facto University of Venice. From that moment
onward, it has stood as a bastion of liberty, protecting its professors
and students from the Inquisition, admitting Jews during centuries
of rampant anti-Semitism, awarding the first degree ever granted to
a woman, the Venetian noblewoman Elena Lucrezia Cornaro Piscopia, doctor of philosophy, in 1678. Foreign students were welcome at Padua from the beginning, at a time when the usual Italian
term for German was *barbarus* and the Swedes were known as
Goths. At Padua, therefore, Bruno maintained his international
contacts, moving as easily among Germans as among Italians. He
renewed his close association with his former students Hieronymus

Besler, from Helmstedt, and Raphael Eglin, from Zurich. But he also had Italian contacts, notably Giovanni Vincenzo Pinelli, the correspondent of Jacopo Corbinelli, his friend from Paris.

He would have learned quickly, if he did not know already, that the university hoped to appoint a new professor in mathematics, and Bruno adapted to the situation by lecturing on mathematics and writing two short treatises on mathematical subjects during his stay, *Readings on Geometry* and *The Art of Deformations*. As these works show, he continued to see mathematics in visual, geometric terms rather than in terms of calculation, or, as would prove to be crucial in Padua, of observational astronomy.

For the chair in mathematics went, two years later, to a candidate from Pisa, Galileo Galilei, as sharp-tongued as Bruno and like him a writer and draftsman of uncommon brilliance, but also, most important of all, a meticulous observer of nature as well as a philosophical speculator. By then, the Nolan was long gone; within a few months he had moved on to Venice. Several months earlier, a Venetian nobleman, Giovanni Mocenigo, had sent Bruno a letter in Frankfurt, asking him for private lessons in the art of memory. Tutoring had never been Bruno's first choice of work, nor could Mocenigo have been his first choice among patrons; his sojourn in Padua shows that the offer was probably a last resort. Even after he had accepted Mocenigo's invitation, Bruno initially kept his distance, living for a time in rented rooms. Eventually, however, he moved into the Ca' Grande, or "Big House," the powerful family's palazzo on the Grand Canal.

Together the two men went to learned gatherings at the palazzo of another, still more distinguished nobleman, Andrea Morosini, to discuss the broad range of subjects that could be considered philosophy at the end of the sixteenth century. Bruno also wandered among the Venetian bookshops, talking to the printers and their customers.

The city must have been a congenial place to a wanderer as sophisticated and well traveled as the Nolan. A merchant republic whose lagoon marked the intersection of several important religious and linguistic borders, Venice treated its residents, permanent and temporary, with conspicuous tolerance; the world's trade in cloth and spices depended on the continuing ability of Turkish Muslims, German Protestants, Levantine Jews, and Venetian Catholics to strike deals with one another, and there were few ports on earth better placed geographically to receive them all. As a general rule, the Venetians let the Muslims live as Muslims, the Jews as Jews, the Protestants as Protestants; fear and discomfiture were bad for business. The ubiquitous mix of religions, dress, and skin colors seems to have made such an inveterate outsider as Giordano Bruno feel less isolated; he began to hear Mass in two grand Gothic churches: Santo Stefano near the Palazzo Mocenigo, and his old haunt, San Zanipolo. Surrounded by the tombs of the doges and paintings by Bellini and Paolo Veronese, and surely surrounded by equally luxuriant music, Bruno listened to Mass, but held back, as ever, from taking Communion. That carefully observed restriction, the literal expression of his Catholic excommunication, clearly bothered him, and once again, as at the very start of his wanderings, he inquired about full readmission into the Church—and this time, he spoke with a Dominican. In the free air of Venice it must all have seemed possible.

In May 1592, as Fra Domenico da Nocera left the sacristy of San Zanipolo, he saw a layman approaching him. At first the man looked unfamiliar, but gradually Fra Domenico, who was regent of the College of San Domenico Maggiore in Naples, recognized his former brother Fra Giordano da Nola. The two of them withdrew to a corner of the huge church, and there Bruno told the story of his life, his presumed defrocking, his contacts with kings, queens, and princes, and his plans. As Fra Domenico eventually reported to the Inquisition:

> He resolved to settle down and put his efforts into composing a book that he had in mind, and to present it, accompanied by the proper recommendations, to the pope; and to obtain from him a pardon for what he had expressed to quiet his conscience, and, finally, the ability to live in Rome, and devote himself to writing and show his abilities and perhaps to obtain a lecture or two.

Fra Domenico also noted, pointedly, that Bruno had always lived "in a Catholic manner."

In his own testimony, Bruno supplied the name of this prospec-

tive book: *On the Seven Liberal Arts*. With its help, as he would
eventually tell his inquisitors, he hoped to capture the pontiff's attention both for the Nolan philosophy and for his own situation:

> I was going to go to Frankfurt again, leaving here, to print some of my
> other works, and one in particular, *On the Seven Liberal Arts*, with the
> idea of taking these and some of my other printed works that I approve of
> (because there are some I don't approve of), and go to present them at
> the feet of His Beatitude, as I understand that he loves people of talent,
> and explain my situation to him, and try to obtain absolution from my
> excesses and the right to wear a clerical habit, but live outside the con-
> vent.

He had already used the theme of the seven liberal arts in his
farewell address to the University of Wittenberg, expounding on
the different ways in which these disciplines, and the university itself, provided a home for wisdom. Perhaps he intended to develop
a similar picture of Clement's pontificate, launching barbs against
Protestant intolerance rather than "the perverse tyranny of the
pope" (as he had in Helmstedt). We will probably never know, because the Nolan's plans to leave again for Frankfurt aroused deep
suspicions in his Venetian host, Giovanni Mocenigo.

As Bruno's works on memory insist from the beginning to the
end of his career, the art was not an easy one to master. It took constant application to learn it and constant exercise to preserve it. A
Venetian patrician like Mocenigo had many other demands on his
time and concentration, and nothing in Mocenigo's subsequent
history suggests that he was either outstandingly bright or outstandingly disciplined in the first place. After seven or eight
months, he began to feel that Bruno was cheating him, taking his
money and accepting his hospitality while holding back the real secrets of the art. They had begun to get on each other's nerves, not
least, Mocenigo family tradition suggests, because Bruno was all too
attentive to Mocenigo's wife.

Bruno himself recounts what happened next:

> It seems to me that I had done enough and taught him what I should on
> the basis of what he had asked me, and therefore I planned to return to

Frankfurt to publish certain works of mine, and on Thursday last I asked his permission to leave. And he, hearing this, and suspecting that I really intended to leave his house to teach the same arts that I have taught him, and more, rather than go to Frankfurt as I said, he pressed me to stay, and when I continued to insist that I wanted to leave, first he began to complain that I had never taught him as much as I had promised, and then he threatened me by telling me that if I did not stay with him of my own free will, he would find a way to make me stay. And the next night, which was Friday, when Signor Giovanni saw that I was still resolved to leave, and that I had already packed my things and arranged to ship them to Frankfurt, he came to see me when I was in bed, with the excuse that he wanted to talk to me, and once he had entered, his servant, named Bortolo, joined him, along with five or six others; I think they were some of the gondoliers who are stationed nearby. And they lifted me out of my bed and carried me up to an attic, and locked me in that attic, while Signor Giovanni told me that if I wanted to stay and teach him the terms for memorizing words, and the terms for geometry, as he had asked earlier, then he would let me out, but otherwise something unpleasant would happen to me. And I replied that I had taught him enough and more than I was obliged to, and that I did not deserve to be treated like this. He left me until the next day, when a captain came with certain men I didn't recognize, and they took me with them to the ground floor of the house, to a storeroom, where they left me until nightfall, and then another captain came with his assistants, and they took me to the prisons of this Holy Office, where I believe I have been brought by the efforts of Signor Giovanni, who, offended by what I have already said, I believe may have reported something about me.

Bruno was right. On May 23, 1592, as Giordano Bruno sat locked in one of his storerooms, Giovanni Mocenigo first went to his confessor, and then drafted a letter to the Inquisition in his large, assertive handwriting, trembling with an anger that sometimes made him press his pen into the paper with particular fury:

I, Zuane Mocenigo, report by obligation of my conscience and order of my confessor that I have heard Giordano Bruno of Nola say, while conversing in my home: that it is a great blasphemy for Catholics to say that bread transmutes into flesh, that he is an enemy to the Mass, that no reli-

gion pleases him, that Christ was a wretch, and that if he did such
wretched work as deluding the people, he could easily have predicted that
he would be hanged, that God has no distinction of persons, as this would
constitute an imperfection in God, that the world is eternal and that
there are infinite worlds, because he says that he wants to do what he is
able to do, that Christ performed apparent miracles and was a magician,
and likewise the apostles, and he had a mind to do as much as they and
more, that Christ showed reluctance to die, and fled death as long as he
could, that there is no punishment of sins, and that the souls created by
nature pass from one animal, and that just as brute animals are born by
spontaneous generation, so are human beings when they are born again
after a flood. He revealed plans to make himself the head of a new sect
under the name of a new philosophy, he said that the Virgin could not
have given birth, that our Catholic faith is full of blasphemies against
God, that friars should have neither the right to debate nor incomes, because they pollute the world and are all asses, that our opinions are the
teaching of asses, that we have no proof that our faith finds merit with
God, and that to lead a good life it is enough to do to others as we would
have them do to us, and that he laughs at all the other sins, and he marvels that God can bear such heresies from Catholics. He says he wants to
tend to the art of divination, and draw the whole world behind him, that
Saint Thomas and all the doctors of the Church know nothing in comparison with him, and he would so enlighten all the best theologians in
the world that they would have not a word to say to him . . . And I rever-
ently kiss the hands of your Reverend Paternity. At home, May 23, 1592

The accusations go on for three pages. Two days later, when
Bruno was already in custody, Mocenigo wrote a second letter:

On that day, when I kept Iordano Bruno under lock and key . . . he told
me that he didn't fear the Inquisition, because he offended no one living
as he did, and he never remembered saying anything bad to me . . . And
because you have done me a great favor by pardoning the lateness of my
accusation, I beg you to excuse it also among those most illustrious lords
[of the Inquisition] with every respect for my good intentions and because
it was impossible for me to bring up everything at one moment, except for
the fact that I had no idea of the man's depravity until I hosted him in my

house, which I did for perhaps two months, because after he came here [to Venice] he was partly in rented rooms and partly in Padua . . . and I had always promised to myself that I would turn him in for the censure of this Holy Office.

The trip from the Palazzo Mocenigo to the Inquisition was not a short one, and it must have been made in a gondola. Since 1560, the Dominican complex of San Domenico di Castello had served the Venetian Inquisition as tribunal and prison. The fourteenth-century Gothic church and its adjoining convent stood on the other end of the city from the Palazzo Mocenigo, just south of the great Venetian Arsenal, where the city's fleets were built, outfitted, and maintained by one of the most efficient industrial operations in the world. The Dominican outpost was remodeled in the six-teenth century for its new purpose, but we can see nothing of those remodelings now: church and convent were razed in 1807 by order of Napoleon, who claimed the land for a public garden. By 1812, the canal that flanked San Domenico had been filled to become a promenade, and every trace of the building had been scraped away. On that occasion, at least, the Venetians obeyed Napoleon's orders with a speed worthy of the Arsenal workers, as eager to erase the memory of the Holy Office as their Corsican overlord. The former site of San Domenico di Castello is now dedicated to the memory of Giuseppe Garibaldi, who fought so fiercely to free Italy from the temporal dominion of the Church. On a nearby building, a marble relief in Gothic style of the saints Dominic, John the Baptist, and Peter Martyr beneath a blessing Christ is the only surviving re-minder of what once stood on this ground.

Venice called itself the Serenissima Repubblica, the "Most Serene Republic." "Serene," as the pedant Manfurio had pointed out in Bruno's *Candlemaker*, was an adjective appropriate only for the heavens; in effect, therefore, serene Venice was a heaven on earth (the seas over which it ruled, as Manfurio noted, had only the right to be termed "calm"). Venetian serenity was famously enforced by the rule of law, spectacularly in the pageantry of its government, cruelly in the New Prisons that adjoined the Doge's Palace. Violent criminals, murderers, thieves, and sexual offenders had the worst of it, thrust into windowless cells along the water-line, some in solitary confinement, some in utter darkness, crawling through the low entrances until they felt the slam of the ironclad wooden door behind them.

The Inquisition's prisoners, who posed less of an immediate physical threat and often came from a higher social stratum, were kept in greater comfort at San Domenico. They had windows to waft away at least some of the stench of seldom-washed bodies, un-washed clothing, slop buckets, and food. But they were crowded into close quarters as they waited for their hearings. And for those who ran afoul of the Venetian Republic, its rule of law did nothing to comfort their madness, heal their tortures, or soften the cruel pageantry of their punishments.

Giordano Bruno's case is one of thirty-five preserved in the same file of the Venetian State Archive, and the nineteenth to come before the Inquisition in the year 1592. By the beginning of December the cases would number seventy-two. The old records are spotty: about half the cases from 1592 still survive; none are preserved from 1593, a handful from 1594. Yet these cases, when taken together, provide a powerful image of the insecurities that plagued Venetian society near the end of the sixteenth century. Most of the accused were literate, workers or professionals, but not noble: in part because Venetian aristocrats protected one another, but also for purely statistical reasons—most Venetians belonged to the working or merchant class.

In their investigations, the inquisitors obeyed strict rules of due process; unless two witnesses backed up an accusation, there was no case. Furthermore, unlike its counterparts in Rome and Naples, the Venetian Holy Office tended, with a few important exceptions, to leave people alone. In 1592, seven people lodged accusations of witchcraft or fortune-telling by "throwing the beans" (*buttare la fava*), against women: Caterina Moretta, Virginia Greca, Lucrezia Baglioni, Paulina Bianchini, Cathe Zaratina "the Slav" ("Schia-vona"), Clara who has no surname, and a whole list submitted by one informer in November. The inquisitors ignored every one of these denunciations. Typically, the accused witches were poor and often illiterate, whereas the men accused of sorcery in the same year were all well educated: the Neapolitan schoolmaster Maximiliano Visconti, accused of necromancy, turned out to have read extensively about astrology, but owned no texts listed on the *Index of Forbidden Books*; neither had a whole set of Capuchin friars who were denounced by a neighbor "to unburden his conscience."

On the other hand, although conviction was impossible on the basis of a single witness, there was no law against preventive detention, as Bruno discovered when Giovanni Mocenigo handed him over to the inquisitors' police. The Franciscan friar Agostino Altomonte spent several months of 1592 and 1593 in prison, after a series of women denounced his sexual assaults. His actions, however unsavory, did not qualify as heresy—indeed his brothers in the convent reported that he lived an exemplary Christian life—and eventually the inquisitors were compelled to absolve him, but only after dragging out his captivity and postponing his verdict as long as they could, the one punishment they could inflict on an obviously reprehensible character. They were equally powerless to help Zuane Zaratan's wife when she denounced him for bigamy: Zuane had run off to live with his new wife long before. The fact that Antonio Benzon had eaten cheese with his bread and water in prison seems to have disturbed neither Antonio himself nor his examiners.

With the Ottoman Empire just across the Adriatic, Venice had become a sanctuary for fugitive Christian slaves; Florentia Podocathara, Demetrio Lecca Bagga, Luigi Hernandez, Zorzi Armeno, and Ser Natalino da Perasto, each bought by Turkish slavers and forced to convert to Islam, asked to be reinstated as practicing Christians. Each one recounted a terrifying story to the inquisitors: Florentia had borne three children to her Turkish master, gently promoted to her "husband" in her testimony, and fled after his death to avoid a second "marriage." Demetrio was sold in Albania at the age of twelve to be brought up as a Janissary, the crack imperial troop made up entirely of converted Christians; at twenty-two, he had already entered a high level of the Turkish civil service in Greece before escaping to Venice by way of Kephallonia. Each of these former slaves was received immediately back into the Church.

The harshness of Venetian rhetoric about "damned Muslims" and the republic's incessant evocations of its victory over the Turks in the Battle of Lepanto played out more leniently in daily life: thus the fact that Battista Brezula had a Turkish wife impressed the inquisitors no more unfavorably in 1591 than it had in 1584; in each instance a single person had informed on him, not enough to make a case. Neither did the Holy Office seem to care much about foreigners whose suspicious neighbors denounced them: they saw no problem with Antoine Noner, denounced as a Huguenot; or the Portuguese convert Antonio Diez, said to have reverted to Judaism; or the alleged Protestant Jacob of Flanders, who sold pewter spoons and, it soon transpired, regularly went to Mass and confession at the huge Dominican church of San Zanipolo, where he may have seen Giordano Bruno mingling with the crowd.

The Holy Office in Venice had only two real concerns: publishing and heresy. No printer in the city was authorized to publish without a license from the inquisitors. This procedure worked two ways: it provided a rudimentary sort of copyright protection, but it also subjected authors and printers to censorship, the most lenient form of censorship to be found in Italy, but censorship nonetheless. This censorship was intimately linked with the Inquisition's chief fear: heresy, or, as they put it, "heretical depravity."

Nine accusations of heresy survive from 1592, including Bruno's, in the Venetian archive's file of thirty-five. These proceedings show that Venice was an emporium for exchanging ideas as much as silks and spices, and it was this traffic, a traffic of books as well as conversations and sermons, that the Holy Office tried to control.

The files show just how actively people discussed religion, and how little guidance the Church provided for any such discussion. Workmen argued in their shops, around the well, or in the tavern; their better-educated neighbors congregated in bookshops. The highest level of society met in noble palazzi, like the group that gathered in the house of Andrea Morosini and included both Giordano Bruno and his accuser, Giovanni Mocenigo. In 1592, with striking regularity, the first witnesses brought in for the Inquisition's nine cases of heresy were booksellers and Dominican priests from San Zanipolo. Both groups responded to the inquisitors' questions with studied evasiveness. The booksellers' attitude is easy to explain: the Inquisition did nothing but interfere with their lucrative business. If its interference mattered less in Venice than elsewhere in Italy, the lack of a Holy Office in the Protestant world meant that northern Europeans were coming to dominate the printing industry, and Venetian printers could see this domination on display twice a year at the Frankfurt book fair.

As for the Dominican friars from San Zanipolo, they represented the most authoritative Dominican community in Venice. The Inquisition's headquarters at San Domenico di Castello served the workers at the Arsenal, whereas San Zanipolo served generations of doges and aristocrats among more humble Venetians. It is not surprising that the inquisitors would bring these illustrious colleagues in to testify, and when they did, it was usually to exonerate the accused. Most cases brought before the Holy Office in Venice seem to have ended in acquittal; most people who were finally found guilty of unorthodox beliefs were assigned a regimen of devotions like daily prayer and abstinence from meat on Fridays and Saturdays, and set free to resume their normal lives. The five people who sometimes crowded with Giordano Bruno in the Inquisition's jail cell at San Domenico were the exceptions to this comparatively lenient rule, and it is no wonder that they got on one another's nerves as violently as they did. With a workload that averaged fewer than a hundred cases a year, most of them inconclusive, the Venetian Inquisition could never have entertained many prisoners at one time, and they were never entertained for long. The prisoners who belonged to religious orders were usually punished by being sent out to a house in the provinces, far from the temptations of Venice: a sentence to life imprisonment that could eventually be commuted by good behavior. Insanity was handled in the same way: the prisoner/patient was institutionalized in some remote religious community. Giordano Bruno's cellmates included one such madman, Fra Celestino Arrigoni da Verona, whose trial records, like those of his other cellmates, do not seem to have survived in Venice.

The ideas that brought nine people to the attention of the Inquisition in 1592 show surprising similarities, and show them at every social level. Giordano Bruno expresses these ideas in their most sophisticated form, but he clearly represents a refined version of some fairly common beliefs. The evident wealth and equally evident corruption of the Church hierarchy had spurred insistent reform movements since the rise of the Franciscan order (founded 1212) and the Dominican order (founded 1216). In the sixteenth century, the Reformation had brought about trenchant changes in the way Christians regarded their religion, with Protestants insisting on a vernacular liturgy and a vernacular Bible, opening service and Scripture alike to the public at large.

By the time Martin Luther conceived his Ninety-five Theses against the papacy in 1517, the culture of critical scholarship that defined the Renaissance had already trained readers of every social stratum to question what they read and apply rules of evidence to extract their answers. It did not take long to discover that only two of the seven sacraments of the Catholic Church, baptism and Communion, had any basis in the Gospels; the other five—marriage, confession, holy orders, last rites, burial—were matters of tradition. When a Waldensian Protestant from the mountains of the Friuli, Marcantonio Pestalozzi, decided to convert to Catholicism in 1591, he spelled out his creed to the Venetian inquisitors:

> I was born and brought up among heretics, of a heretic mother and father, and in a village where we have another faith . . . and in those places they hold to and believe in the Gospels but not in the sacraments, and for that reason they are called Evangelicals and they call the Catholics papists. In my faith I have believed up to now that neither the pope nor any other priest has authority to absolve us from sin, but only God alone. And I have not believed that the Mother of Grace or the saints have any authority to intercede for us. And I have not believed that there is a purgatory. I have not believed that Confession is necessary, but that it is an invention of the pope to make money.
>
> I have not believed that baptism is necessary, and if a child dies unbaptized, it is saved because it was blessed in its mother's womb, and this is what I have heard preached. I have believed that the Host that the

Catholics consecrate, who are called papists in those parts, is not the real body of Christ, because we take the holy meal four times a year and after the minister's sermon he takes up bread baked in the oven and gives it to each person, saying, "Take this bread in memory of the body of Christ who died for our sins."

Another Protestant they examined, Girolamo Celeste, maintained in 1591 that salvation could be obtained by good works; a third, Serafino de Magris, had begun to form his own opinions about the sacraments and the simple apostolic life by reading a vernacular translation of the Bible. The Protestant overtones of many of Bruno's own statements, combined with his long sojourns in Protestant countries, could not have been lost on either the Venetian inquisitors or their Roman counterparts.

Multiple worlds were also familiar terrain for the inquisitors: they appeared in a book that Giovanni da Gara had hoped to print in Venice, at least until he presented the project to the inquisitor Sebastiano Barbadico. The text had been written and printed about a hundred years earlier, by Rabbi Abarbanel (father of the popular sixteenth-century writer Leone Ebreo, whose *Dialogues on Love* helped to inspire Bruno's *Heroic Frenzies*). But by the time this venerable Jewish author came up for discussion again, on June 9, 1592, Giordano Bruno was already in prison. As the Inquisition's special consultant for the case warned:

In this book I have found the following false conclusions: that there have been and shall be many worlds, and that finally there shall be two consumptions, an individual one for each world at the end of seven thousand years, and another general at the beginning of fifty thousand years, during which time the souls of the just shall unite with God without a multiplication either of angels or of souls, and the souls of the impious, if they have not already been purged by that time, shall be converted into mind, as if they were corruptible bodies, and there are other errors regarding these conclusions to my mind . . . Furthermore, in the same book he maintains that the sensitive soul of animals and the vegetative soul of trees have not been created by God, but by a minister of God, whom he calls the operating intelligence, and in this way there come to be two

creations, and these are the things that I think are repugnant to our
Catholic faith.

Bruno's heretical propositions, in other words, could not have
struck the inquisitors as the theories of a lone philosopher; instead,
they seemed to draw together a whole series of heretical themes
with a cogency and an overarching structure that reflected his own
training in the mighty mental architectures of Thomas Aquinas.
Furthermore, unlike the humble Protestant workers Marcantonio
Pestalozzi and Girolamo Celeste, Bruno came from the centers of
Protestant power, almost to a one: Geneva, London, Wittenberg,
and that prime source of all dangerous ideas, the Frankfurt book
fair.

The other men confined in the same cell with Giordano Bruno
could not have found much comfort in his company. Garrulous, betrayed, terrified, he talked constantly, to them and to God. He
would awaken in the night, cursing God, Christ, and his own fate
in a string of blasphemies: "Traitor! Take that, wretched dog fucked
cuckold! Look how you run the world!" giving heaven the finger
before going back to sleep. The Neapolitan carpenter Francesco
Vaio, a simple layman, may have ignored the elaborate theological
arguments that sometimes raged around him in Latin as well as a
hodgepodge of Italian dialects, but most of the others, including a
pair of friars, responded more actively to Bruno's constant needling
and casual blasphemy. By September, a volatile Capuchin brother
named Fra Celestino Arrigoni had entered the cell, and the atmosphere grew more tense than ever. Fra Celestino already had a
record with the Inquisition and a history of mental instability. As a
relapsed heretic, he had little hope of a lenient sentence, and his
fear and his short temper made him as irritating as Bruno in his
own way; at one point during an argument Bruno actually slapped
him. Mostly, however, they bickered about theology, the habit that
had earned them both their prison terms in the first place.

Aside from one brief interrogation in jail, Bruno was taken six
times for questioning into the chamber of the Ducal Palace reserved for such inquisitions, the Hall of the Council of Ten. The
deceptively attractive Bridge of Sighs had not yet been built across

the canal that divided the palace from the New Prisons (it was constructed in 1604), but the secret back staircase and the narrow, well-guarded passages through which prisoners could be spirited into various chambers under guard were already in place. Bruno's three judges and the court recorder sat beneath a large oil painting of Jupiter casting down the rebellious giants; on the room's two side walls, images of the pope and the doge reinforced the suggestion that for all the city's political independence, Venetian serenity lay firmly on the side of the Catholic Church. Above their heads, an inlaid wooden frieze praised "WHAT UNCORRUPTED RELIGION BORE AND UNCONQUERED VIRTUE BROUGHT UP"—"QUOD IN- CORRUPTA RELIGIO PEPERIT INVICTAQUE VIRTUS EDUCAVIT." In its own way, the opulent decoration of the Ducal Palace proclaimed the stern sobriety of Venetian justice no less ominously than the stark severity of the New Prisons.

Bruno's interrogators, like the paintings around them, repre- sented the power of the republic ranged alongside the power of the Church in the pursuit of justice: they included the papal nuncio Ludovico Taverna; the patriarch of Venice, Lorenzo Priuli; and the Venetian inquisitor Giovanni Gabriele de Sentis. Yet despite the prominent papal portraits in the chamber where they sat, the two Venetians, at least, were eager on principle to protect their repub- lic's spiritual life from papal rule, just as the doge was committed to preserving the republic's political autonomy.

At the outset, Bruno's position must have looked reasonably fa- vorable; his arrest depended on the report of a single informer, his former host Mocenigo, and the Inquisition regarded the testimony of any single witness, even an aristocrat, as insufficient grounds for a conviction of heresy. Both the philosopher and his interrogators may well have assumed that his arrest would eventually result in no more than a reprimand and release (as in fact happened with sev- eral of his cellmates).

The initial line of questioning involved establishing who Bruno was, and then sounding out his response to the charges that Mocenigo had piled up in his first letter of accusation.

Mocenigo had also suggested three possible witnesses to corrob- orate his charges, and these three—two booksellers and a Venetian nobleman—were actually summoned to appear in court just before Bruno made his first deposition on May 26. None of the three, however, was much inclined to support Mocenigo's accusations; a disagreeable man in his own right, he had done them no favor by referring them to the Holy Office. The first to be questioned was Giovanni Battista Ciotti, a Sienese printer whose Venetian bookshop must have been one of the city's intellectual centers in the late sixteenth century. A good friend of the Servite friar Paolo Sarpi, whose scathing history of the Council of Trent would one day earn him a position next to Giordano Bruno on the *Index of Forbidden Books*, Ciotti made his testimony as studiously bland as possible. He did, however, furnish some secondhand rumors for the inquisitors' ears:

> I know this Giordano Bruni of Nola, or Naples, and he is a little skinny man with a bit of black beard, around forty years old . . . When I have conversed with said Giordano here and in Frankfurt, as I have said, he has never said anything to make me think that he was not a Catholic and a good Christian. But when I was in Frankfurt, I spoke to various scholars . . . who said to me, in essence, that said Giordano made grand claims about memory and having other such secrets, but no one had ever seen him do anything with anyone; indeed, that everyone who had anything to do with him on these subjects ended up dissatisfied; and they also told me, "I don't know how it is in Venice, but here he is thought to be a man without religion."

The second bookseller, Giacomo Brictano, was an expatriate from Antwerp who offered his questioners a good deal more than the cagey Ciotti:

> Said Giordano . . . in Frankfurt spent most of his time writing and going around talking riddles and astrologizing new things . . . He read heretical teachers, because everyone in that city is a heretic, generally speaking . . . With me said Giordano has never said anything, nor have I ever noticed anything that would make me think that he was anything but a good Christian; however, the prior of the Carmelites in Frankfurt told me, when I asked what kind of man said Giordano was, that he had won-

derful talent, an education, and was a universal man, but that he had no
religion so far as he could tell.

Bruno's own initial deposition revealed that he had been a fugitive from the Inquisition in Naples and Rome since 1576, and for
just as long he had doffed his Dominican habit and, as he said, "left
religion." The inquisitors would have understood *"religione"* in his
statement to mean the Dominican Order, but *religione* could also
mean religion itself, and Bruno, looking back, may have meant it
both ways. In the context of the booksellers' nearly identical statements, Bruno's mention of "leaving religion behind" must have
taken on a more general significance than abandoning the Dominicans.

As questioning continued, Bruno revealed how thoroughly his
strange life had accustomed him to speaking his mind; he admitted
some of his doubts about orthodox Christian faith with what must
have seemed shocking frankness. At the same time, his Dominican
training showed through in the cleverness of his other arguments,
some of them evidently devised to mask, or at least to obscure, his
real beliefs. Alternately, then, the prisoner seemed recklessly bold
and cannily calculating. The case, as it proceeded, grew more and
more complex, not least because Bruno's ideas seemed to echo, in
the most sophisticated terms, what the Inquisition was hearing in
its other cases.

Furthermore, Bruno's arrest had reached the attention of the
Roman Inquisition, which began to press Venice for his extradition. Under normal circumstances, Venice rejected any interference with its sovereignty from Rome in matters of church or state.
In 1592, however, the Most Serene Republic had less room to maneuver than usual, with an unstable political situation in Europe
and a new pope who showed no sign of willingness to compromise
on any question of politics or religion.

Bruno seems to have had no sense that he might be in serious
trouble. Accustomed as he was to the lordly prerogatives of San
Domenico Maggiore in Naples and to the courts of Europe, he may
have overestimated the inquisitors' tolerance of new ideas. Although Venice itself may have been an international port, its soci-

ety was tightly closed and conservative. After so many years on his own, he may also have grown inured to the novelty of his own thoughts; if his vision of the cosmos sent a thinker as bold as Kepler into an existential panic, it was still more likely to upset theologians and state officials who had enough trouble keeping order in Venice, let alone the whole universe.

Besides misjudging the intellectual flexibility of his Dominican captors, Bruno had not quite grasped how much times had changed in Italy, even in the free republic of Venice. He had lived in Naples under a series of repressive popes, but had done so in a Neapolitan convent that found its own ways to get around the Spanish rules; true to form, San Domenico Maggiore would foment yet another revolt against Spain in 1599, as his own trial reached its endgame.

In Rome, the militant pope Pius V, who had heard Bruno recite in Hebrew and perform feats of memory, had been superseded by figures of equal intransigence, at least on matters of religion. Gregory XIII had reformed the calendar with the help of Christoph Clavius, but he undertook that scientifically significant move for the most religiously conservative of reasons: to ensure that Easter fell at the correct time of year. Clement VIII, like Gregory before him, mixed intellectual enthusiasm with an increasing religious rigor, brought on in part by the growing economic power of Protestant nations, but also by a series of disturbances by Protestant agitators in Rome itself.

For some reason, in any event, Bruno answered his inquisitors frankly as they brought Mocenigo's accusations, one by one. Some of his answers must have shocked them.

To this day, Italian blasphemy is a regional matter; what sounds horrific in Rome is casual conversation in Tuscany ("syphilitic Madonna," "hang God," "dog God"), or Bergamo ("shit Host"), or Florence ("pathic Madonna"). Strikingly, most Roman invective, like that of Sicily, is phallic rather than religious, aside from the occasional "pig Madonna." Bruno's rich repertory of Neapolitan curses may have jarred on Giovanni Mocenigo's Venetian ears as harshly as the accent in which Bruno pronounced them.

Unfortunately, however, Bruno's unbridled tongue also covered matters of theology, most damningly his remarks about the Holy

Trinity. In his third deposition before the inquisitors, on June 2, 1592, he admitted that he "in effect . . . harbored doubts" about his Lord already as a novice friar. That statement would dog him for the rest of his trial. It was enough in itself to earn him a condemnation for heresy, and may be one of the reasons that he was kept in prison. Bruno denied most of Mocenigo's other accusations outright, and where the inquisitors had no more evidence to pursue, they could do nothing more. Prisoner and inquisitors began searching for an agreement that could resolve their impasse. Bruno indicated his willingness to retract his more troublesome propositions, trusting, probably, that he could get off with a reprimand. Venice, after all, was famous for its independence and its tendency to live and let live so long as the lanes of commerce stayed open. He offered his repentance with the same eager familiarity that he had used to present his ideas, in all their originality. With only one accuser ranged against him and a sincere pledge to mend his ways, he would normally have stood a good chance of gaining his release.

Bruno could also have been relatively confident that his encounter with the Venetian Inquisition would remain confined to Venice. To its utmost ability, the Venetian Church resisted interference from Rome, a city with no head for business. Because of the relatively lenient standards that Venetian censors applied to the manuscripts submitted to their scrutiny, they had managed to save the city's printing industry. The strong inquisitorial presence in places like Florence and Rome had drastically reduced the number of publishing houses, and in many small towns the printing industry had been destroyed altogether by rigid censorship. It was hard to believe, in the waning sixteenth century, that Italian printing had once been the glory of Europe. It is telling, also, that Bruno planned to publish his next book not in Venice but in Frankfurt.

As the months dragged by, Giordano Bruno, in his prison cell, began to speak about how Jesus behaved in the hour before his capture by the authorities of Roman Judaea. In the Garden of Gethsemane, in a moment of agonized, desperate prayer, Jesus had asked God to spare him the ordeal he was about to endure. This prayer, Bruno crowed to his cellmates, resisted the will of God, an act that made Christ a mortal sinner like the rest of them:

Matteo Silvestri, fellow prisoner: "He had a huge argument with Fra Celestino and Fra Giulio, insisting that Christ had committed a mortal sin
in the Garden when he prayed: 'Father, let this cup pass me by.' About
this there was a huge commotion in prison, because at that moment
Francesco Napolitano, Lame Graziano, those two friars and I were all in
prison."

At the same time, however, that bleak Venetian prison plunged
Bruno into his own agony in the garden. He, too, prayed for the
cup to pass, in his own words: "I despise you, fucked cuckold, done
and undone!" His cellmates' pious prayers drove him into the same
kinds of rages that had first brought him to the attention of the Inquisition in Naples:

When the prisoners who were friars said the breviary, he said that these
whispering friars had no idea what they were saying, and when he had the
breviary in hand, it made his head ache, because it was badly put together, like a lute out of tune . . . and the person who compiled it was a
great fucked cuckold.

Unlike the Christ in the Gospel who immediately resigned
himself to his fate, Giordano Bruno also took more practical action
to avoid his doom. As he well knew, if he were to admit error and
publicly repent, he could not be sentenced to death. Therefore, at
the end of his final deposition before the Venetian inquisitors, on
July 30, 1592, he made an abject confession. Its text is still preserved in the Venetian State Archive, along with the detail that
Bruno threw himself to his knees at the end of his speech as the inquisitors pressed him to stand:

He replied: "I willingly confess my errors now, and am here in the hands
of Your Illustrious Lordships to receive the remedy for my health; about
my repentance for my misdeeds I could never say enough or express my
intentions as effectively as I would wish." Then, on his knees, he said: "I
humbly beg pardon of the Lord God and Your Illustrious Lordships for all
the errors I have committed, and am ready to carry out whatever your
prudence shall have deliberated and judged expedient to my soul . . . and

if by the mercy of God and Your Most Illustrious Lordships I am allowed to live, I promise to make a notable reform of my life, and repay every scandal with edification."

For the moment, the Venetian inquisitors had no choice but to let Bruno live. But they did not release him from prison. Instead, they turned to face the Inquisition in Rome.

CHAPTER TWENTY-FIVE

The Witness

SMITHO: There were two of them?

PRUDENZIO: *Ut essent duo testes.*

FRULLA: What do you mean by those testes?

PRUDENZIO: Witnesses, proven testifiers to the Nolan competence.

—*The Ash Wednesday Supper*, dialogue 1

To long for that which comes not. To lye a bed and sleepe not. To serve well and please not. To lye in iayle and hope not. To bee sick and recover not. To loose ones waye and knowe not. To waite at doore and enter not, and to have a friend we trust not; are ten such spites as hell hath not.

—John Florio, *Second Frutes* (1591)

When the Roman Inquisition asked Venice to extradite a prisoner, as it did on occasion, the Venetians normally refused. Rome let them refuse because Venice meant money and all that money could buy, including, notably, military security: the Venetian fleet had bested the Turks at Lepanto in 1571, and no pope as yet had been inclined to forget that favor.

But by 1592, Lepanto lay nearly a generation in the past, and German Protestants loomed as large on the threshold of Roman fear as the infidel. News about Bruno's arrest had traveled to Rome, and in 1592 the Holy Office requested his extradition, not least because of his German connections. For once, Venice hinted that it might be willing to negotiate. The republic needed money, and it needed Rome as an ally against Germany and Spain, which now ruled Milan and pressed insistently against Venetian-held lands in northern Italy. Besides, Bruno's offers to retract his statements may well have sounded more expedient to his examiners than sincere: for once, the bargain he had to offer if they used him to reassert Venetian independence could not compare with the offers coming from Rome. The diplomatic process that procured Giordano Bruno's extradition to Rome took months, from the end of July to the middle of February of the following year. On February 20, 1593, Giordano Bruno was loaded onto a ship and sailed down the coast to Ancona, made the trip westward over the Apennines along the ancient course of the Via Flaminia, and reached the prisons of the Roman Inquisition seven days later, on February 27. He would spend just under seven years inside this forbidding palazzo just off Saint Peter's Square, as workmen continued to put the final touches on the facade of the huge basilica, almost ninety years in the making. As a bargaining chip, he was probably treated with some care, in transit and on arrival. As a former courtier in Paris, London, Prague, and Braunschweig, he might still have powerful protectors in those places. Both in Venice and in Rome he seems to have baffled the authorities, a perpetual wanderer with a perpetual power to charm people—and to repel them.

The Holy Office locked him into a cell of their palazzo just south of Saint Peter's Basilica, on the square newly dominated by the pink granite obelisk of Caligula, moved to the site by Domenico Fontana only five years before. His cell, private, windowed, in a building perched on dry ground rather than a canal, was in every way an improvement over his crowded pen in Venice. A later report criticizes those cells for their spaciousness and the opportunity they afforded prisoners for conversation; for the moment, at least, Bruno's physical circumstances were tolerable. He was permitted to read only what pertained to his impending trial, assigned a pen, but forbidden a compass or penknife.

The Roman Inquisition kept its prisoners well by the standards of the time. A team of inspectors came through every six months to ensure that the inmates were properly fed, clothed, and housed; Bruno was issued a warm mantle and a beret to keep off a dank Ro-

man winter that could hardly have compared in severity with the
Venetian winter he had just spent by the Arsenal. But the Holy Office in Rome also practiced juridical torture in its chambers, and it
regularly handed over convicted heretics to the city prison of Tor
di Nona, where they could contemplate the impaled heads of former inmates as they crossed the ancient Roman bridge built by the
emperor Hadrian fourteen centuries before. Because the Inquisition
itself claimed to shed no blood, its punishments were exacted here
by the state's "secular arm." Blood flowed in Tor di Nona in abun-
dance, and the piazza between the prison and the bridge was one of
Rome's most active execution grounds.

In the spring of 1593, Giordano Bruno had no immediate reason to fear being transferred to Tor di Nona. Unless new evidence
emerged, his case with the Inquisition could proceed no further
than it had already. The Roman inquisitors could do no more than
to review records from the Venetian proceedings and begin to assemble a more accurate collection of Bruno's writings than the
Venetians had been able to do.

Within a few months, however, in the fall of 1593, a second
witness made his appearance: Bruno's old cellmate and frequent adversary from Venice, Fra Celestino Arrigoni da Verona, newly
transferred from prison to a Capuchin convent in the Marches, the
region along the east coast of Italy, where he had been put under
observation; in modern terms, the troubled friar had been institutionalized. Convinced (wrongly) that Bruno had incriminated him
in his own interviews with the inquisitors, Fra Celestino, in a combination of vindictive rage and fear for his life, wrote a letter to
the Roman Inquisition reporting his conversations with Bruno
in prison. Although in the normal social world both Giovanni
Mocenigo and Fra Celestino were unstable individuals and recognized as cranks, in the world of the Inquisition they still provided
the necessary two witnesses for prosecuting a heretic. (In 1599,
Bruno once again crossed paths with his accuser Fra Celestino da
Verona, whose years under close supervision had not brought his
behavior into much better control. The Capuchin had been arrested again for heresy and taken to Rome. This time he was on
trial as a recidivist rather than as a first-time offender. He was condemned and burned at the stake in the same year.)

Fra Celestino's report to the inquisitors was hardly a trenchant critique of the Nolan philosophy; it provided the kind of evidence that the Venetian Inquisition tended to throw away if at all possible. But the mad Capuchin was a witness nonetheless, and as such he changed the nature of the case against Giordano Bruno:

He [Fra Celestino] says that he deposes against Giordano, because he suspects that he has been slanderously denounced by the same, and informed against Giordano in writing. He reports that Giordano has said:

1. That Christ committed a mortal sin when he made his prayer in the Garden refusing the will of the Father, when he said: "Father, if possible, let this cup pass me by."
2. That Christ was not put on a cross, but hanged on two beams as was done in those days, and called a *forca*.
3. That Christ is a dog cuckold fucked dog; he said that the ruler of this world was a traitor, because he could not rule it well, and raising his hand he gave the finger to heaven.
4. That there is no hell, that no one is damned to eternal punishment, but in time everyone shall be saved, citing the prophet: Shall God be angry forever?
5. That there are many worlds, and all the stars are worlds, and believing that this is the only world is supreme ignorance.
6. That when bodies die their souls transmigrate from one world to the other, in the many worlds, and from one body to another.
7. That Moses was a shrewd magician and because he was so experienced in the art of magic, he easily beat the magicians of Pharaoh, and that he only pretended to talk to God on Mount Sinai, and that the law he gave to the Hebrew people was made up and created by himself.
8. That all the prophets were shrewd men, but false and lying, and because of that they came to a bad end; that is, they were condemned by law to a shameful death, as they deserved.
9. That praying for intercession to the saints is a ridiculous thing, not to be done.
10. That Cain was a good man, and that he was right to kill Abel his brother, because Abel was a wretch and a butcher of animals.
11. That if he had to go back to being a Dominican friar, he wanted

to blow up the monastery, and when he had done that, he wanted to return to Germany or England among the heretics where he could live in his own way more comfortably and plant his new and infinite heresies there. And I intend to produce as witnesses Francesco Girolami, Silvio, canon of Chioggia, and Fra Serafino of Acquasparta.

12. The person who compiled the breviary is an ugly dog fucked cuckold, shameless, and the breviary is like an out-of-tune lute, and in it there are many things that are profane and irrelevant, and therefore it is not worth reading by serious men, but ought to be burned.

13. That nothing of what the Church believes can be proved. As witnesses, he named Fra Giulio da Salò, Francesco Vaio, and Matteo d'Orio, cellmates.

Now the inquisitors tracked down all of Bruno's former cellmates from Venice to question them about their conversations in prison. More than a year had elapsed, and one of them, Francesco Vaio, had died in the meantime. Although Fra Celestino's reports were invariably more lurid than the others', the testimony of all the witnesses was consistent, dangerously so for Bruno's position.

It is most likely that the original records for Bruno's trial in Rome no longer exist. Napoleon Bonaparte, who had ordered the razing of San Domenico di Castello in Venice, also attacked the memory of the Inquisition in Rome. Many of its records were bundled up in the Vatican and taken off to Paris, only to be shipped back in 1814, in the aftermath of Waterloo. A good deal was lost in transit in both directions; carts were upset en route, and some papers seem to have been turned into cardboard. What does survive in the Holy Office is a summary of Bruno's trial, divided according to the various points, twenty-nine of them, that counted as heretical. This *Summary* was first discovered in 1941 by the head of the Vatican's Secret Archive, Angelo Mercati, who published it with an extensive, vituperative commentary. It quotes extensive passages both from the Venetian records of Bruno's trial and from the missing Roman papers, and from these we can reconstruct the general course of the proceedings.

The first of Bruno's Venetian cellmates to be recalled in this second phase of the trial was Fra Giuliano da Salò:

> When Giordano was discussing with the prisoner Fra Celestino, I heard him say that Christ Our Lord had committed a mortal sin in this world because he wanted to oppose the will of the Father, when he prayed in the Garden, saying, "If possible, let this cup pass from me," and Francesco Marangon of Naples was there, too, and I said to him: "Listen to what blasphemies this man says!" and I think this was September 1592.

The Roman inquisitor, confronted with the transcripts of Bruno's Venetian depositions, began to realize how little they knew about him. He had mentioned books and treatises to his examiners, but in fact the Holy Office in Rome had no idea what he had written, nor how much. They questioned him, and for once the master of memory hesitated. It would take the inquisitors years to assemble an adequate list, as Bruno waited in his Roman cell, watching prisoners come and go through the purgative system of the Holy Office. For most the experience lasted a few months. Most were let off with a reprimand, but some faced the full brutality of sixteenth-century Italian justice.

The punishment of criminals in Rome, as elsewhere in Europe, was a public spectacle designed to deter citizens from wrongdoing. (An exception was Alfonso Cardinal Petrucci, discreetly strangled with a scarlet cord in the depths of Castel Sant'Angelo for attempting to assassinate Pope Leo X in 1517. The executioner was a huge Moor, who, as an infidel, could kill a prince of the Church without ulterior fear for the fate of his immortal soul.) In unconscious obedience to ancient Roman religious belief, lower-class criminals were hanged, aristocrats beheaded (a procedure that had once been thought to leave them in possession of their souls). Traitors, sex offenders, witches, and heretics were treated more theatrically and more severely, traitors drawn and quartered, the others burned in a civic version of the Lord's refining fire.

Two years into Bruno's Roman imprisonment, a Scots priest was hauled into the Holy Office for interrogation. Unlike most of his fellow prisoners, he may already have been manhandled by his cap-

tors, for his offense had been one of action rather than ideas. Walter Merse, an Anglican, had interrupted the Mass. By elevating the
Host, the Catholic priest had committed idolatry in the Protestant's eyes, and Merse had begun to shout his objections; neither
did the Scotsman agree with the Catholic claim that the conse-
crated bread had turned into the literal body of Jesus Christ. His
experience in the prisons of the Holy Office did not change his
mind. When he was finally convicted in the following year, he
was burned alive in a shirt soaked with pitch (as described in
Chapter 1).

In Bruno's case, for the time being the inquisitors decided that
they needed more information about him and his writings. They
asked him for a list of his publications and searched on their own
for copies of his books, suspecting, correctly, that he might not give
them a complete list. Bruno, for his part, was allowed the paper,
pen, ink, and compasses to draft his defense. In this state of suspen-
sion, his imprisonment dragged on for another several years.

CHAPTER TWENTY-SIX

The Adversary

Well, I am answer'd: now tell me who made the world?
—Christopher Marlowe, *Doctor Faustus*

I hardly ever read a book without wanting to give it a good censoring.
—Robert Cardinal Bellarmine to Antonio Possevino, 1598

The prelates who examined Giordano Bruno for the Inquisition were Catholic priests who saw obedience as a supreme virtue. They offered that obedience not only to God but also to various kinds of established authority: the Church, Scripture, and, if only on occasion, the state. The grand inquisitor, Cardinal Santori, had known Bruno in Naples at the convent of San Domenico, where they had received the same training in theology and argumentation. Each in his turn had also absorbed the powerful convent's culture of independence and, on occasion, revolution. Santori, in fact, had joined the Neapolitan revolt of 1563, when the friars of San Domenico led the city's resistance to an attempt to impose the Spanish Inquisition. As inquisitor, he would defend this youthful action as a defense of Roman, and hence papal, authority: the revolt had ensured that Naples, and the inquisitors at San Domenico, would continue to observe the rules of the Roman Inquisition. It seems unlikely, however, that obedience to Rome had ranked high among the young Santori's motives in 1563. The young rebel had grown into an old conservative, but a canny one.

The fact that Bruno's trial dragged on year after year suggests that Santori and his fellow inquisitors could find no plausible way to obtain a conviction. By Roman rules, they could not turn Bruno's trial into an endgame without observing due process. They found their solution in the person of the Jesuit theologian Roberto Bellarmino of Montepulciano, known in English as Robert Bellarmine, by all reports the most incisive theological mind of the outgoing sixteenth century. In 1599, six years into Bruno's imprisonment, Pope Clement VIII granted Bellarmine a cardinal's hat, making it possible to appoint him directly to the board of inquisitors general, which he had been serving as a consultant since 1592, the very first Jesuit to join the Dominicans in their traditional undertaking. For Santori, who had spent the first decades of his life under a despotic monarchy in the Kingdom of Naples, it is easy to see how obedience must have been inculcated in him from childhood (and how badly the lesson took at first). But Robert Bellarmine came from Montepulciano in Tuscany, where local tradition looked back to the Etruscans for a model of republican liberty, even after a Medici despot proclaimed himself Grand Duke of Etruria in 1538.

A fifteenth-century Tuscan chronicle reported that Robert Bellarmine's family had descended from two handsome Armenians—in Italian, "belli Armeni"—who had helped the Etruscan warlord Lars Porsenna found a hilltop city some five hundred years before the birth of Christ. For its supreme civility, Porsenna's utopia was called Mons Politicus—"Civic Mountain"—a name that would be transformed over the centuries into Montepulciano. And in fact sixteenth-century Montepulciano came as close as any contemporary city to a real Mons Politicus. For centuries it had been a pawn in power struggles between Florence and Rome, but a Florentine victory in 1511 allowed its citizens to concentrate at last on making money off the fertile lands beneath them, the silt-rich remnants of an Etruscan lake. To commemorate their prize, the Florentines erected a marble column near the town's lower gate, topped by a marble image of the Florentine lion, the Marzocco, and a terra-cotta statue of Lars Porsenna himself. Born in one of the magnificent town's most elegant palazzi, Robert Bellarmine followed the career that most wealthy Italian families dictated for their second sons: joining the Church. It was the easiest way to curb any future claims to an inheritance. Robert Bellarmine was not the first of his line to do so; his maternal uncle Marcello Cervini had been appointed cardinal in 1539 and was elected pope in 1555 (he took ill after his coronation and died after a reign of three weeks).

Six years older than Giordano Bruno, Robert Bellarmine entered religious life in 1560, at the age of eighteen. Rather than one of the traditional orders, he chose the newest, and in many ways the most exciting: the Society of Jesus, officially recognized by Pope Paul III only in 1539. Those first Jesuits were forbidden to take higher office in the Church, and Bellarmine would later say (albeit as cardinal) that he had entered the order specifically to avoid any chance of undeserved promotion, thereby emphasizing, as he so often did in his long life, his great personal modesty. Most other Jesuits had been attracted by other qualities about the Society—namely, its energy, its sense of spiritual mission, and its intellectual rigor. They were pioneers in a literal sense: foot soldiers for a militant Church, and their combination of brains and bravery soon made them a power to reckon with.

That pioneer spirit pervaded Jesuit life; the Society prepared its members to go on mission anywhere in the world, and many of them did, sometimes facing torture and death with the remarkable physical courage of their founder, the onetime soldier Ignatius of Loyola, sometimes meeting alien cultures with an adaptability that terrified their more conservative brethren. Devoted to a religion in which God was supposed to have taken on human form, they always combined their intellectual feats with a certain physicality: each Father literally strove to embody the whole Church in himself, trained by the founder's *Spiritual Exercises* to extend his imagination through all the senses to the extremes of heaven and hell. The *Spiritual Exercises* also acted as a form of memory training; the Jesuits aspired to the same command of their mental powers as Bruno did through the Nolan philosophy.

One of Bellarmine's classmates at the Society's Roman College, the German Christoph Clavius, would become a famous professor of mathematics at that same institution. Bellarmine himself felt the pull of natural philosophy in an age when the structure of nature and the universe was coming increasingly into question and provoking increasingly interesting discoveries. But unlike Clavius, who changed his mind over the years with every change in empirical data, Bellarmine gravitated early toward a world of certainty. He focused his talents at the college on mastering Christian doctrine, whose essential information had already been supplied once and for all by Scripture. He would eventually scour the Church Fathers, Thomas Aquinas, and, on occasion, Jewish scholarship to advance his understanding of the Christian mission, but his basic impulse, as he admitted to his fellow Jesuit Antonio Possevino, was a repressive one, whereas many of his fellow Jesuits seemed more inclined to limitless exploration and ecstatic wonder. As Clavius's students Matteo Ricci and Adam Schall von Bell plunged into the center of Chinese society—dressing as mandarins, serving at court in Beijing, publishing in Chinese for Chinese readers—and as Clavius himself, German by birth, Portuguese-educated, teaching in Italy, corresponded with the astronomers of Europe about the structure of space, Bellarmine justified his own ignorance of French and German (and this after spending a few years at Louvain!) by insisting that Latin was the only language fit for learned discourse.

He described his mission in the Holy Office as that of teaching, noting that just as resistant schoolboys could expect to be beaten by their masters, so could resistant Christians expect to be punished for persisting in their errors. This is what he says, for example, in reviewing a censor's comments on a book by the Protestant scholar Justus Lipsius:

> The censor is wrong to say that this author says "We need a teacher, not a torturer," and he is wrong to apply this statement to the Holy Office. For the author says this: "In these matters, first a teacher is needed": where he first wants to instruct and teach—which is what happens in the Holy Office, and then, if they are not teachable, to punish.

Robert Bellarmine's idea of obedience took a highly personal form, despite the clear prescriptions enjoined by his order: Ignatius of Loyola had decreed that if the Church were to tell him that black was white, he would obey and agree. Bellarmine's obedience was more selective. He had evolved his own model of the cosmos early, when he studied at the order's Roman College alongside Christoph Clavius. In some ways, his ideas about natural philosophy were far more radical than those of his mathematical colleague. Bellarmine had come to see interplanetary space as a liquid, even though the standard Jesuit curriculum endorsed Aristotle's picture of the heavens as a set of concentric crystalline spheres. In its defense, Bellarmine's liquid space ensured that the biblical account of "waters over the heavens" (*mayim b'shamayim*) was literally true, suggesting that in a pinch he would prefer a literal reading of the Bible to the force of Jesuit tradition. In the meantime, however, he followed the work of Galileo's Roman friend Count Federico Cesi with great interest, for Cesi also believed in liquid space.

As a theologian, Bellarmine's greatest gift was his ability to reduce theological disputes to a set of clearly expressed arguments; once he had outlined both sides of a question, he could press home his own position with relentless ingenuity—and perhaps a bit of reckless self-satisfaction, for when he tried this technique in 1589 against a reigning pope, Sixtus V, he found himself denounced before the Inquisition. Sixtus's timely death in 1590 freed Bellarmine from the Inquisition's toils and his latest work, the *Disputations*, from a threatened appearance on the *Index of Forbidden Books*. Thereafter he rose quickly to a position as the most powerful theologian in the Catholic Church, and in that position consulted for the Inquisition, although as a Jesuit he could not take part as an actual inquisitor: only Dominicans could.

A Jesuit could not be an inquisitor, but a cardinal was another matter. Hence Robert Bellarmine, elevated to cardinal, became the first Jesuit inquisitor, as well as one of the first Jesuit cardinals. His elevation in 1599 also brought him into direct contact with the troubling case of Giordano Bruno. Like Alexander the Great, who resolved the ancient puzzle of the Gordian knot by one slice of his sword in place of a patient unraveling, Robert Cardinal Bellarmine proceeded to cut through the knotty tangles of Giordano Bruno's philosophy.

Fulfilling his self-stated mission to censor, teach, and, if neces-

sary, punish, Bellarmine distilled Bruno's heresies to eight propositions, which Bruno was then invited to abjure. The "propositions"
in this kind of argumentation (a legacy from the Inquisition's Dominican, Scholastic roots) could be as short as a sentence or as
long as a printed page; Bellarmine must have written out the
propositions for Bruno as summaries drawn from what he and the
inquisitors knew of the Nolan philosopher's writings and his oral
testimony. The cardinal may also have supplied his own refutations
of those propositions in order to teach Bruno the "correct" opinion.
This, at least, is the kind of exchange we can see in connection
with another set of eight propositions drawn up by Bellarmine in
another context. Giovanni Marsilio's *Defense in Favor of the Reply
to Eight Propositions Against Which the Most Illustrious and Reverend
Lord Cardinal Bellarmine Has Written* (1606) begins its reply to the
cardinal by describing Bellarmine's style of argument, or, as Marsilio calls it, his "arts." Written by an independent-minded Venetian, this *Defense* suggests how the cardinal's teaching method
might also have struck the proud and independent-minded Bruno:

> The first technique is that, no sooner had said treatise appeared in print,
> than it was banned by the congregation appointed to such business in
> Rome, among whose number the Lord Cardinal appears, without identi-
> fying the reason for said prohibition, but only certain general headings
> and concerns . . .
>
> The second is that for an author's words he fabricates an interpreta-
> tion contrary to [the author's] meaning and intention, in order to extract
> conclusions to reprove them now as heretical, now as schimastic, now as
> erroneous, now as impudent, now as scandalous, now as harmful, with
> this formula: "If the author means this," he says (but the author means it
> otherwise), "then the proposition is heretical, wrong, etc." . . .
>
> The third is that he mixes up his material so that from that chaos of
> confusion he can draw similar conclusions . . .
>
> The fourth is to say: The author doesn't know logic . . .
>
> The fifth is to ascribe common printer's errors not to the printer but
> to the author, and to make digressions over these, truly unworthy of the
> doctrine and authority of this Lord . . .
>
> The sixth is to take the road of supposition, as, for example, he sup-

poses that the pope has supreme authority over Christians in temporal matters, and that temporal power is subordinate to spiritual power, and other matters of this sort, which he not only assumes as certain, and does not prove them, but also asserts that to deny them is heresy, without citing any text, Scripture, or definition by the Church.

Unfortunately, the eight propositions Bellarmine drew up for Bruno disappeared with the other records of his trial. However, the surviving *Summary*, drafted at the beginning of March 1598, may provide one clue to what those propositions were, and Marsilio's remark about Bellarmine's fondness for the "road of supposition," as we shall see, may provide another.

The *Summary* groups Bruno's questionable opinions under twenty-nine subject headings and a thirtieth heading for miscellaneous remarks. Of these twenty-nine accusations, Bruno openly admitted to four: he had read forbidden books, eaten meat on fast days, traveled to Protestant lands and heard Protestant sermons, and denied that the "sin of the flesh" was a mortal sin.

Most of the *Summary*'s headings concern casual remarks he made in prison and elsewhere. Under interrogation, however, he readily denied having spoken ill of the holy Catholic faith and its ministers, of Christ, of transubstantiation, Mass, hell, the three Magi, Cain and Abel, Moses, the prophets, the decisions of the Church, the doctors of the Church, the invocation of saints, relics of saints, holy images, the virginity of Mary, the breviary, the punishment of sin, and the pope. Like many of his contemporaries (and like many contemporary Italians), he clearly made occasional irreverent remarks on all these subjects and blasphemed with gusto—a habit he also denied—but he insists repeatedly that he was joking when he made such comments, and the shock he expresses at hearing his own raw language sounds genuine.

For example, Giovanni Mocenigo reported in his first letter: "I have heard Giordano Bruno of Nola say . . . that Christ was a wretch, and that if he did such wretched work as deluding the people, he could easily have predicted that he would be hanged . . . that Christ showed reluctance to die, and fled death as long as he could."

The Venetian inquisitors reported the accusation to Bruno:

> He was asked if he had ever argued . . . that Christ was not God but a
> wretch, and as he went about his wretched ways he could have predicted
> his own death, even if he showed later that he died against his will.
>
> He replied: "I can't believe I'm being asked this; I never had such
> opinions, nor said anything of the sort" . . . And as he spoke, he became
> extremely upset, repeating, "I don't know how they can accuse me of such
> things."

On some subjects, however, Bruno would not back down even
under duress. The Roman *Summary* describes those categories as:

> On the Trinity, divinity, and incarnation.
> That there are multiple worlds.
> On the souls of men and beasts.
> On the art of divination.

It seems unlikely that Bellarmine's eventual eight propositions
reflected the *Summary*'s headings precisely, but certainly these last
four categories are more likely to have aroused the Inquisition's interest than the infractions Bruno had admitted outright. In the first
place, Bruno himself explains repeatedly that the lapses he committed in Protestant lands (eating meat, hearing Protestant sermons, reading forbidden books) were necessary concessions to local
custom; furthermore, because he so readily admitted that the actions were wrong, they provided relatively little opportunity for
profound "instruction" on the part of the inquisitors. On the other
hand, his stated beliefs about the Trinity, reincarnation, divination,
and multiple worlds were complex, unorthodox, and forcefully argued. These, and perhaps Bruno's stubborn leniency about the "sin
of the flesh," would have posed the most obvious challenge to Bellarmine's own censorious skill.

Our only concrete clue to the substance of the propositions
comes from the text of Bruno's sentence: "That you said that it is a
great blasphemy for Catholics to say that bread transmutes into
flesh, etc. et infra."

The wording of this passage from the sentence is taken directly from Giovanni Mocenigo's first letter of accusation, showing that, six years after the fact, this single document still continued to form the backbone for Bruno's trial. Mocenigo's subsequent behavior in Venice had revealed him as a malevolent crank, but the trial of his former houseguest had long since taken on a life of its own in Rome. The Roman inquisitors knew Giovanni Mocenigo only on paper, as the writer of three indignant letters in the summer of 1592.

Mocenigo's charge about transubstantiation was one of the items that Bruno emphatically denied under questioning; the Roman Inquisition, therefore, must not have been convinced by his protestations. If Bellarmine's other propositions followed the same pattern as the first—that is, they were drawn from Mocenigo's original accusation and elaborated by the *Summary*—then we can create a reasonably plausible list by combining these two sources. Here, for example, are seven other accusations that might be described under the "etc. et infra" of Bruno's sentence, listed in the order that they appear in Mocenigo's letter, but recorded as they have been paraphrased under their respective headings in the *Summary* that guided the inquisitors in their final deliberations in 1598:

2 (*Summary* heading 3). About Christ. Giovanni Mocenigo, informer: "I have sometimes heard Giordano say in my house that Christ was a wretch, and that, if he did wretched things to seduce the people, he could perfectly well have predicted that he would have to hang, and that Christ performed illusory miracles and that he was a magician, that Christ showed he was unwilling to die, and fled to the extent that he could."

3 (*Summary* heading 2). About the Trinity, divinity, and incarnation. Giovanni Mocenigo, informer: "I have sometimes heard Giordano say in my house that there is no distinction of persons in God, and that this would be an imperfection in God."

4 (*Summary* heading 7). That there are multiple worlds. Giovanni Mocenigo, informer: "I have sometimes heard Giordano Bruno say in my house that there are infinite worlds, and that God makes infinite worlds continually, because, he says, he wants to do so as much as he can."

5 (*Summary* heading 22). About the souls of men and beasts. Giovanni Mocenigo, informer: "I have sometimes heard Giordano say in my house that the souls created by the work of nature pass from one animal to another, and that, just as brute animals are born of corruption, so are men, when they return to be born after the floods."

6 (*Summary* heading 1). That Brother Giordano has bad feelings about the holy Catholic faith, against which, and its ministers, he has spoken ill. Giovanni Mocenigo, informer in Venice: "I have sometimes heard Giordano say in my house that no religion pleases him. He has shown that he plans to make himself the creator of a new sect under the name of 'new philosophy' and has said that our Catholic faith is full of blasphemies against the majesty of God, and that it is time to remove the discussion and the income from friars, because they defile the world, that they are all asses, and that our opinions are the doctrine of asses, that we have no proof that our faith has any merit with God, and that he marvels at how many heresies God tolerates among Catholics."

7 (*Summary* heading 24). That sins are not to be punished. Giovanni Mocenigo, informer: "I have sometimes heard Giordano say in my house that there is no punishment for sins, and he has said that not doing to others what we do not want them to do to us is enough [advice] to live well."

8 (*Summary* heading 23). About the art of divination. Giovanni Mocenigo, informer: "I have sometimes heard Giordano say in my house that he wants to pay attention to the art of divination and he wants all the world to follow after him, and when I kept him locked up to report him, he asked me to give back a copy of a book of spells that I had found among his papers."

As the records of the Venetian Inquisition reveal, several of these propositions had appeared, more modestly expressed, in the trials of other people who came before the Holy Office in the same year as Giordano Bruno. Bruno's opinions struck, then, at the papacy's worst fears about Protestants on one side, renegade natural philosophers on another, and on yet another, those ancient objects of fear, the Jews.

The Protestant congregations in neighboring Lombardy, like the one that produced the convert Marcantonio Pestalozzi, specifically rejected transubstantiation, intercession by the Virgin and the saints, purgatory, confession, and even baptism; multiple worlds existed in Jewish mysticism; and most Protestants shared Bruno's reported skepticism about the Roman Church and its rituals, echoing his desire to strip its precepts to the apostles' simple life or to the Golden Rule. In the Roman phase of Bruno's trial, the Protestant position on papal authority became particularly crucial. As Pestalozzi had declared to his Venetian inquisitors: "In my faith I have believed up to now that neither the pope nor any other priest has the authority to absolve us from sin, but only God alone."

When Giovanni Marsilio rendered his own account of Bellarmine's rhetorical "arts," the sorest point of contention was precisely this one: the source of the Church's authority. Marsilio was not the only contemporary who found Cardinal Bellarmine a little too ready to identify his own opinions automatically with those of the institution he represented. Prelates from Pope Sixtus V to Decio Cardinal Azzolini detected something insufferably arrogant about this Tuscan Jesuit and took action accordingly: Sixtus, pulled up short by Bellarmine for errors in one of the publications he had sponsored, had retaliated by putting the censor's *Disputations* on the *Index of Forbidden Books*; Azzolini, for his part, squelched an early attempt at canonization (in fact, Bellarmine would be canonized only in 1930).

Bruno showed no greater willingness than Pope Sixtus or Giovanni Marsilio to bow to the Church's chosen censor; he wanted confirmation of that authority from the pope, as the text of his sentence reveals, addressing him: "You replied that if the Holy See and the Holiness of Our Lord had declared the eight propositions as definitively heretical, or that His Holiness knew them to be such, or that they had been so defined by the Holy Spirit, then you were disposed to revoke them."

Not only was Bruno's statement openly defiant, but it also veered perilously close to the Italian secular ritual of giving the lie. When two men began the escalating exchange of insults that led to a duel, the final insult, the phrase that automatically provoked the challenge, was *"menti per la gola"*—"you lie through your throat." In 1606, Giovanni Marsilio would more delicately describe Bellarmine's authoritarian tendencies as taking the "road of supposi-tion." But there is nothing delicate about Bruno's retort. It is an open challenge, and by specifically proclaiming his skepticism about the eight propositions, he ensured that the whole Inquisition knew that his challenge to this philosophical duel was aimed straight at Robert Cardinal Bellarmine.

CHAPTER TWENTY-SEVEN

Gethsemane

And they came to a place which was named Gethsemane: and he saith
to his disciples, Sit ye here, while I shall pray. And he taketh with him
Peter and James and John, and began to be sore amazed, and to be very
heavy; And saith unto them, My soul is exceeding sorrowful unto
death: tarry ye here, and watch. And he went forward a little, and fell
on the ground, and prayed that, if it were possible, the hour might pass
from him. And he said, Abba, Father, all things are possible unto thee;
take away this cup from me: nevertheless not what I will, but what thou
wilt. —Mark 14:32–36

I remember him saying that the apostles showed more constancy than
Christ, because they showed themselves ready to die and Christ prayed
not to die. —Giovanni Mocenigo, accuser

As Bruno showered opprobrium on the figure of Jesus, their
lives, ironically, took an increasingly parallel course.
Bruno's statements seem to regard Jesus as a symbol of the
institutional Church rather than as a defiant figure in his own
right, the flouter of Jewish Law who dined with publicans and sin-
ners and described himself as a prophet without honor in his own
country. But Giordano Bruno had also spent much of his life contemplating the acts, words, and death of Jesus, and the deeper sig-

nificance of those meditations did not leave him in the prisons of the Inquisition. In many ways, his own passion not only paralleled but also imitated, whether consciously or instinctively, the passion of Christ.

At times, that imitation of Christ all but carried him away, as Giovanni Mocenigo would testify. It is strange to imagine the two of them in a gondola bound for Andrea Palladio's magnificent church of San Giorgio Maggiore, the excitable little Neapolitan bragging more and more extravagantly beneath a building whose calm harmonies and massive proportions could not provide a starker contrast:

> Giovanni Mocenigo, accuser: Once when I was going with Giordano to San Giorgio Maggiore, he said that there was no reason to marvel at the miracles of Christ, because he intended to do even greater things, and he added that it was no miracle that Christ predicted his own death, because with all his misdeeds, he would have to be strung up. In the matter of Christ's miracles he said that he knew how Christ had performed his miracles, and using the same art he intended to do as much and more, but he did not say that Christ was a magician or whether his miracles were real or apparent so far as I remember. But I do remember that because he knew the Hebrew language, he wanted to infer that Christ, who had little knowledge of this language, performed these miracles. I remember him saying that the apostles showed more constancy than Christ, because they showed themselves ready to die and Christ prayed not to die.

Sixteenth-century prisoners were routinely called upon to remember the passion of Christ and his agony in the Garden of Gethsemane; such meditations were seen as a way of steeling them for their own destinies, which often included punishments as brutal and violent as those of ancient Rome. Typically, Bruno laced his meditations with bravado and antiquarian precision:

> Francesco Graziani, cellmate in Venice: I heard him say that Christ had died a shameful death and that all the prophets and Christ died like wretches because everything they had done was a fiction . . . Seeing that the others and I crossed ourselves, he said there was no reason to make

this sign, because Christ was not put on a cross, but on a pillory, on which they used to hang their condemned criminals, and the form of the cross that we have today is the sign that was sculpted on the breast of the goddess Isis, and that that sign had always been held in veneration by the ancients, and the Christians had robbed the ancients by pretending that the wood to which Christ had been nailed had taken that form.

He also treated his cellmates to his own variety of gallows humor:

Matteo Silvestri, cellmate: When he saw us make the sign of the cross, he laughed, and many times when he heard me chant the psalms, and especially chanting the psalm "My God, my God, why hast thou forsaken me?" he yelled at me, saying, "What kind of desperate psalm is this? Shut up, or you'll go to jail!"

The Nolan philosophy offered the Nolan philosopher a way to live in a boundless universe, but when it came to facing down the conventional forces of a world that might no longer have seemed to be "fine as it is," he turned, ironically, instinctively, to something closely resembling Christian morality. Not the morality of his inquisitors, to be sure, but the morality of generations of martyrs, beginning with Jesus himself. In the prison of the Holy Office, Giordano Bruno found his own Gethsemane. Like the Jesus who, "sorrowful unto death," prayed for any possible deliverance from his situation, the philosopher from Nola tried to bargain his fate with Robert Bellarmine, and then, just like the fearful, despondent Christ he had once derided as a *tristo*, he changed his mind.

On the edge of Oxford's Corn Market, on October 16, 1555, Hugh Latimer, bound to the stake, had called over to Nicholas Ridley, condemned to burn with him, "Be of good cheer, Master Ridley, and play the man; for today, God willing, we shall light such a candle in England as shall never go out." Whether or not Bruno had read John Foxe's account of their deaths in his *Book of Martyrs*, he would certainly have known about it from his Anglican hosts at Oxford, just as he knew the stories of early Christian martyrdom from his youth in Naples: Sebastian, bristling with arrows; Peter, crucified upside down; Paul, decapitated; Stephen, stoned; the virgin saints, tortured, healed, and finally decapitated— Catherine with her wheel, Agatha with her severed breasts, Margaret, Ursula, Lucy, Agnes, Cecilia; the Dominican Peter Martyr, skull split by bandits. Like it or not, Bruno had been schooled in resistance, a resistance, he had always been told, that bore extreme witness to an ultimate truth.

In his own way, in his own terms, Giordano Bruno now began to prepare his own martyrdom. If he truly believed his own philosophy, his own death formed an infinitesimal part of the eternal life of the universe, but, like Jesus in the garden, he could not face that truth without passing through a sorrow unto death. Like his God, who would even pardon the demons, Bruno eventually came to pardon, at least by emulation, the Christ figure he had contended with ever since the age of eighteen.

ḥell's Purgatory

Whither shall I go from thy spirit? or whither shall I flee from thy presence?
If I ascend up into heaven, thou art there: if I make my bed in hell, behold,
    thou art there.
If I take the wings of the morning, and dwell in the uttermost parts of the sea;
Even there shall thy hand lead me, and thy right hand shall hold me.
If I say, Surely the darkness shall cover me; even the night shall be light
    about me.
Yea, the darkness hideth not from thee; but the night shineth as the day: the
    darkness and the light are both alike to thee.
                  —Psalm 139:7–12

TEOFILO: To you, Smitho, I will send the Nolan's dialogue called *Hell's
Purgatory*, and there you will see the fruit of redemption.
            —*The Ash Wednesday Supper*, dialogue 5

And what communion hath light with darkness?
            —2 Corinthians 6:14

I n the end, Giordano Bruno seems to have decided that all the debates with his inquisitors about questions of doctrine, cosmology, and even philosophy were beside the point. The only question that mattered was whether the Inquisition could justify its claim to authority over him. Aside from slapping his crazy cell-mate, Fra Celestino, Bruno had done nothing in his life except talk, write, and argue. If he ever acted as a spy, we have no record of it. Although he moved at times in powerful political circles, he had fomented no rebellions, killed no one, tortured no one, stolen nothing. He may have ridiculed his cellmates in Venice for reciting the breviary, but he had never, like the Protestant agitator Walter Merse, interrupted the Mass or profaned the Host. He had observed the terms of his excommunications, Catholic, Calvinist, and Lutheran, as scrupulously as any believer. Nevertheless, his inquisitors, late in the game, discussed subjecting him to torture; technically, this meant ordering that he be examined *stricte*, "strictly." It was his sixteenth interrogation, six years into his imprisonment. Their motive could no longer have been primarily to extract information; Bruno had readily told them his beliefs, in great detail. He had been much less willing, however, to retract those beliefs. Torture might make him do so, if only for the moment of his duress. Thus the recommendation to interrogate him *stricte*, endorsed by every one of his inquisitors, seems mostly to express their frustration with the case; it was an opportunity to watch their clever, obstinate victim bend at last, hanging from a beam by arms tied together behind his back.

It is not clear that Bruno was ever tortured physically (neither is it clear that he was not), but in any case listening to the discussion of torture at the end of his sixteenth interrogation must have been a torture in itself. Some prisoners talked as soon as they saw the instruments that were to be used against them. But inflicting physical harm on a prisoner who had given information willingly was, as the cardinals and Bruno well knew, an outrage against the Inquisition's own ideas of due process.

It was at this point in his long trial, when the cardinals resorted to pure coercion, that Bruno, like many of the Inquisition's victims before and after him, began to contest their very right to sit in judgment at all. Abruptly, as the records seem to show, he turned from an apparent willingness to negotiate with his inquisitors to radical defiance, both of Christian dogma and of the Inquisition's right to enforce it.

The initial negotiations began in mid-January 1599, as his inquisitors would remind him in their final sentence:

> [Eight] propositions were presented to you on the eighteenth of January 1599 in the congregation of the lord prelates held in the Holy Office, and you were assigned the limit of six days in which to deliberate and then answer whether you wanted to abjure said propositions or not.

Bruno's reply a week later only incensed them:

> You replied that if the Holy See and the Holiness of Our Lord [that is, the pope] had declared eight propositions as definitively heretical, or that His Holiness knew them to be such, or that they had been so defined by the Holy Spirit, then you were disposed to revoke them; and then you presented a document addressed to His Holiness and to us, which, as you said, concerned your defense.

This strategy silenced the cardinals for another ten days. However, Bruno's appeal to the pope over their heads seems to have failed; if Clement VIII read the document that Bruno submitted to him, he gave no sign of it. At the beginning of February, the inquisitors returned again to Bellarmine's propositions, again demanding an abjuration. Now Bruno seemed to take a more conciliatory line— except that he still insisted on speaking directly with the pope:

> Subsequently, on the fourth of February 1599, it was ordered that the eight propositions be proposed to you again, as in effect they were proposed to you on the fifteenth of said month, and if you were to recognize them as heretical and desire to abjure them, you would be received in penitence, otherwise, that a term of forty days would be set for you to repent; and you said at the time that you recognized the said eight propositions as heretical and that you were ready to detest and abjure them at a time and place acceptable to the Holy Office, and not only the said eight propositions, but that you were also prepared to perform every obedience with regard to the others that were proposed to you, but afterward, after you had handed over other documents to the Holy Office addressed to the Holiness of Our Lord and to us.

"From which," the inquisitors concluded, "it is manifestly apparent that you stubbornly persevered in your aforementioned errors."

Bruno had to know that he would pay for having "stubbornly persevered" with his death. Thus his own agony in prison, like Jesus' agony in the garden, ended with the resolve to drink the bitter cup he had prayed would pass him by.

Bruno's own view of divine justice could not have diverged more radically from that of the Church, a fact that had emerged early in his trial:

> Francesco Graziano, fellow prisoner in Venice: "He said that neither hell nor purgatory existed, but if one of them had to exist, it would be purgatory, which was more reasonable than hell, for even if the fire were eternal, it did not follow that the punishment would be eternal, because in the end everyone would be saved, and that God's wrath was not eternal. He cited [Jeremiah 3:5] *Will he reserve his anger forever?* and also said that at the end of the world even the demons would be saved, because [Psalm 36:6] *O LORD, thou preservest man and beast.* And if I argued with him, he said that I was a beast and a goatherd, and that I knew nothing."

The Nolan philosopher's last known act, as the eyewitness Gaspar Schoppe reported, was to turn his head away from the crucifix put before his eyes when he mounted the stake. Bound, with his tongue stopped (probably by a leather bridle, possibly by an iron spike), he could do no more than launch what Schoppe called "a fierce expression," and that expression in that public place must have read as contempt for the crucified image as well as for the Church his executioners claimed to represent.

His teacher Fra Teofilo da Vairano had written eloquently and broadly about the membership of the Church as a gathering of all humankind. Bruno himself had written about "that law of love that is spread far and wide . . . which derives . . . from God the father of all things, so that it is in harmony with all nature, and teaches a general philanthropy by which we love even our enemies, lest we become like brutes and barbarians, and are transformed into his image who makes his sun rise over good and bad, and pours out a rain of grace upon the just and the unjust."

"This," he had told Rudolf II, "is the religion that I observe, which is without controversy and beyond all dispute, whether of the spirit's inclination or the principle of ancestral or national custom." If the inquisitors killed him for observing it, they would have to explain to the world how they could do so in the name of love, forgiveness, and the Gospel. As Saint Paul wrote, "What communion hath light with darkness?"

CHAPTER TWENTY-NINE

The Sentence

ROME, 1600

Ah, snake! You cannot flee, try as you might;
Slink toward your lair; it's lost now to decay.
Summon your strength; you'll find that it's too slight.
Await the sun; dark clouds obscure the day.
Cry to the peasant: how he hates your bite!
Call Fortune; fool! She's turned her ear away.
Escape, home, strength, stars, man, or destiny:
Not one of them from death can set you free.
—*The Heroic Frenzies*, dialogue 1.5

You may be more afraid to bring that sentence against me than I am to
accept it. —Giordano Bruno, at his condemnation

G iordano Bruno's conviction for heresy hinged on two points: his refusal to believe that the bread of Communion was literally transformed into the body of Christ; and his refusal to renounce as heretical the eight propositions distilled from his writings by Robert Bellarmine. But the eight propositions in themselves did not motivate his sentence. In his last defenses, Bruno declared that the inquisitors had no right to dictate what was heresy and what was not. It was this denial of their authority that sealed his fate: "You replied that if the Holy See and the Holiness of Our Lord had declared the eight propositions as definitively heretical, or that His Holiness knew them to be such, or that they had been so defined by the Holy Spirit, then you were disposed to revoke them."

Needless to say, neither pope nor Holy Spirit intervened to pronounce in a way that Bruno regarded as binding. As for the cardinals, they understood from the outset that the Holy Spirit was present wherever two or more of them gathered together; the Gospel of Matthew said as much for any group of Christians, let alone the Princes of the Church who made up its "sacred Senate": "Jesus said . . . where two or three are gathered together in my name, there am I in the midst of them." Bruno's own ordination as a priest and his ordination as a Dominican priest granted him the right to interpret Scripture on behalf of Holy Mother Church, but by insisting on his own rights to do so in the face of the cardinal inquisitors, he sounded like—was—a Protestant. His invocation of the pope could not negate his refusal to accept every other level of Catholic ecclesiastical authority.

Bruno's position on transubstantiation was also thoroughly Protestant, as the Church of England proclaimed in article 28 of its Thirty-nine Articles of Religion:

> Transubstantiation (or the change of the substance of Bread and Wine) in the Supper of the Lord, cannot be proved by holy Writ; but is repugnant to the plain words of Scripture, overthroweth the nature of a Sacrament, and hath given occasion to many superstitions. The Body of Christ is given, taken, and eaten, in the Supper, only after an heavenly and spiritual manner.

Thomas Aquinas himself had been inclined to agree with Thomas Cranmer and Giordano Bruno rather than Robert Bellarmine on this issue; he insisted that the body of Christ existed in the Host "in symbol, not in actuality"—"*signis tamen et non rebus.*" On many matters, Bruno was a radical thinker. On this particular matter, he was not.

Because Bruno refused to acknowledge the inquisitors' authority, they could only respond by showing him their power, which they did by forcing him to his knees as they read him his sentence:

We proclaim in these documents, state, pronounce, sentence, and declare you, the aforementioned Fra Giordano Bruno, to be an impenitent, pertinacious, and obstinate heretic, and for that reason to incur all the ecclesiastical censures and penalties of the sacred canons, laws, and constitutions, in general and in particular, as those are imposed on such confessed, impenitent, pertinacious, and obstinate heretics; and as such we degrade you in words and declare that you should be degraded, just as we order and command that you now be degraded from all the major and minor ecclesiastical orders to which you have been admitted, according to the order of the holy canons; and that you should be expelled, as we now expel you, from our ecclesiastical bar and from our holy and immaculate Church, of whose mercy you have rendered yourself unworthy.

Bruno's reaction shows how clearly he understood the situation. A German convert to Catholicism, Gaspar Schoppe, was in the audience that attended Bruno's sentencing and left a description: "He made no other reply than, in a menacing tone, [to say], 'You may be more afraid to bring that sentence against me than I am to accept it.'"

The Church in 1600 had good reason to be afraid. Catholic power in Europe was more precarious than ever, not only pitted against the Protestants of northern Europe but also menaced by the thriving empire of the Ottoman Turks. The jubilee in Rome was normally an occasion for the city to present its most attractive face to pilgrims coming to collect indulgences and less devout visitors coming to see the show. Clement VIII, an apparently enlightened cardinal who became an authoritarian pope, used his jubilee for more basic displays of power, relying on help from the civic authorities headed by the governor of Rome. In a series of spectacular public executions, he gave dramatic proof of his, and therefore Rome's, devotion to the principles of Church and family.

Thus in 1599, when the wife and children of the noble Cenci family were accused of plotting to kill their tyrannical, violent patriarch, they were all arrested, put into prison, and examined under torture. The investigators spared neither the teenage Beatrice Cenci, who had been molested repeatedly by her father, nor her younger brother, still a child. Their prosecution served to confirm, through an unforgettable public drama, that paternal rights were the only valid basis of family life. Each one of the Cenci was therefore sentenced to death by public execution. The spectacle took place, as it often did, in the piazza in front of the Tor di Nona prison. Beatrice and her mother were simply beheaded, although in the case of Beatrice the decapitation was not so simple—it took three blows of the ax. The males of the family were drawn and quartered, after having their flesh torn with hot pincers.

The Cenci, for all the public clamor of their trial and punishment, had tried to resolve their private travails privately, by a discreet assassination; it was the pope and the papal government that decided to bring their case out into the open. But the Protestant agitators who began to disrupt Catholic Masses in preparation for the jubilee intended their actions as public actions from the outset, as deliberate defiance of Catholic power both in the world around them and in the realm of the spirit.

The Inquisition's response to these provocations was increased violence. Walter Merse, the Scotsman, had been burned alive at the stake just before the Cenci executions. Then it was the turn of Bruno's former cellmate Fra Celestino da Verona.

The decision to burn Giordano Bruno was more complex, and required long deliberation. It seems likely that the inquisitors' slow pace was dictated by more than an insistence on correct procedure. In the first place, Bruno, however heretical his propositions may have sounded to their ears, had been a formidable opponent. With the exception of Bellarmine (and perhaps not even he), they may not quite have understood his philosophy. Second, Bruno seems to have forged influential connections throughout much of Europe. His travels had taken him to the Continent's largest cities and into the presence of an impressive number of kings and queens—Henri III and Henri IV in Paris, Elizabeth I in London, Rudolf II in Prague—not to mention a succession of landgraves, dukes, and electors, as well as a pair of popes, Pius V at the promising start of his career and Clement VIII at its tragic ending. Pope Clement and the inquisitors may well have taken time to consider exactly what kind of risk they ran in executing Bruno, and consequently how public, and how dramatic, they should dare to make his death. It was Bellarmine, in fact, who would live to regret their decision.

Article 20 of the Church of England's Articles of Religion declares:

> The Church hath power to decree Rites or Ceremonies, and authority in Controversies of Faith: and yet it is not lawful for the Church to ordain any thing that is contrary to God's Word written, neither may it so expound one place of Scripture, that it be repugnant to another. Wherefore, although the Church be a witness and a keeper of Holy Writ, . . . it ought not to decree any thing against the same.

Giordano Bruno's vision of the universe has long since been accepted by Christian creeds of every stripe, proving the Nolan's argument that insisting upon any more limited creation diminishes the grandeur of God. The same kind of grandeur distinguished Bruno's view of divine mercy as an absolute certainty. However strenuously he continued to contest Christianity, he had absorbed the Christian Gospels through and through: "Then came Peter to [Jesus], and said, Lord, how oft shall my brother sin against me, and I forgive him? till seven times? Jesus saith unto him, I say not unto thee, Until seven times: but, Until seventy times seven."

The Inquisition would take a less forgiving view of the Nolan and his philosophy. His sentence defined him irrevocably as a heretic, but this was only the beginning of his ritual separation from the Church. In the course of his life, he had taken a whole series of religious vows, and in a ceremony known as "solemn degradation," performed immediately after the sentencing, he was formally stripped of them, one by one. A degradation usually took two or three hours, and the bishop who performed Bruno's degradation on February 8, 1600, was well paid for his time. First he took away the symbols of Bruno's priesthood—the paten and chalice of Communion and the chasuble—as he pronounced the terrible formulas that cast the Nolan permanently from the priesthood and forbade him to say Mass. Next he took away the deacon's stole and New Testament, forbidding him to pronounce on Scripture, then a subdeacon's alb and maniple, an acolyte's candle, stripped off Bruno's Dominican scapular, and then his white habit, and finally, to eliminate any trace of a friar's tonsure (if it still existed), shaved his head and face.

At last he consigned the bald heretic, now hastily dressed in layman's clothing, to the secular arm of Rome's government—that is, to a bailiff—urging the Roman authorities all the while to use mercy and avoid the shedding of blood. Only then, after an ordeal of several hours, was the prisoner bundled off from a cardinal's palazzo in Piazza Navona to the dank riverside cells of the prison of Tor di Nona. There followed eight days of appeals to repent by successive teams of friars: Dominicans, Bruno's former order; Augustinians, the order of his beloved teacher Fra Teofilo da Vairano; and Franciscans, the friars who shared his belief that God was to be found everywhere in nature. And then, on February 17, 1600, it was all over. At dawn on Ash Wednesday, Giordano Bruno mounted a donkey and rode forth to the stake.

The Field of Flowers

Is it nothing to you, all ye that pass by? Behold, and see if there be any
sorrow like unto my sorrow.   —Lamentations of Jeremiah 1:12

Dispatch from Rome, February 19, 1600:

Thursday morning in Campo de' Fiori that wicked Dominican friar from
Nola was burned alive, the one mentioned before: the most obstinate of
heretics, and because in his imagination he had formed certain beliefs contrary to our faith, and in particular about the Holy Virgin and the saints,
the wicked man wanted to die obstinate in those beliefs. And he said that
he died a martyr, and willingly, and that his soul would ascend with the
smoke into paradise. Well, now he will see whether he spoke the truth.

Giordano Bruno, *On the Immense and the Numberless*:

Hence as I make my journey, secure and sufficiently happy,
Suddenly I am raised aloft by primordial passion;
I become Leader, Law, Light, Prophet, Father, Author, and Journey,
Rising above this world to the others that shine in their splendor.
I wander through every part of that ethereal country;
Then, far away, as they gape at the marvel, I leave them behind me.

Epilogue: The Four Rivers

Opus doctore est, non tortore.

A teacher is what's needed, not a torturer.
— Justus Lipsius, paraphrased

Giordano Bruno's execution was designed to show the world that he had died a lone fanatic, not only defrocked and degraded by formal Church procedure, but also literally stripped bare of every worldly object before he was tied to the stake. If he had friends or sympathizers among the crowds who watched him burn to death, no one noticed them. Like the animals and people who were victims of the ancient Roman games, Giordano Bruno, or that part of him that had not been transformed into ether, was swept up with the ashes of his pyre and dumped into the Tiber. It would take a separate decree of the Holy Office to consign his writings, "every one of them"—"*omnia scripta*"—to the *Index of Forbidden Books*. And then Giordano Bruno was supposed to disappear.

But the reach of the *Index* stopped at the borders of Spain and Italy. Furthermore, a misprint in the Spanish version of the *Index* meant that in the Iberian Peninsula and the New World the forbidden author became "Iordanus Bruerus Holanus," so that in theory some daring soul could have argued that no prohibition affected the reading of "Iordanus Brunus Nolanus." There is no record, however, that anyone tried to do so. The error was reprinted, in issue after issue of the Spanish *Index*, suggesting that the list was neither read nor proofread with any particular care.

In Italy, meanwhile, powerful people could read whatever they liked. Francesco Cardinal Barberini, whose uncle Urban VIII led Galileo's prosecution for heresy, owned a copy of *Cause, Principle, and Unity*. The library in the Jesuits' Roman College must have contained several of Bruno's books as well, because seventeenth-century Jesuit authors cite them.

An exchange between Kepler and Galileo in 1610 shows that Galileo had also read Giordano Bruno's work on cosmology, and until 1601 it had been perfectly legal to do so. In 1610, when Galileo wrote his *Starry Messenger* to announce that the telescope had shown him moons around Jupiter and craters on the lunar surface, he sent a copy of the new book to Kepler in Prague. Kepler responded almost immediately in a long letter; this Galileo published in Florence as a small book in itself. In his letter, Kepler tellingly associates Bruno's ideas about the infinite universe with prison and displacement, as if the philosopher's thoughts automatically brought on the confinement and exile of which Bruno's life had seemed to consist rather than, as Bruno had seen it, a deliverance from all bondage and all strangeness:

> In the first place, I rejoice that you have restored me not a little by your labors. If you had found planets circling one of the fixed stars, there among Bruno's infinities I had already prepared my prison shackles, that is, my exile in that Infinity. Thus you freed me from the great fear that I had conceived when I first heard about your book . . . because you say that these four planets run their course around Jupiter rather than one of the fixed stars.

Evidently, Kepler had no intention of giving up his own vision of a finite universe laid out according to musical intervals, until the day when observation would force him to revise it.

Another of Kepler's comments to Galileo is, if anything, more revealing. The discoveries proclaimed by *The Starry Messenger* depended on the invention of a mechanical device, the telescope, in 1609. Making those observations, however, was by no means easy, and interpretation more difficult still. *The Starry Messenger* proves that Galileo was a superb technician, a superb observer, and a superb draftsman as well as an eloquent writer. His telescope boasted finer lenses than the Belgian original on which he based his design; his drawings of the moon's surface are also extraordinary works of art. Some editions of *The Starry Messenger* show the constellation of the Pleiades bursting the margins of the page, just as contemporary cosmology was beginning to burst the margins of the universe. Yet Kepler tells Galileo that he himself is more impressed by the ingenuity of a thinker like Bruno, who predicted what the telescope would eventually reveal, than Galileo, who plied the telescope with such skill. Bruno's gift for speculation, he suggests, is more truly godlike than Galileo's empirical observations:

> For the glory of this world's Architect greatly exceeds that of the person, however ingenious, who contemplates it. The former, after all, drew the principles of its creation from within himself, whereas the latter, after great effort, scarcely recognizes the expression of such principles in that same creation. Certainly those who can conceive the causes of phenomena in their minds before the phenomena themselves have been revealed are more like Architects than the rest of us, who consider causes only after they have seen the phenomena. Do not, therefore, Galileo, begrudge our predecessors their proper credit . . . you refine a doctrine borrowed from Bruno.

Kepler's admonition is not entirely fair; Galileo, writing in Italy, had good reason not to have mentioned his readings among Bruno's banned books. Within six years, the Tuscan astronomer would be negotiating himself with Cardinal Bellarmine and the Holy Office. However, Kepler's preference for speculation over experimentation was common to his time; Galileo, however strongly he advocated empirical observation, also made purely conceptual experiments. In fact, one of his most famous thought problems, involving motion, had also exercised Giordano Bruno.

Another of Galileo's most vivid pronouncements had to do with the importance of mathematics to scientific investigation, although he calls this activity not science but philosophy in his 1623 book on comets, *The Assayer*:

> Perhaps [my adversary] thinks that philosophy is a book, and one man's imaginings, like the *Iliad*, and *Orlando Furioso*, books in which the least important matter is whether the contents are true. Signor Sarsi, it's not like that. Philosophy is written in this great book that stands continually open before our eyes (I mean the universe), but you cannot understand it until you learn to understand its language, and know the script in which it is written. It is written in the language of mathematics, and the letters are triangles, circles, and other geometric figures, and without these means it is impossible for a person to understand one word; [to be] without them is to wander vainly through a dark labyrinth.

Galileo's statement has been quoted ever since the eighteenth century because of its striking imagery, and because of the rigorous experimentation by which his science bore it out. Yet the idea that mathematics underpinned philosophy was as old as Pythagoras (and was so pervasive in Greco-Roman culture that the practical Roman architect Vitruvius could praise Plato first and foremost as a mathematician). In the generation before Galileo, Giordano Bruno had already made the same case for the preeminence of mathematics in philosophy. The Nolan philosophy, however, made scant use of calculations or empirical observations. Instead, it relied on mental geometries that are strange to us, and foresaw the need for new kinds of mathematics to account for the conditions of an expanded universe. Bruno's mathematical world is in some respects entirely alien to modern science; in other respects (especially in the recognizably Platonic emphasis of string theory on unity and elegance) it is uncannily familiar.

Modern science, and the history of science, have emphasized the differences between Galileo and Bruno, but there are also profound similarities between the two, as both Johannes Kepler and Robert Bellarmine recognized from their different perspectives.

Another figure neglected until recently, the German Jesuit

Athanasius Kircher, was also a reader of Bruno who presented elements of the Nolan philosophy to a wider public. Among a welter of fanciful ideas, Kircher also made some real progress in the sciences: he is now acknowledged as the inventor of plate tectonics, as the first person to propose a microbial origin for bubonic plague, and as the first scholar to suggest that Coptic, the liturgical language of Egyptian Christians, would provide the key to deciphering Egyptian hieroglyphics. With dozens of books to his name, many of them lavish picture books, he was also one of the most influential writers on natural philosophy in the entire seventeenth century, an author whose books were literally distributed worldwide through the global networks of the Society of Jesus.

As a literary figure, Bruno also continued to exert influence beyond his imprisonment and execution; his impact on Galileo's *Dialogue Concerning the Two Chief World Systems* is evident in the later dialogue's subject matter and its sparkling style. The extent of his effect on English literature is harder to gauge, but from Shakespeare's *Antony and Cleopatra* to an early-seventeenth-century motet like Orlando Gibbons's "O Thou, the Central Orb" (in which God is addressed as "the central orb of righteous love / pure beam of the on high / eternal light to this our bleak world") it is possible to see glimmers of the Nolan philosophy.

By bearing steadfast witness to his own beliefs, Bruno also influenced the Church away from a policy of punishment toward a policy of persuasion. For the jubilee year of 1650, rather than scheduling the immolation of heretics, Pope Innocent X commissioned projects to beautify Rome, redecorating churches and installing a monumental fountain in Piazza Navona. There, thanks to the collaboration of the great sculptor Gian Lorenzo Bernini and the Jesuit Athanasius Kircher, an Egyptian obelisk stands above a travertine mountain whose slopes bear personifications of four rivers, representing four continents of the world, amid a burgeoning population of stone plants, animals, and sea monsters. At the obelisk's peak flies a gilded bronze dove with an olive branch in its beak. The dove symbolizes the pope's family, which had a dove in its coat of arms, but in 1650, with the Thirty Years' War newly ended, it would be hard not to think about the dove in its usual role as a symbol of peace, as a kind of Christian hieroglyph of that idea. The fountain's design, however, celebrates not so much the temporal peace of 1648 as peace of another kind: the partnership of natural philosophy—science—and religion. Only profound knowledge of nature's laws could pump water into the middle of a city square in this profusion, or carve graceful texts into the surface of granite. But only faith could inspire the effort of carving granite in the first place. Mastery of physics keeps the obelisk standing above a hollow shell of travertine, but Bernini had no doubt that what guided his hand to create that hollow shell was divine inspiration. The *Fountain of the Four Rivers* simply could not exist if its makers did not believe that science and religion belonged together. Only a few blocks from the place where Giordano Bruno perished by fire, this assemblage of stone, water, and bronze suggests another kind of response to the challenges of his philosophy, joyful, generous, thoughtful, and surpassingly beautiful.

APPENDIX

NOTES

BIBLIOGRAPHY

ACKNOWLEDGMENTS

INDEX

Appendix: Bruno's Sentence

A copy of the sentence leveled against Friar Iordanus of Nola, consigned to the Most Illustrious Governor of the City of Rome:

We, Lodovico Madruzzo, bishop of Santa Sabina, Giulio Antonio Santori, bishop of Palestrina called of Santa Severina, Pietro Dezza, titular cardinal of San Lorenzo in Lucino, Domenico Pinello, titular cardinal of San Crisogono, Friar Hieronymo Bernerio d'Ascoli, titular cardinal of Santa Maria Sopra Minerva, Paolo Sfondrato, titular cardinal of Santa Cecilia, Lutio Sasso, titular cardinal of Santi Quirico e Giulitta, Camillo Borghese, titular cardinal of Santi Giovanni e Paolo, Pompeo Arrigone, titular cardinal of Santa Balbina, and Roberto Bellarmino, titular cardinal of Santa Maria in Via, summoned by the mercy of God cardinal priests of the Holy Roman Church in all the Christian republic, inquisitors general against heretical depravity, specially deputed by the Holy Apostolic See:

Because you, Fra Giordano, son of the late Giovanni Bruno of Nola in the Kingdom of Naples, professed priest of the order of Saint Dominic, at the age of circa fifty-two years, were denounced to the Holy Office in Venice eight years ago:

That you said that it was a great blasphemy to say that bread transubstantiates into flesh, etc. et infra.

These propositions were presented to you on the eighteenth of January 1599 in the congregation of the lord prelates held in the Holy Office, and you were assigned the limit of six days in which to deliberate and then answer whether you wanted to abjure said propositions or not, and then on the twenty-fifth of said month, when the same congregations had assembled again in the same place, you replied that if the Holy See and the Holiness of Our Lord had declared eight propositions as definitively heretical, or that His Holiness knew them to be such, or that they had been so defined by the Holy Spirit, then you were disposed to revoke them; and then you presented a document addressed to His Holiness and to us, which, as you said, concerned your defense, and subsequently, on the fourth of February 1599, it was ordered that the eight propositions be proposed to you again, as in effect they were proposed to you on the fifteenth of said month, and if you were to recognize them as heretical and desire to abjure them, you would be received in penitence, otherwise, that a term of forty days would be set for you to repent; and you said at the time that you recognized the said eight propositions as heretical and that you were ready to detest and abjure them at a time and place acceptable to the Holy Office, and not only the said eight propositions, but that you were also prepared to perform every obedience with regard to the others that were proposed to you, but afterward, after you had handed over other documents to the Holy Office addressed to the Holiness of Our Lord and to us, from which it is manifestly apparent that you stubbornly persevered in your aforementioned errors.

And because notice has been given that you were denounced to the Holy Office in Vercelli, and when you were in England you were reputed to be an atheist and that you had written a book about the Triumphant Beast, on the tenth of the month of September 1599 you were given the term of forty days in which to repent, after which proceedings would be taken against you as the holy canons order and command; and because you nonetheless remained obstinate and impenitent in your errors and heresies, the Right Reverend Father Ipolito Maria Beccaria, general, and Father Fra Paolo Isaresio della Mirandola, procurator of your order, so that they admonish and persuade you to recognize your most grave errors and heresies; nonetheless, you have always stubbornly and obstinately persevered in these said erroneous and heretical opinions of yours.

For which reasons, having seen and considered the trial mounted against you, and the confessions of your errors and heresies with stubborn persistence—although you deny that they are such—and all the other matters to be seen and considered: your case having been presented before our general congregation in the presence of the Holiness of Our Lord on the twenty-second of January last, and voted and resolved, we have arrived at the following sentence:

Therefore, invoking the name of Our Lord Jesus Christ and of his most glorious mother ever virgin Mary, in the case and cases aforementioned pending at present before this Holy Office between the Reverend Giulio Monterentii, doctor of law, fiscal procurator of said Holy Office on one side, and you the aforesaid Fra Giordano Bruno, a felon examined, tried, found guilty, impenitent, obstinate, and pertinacious on the other, by this our definitive sentence, on the counsel and opinion of the Reverend Fathers who are masters of sacred theology and doctors of canon and civil law, our consultants, we proclaim in these documents, state, pronounce, sentence, and declare you, the aforementioned Fra Giordano Bruno, to be an impenitent, pertinacious, and obstinate heretic, and for that reason to incur all the ecclesiastical censures and penalties of the sacred canons, laws, and constitutions, in general and in particular, as those are imposed on such confessed, impenitent, pertinacious, and obstinate heretics; and as such we degrade you in words and declare that you should be degraded, just as we order and command that you now be degraded from all the major and minor ecclesiastical orders to which you have been admitted, according to the order of the holy canons; and that you should be expelled, as we now expel you, from our ecclesiastical bar and from our holy and immaculate Church, of whose mercy you have rendered yourself unworthy; and that you should be released to the secular court, as we now release you to the court of Your Honor, Monsignor Governor of Rome here present, to punish you with the appropriate punishments, heartily enjoining you to mitigate the rigor of the law about the punishment of your person, that it should be without danger of death or mutilation of limb.

Furthermore, we condemn, reprove, and prohibit all the books aforementioned and all other books and writings of yours as heretical and erroneous and containing many heresies and errors, ordering that all those that have up to now and in the future shall be consigned to the Holy Office shall be publicly destroyed and burned in the piazza of Saint Peter's, before the stairs, and as such they shall be posted on the *Index of Prohibited Books*, as we now order be done.

And thus we state, pronounce, sentence, declare, degrade, command, and order, expel, and release and pray that in this and in every other most binding way and form that we can and ought reasonably to do.

So pronounce we the undersigned Cardinals Inquisitors General:

> Ludovicus Cardinal Madruzzi
> Iulius Antonius Cardinal Santa Severina
> Petrus Cardinal Dezza
> Dominicus Cardinal Pinellus
> Fra Hieronymus Cardinal d'Ascoli
> [Paulus Cardinal Sfondrato]
> Lutius Cardinal Sasso
> Camillus Cardinal Borghese
> Pompeius Cardinal Arrigoni
> Robertus Cardinal Bellarminus

The aforementioned sentence was rendered and given by the aforementioned Most Illustrious and Most Reverend Lord Cardinals Inquisitors General sitting at the bench in Rome in the general congregation of the Holy Roman and Universal Inquisition held in the presence of the aforementioned Most Illustrious and Most Reverend Lord Cardinals Inquisitors General in the palazzo that is the habitual residence of the aforementioned Most Illustrious and Most Reverend Lord Cardinal Madruzzi by the Church of Sant'Agnese in Agone, in the year of our Lord's birth 1600, on the eighth day of the month of February . . . cited yesterday for today and sent by a courier of Our Most Holy Lord the Pope to the aforementioned Brother Jordano, summoned to hear said sentence.

And on the same day, by an order of the Most Illustrious and Reverend Lord Cardinals Inquisitors General, said Fra Jordano having been led out of the jail of the Holy Inquisition and conducted to the palazzo that is the habitual residence of the aforementioned Most Illustrious and Most Reverend Lord Cardinal Madruzzi, and with himself present and hearing said sentence recorded by myself the Notary, by their order, in a loud and intelligible voice, it was read and published.

Notes

References to Bruno's works cite the section of the work in which the passage is found rather than pages of a particular edition. Like most sixteenth-century works, Bruno's are divided into small sections, so that tracing an individual reference is never difficult.

PROLOGUE: THE HOODED FRIAR
3 statue of a hooded friar: See Berggren, "Visual Image of Giordano Bruno."
7 "It is not our place": Angelo Cardinal Sodano, "Letter [Feb. 14, 2000] of the Cardinal Secretary of State . . . to the Principal of the Pontifical Theological Faculty of Southern Italy," www.vatican.va/roman_curia/secretariat_state/documents/re _segst_doc_20000217_sodano-letter_it.html.

1: A MOST SOLEMN ACT OF JUSTICE
9 For a public execution: See Ricci, *Giordano Bruno*, pp. 542–57; Spampanato, *Vita*, pp. 579–98; Firpo, *Il processo*, pp. 87–104.
10 Protestant troublemakers: See also the *Avvisi di Roma*.
11 "Today we thought": *Avvisi di Roma*.
11 the burning of a Scottish heretic: His name was Walter Merse, and his death is reported in a compilation of executions effected in Rome under various popes, including Clement VIII; Biblioteca Apostolica Vaticana, MS Urb. Lat. 1645, 337r–340v. The passage cited is found on 340r.

2: THE NOLAN PHILOSOPHER
14 Bruno's home: Spampanato, *Vita*, pp. 1–66; Ricci, *Giordano Bruno*, pp. 7–32.
15 discuss how to live wisely: Bruno, *Heroic Frenzies*, pt. 1, dialogue 2.
16 "Once, when I was a boy": Bruno, *On the Immense and the Numberless*, 3.1.
17 as if he were still there: Bruno, *Expulsion of the Triumphant Beast*, pt. 3, dialogue 1.

3: *"NAPOLI È TUTTO IL MONDO"*

My special thanks to Eugenio Canone, Maria Ann Conelli, Mario Pereira, Livio Pestilli, Sebastian Schütze, and John Marino for information about all things Neapolitan.

19 umbrella pine: This is the description of Pliny the Younger, an eyewitness to the eruption of A.D. 79, *Letters*, 6.16; see also 6.20.

19 rivers of fire: In fact, a flood in 1504 had generated a Nolan proverb about fearing water more than fire; see Bruno, *Candlemaker*.

20 "It was almost as if": Bruno, *On the Immense and the Numberless*, 3.1.

20 wine: Bruno specifically mentions the *asprinio* of Nola and the "greco" of Vesuvius in *Expulsion of the Triumphant Beast*, dialogue 3.

21 *"benigno cielo"*: The line comes from *Ash Wednesday Supper*, dialogue 4; see the epigraph to chap. 17.

21 Beneath that benign heaven: Spampanato, *Vita*, pp. 66–243; Ricci, *Giordano Bruno*, pp. 32–51; Nino Leone, *La vita quotidiana a Napoli al tempo di Masaniello* (Milan: Fabbri, 1998).

21 Naples's sixteenth-century population: See Chase-Dunn and Willard, "Systems of Cities and World-Systems": In 1550, "Ottoman Constantinople was once again the largest city with a population of 660,000. Cairo was now second with 360,000, down 40,000 since 1500. [Tabriz, with about 275,000, would have been third.] Paris was growing again with 210,000. Naples was in fifth place with 209,000." By 1575, Cairo's population had shrunk and that of Paris and Naples had grown.

23 Spanish Inquisition: Ricci, *Giordano Bruno*, pp. 47–48; Olga Casale, introduction to Giovanni Battista Pino, *Ragionamento sovra del asino*, ed. Olga Casale (Rome: Salerno Editrice, 1982).

23 "the influence": Ricci, *Giordano Bruno*, p. 33.

23 "To whom shall I dedicate": Bruno, *Candlemaker*, "To Signora Morgana B."

4: *"THE WORLD IS FINE AS IT IS"*

25 "The comedy will have": Bruno, *Candlemaker*, proprologue.

26 "Consider that, like virgins": Ibid., act 2, scene 3.

27 "It is common opinion": Ibid., act 5, scene 19.

28 "O gentle master": Ibid., act 2, scene 1.

5: *"I HAVE, IN EFFECT, HARBORED DOUBTS"*

29 San Domenico Maggiore: Miele (who is himself a member of the congregation of San Domenico Maggiore), "L'organizzazione degli studi"; Miele, "Indagini sulla comunità conventuale"; Spampanato, *Vita*, pp. 147–93.

29 Oziosi: I am indebted to Mario Pereira, "The Accademia degli Oziosi" (master's thesis, University of Chicago, 1997).

30 weapons: Spampanato, *Vita*, pp. 196–212, 619–25.

30 Fra Teofilo Caracciolo: Ibid., pp. 200–201.

30 Gregory XIII: Cited in ibid., p. 200.

31 less accommodating: Canone, *Giordano Bruno, 1548–1600*, p. 37.

31 Council of Trent: O'Malley, *Trent and All That*; Gleason, *Gasparo Contarini*.

33 "I have, in effect, harbored doubts": Firpo, *Il processo*, p. 170.

33 Fra Giordano Crispo: Spampanato, *Vita*, p. 125.

34 expulsion: Miele, "L'organizzazione degli studi," pp. 49–50.

35 project he must have: An excellent account is in O'Malley, *Praise and Blame in Renaissance Rome*.

35 "Is it nothing to you": The sorrows of Don Carlo Gesualdo, always a strange, aloof man, finally took him to the verge of madness; he would shock the residents of Piazza San Domenico one morning in 1590 when he opened his palazzo's huge wooden door and laid out the naked, ravaged bodies of his earthy young wife, Maria d'Avalos, and her dashing lover, Fabrizio Carafa, whom he had stabbed the night before when he discovered them in bed together, as well as the body of the young daughter he now suspected might have been Fabrizio's child rather than his own.

6: "I CAME INTO THIS WORLD TO LIGHT A FIRE"

39 Bernardino of Siena: Iris Origo, *The World of San Bernardino* (New York: Harcourt, Brace & World, 1962); Bolzoni, *Web of Images*.

39 Mariano da Genazzano: O'Malley, *Praise and Blame in Renaissance Rome*.

39 Giles of Viterbo: O'Malley, *Giles of Viterbo*; Martin, *Friar, Reformer, and Renaissance Scholar*.

41 Fra Teofilo da Vairano: Giovanni Mercati, *Prolegomena*, pp. 121–23; Carella, "Tra i maestri"; Ricci, *Giordano Bruno*, pp. 40–46.

42 "what we have been taught": Teofilo da Vairano, *De gratia Novi Testamenti*, c. 130r.

43 As it survives today: Probably about half the text of *De gratia Novi Testamenti* has been preserved.

44 "God is love": Pope Benedict XVI, *God Is Love (Deus caritas est)* (Fort Collins, Colo.: Ignatius Press, 2006).

7: FOOTPRINTS IN THE FOREST

45 Marsilio Ficino: James Hankins, *Plato in the Italian Renaissance* (New York: Columbia University Press, 1994); Allen, *Marsilio Ficino and the Phaedran Charioteer*.

46 Bruno's work: For Bruno's relationship to the Augustinians of San Giovanni a Carbonara, see Rowland, "Giordano Bruno and Neapolitan Neoplatonism." For Platonic influence on Bruno, see also Bönker-Vallon, "Unità nascosta."

46 In one manuscript from the Seripando library: Now Naples, Biblioteca Nazionale, MS 13.D.43.

46 "girded in chestnut": Bruno, *On the Immense and the Numberless*, 3.1; see chaps. 2 and 3.

47 Calcidius: Van Winden, *Calcidius on Matter*.

47 "That hunter": Marsilio Ficino and Giovanni Cavalcanti to Giorgio Antonio Vespucci, in Ficino, *Opera omnia*, vol. 1.2.631.

48 Seripando's own copy: Naples, Biblioteca Nazionale, MS 8.F.8.

48 *The "Sentences" According to the Mind of Plato: Sententiae ad mentem Platonis.* See

Gionta, " 'Augustinus Dux meus' "; O'Malley, *Giles of Viterbo*, pp. 15–16, 25, 197; Pfeiffer, *Zur Ikonographie von Raffaels Disputa*; Rowland, "Intellectual Background of the *School of Athens*."

49 "Sometimes, however": Giles of Viterbo, *Sententiae*, 37v.

50 a specific sum: Ibid., 37v–38r.

50 "God . . . created": Ibid., 39r.

51 "Those blessed souls": Ibid., 155r–v.

52 "I bear what I've become": Giles of Viterbo, "La caccia bellissima dell'amore," D iiir–v.

8 : A THOUSAND WORLDS

For this chapter, I am indebted to Brian Copenhaver, Peter Mazur, and James Nelson Novoa.

53 all Jews: The Italian periodical *Zakhor*, issued annually, has articles on Jewish life in Italy; see also Cooperman and Garvin, *Jews of Italy*.

55 de Monte's learning and eloquence: Spampanato, *Vita*, pp. 188–89.

55 "Judaizing": This is the subject of a Ph.D. thesis by Peter Mazur, forthcoming from Northwestern University.

56 his readings in Kabbalah: See de León-Jones, *Giordano Bruno and the Kabbalah*; Idel, *Kabbalah*; Secret, *Hermétisme et Kabbale*.

56 Giles of Viterbo: O'Malley, *Giles of Viterbo*; Martin, *Friar, Reformer, and Renaissance Scholar*.

56 "all are elected by God": Teofilo da Vairano, *De gratia Novi Testamenti*, 158v.

56 "Let no one think": Ibid., 144r–166r, esp. 145r, 150r.

57 "to show me a single proof": Ibid., 194v.

57 charity should guide religion: Ibid., 130r.

57 "To get to the individual": Ibid., p. 168.

57 "As for the second person": Ibid., p. 170.

58 the certainties of dogma: The fact that Bruno was encouraged in his opinion by Saint Augustine may suggest, once again, the influence of the Augustinian Teofilo da Vairano. The conclusion that Bruno drew from Augustine, however, that God does not consist in the separate person of Jesus of Nazareth, is evidently his own: Teofilo's one surviving work, *On the Grace of the New Testament*, is, as its name suggests, a devotedly Christian tractate, as were the works of Teofilo's Augustinian forebears Egidio da Viterbo and Girolamo Seripando.

58 Ecclesiastes: Bruno habitually adapts Ecclesiastes 1:9, whose full text states: "The thing that hath been, it is that which shall be; and that which is done is that which shall be done: and there is no new thing under the sun."

59 freethinking Catholics: I owe this information to Peter Mazur.

59 "Do not infer": Bruno, *Expulsion of the Triumphant Beast*, dialogue 3.

59 It is tempting: See, for example, Giovanni Gentile's note to this passage in Giovanni Aquilecchia's edition of Bruno's Italian dialogues, p. 722 n. 2, referring to the Nolan's "hatred for the Jews." (It may be worth noting that although Gentile was Mussolini's minister of education, he protected the Jewish scholar Paul Oskar Kristeller until the latter could escape to the United States; his reading of this passage should be imputed not to personal anti-Semitism but rather to the resonant name of Sophia.)

60 "He said that God": Firpo, *Il processo*, p. 268.
61 "He rides upon a cloud": Biblioteca Apostolica Vaticana, MS Vat. Lat. 5198, 247r.

9: ART AND ASTRONOMY
62 Remembering would become: Yates, *Art of Memory*; Carruthers, *Book of Memory*; Bolzoni, *Gallery of Memory*; Rossi, *Clavis universalis*.
62 Thomas Aquinas: Carruthers, *Book of Memory*, pp. 2–7, 201–4, and passim.
62 perform feats of recall: Ricci, *Giordano Bruno*, pp. 90–97.
63 The basic principle: Yates, *Art of Memory*, pp. 1–49.
64 Ramon Llull: Ibid., pp. 173–98; Rossi, *Clavis universalis*; Ricci, *Giordano Bruno*, pp. 150–65.
64 "We created this Art": Llull, *Ars compendiosa Dei*, p. 1308.
65 San Domenico Maggiore: Canone, *Magia dei contrari*, pp. 95–118.
66 *On the Sphere*: Canone, "Variazioni Bruniane."
66 Copernicus: Michel, *Cosmology of Giordano Bruno*; Gatti, *Giordano Bruno and Renaissance Science*; Blackwell, *Galileo, Bellarmine, and the Bible*; Granada, "Digges, Bruno, e il copernicanesimo in Inghilterra."
67 Telesio had been living: The palazzo of the Duke of Nocera on the Via Medina was destroyed by the urban renewal program of *risanamento* in the late nineteenth century; see Alisio, *Napoli e il risanamento*, p. 133.
67 two mechanical forces, heat and cold: Spruit, "Telesio's Reform."
67 Another view of astronomy: Lattis, *Between Copernicus and Galileo*.
67 Clavius: Ibid.; Baldini, *Legem impone subactis*; Baldini, *Christoph Clavius e l'attività scientifica dei Gesuiti nell' età di Galileo*.
67 commentary on Sacrobosco's *On the Sphere*: Clavius, *Bambergensis* (1570).

10: TROUBLE AGAIN
70 For his own ordination: Spampanato, *Vita*, pp. 162–64, 697.
71 series of theses: Ibid., p. 180.
71 And then, early in 1576: Ricci, *Giordano Bruno*, pp. 100–105, 173–74.
71 As he later told his Venetian inquisitors: Firpo, *Il processo*, p. 157.
71 Bruno moved to Rome: Ricci, *Giordano Bruno*, pp. 104–15.
72 to defend Arius: Firpo, *Il processo*, pp. 170–71.
72 "never made a public denial": Ibid., pp. 167, 170.
74 (as a papal bull put it in 1451): Netanyahu, *Origins of the Inquisition*, p. 1011.
74 obeyed the Spanish crown: Indeed, popes like Sixtus IV and Julius II protested vigorously against the excesses of the Spanish inquisitors; ibid., pp. 1027–40.
74 Roman branch of the Inquisition: Ricci, *Giordano Bruno*, p. 47.
75 attempt to impose the Spanish Inquisition: Ibid., pp. 33, 47–61.
75 But a search of the latrine: Ibid.
75 interconnecting cisterns: The cisterns of Naples can be seen on excellent guided tours, departing from the Spanish Quarter, and underneath the church of San Paolo Maggiore.
75 "He told me": Ricci, *Giordano Bruno*, p. 144.
76 exactly ten years: Even so, Bruno was formally degraded (that is, ritually stripped of his friar's habit and expelled from the priesthood) at his execution.

11: HOLY ASININITY

77 "I myself saw the friars": Spampanato, *Vita*, also citing Bruno's *Candlemaker* (act 1, scene 1) and *Expulsion of the Triumphant Beast*, dialogue 3. In the name of the blessed donkey's tail that the Genoese venerate: *Candlemaker*, act 1, scene 1.

78 display the bone of a dog: Firpo, *Il processo*, pp. 278–79.

78 "A mixture of desperate souls": Bruno, *Ash Wednesday Supper*, dialogue 2.

79 *Asinità*: Ordine, *La cabala dell'asino*.

80 "The Donkey's Testament": Biblioteca Apostolica Vaticana, MS Vat. Lat. 3370, 264v–265r.

81 "Blest asininity": Bruno, *Kabbalah of the Horse Pegasus*, letter of dedication.

81 Jews: De León-Jones, *Giordano Bruno and the Kabbalah*, pp. 109–36.

82 "Learned Jews explain": *Digression in Praise of the Ass*, cited by Gentile in Aquilecchia's edition of Bruno's *Dialoghi italiani*, pp. 838–39.

82 *Discourse on the Ass*: Pino, *Ragionamento sovra del asino*; see also Ordine, *La cabala dell'asino*, pp. 114–21.

82 Lazarillo de Tormes: Maiorino, *Picaresque*; Bjornson, *Picaresque Hero in European Fiction*; Parker, *Literature and the Delinquent*; see also Eisenberg, "Does the Picaresque Exist?"

84 *Don Giovanni*: Rowland, "What Communion Hath Light with Darkness?"

84 Wheel of Fortune: Ciliberto, *La ruota del tempo*.

84 seashells in the soil of Monte Cicala: Bruno, *Ash Wednesday Supper*, dialogue 5.

85 "Once upon a time": Bruno, *Candlemaker*, act 2, scene 4.

12: THE SIGNS OF THE TIMES

87 "I stayed in Noli": Firpo, *Il processo*, pp. 157, 159.

88 Mauro Fiorentino: Canone, "Variazioni Bruniane."

88 Juan de Ortega: Rowland, "Abacus and Humanism."

89 Clavius: Vetere and Ippoliti, *Il Collegio romano*; Clavius, *Bambergensis* (1581).

89 "Many absurd and erroneous things": Clavius, *Bambergensis* (1570), p. 437, cited in Canone, *Giordano Bruno, 1548–1600*, p. 63.

89 softened his stance on Copernicus: Baldini, *Legem impone subactis*, pp. 127–53.

89 "Father Malaperti and Father Clavius": Kircher's statement is found in a letter from the French scholar Nicolas-Claude Fabri de Peiresc to the French royal astronomer, Pierre Gassendi, Aug. 27, 1633, Peiresc, *Lettres*.

90 "There I stayed for a month and a half": Firpo, *Il processo*, p. 159.

90 *On the Signs of the Times*: Ricci, *Giordano Bruno*, pp. 116–19.

90 Sebastian Brant's illustrated page: Rowland, "Contemporary Account of the Ensisheim Meteorite."

90 Gerolamo Cardano's cheap pamphlet: Grafton, *Cardano's Cosmos*.

92 "Above the clouds": Bruno, *Heroic Frenzies*, pt. 1, dialogue 5, emblem 3.

93 Lucretius's great Latin poem: Although written in 1930, George Hadzsits's *Lucretius and His Influence* remains unsurpassed.

93 Hubertus Grifanius: Spampanato, *Vita*, p. 650.

93 Fra Remigio Nannini: Ibid., p. 275.

94 sins of the flesh: Firpo, *Il processo*, pp. 288–89.

95 "We painters take the same license": Archivio di Stato, Venice, Sant'Uffizio 33, July 18, 1573.

13: A LONELY SPARROW

96 "When I left here": Firpo, Il processo, p. 160.

97 "Once I arrived there": Ibid.

98 Gian Galeazzo Caracciolo: Spampanato, Vita, pp. 281–84.

98 attended Calvinist services: Firpo, Il processo, pp. 160–61.

98 "the Word of God": Article 24 of the Thirty-nine Articles of Religion: "It is a thing plainly repugnant to the Word of God, and the custom of the Primitive Church to have public Prayer in the Church, or to minister the Sacraments, in a tongue not understood of the people."

100 enrolled in the University of Geneva: Spampanato, Vita, p. 286.

100 Antoine de La Faye: Ibid., pp. 290–93.

100 "turn away . . . from the opinions of Aristotle": Ibid., p. 294.

100 "treating exclusively questions of knowledge": Ibid., p. 295.

102 "My lonely sparrow": Heroic Frenzies, pt. 1, dialogue 4.

14: THIRTY

104 "I went to Lyon": Firpo, Il processo, p. 161.

105 France . . . was a battleground: Ricci, Giordano Bruno, pp. 142–50.

105 The list of courses: Firpo, Il processo, p. 161.

106 Fibonacci: Rowland, "Abacus and Humanism."

106 "No human investigation": Biblioteca Apostolica Vaticana, MS Urb. Lat. 1270, 1v.

107 "Philosophy is written": Galilei, Il saggiatore, p. 24.

108 "Have it as you like": Bruno, Ash Wednesday Supper, dialogue 1.

109 Aristarchus: Michel, Cosmology of Giordano Bruno.

109 The Arab astronomers: Ibid.

109 Nicolaus Cusanus: Ricci, Giordano Bruno, pp. 283–91.

109 On the None Other: Nicolaus Cusanus, De non aliud, 1.1: "Non aliud non est aliud quam non aliud."

109 On Learned Ignorance: Gatti, Giordano Bruno and Renaissance Science.

110 Song of Songs: An excellent account of the allegorical interpretations of the Song can be found in the Anchor Bible edition: Marvin H. Pope, ed., Song of Songs: A New Translation with Introduction and Commentary (Garden City, N.Y.: Doubleday, 1980).

111 "Against Love's blows": Bruno, Heroic Frenzies, pt. 2, dialogue 1, emblem 9.

113 Francisco Sánchez: Canone, Giordano Bruno, 1548–1600, pp. lxxxv, 79–83.

114 In the secrecy of a confessional: Firpo, Il processo, pp. 174, 176.

114 without involving the Inquisition: Ricci, Giordano Bruno, p. 382. Pope Sixtus V revoked this privilege in 1587.

114 Fra Domenico Vita: Firpo, Il processo, p. 163.

114 "he despised . . . all the philosophy": Spampanato, Vita, p. 652, from the journal of Guillaume Cotin, Dec. 11, 1585.

115 imprisoned emissaries: Spampanato, Vita, pp. 303–6.

15: THE GIFTS OF THE MAGI

117 "If you knew the Author": Bruno, *Candlemaker*, antiprologue.

117 As a child in Nola: *On Natural Magic*, par. 50, cited from *Opere magiche*, p. 234.

118 "Certainly in the interior regions": Bruno, *On the Immense and the Numberless*, 4.11.

118 read the future: Bonnici, "Superstitions in Malta."

118 Sorcerers and magicians: Stephens, *Demon Lovers*.

119 "A Greek who healed spleens": Bonnici, "Superstitions in Malta," p. 13 n. 54, from Archivium Inquisitionis Melitensis, *Processi*, MS 61 n. 209, May 20, 1649, f. 1048r–v.

120 "fascination": Onians, *Origins of European Thought*.

120 "I gave a course": Firpo, *Il processo*, pp. 161–62.

121 Johann von Nostitz: Canone, *Giordano Bruno, 1548–1600*, pp. 85–86.

122 These three works: See Sturlese, *De umbris idearum*, p. ix. Bruno also published his play *The Candlemaker* in the same year. The order of publication can be established by the fact that *The Song of Circe* mentions *On the Shadows of Ideas*, and *On the Compendious Architecture* mentions *The Song of Circe*; see Sturlese, *De umbris idearum*, p. ix.

122 "Just as painting": Bruno, *On the Shadows of Ideas*, par. 101.

123 corrections in Bruno's own hand: See Sturlese, *De umbris idearum*, pp. xii–xiv, xxvi–liv.

123 "clever application of thought": Bruno, *On the Shadows of Ideas*, par. 119.

123 "a distilled and developed order": Ibid.

123 He describes one system: Rita Sturlese presents this ingenious reconstruction in *De umbris idearum*, pp. liv–lxxiii.

124 "Pharfacon, Doctor of Civil and Canon Law": Bruno, *On the Shadows of Ideas*, par. 11.

125 "a habit of the reasoning soul": "*Habitus quidam ratiocinantis animae*," in ibid., par. 87.

125 "A technical extension": Ibid., par. 105.

125 "Just as a hand joined to an arm": Ibid., par. 68.

125 "This art can be called nothing else": Ibid., par. 17.

126 "A footprint is not an idea": Vat. Lat. 6325, 39v.

126 Giles goes on: Vat. Lat. 6325, 111v, 61r.

126 "Shadow is not of darkness": Sturlese, *De umbris idearum*, p. 26.

126 "Nor does Nature suffer": Ibid., p 36.

127 "A clearer soul": Ibid., p. 103.

127 "The light . . . contains all species": Bruno, *On the Shadows of Ideas*, par. 65.

128 "We decided that this art": Ibid., par. 86.

128 "Time takes away all": Bruno, *Candlemaker*, "To Signora Morgana B."

129 "O you who suckle": Bruno, *Candlemaker*, "The Book, to the Drinkers from the Spring of Pegasus."

129 "You, cultivator of the field": Bruno, *Candlemaker*, "To Signora Morgana B."

130 when they are acted out: A superb example was *The Drinking Party*, a version of Plato's *Symposium* produced for BBC television in 1965, written by Leo Aylen, directed by Jonathan Miller, with Leo McKern as Socrates, and Barry Justice, Michael Gough, Alan Bennett, Roddy Maude-Roxby, John Fortune, Robert Gillespie, Julian Jebb, and Darroll Richards as the symposiasts.

130 Bruno's philosophical drama: The director Luca Ronconi's 2002 production of *The Candlemaker* for the Teatro Piccolo in Milan, apparently successful in that setting, was much less compelling at the Teatro India in Rome, where a deep stage made much of the dialogue unintelligible. Under such conditions, the absence of proper sustenance at the theater bar made dinner an altogether more tempting proposition than seeing the play through to the end.

131 "Back when we could still touch hands": Bruno, *Candlemaker*, "To Signora Morgana B."

16: THE SONG OF CIRCE

133 "Off-the-cuff": Raphael Eglin, preface to Giordano Bruno, *Summa terminorum metaphysicorum*, A2r.

133 "There is only one difficulty": Bruno, *The Song of Circe*, ed. Imbriani and Tallarigo, p. 216.

133 "This art requires much less work": Ibid., p. 182.

134 San Felice Circeo: See the description of Circe's promontory in Bruno, *Heroic Frenzies*, pt. 2, dialogue 5.

135 "Sun, who alone": Bruno, *Song of Circe*, p. 188.

136 "What will you reply": Bruno, *On the Shadows of Ideas*, par. 10.

137 Cicero had noted: Cicero, *De oratore*, 1.42.187–89.

137 Henri had signed a truce: Spampanato, *Vita*, pp. 328–29.

137 "If her Highness endure": Aquilecchia, "Giordano Bruno in Inghilterra," pp. 23–24.

17: "GO UP TO OXFORD"

This chapter owes a particular debt to Mordechai Feingold.

139 Henry Cobham: Aquilecchia, "Giordano Bruno in Inghilterra," pp. 23–24.

140 a spy installed in the French embassy: This spy was not Giordano Bruno himself. John Bossy's attempt to propose such a theory in *Giordano Bruno and the Embassy Affair* is as baseless as it is transparently sectarian (for his putative Bruno is not only a spy but also a sadistic torturer of Catholics). The real spy's stream of letters, clearly dated, written in a French rather than an Italian hand, begins in April 1583, that is, before Bruno arrived in England.

141 ambassador maintained his residence: In *Giordano Bruno and the Embassy Affair*, John Bossy has proposed that the embassy was located in Salisbury Court rather than Butcher Row. Ricci, with admirable objectivity, notes that the speciousness of Bossy's major argument (namely, that Bruno was a spy) should not detract from the more genuine results of his research; see *Giordano Bruno*, pp. 580–81 n. 8.

142 John Florio: Wyatt, *Italian Encounter with Tudor England*; Gatti, *Renaissance Drama of Knowledge*.

142 "As for critiks": Florio, *Second Frutes*, A2.

143 His opportunity to "make [him]self known": The following discussion owes a great debt to Feingold, "Bruno in England Revisited." My thanks to Mordechai Feingold for sending me this article, among others.

144 It was not a good time: This is brought out by Feingold, ibid.

144 "or that a scholer would faine read his lesson": Florio, *Worlde of Wordes* s.v. *boccata*.

145 "When that Italian Didapper": Cited in Aquilecchia, "Giordano Bruno in Inghilterra," pp. 33–34.

145 "Philotheus Jordanus Brunus Nolanus": Bruno, *Explication of Thirty Seals*, pp. 76–78.

146 "Not long after returning againe": Aquilecchia, "Giordano Bruno in Inghilterra," p. 34.

147 "Be circumspect how you offend schollers": Florio, *Second Frutes*, p. 97.

147 "To the Malcontent": Bruno, *Ash Wednesday Supper*, immediately following the title page.

18: DOWN RISKY STREETS

149 John Charlewood: Provvidera, "On the Printer."

150 "Did they speak good Latin?": Bruno, *Ash Wednesday Supper*, dialogue 1.

150 Fulke Greville: Ibid.

151 "Next Wednesday": Ibid.

151 "But, I pray you": Ibid.

151 "Up to now": Ibid.

152 "England can brag": Ibid.

152 sharing a goblet: Ibid., dialogue 2.

153 the Nolan's ability to shed light: See Gatti, *Giordano Bruno and Renaissance Science*, pp. 49–78.

153 "Now, what shall I say of the Nolan?": Bruno, *Ash Wednesday Supper*, dialogue 1.

153 "Now, in order": Ibid.

154 "blind visions of vulgar philosophers": Some historians of science have taken Bruno's denunciation in this passage of "vain astronomers [*mathematici*]" and "vulgar philosophers" as a statement of contempt for mathematicians, compounded, then, by his misinterpretation of a passage from Copernicus later in *The Ash Wednesday Supper*, to build up a picture of Bruno as unscientific or antiscientific. But he is not saying that all *mathematici* are vain, any more than the Nolan philosopher, of all people, is saying in this same passage that all philosophers are vulgar. He is saying that it is useless for astronomers to have concentrated their attention on one star and its planets in the face of plain empirical evidence that the stars are infinite in number. The statement may not be courteous, but it certainly shows competence in, rather than hostility to, natural philosophy.

155 He called it a banquet: In the letter of dedication, and, of course, in his very choice of title, *The Ash Wednesday Supper*.

156 "Spread your wings, Teofilo": Bruno, *Ash Wednesday Supper*, dialogue 2.

157 "Now what customs have I named": Bruno, *Cause, Principle, and Unity*, dialogue 1.

157 Alexander Dicson: Clucas, "In Campo Fantastico."

158 "As I was studying": Bruno, *Cause, Principle, and Unity*, dialogue 2.

158 "You humanists": Ibid.

19: THE ART OF MAGIC

160 "the Academic of no Academy": The self-identification comes from the *Candlemaker's* act 1, scene 2. We do not know the source of the poem.

161 "The point on which we should fix": Bruno, *Ash Wednesday Supper*, dialogue 2.

162 These Hermetic books: Festugière, *La révélation d'Hermès Trismégiste*; Fowden, *Egyptian Hermes*; Yates, *Giordano Bruno and the Hermetic Tradition*; Gentile, *Marsilio Ficino e il ritorno di Ermete Trismegisto*.

163 "Do you not know": Bruno, *Expulsion of the Triumphant Beast*, dialogue 3.

164 "And the devil that deceived them": Revelation 20:10, 21:1.

165 This is not to say: In *Giordano Bruno and the Hermetic Tradition*, Frances Yates argued that Bruno was trying to resurrect a kind of Egyptian religion, whereas most contemporary Bruno scholars regard the Nolan philosopher as a philosopher rather than a religious reformer.

166 "The stupid, insensitive idolaters": Bruno, *Expulsion of the Triumphant Beast*, dialogue 3.

167 "You can see, then, how a simple divinity": Ibid.

170 Elizabeth fought back: Elizabeth wrote in Spanish, French, Italian, Greek, and Latin as well as English; see Mueller and Marcus, *Elizabeth I*.

171 "How can my Muse": William Shakespeare, Sonnet 38.

171 "Here Giordano speaks": Bruno, *Expulsion of the Triumphant Beast*, dedication.

20: CANTICLES

175 "It is truly, O most generous Sir": Bruno, *Heroic Frenzies*, dedication.

176 Penelope Devereux: Spampanato, *Vita*, pp. 385, 386.

177 "I mean for the world": Bruno, *Heroic Frenzies*, dedication.

178 Tansillo: Rubino, *Tansilliana*; Erasmo Pércopo, introduction to *Canzoniere*, by Tansillo.

178 "With pretty blazes": Bruno, *Heroic Frenzies*, pt. 1, dialogue 3.

179 "Felonious child of Love and Rivalry": Ibid., dialogue 1.

179 "Finally, I mean to say": Ibid., dedication.

181 "In this poetry, however": Ibid.

182 "because two women are introduced": Ibid., dedication.

183 "These are the lesser mysteries": Plato, *Symposium*, 210A.

183 Marcantonio Epicuro's poem: Gentile, in Bruno, *Dialoghi italiani*, p. 973 and passim.

183 Seripando's library: An inventory of the library is preserved in the Biblioteca Corsiniana in Rome, MS 671 (34B15), 132–69, with an "extremely inaccurate" copy in the Vatican Library, MS Vat. Lat. 11310. See Giovanni Mercati, *Prolegomena*, pp. 120–23.

183 The fact that there are two eyes: Canone, "Le 'due luci.' "

184 "But here contemplate": Bruno, *Heroic Frenzies*, dedication.

184 "As day and night": Ibid., pt. 2, dialogue 5.

185 " 'O Jove, I envy not your firmament' ": Ibid., "Song of the Illuminati."

187 "like those Irish exiles": Spampanato, *Vita*, p. 387.

21: SQUARING THE CIRCLE

188 a menacing, unstable place: Ricci, *Giordano Bruno*, pp. 373–76.

188 "[I presented myself to a confessor]": Firpo, *Il processo*, pp. 176, 196–97.

189 Sixtus V: Fagiolo and Madonna, *Sisto V.*

191 Jacopo Corbinelli: Ricci, *Giordano Bruno*, pp. 382–97.

191 "December 7: Jordanus came back again": Spampanato, *Vita*, pp. 650–51.

192 Harold Urey: As a high school student, I heard Urey make this statement in the question period following a lecture at the University of California, Irvine, in the late 1960s.

192 Mordente came originally: Aquilecchia, *Due dialoghi sconosciuti*, pp. vii–xxiii; Ricci, *Giordano Bruno*, pp. 380–90.

194 his friendship with John Florio: Wyatt, *Italian Encounter with Tudor England.*

194 "I'd gladly have them translated": Bruno, *Cause, Principle, and Unity*, dialogue 1.

195 "Is it not then possible": "A Dream," cited from Aquilecchia, *Due dialoghi sconosciuti*, p. 57.

195 Giovanni Botero: Spampanato, *Vita*, pp. 328–29.

196 "Why don't you think it right": Bruno, *The Triumphant Idiot*, cited from Aquilecchia, *Due dialoghi sconosciuti*, p. 5.

196 "This man who mentions": Ibid., p. 16.

197 The reports of that debate: Ricci, *Giordano Bruno*, pp. 390–97.

198 Marburg: Spampanato, *Vita*, pp. 411–14, 663, 664.

198 University of Wittenberg: Ibid., pp. 414–22.

22: CONSOLATION AND VALEDICTION

199 Alberico Gentili: Feingold, "Bruno in England Revisited," p. 332.

200 "I happen to have heard": Spampanato, *Vita*, p. 419.

201 Paracelsus: Ricci, *Giordano Bruno*, pp. 406–8.

201 "On behalf of such a university": Bruno, *The Llullian Combinatory Lamp*, ed. Tocco and Vitelli, p. 230.

201 *The Lamp of Thirty Statues*: This work was finally published in Florence in 1891.

202 Polycarp Leyser: Ricci, *Giordano Bruno*, 403–4.

202 Nicodemus Frischlin: Canone, *Giordano Bruno, 1548–1600*, p. 145.

202 Rudolf II: Ricci, *Giordano Bruno*, pp. 410–15.

204 "Venus, third heaven's goddess": Bruno, *Heroic Frenzies*, pt. 1, dialogue 5, emblem 11.

204 "Hear Solomon": Wisdom 7:8–10. Douai-Rheims version.

204 "*Her have I loved*": Ibid. 8:2.

205 "I came myself": Bruno, *Valedictory Oration*, pp. 21–22.

205 Saint Vitus: Ianneci, *Il Libro di San Vito.*

205 John Dee: French, *John Dee*; Woolley, *Queen's Conjuror.*

206 Don Guillén de Haro de San Clemente: Ricci, *Giordano Bruno*, pp. 417, 419.

207 "It happens that, against every reason": Bruno, *One Hundred and Twenty Articles Against Mathematicians and Philosophers*, ed. Tocco and Vitelli, p. 4.

208 "As for the liberal arts": Ibid.

209 "On November 21": Ricci, *Giordano Bruno*, p. 411.

209 Hieronymus Besler: Ibid., p. 410 and passim thereafter.

209 National Library of Moscow: MS Noroff 36. The texts contained in the manuscript have been transcribed and edited twice: by Tocco and Vitelli in 1891, and
recently by Simonetta Bassi, Elisabetta Scapparone, and Nicoletta Tirinnanzi. A
full study of the manuscript still needs to be undertaken.

210 "God flows into the angels": Bruno, *On Mathematical Magic*, par. 1, cited from
Opere magiche, p. 4.

210 "I, for the exaltation of my goal": Bruno, *Heroic Frenzies*, pt. 1, dialogue 3.

211 "Whoever comes across this book": The notes were discovered by Paul Richard
Blum in the Herzog August Bibliothek, Wolfenbüttel. T 1066 Helmst. 2.o, a
copy of Paracelsus, *Astronomia magna; oder, Die ganze Philosophia sagax der grossen
und kleinen Welt* (Frankfurt: Sigismundus Feyerabend, 1571). My thanks to Paul
Richard Blum for pointing them out.

212 "The things that seem appropriate": Bruno, *On Mathematical Magic*, par. 22, cited
from *Opere magiche*, p. 72.

212 "This supreme concern": Preface to Bruno, *De Lampade combinatoria Lulliana et
specierum scrutinio*, ed. F. Tocco and H. Vitelli, *Jordani Bruni Nolani Opera Latina*,
Vol. 2.3 (Florence: Le Monnier, 1890), p. 229 (a2r).

212 "That severed head of the Gorgon": Ibid., (a2v).

23: INFINITIES

215 *On the Immense and the Numberless*: Published in Frankfurt in 1591 as *De Innumerabilibus, immenso, et infigurabilis, sen, De Universo et mundis*, the poem was republished in 1879 by Francesco Fiorentino as *De Immenso et Innumerabilibus*,
which is now the usual short title for the work.

215 *On the Immense* traced a biography: Gatti, *Giordano Bruno and Renaissance Science*, pp. 29–37, 61–89, 100–117.

216 Atoms were the last piece . . . to fall into place: Ibid., pp. 128–42.

217 "I write for other than the crowd": Bruno, *On the Immense and the Numberless*, 5.1.

217 "I hate the profane crowd and shun it": Horace, *Odes* 3.1.1: *"Odi profanum vulgus
et arceo."*

217 "seeds of things": See also Horowitz, *Seeds of Virtue and Knowledge*.

218 "Principle of existence": Bruno, *On the Immense and the Numberless*, 6.5.

218 "Never shall you see the face": Ibid., 1.7.

218 "Sun and Earth are the primal animals": Ibid., 4.9.

219 "Isn't it the mother of all follies": Ibid., 3.3.

219 "Now, if you please, ask me": Ibid., 3.1.

219 "Past time or present": Ibid., 1.12.

220 "Bacchus and Ceres are thus": Ibid., 6.5.

221 "Hence, as I make my journey": Ibid., 19–24.

24: RETURN TO ITALY

223 Padua: Grendler, *Universities of the Italian Renaissance*, pp. 3–40, 366–71, 408–19.

223 Elena Lucrezia Cornaro Piscopia: Maschietto, *Elena Lucrezia Cornaro Piscopia*;
Guernsey, *Lady Cornaro*.

224 Giovanni Vincenzo Pinelli: Ricci, *Giordano Bruno*, pp. 383–85.
224 *Readings on Geometry* and *The Art of Deformations*: Aquilecchia, *Praelectiones geometricae, e Ars deformationum.*
224 Giovanni Mocenigo: Ricci, *Giordano Bruno*, pp. 480–88.
224 Andrea Morosini: Ibid., pp. 478–80.
225 he began to hear Mass: Firpo, *Il processo*, p. 174.
225 Fra Domenico da Nocera: Ibid., pp. 21, 164–65.
226 "I was going to go to Frankfurt": Ibid., p. 163.
226 "It seems to me that I had done enough": Ibid., p. 155.
227 "I, Zuane Mocenigo": Venice, Archivio di Stato, Sant'Uffizio 69, Case 19, May 23, 1592, 1r–3r; Firpo, *Il processo*, pp. 143–45.
228 "On that day, when I kept Iordano Bruno": *Il processo*, p. 145.
229 New Prisons: The Dominican convent of San Domenico a Castello, which contained the inquisitorial prison, was demolished by Napoleon, along with forty-seven other parish churches.
234 "I was born and brought up among heretics": Deposition of Marcantonio Pestalozzi, Venice, Archivio di Stato, Sant'Uffizio 68, Case 59, July 11, 1591.
235 "In this book I have found the following": Deposition of the Reverend Father Sebastiano Taiapetra, professor of Hebrew, Venice, Archivio di Stato, Sant'Uffizio 69, Case 25, June 9, 1592.
236 "Traitor! Take that": Firpo, *Il processo*, pp. 282–83.
236 Fra Celestino Arrigoni: Firpo, *Il processo*, pp. 42–49.
238 Giovanni Battista Ciotti: Ciotti would also publish the third edition of Christoph Clavius's commentary on Euclid (with a false Cologne imprint), *Euclidis Elementorum libri XV.*
238 "I know this Giordano Bruni": Firpo, *Il processo*, pp. 149, 151.
238 "Said Giordano . . . in Frankfurt": Ibid., pp. 152–53.
242 "Matteo Silvestri": Ibid., pp. 263–64.
242 "When the prisoners who were friars": Ibid., p. 281.
242 "He replied": Ibid., pp. 198–99.

25: THE WITNESS
244 *"Ut essent duo testes"*: "So that there would be two witnesses."
244 Lepanto lay nearly a generation in the past: Ricci, *Giordano Bruno*, pp. 480–88.
245 On February 20, 1593: Firpo, *Il processo*, p. 40.
245 A later report criticizes those cells: Ibid. Visits to the cells are recorded in ibid., pp. 217–346.
245 Bruno was issued a warm mantle: Ibid., p. 217.
246 Fra Celestino . . . wrote a letter to the Roman Inquisition: Ibid., pp. 42–47.
247 "He [Fra Celestino] says that he deposes": Ibid., pp. 47–48.
247 "he gave the finger": The usual Italian gesture, the *fica* (vulva), is made by inserting the thumb between index and middle finger. In this case, the inquisitors literally call the act *digitum ostendere*, "showing the finger," a gesture that was already known in ancient Rome; see Suetonius, *Life of Augustus*, 45.4.
249 "When Giordano was discussing": Firpo, *Il processo*, p. 263.

249 no idea what he had written, nor how much: Canone, "L'editto di proibizione," p. 57.

249 in possession of their souls: See Onians, *Origins of European Thought*.

26: THE ADVERSARY

251 Cardinal Santori: Ricci, "Giovinezza di un inquisitore."

252 Robert Bellarmine: Godman, *Saint as Censor*; Galeota, *Roberto Bellarmino arcivescovo di Capua*; Baldini, *Legem impone subactis*, pp. 285–346.

253 Those first Jesuits: O'Malley, *First Jesuits*.

253 great personal modesty: The shrewd seventeenth-century cardinal Decio Azzolini would say that Bellarmine's autobiography "has many signs of vanity"—"*hà molta apparenza di vanità.*" See Godman, *Saint as Censor*, p. 50 n. 8, where he cites *Voto del Cardinale Decio Azzolini . . . nella Causa Romana di beatificazione e canonizzazione del Roberto Cardinale Bellarmino* (Rome, 1749), pp. 54, 65.

254 "The censor is wrong to say": The text is quoted in Godman, *Saint as Censor*, p. 301.

255 Bellarmine's liquid space: A concise summary of Bellarmine's cosmological views is provided in Blackwell, *Galileo, Bellarmine, and the Bible*, pp. 40–45.

255 the first Jesuit inquisitor: The prohibition on Jesuits joining the Inquisition was lifted in 1587, in order to appoint Bellarmine; see Godman, *Saint as Censor*, p. 74.

256 Giovanni Marsilio's *Defense*: *Difesa di Giovanni Marsilio*, 3r–4r ff.: "Dell'Arti usate dal Signor Cardinale."

258 "He was asked if he had ever argued": Firpo, *Il processo*, p. 175.

259 2 (*Summary* heading 3). "About Christ": Ibid., p. 259.

259 3 (*Summary* heading 2). "About the Trinity, divinity, and incarnation": Ibid., p. 253.

259 4 (*Summary* heading 7). "That there are multiple worlds": Ibid., p. 267.

260 5 (*Summary* heading 22). "About the souls of men and beasts": Ibid., p. 283.

260 6 (*Summary* heading 1). "That Brother Giordano has bad feelings": Ibid., p. 247.

260 7 (*Summary* heading 24). "That sins are not to be punished": Ibid., p. 287.

260 8 (*Summary* heading 23). "About the art of divination": Ibid., p. 286.

261 "You replied that if the Holy See": Ibid., pp. 340–41.

261 the final insult: Muir, *Mad Blood Stirring*, p. 257.

27: GETHSEMANE

264 "Giovanni Mocenigo, accuser": Firpo, *Il processo*, p. 259.

264 "Francesco Graziani, cellmate in Venice": Ibid., p. 263.

265 "Matteo Silvestri, cellmate": Ibid.

265 Corn Market: Foxe, *Acts and Monuments*, bk. 11, p. 1770. Hugh Latimer's famous remark to Nicholas Ridley at the stake does not appear in the first edition (1563) of *Foxe's Book of Martyrs*, but only from 1570 onward; hence, like Galileo's "*Eppur si muove,*" it may be apocryphal.

28: HELL'S PURGATORY

268 discussed . . . torture: Firpo, *Il processo*, pp. 78–79.

269 "[Eight] propositions": Ibid., pp. 82–104.

270 "Francesco Graziano, fellow prisoner in Venice": Firpo, *Il processo*, p. 266.

29: THE SENTENCE

273 "Jesus said": Matthew 18:20.

274 "We proclaim in these documents": The text of Bruno's sentence is printed in Firpo, *Il processo*, pp. 339–44.

274 the noble Cenci family: Brigante Colonna and Chiorandi, *Il processo Cenci*.

30: THE FIELD OF FLOWERS

278 "Thursday morning": *Avvisi di Roma*, 110r–v; Firpo, *Il processo*, p. 356.

278 "Hence as I make my journey": Bruno, *On the Immense and the Numberless*, 1.19–24:

> *Quapropter dum tutus iter sic carpo, beata*
> *Conditione satis studio sublimis avito*
> *Reddor Dux, Lex, Lux, Vates, Pater, Author, Iterque:*
> *Adque alios mundo ex isto dum adsurgo nitentes,*
> *Aethereum campumque ex omni parte pererro,*
> *Attonitis mirum et distans post terga relinquo.*

EPILOGUE: THE FOUR RIVERS

280 "In the first place": Kepler, *Dissertatio cum nuncio sidereo*, 9v.

281 "For the glory of this world's Architect": Ibid., 10r.

282 "Perhaps [my adversary]": Galilei, *Il saggiatore*, p. 24.

282 the idea that mathematics underpinned philosophy: Leonardo da Vinci, *Note sulla pittura*, 1r. See also Napolitano Valditara, *Le idee, i numeri, l'ordine*.

Bibliography

Any biographer of Bruno is indebted to two excellent, extensive Italian biographies: Vincenzo Spampanato, *Vita di Giordano Bruno*, with an afterword by Nuccio Ordine (Messina: Giuseppe Principato, 1922; Rome: Gela Editrice, 1988), and Saverio Ricci, *Giordano Bruno nell'Europa del Cinquecento* (Rome: Salerno, 2000).

Shorter biographies, also excellent, exist in Italian by Michele Ciliberto, *Giordano Bruno* (Rome: Laterza, 1990; 2nd ed. 1992), and Giovanni Aquilecchia, *Giordano Bruno* (Rome: Istituto della Enciclopedia Italiana, 1971), and in German by Paul Richard Blum, *Giordano Bruno* (Munich: C. H. Beck, 1999).

The surviving records of Bruno's trial were edited in 1941 by Angelo Mercati, archivist of the Archivio Segreto Vaticano, with a fierce apologetic agenda, *Il sommario del processo di Giordano Bruno*, Studi e Testi 101 (Vatican City: Biblioteca Apostolica Vaticana), and in 1993 by Luigi Firpo, with welcome objectivity, *Il processo di Giordano Bruno* (Rome: Salerno Editrice), republished and annotated with French translation as *Giordano Bruno, Documents I, Le Procès*, introduction and text by Luigi Firpo, translation and notes by A.-Ph. Segards, Paris: Les Belles Lettres, 2000.

The specialized literature on Bruno has grown exponentially in the past thirty years, with its own journal, *Bruniana & Campanelliana*, edited in Rome by Eugenio Canone and Germana Ernst, which provides an annual list of recent publications ("Schede") on Bruno. The references compiled below emphasize, where possible, general sources in English.

Many English-speaking readers have first been introduced to Bruno by the work of the late Frances Yates, still marvelous to read. The most cogent disagreement with Yates's point of view is that presented by Hilary Gatti, *Giordano Bruno and Renaissance Science* (Ithaca, N.Y.: Cornell University Press, 1999).

Bruno's influence on nineteenth-century Italy is traced by Anna Foa, *Giordano Bruno* (Bologna: Il Mulino, 1998); Eugenio Canone, ed., *Brunus redivivus: Momenti della fortuna di Giordano Bruno nel XIX secolo* (Pisa: Edizioni dell'Ateneo, 1998); and Lars Berggren, "The Visual Image of Giordano Bruno," in Hilary Gatti, ed., *Giordano Bruno, Philosopher of the Renaissance* (Aldershot: Ashgate, 2002), pp. 16–49.

TRANSLATIONS OF BRUNO'S WORKS INTO ENGLISH

The Ash Wednesday Supper. Translated by Edward Gosselin and Lawrence Lerner. Toronto: University of Toronto Press, 1995.

The Ash Wednesday Supper. Translated by Stanley Jaki. The Hague: Mouton, 1975.

Cause, Principle, and Unity. Translated by Richard Blackwell and Robert de Lucca. Cambridge: Cambridge University Press, 1998.

The Expulsion of the Triumphant Beast. Translated by Arthur Imerti, with a foreword by Karen Silvia de León-Jones. Lincoln, Neb.: Bison Books, 2004.

On the Infinite Universe and Worlds. Translated by Dorothea Waley Singer as part of her *Giordano Bruno: His Life and Thought. With Annotated Translation of His Work "On the Infinite Universe and Worlds."* New York: Henry Schuman, 1950.

New translations of *The Ash Wednesday Supper,* by Hilary Gatti, *On the Infinite Universe and Worlds,* by Arielle Saiber, and my own of *The Heroic Frenzies* are forthcoming from the Lorenzo Da Ponte Italian Library, University of Toronto Press, with David Marsh as editor.

ARCHIVAL SOURCES

Archivio di Stato, Venice, Sant'Uffizio 33 (1572).
Archivio di Stato, Venice, Sant'Uffizio 68 (1592).
Archivio di Stato, Venice, Sant'Uffizio 69 (1592).

EDITIONS OF BRUNO'S WORKS

For a more complete list up to 2000, see Saverio Ricci, *Giordano Bruno nell'Europa del Cinquecento* (Rome: Salerno, 2000), pp. 618–20.

ITALIAN WORKS

Dialoghi filosofici italiani. Edited by Michele Ciliberto. Milan: Meridiani Mondadori, 2000.

Dialoghi italiani, nuovamente ristampate con note da Giovanni Gentile. Edited by Giovanni Aquilecchia. Florence: Sansoni, 1985.

Oeuvres complètes de Giordano Bruno. Critical editions with facing French translation. Vols. 1–7. Paris: Les Belles Lettres, 1993–99.

Opere italiane, testi critici di Giovanni Aquilecchia. Edited by Nuccio Ordine. Turin: UTET, 2002.

LATIN WORKS

Due dialoghi sconosciuti e due dialoghi noti: Idiota triumphans; De somnii interpretatione; Mordentius; De mordentii circino. Edited by Giovanni Aquilecchia. Rome: Edizioni di Storia e Letteratura, 1957.

Explication of Thirty Seals, Triginta sigilli. Edited by Felice Tocco and H. Vitelli. Vol. 2.2 of *Jordani Bruni Nolani opera latine conscripta.* Florence: Le Monnier, 1890.

Jordani Bruni Nolani opera latine conscripta. Edited by Francesco Fiorentino, Felice

Tocco, H. Vitelli, Vittorio Imbriani, and Carlo Maria Tallarigo. Naples: Domenico Morano, 1879–91.

On the Immense and the Numberless, De immenso et innumerabilibus. Edited by Francesco Fiorentino. Vol. 1.1.4 of *Jordani Bruni Nolani opera latine conscripta.* Naples: Domenico Morano, 1879; and vol. 1.2.1. Naples: Domenico Morano, 1884.

Opere iconografiche. Edited by Michele Ciliberto and Mino Gabriele. Milan: Adelphi, 2001.

Opere magiche. Edited by Michele Ciliberto, Simonetta Bassi, Elisabetta Scapparone, and Nicoletta Tirinnanzi. Milan: Adelphi, 2000.

Opere mnemotecniche. Edited by Michele Ciliberto and Marco Matteoli. Milan: Adelphi, 2004.

Praelectiones geometricae, e Ars deformationum. Edited by Giovanni Aquilecchia. Rome: Edizioni di Storia e Letteratura, 1964.

Valedictory Oration, Oratio Valedictoria. Edited by Francesco Fiorentino. Vol. 1.1.1 of *Jordani Bruni Nolani opera latine conscripta.* Naples: Domenico Morano, 1879.

OTHER WORKS

Alisio, Giancarlo. *Napoli e il risanamento: Recupero di una struttura urbana.* Naples: Edizioni Banco di Napoli, 1980.

Allen, Michael J. B. *Marsilio Ficino and the Phaedran Charioteer.* Berkeley: University of California Press, 1981.

Aquilano, Serafino Ciminelli. Biblioteca Apostolica Vaticana. MS Vat. Lat. 5159.

———. *Opera dello elegantissimo poeta Seraphino Aquilano.* Venice: Bindoni, 1556.

Aquilecchia, Giovanni. "Giordano Bruno in Inghilterra (1583–1585)." *Bruniana & Campanelliana* 1 (1995), pp. 21–42.

———, ed. *Due dialoghi sconosciuti e due dialoghi noti: Idiota triumphans; De somnii interpretatione; Mordentius; De mordentii circino.* Rome: Edizioni di Storia e Letteratura, 1957.

———, ed. *Praelectiones geometricae, e Ars deformationum.* Rome: Edizioni di Storia e Letteratura, 1964.

Avvisi di Roma. Biblioteca Apostolica Vaticana, MS Urb. Lat. 1068.

Baldini, Ugo. *Legem impone subactis: Studi su filosofia e scienza dei Gesuiti in Italia, 1540–1632.* Rome: Bulzoni Editore, 1992.

———, ed. *Christoph Clavius e l'attività scientifica dei Gesuiti nell'età di Galileo: Atti del convegno internazionale (Chieti, 28–30 aprile 1993).* Rome: Bulzoni Editore, 1995.

Berggren, Lars. "The Visual Image of Giordano Bruno." In Hilary Gatti, ed., *Giordano Bruno, Philosopher of the Renaissance,* pp. 16–49. Aldershot: Ashgate, 2002.

Bjornson, Richard. *The Picaresque Hero in European Fiction.* Madison: University of Wisconsin Press, 1977.

Blackwell, Richard J. *Galileo, Bellarmine, and the Bible.* Notre Dame, Ind.: University of Notre Dame Press, 1991.

Bolzoni, Lina. *The Gallery of Memory: Literary and Iconographic Models in the Age of the Printing Press.* Translated by Jeremy Parzen. Toronto: University of Toronto Press, 2001.

————. *The Web of Images: Vernacular Preaching from Its Origins to St. Bernardino da Siena*. Aldershot: Ashgate, 2004.

Bönker-Vallon, Angelika. "Unità nascosta e autoconoscenza: La presenza della tradizione del neoplatonismo negli *Eroici furori*." *Bruniana & Campanelliana* 9, no. 2 (2003), pp. 281–94.

Bonnici, Alexander. "Superstitions in Malta Towards the Middle of the Seventeenth Century in the Light of the Inquisition Trials." *Melita Historica: Journal of the Malta Historical Society* 4, no. 3 (1966), pp. 145–83.

Brigante Colonna, Gustavo, and Emilio Chiorandi. *Il processo Cenci*. Milan: Mondadori, 1934.

Canone, Eugenio. *Il dorso e il grembo dell'eterno: Percorsi della filosofia di Giordano Bruno*. Pisa: Istituti Editoriali e Poligrafici, 2003.

————. "Le 'due luci': Il concerto finale degli *Eroici furori*." *Bruniana & Campanelliana* 9, no. 2 (2003), pp. 295–318.

————. "L'editto di proibizione delle opere di Bruno e Campanella." *Bruniana & Campanelliana* 1 (1995), pp. 43–62.

————. *Magia dei contrari: Cinque studi su Giordano Bruno*. Rome: Edizioni dell'Ateneo, 2005.

————. "Variazioni Bruniane. I. Giordano Bruno e Mauro Fiorentino." *Bruniana & Campanelliana* 7 (2001–2), pp. 547–56.

————, ed. *Brunus redivivus: Momenti della fortuna di Giordano Bruno nel XIX secolo*. Pisa: Edizioni dell'Ateneo, 1998.

————, ed. *Giordano Bruno, 1548–1600: Mostra storico documentaria, Roma, Biblioteca Casanatense, 7 giugno–30 settembre 2000*. Florence: Leo S. Olschki, 2000.

Canone, Eugenio, and Ingrid D. Rowland, eds. *The Alchemy of Extremes: The Laboratory of the "Eroici furori" of Giordano Bruno*. Pisa: Accademia Editoriale, 2007.

Carella, Candida. "Tra i maestri di Giordano Bruno: Nota sull'agostiniano Teofilo da Vairano." *Bruniana & Campanelliana* 1 (1995), pp. 63–82.

Carruthers, Mary. *The Book of Memory: A Study of Memory in Medieval Culture*. Cambridge: Cambridge University Press, 1992.

Chase-Dunn, Christopher, and Alice Willard. "Systems of Cities and World-Systems: Settlement Size Hierarchies and Cycles of Political Centralization, 2000 BC–1988 AD." www.jhu.edu/~soc/pcid/papers/17/pcidpap17.htm (accessed May 9, 2001).

Ciliberto, Michele. *Giordano Bruno*. Rome: Laterza, 1990; 2nd ed. 1992.

————. *L'occhio di Atteone: Nuovi studi su Giordano Bruno*. Rome: Edizioni di Storia e Letteratura, 2002.

————. *La ruota del tempo: Interpretazione di Giordano Bruno*. Rome: Editori Riuniti, 1986; 2nd ed. 1992.

Clavius, Christoph. *Christophori Clavii Bambergensis ex Societate Iesu in sphaeram Ioannis de Sacro Bosco commentarius*. Rome: Apud Victorium Helianum, 1570.

————. *Christophori Clavii Bambergensis ex Societate Iesu in sphaeram Ioannis de Sacro Bosco commentarius*. Rome: Ex officina Dominici Basa, 1581.

————. *Euclidis Elementorum libri XV . . . Auctore Christophoro Clavio Bambergensi*. Cologne [really Venice]: Iohannes Baptista Ciotti, 1591.

Clucas, Stephen. "*In Campo Fantastico*: Alexander Dicson, Walter Warner, and Brunian Mnemonics." In Michele Ciliberto and Nicholas Mann, eds., *Giordano*

Bruno, 1583–1585: The English Experience, pp. 37–59. Florence: Leo S. Olschki, 1997.

Cooperman, Bernard Dov, and Barbara Garvin, eds. *The Jews of Italy: Memory and Identity.* Bethesda: University Press of Maryland, 2000.

de León-Jones, Karen Silvia. *Giordano Bruno and the Kabbalah: Prophets, Magicians, and Rabbis.* New Haven, Conn.: Yale University Press, 1997.

Eisenberg, Daniel. "Does the Picaresque Exist?" *Kentucky Romance Quarterly* 26 (1979), pp. 203–19.

Fagiolo, Marcello, and Maria Luisa Madonna, eds. *Sisto V.* Vol. 1, *Roma e il Lazio.* Rome: Istituto Poligrafico e Zecca Dello Stato, 1992.

Feingold, Mordechai. "Bruno in England Revisited." *Huntington Library Quarterly* 67, no. 3 (2004), pp. 329–46.

Festugière, André Jean. *La révélation d'Hermès Trismégiste.* Paris: Gabalda, 1949–54.

Ficino, Marsilio. *Opera omnia.* Basel: Henricus Petri, 1561; Turin: Bottega d'Erasmo, 1959.

Firpo, Luigi. *Il processo di Giordano Bruno.* Rome: Salerno Editrice, 1993.

Florio, John. *Florios Second Frutes: To be gathered of twelve Trees, of divers but delightsome tastes to the tongues of Italians and Englishmen: To which is annexed his Gardine of Recreation, yeelding six thousand Italian proverbs.* London: Printed for Thomas Woodcock, 1591.

Florio, John. *A Worlde of Wordes* (1598).

Foa, Anna. *Giordano Bruno.* Bologna: Il Mulino, 1998.

Fowden, Garth. *The Egyptian Hermes: A Historical Approach to the Late Pagan Mind.* Princeton, N.J.: Princeton University Press, 1986.

Foxe, John. *Acts and Monuments of These Latter and Perilous Days, Touching the Church [Foxe's Book of Martyrs].* London: John Day, 1583.

French, Peter. *John Dee: The World of an Elizabethan Magus.* London: Dorset Press, 1989.

Galeota, Gustavo. *Roberto Bellarmino arcivescovo di Capua, teologo e pastore della riforma cattolica: Atti del convegno internazionale di studi, Capua, 28 settembre–1 ottobre 1988.* Capua: Stabilimento A.C.M., 1990.

Galilei, Galileo. *Il saggiatore, nel quale con bilancia esquisita e giusta si ponderano le cose contenute nella Libra Astronomica e Filosofica di Lotario Sarsi Sigensano scritto in forma di lettera al Illustrissimo et Reverendissimo Monsignore Domino Virginio Cesarini Accademico Linceo Maestro di Camera di Nostro Signore dal Signore Galileo Galilei Accademico Linceo Nobile Fiorentino Filosofo Matematico Primario del Serenissimo Gran Duca di Toscana.* Rome: Appresso Giacomo Mascardi, 1623.

Gatti, Hilary. "The Ending of the *Eroici furori.*" In Eugenio Canone and Ingrid D. Rowland, eds., *The Alchemy of Extremes: The Laboratory of the "Eroici furori."* Pisa: Accademia Editoriale, 2007.

———. *Giordano Bruno and Renaissance Science.* Ithaca, N.Y.: Cornell University Press, 1999.

———. *The Renaissance Drama of Knowledge: Giordano Bruno in England.* London: Routledge, 1989.

———, ed. *Giordano Bruno, Philosopher of the Renaissance.* Aldershot: Ashgate, 2002.

Gentile, Sebstiano, ed. *Marsilio Ficino e il ritorno di Ermete Trismegisto.* Florence: Centro Di, 1999.

Giles of Viterbo [Egidio Antonini da Viterbo]. "La caccia bellissima dell'amore." Venice: Ravano, 1535.

——. *Sententiae ad mentem Platonis*. Biblioteca Apostolica Vaticana, MS Vat. Lat. 6525.

Gionta, Daniela. " 'Augustinus Dux meus': La teologia poetica 'ad mentem Platonis' di Egidio da Viterbo OSA." *Atti del Congresso internazionale su S. Agostino nel XVI centenario della conversione, Roma, 15–20 settembre 1986*, vol. 3, pp. 187–201. Rome: Istituto Storico Agostiniano, 1987.

Gleason, Elisabeth. *Gasparo Contarini: Venice, Rome, and Reform*. Berkeley: University of California Press, 1993.

Godman, Peter. *The Saint as Censor: Robert Bellarmine Between Inquisition and Index*. Studies in Medieval and Reformation Thought 80. Leiden: Brill, 2000.

Grafton, Anthony. *Cardano's Cosmos: The Worlds and Works of a Renaissance Astrologer*. Cambridge, Mass.: Harvard University Press, 2001.

Granada, Miguel Angel. "Digges, Bruno, e il copernicanesimo in Inghilterra." In Michele Ciliberto and Nicholas Mann, eds., *Giordano Bruno, 1583–1585: The English Experience*, pp. 125–55. Florence: Leo S. Olschki, 1997.

Grendler, Paul F. *The Universities of the Italian Renaissance*. Baltimore: Johns Hopkins University Press, 2002.

Guernsey, Jane Howard. *The Lady Cornaro: Pride and Prodigy of Venice*. Clinton Corners, N.Y.: College Avenue Press, 1999.

Hadzsits, George D. *Lucretius and His Influence*. New York: Cooper Square, 1930.

Holleran, James V. *A Jesuit Challenge: Edmund Campion's Debates at the Tower of London in 1581*. New York: Fordham University Press, 1999.

Horowitz, Maryanne Cline. *Seeds of Virtue and Knowledge*. Princeton, N.J.: Princeton University Press, 1997.

Ianneci, Dario. *Il Libro di San Vito: Storia, leggenda, e culto di un santo medioevale*. Salerno: Edizioni Ofanto, 2000.

Idel, Moshe. *Kabbalah: New Perspectives*. New Haven, Conn.: Yale University Press, 1988.

Kepler, Johannes. *Dissertatio cum nuncio sidereo nuper ad mortales misso Galilaeo Galilaeo, mathematico Patavino . . . Huic accessit Phaenomenon singulare de Mercurio ab eodem Keplero in sole deprehenso*. Florence: Apud Io[hannem] Antonium Caneum, 1610.

Lattis, James M. *Between Copernicus and Galileo: Christoph Clavius and the Collapse of Ptolemaic Cosmology*. Chicago: University of Chicago Press, 1995.

Leonardo da Vinci. *Note sulla pittura*. Biblioteca Apostolica Vaticana, MS Urb. Lat. 1270.

Llull, Ramón. *Ars compendiosa Dei* (1308). In Ramón Llull, *Opera Latina*, vol. 13. Edited by Fredericus Stegmüller. Palma de Mallorca: Maioricensis Schola Lullistica, del Consejo Superior de Investigaciones Científicas, 1959– .

——. *Raymundi Lullii Opera ea quae ad adinventam ab ipso Artem Universalem, Scientiarum Artiumque Omnium Brevi compendio, firmaque memoria apprehendarum, locupletissimaque vel oratione ex tempore pertractandarum, pertinent*. Regensburg: Lazarus Zetzner, 1617.

Maggi, Armando. "The Language of the Visible: The *Eroici furori* and the Renaissance Philosophy of *Imprese*." *Bruniana & Campanelliana* 6, no. 1, (2000), pp. 115–44.

Maiorino, Giancarlo, ed. *The Picaresque: Tradition and Displacement.* Minneapolis: University of Minnesota Press, 1996.

Manning, John. *The Emblem.* London: Reaktion Books, 2004.

Marsilio, Giovanni. *Difesa di Giovanni Marsilio a favore della risposta dell'otto proposizioni contro la quale ha scritto l'Illustrissimo et Reverendissimo Signore Cardinal Bellarmino.* In Venetia: Appresso Roberto Meietti, 1606.

Martin, F. X. *Friar, Reformer, and Renaissance Scholar: Life and Work of Giles of Viterbo, 1469–1532.* Villanova, Pa.: Augustinian Press, 1992.

Maschietto, Francesco Ludovico. *Elena Lucrezia Cornaro Piscopia (1646–1684): Prima donna laureata nel mondo.* Padua: Antenore, 1978.

McCoog, Thomas M. *The Reckoned Expense: Edmund Campion and the Early English Jesuits: Essays in Celebration of the First Centenary of Campion Hall, Oxford (1896–1996).* Woodbridge, U.K.: Boydell Press, 1996.

Mercati, Angelo. *Il sommario del processo di Giordano Bruno.* Studi e Testi 101. Vatican City: Biblioteca Apostolica Vaticana, 1941.

Mercati, Giovanni. *Prolegomena de fatis Bibliothecae Monasterii Sancti Columbani Bobiensis et de codice ipso Vat. Lat. 5757.* In *Marci Tulli Ciceronis De re publica libri e codice rescripto Vaticano Latino 5757,* vol. 23, pp. 120–23. Codices e Vaticanis Selecti. Vatican City: Biblioteca Apostolica Vaticana, 1934.

Michel, Paul-Henri. *The Cosmology of Giordano Bruno.* Translated by R. E. W. Maddison. Ithaca, N.Y.: Cornell University Press, 1973.

Miele, Michele. "Indagini sulla comunità conventuale di Giordano Bruno (1556–1576)." *Bruniana & Campanelliana* 1 (1995), pp. 157–204.

———. "L'organizzazione degli studi dei Domenicani di Napoli al tempo di Giordano Bruno." In Eugenio Canone, ed., *Giordano Bruno: Gli anni napoletani e la "peregrinatio" europea: Immagini, testi, documenti,* pp. 29–50. Cassino: Università degli Studi, 1992.

Mueller, Janel, and Leah Marcus. *Elizabeth I: Autograph Compositions and Foreign Language Originals.* Chicago: University of Chicago Press, 2003.

Muir, Edward. *Mad Blood Stirring: Vendetta and Factions in Friuli During the Renaissance.* Baltimore: Johns Hopkins University Press, 1998.

Napolitano Valditara, Linda. *Le idee, i numeri, l'ordine: La dottrina della mathesis universalis dall'Accademia antica al neoplatonismo.* Padua: Bibliopolis, 1988.

Netanyahu, Benzion. *The Origins of the Inquisition in Spain in the Fifteenth Century.* New York: New York Review Classics, 2002.

O'Malley, John W. *The First Jesuits.* Cambridge, Mass.: Harvard University Press, 2005.

———. *Giles of Viterbo on Church and Reform.* Leiden: Brill, 1968.

———. *Praise and Blame in Renaissance Rome: Rhetoric, Doctrine, and Reform in the Sacred Orators of the Papal Court, c. 1450–1521.* Duke Monographs in Medieval and Renaissance Studies 3. Durham, N.C.: Duke University Press, 1979.

———. *Trent and All That: Renaming Catholicism in the Early Modern Era.* Cambridge, Mass.: Harvard University Press, 2002.

Onians, Richard Broxton. *The Origins of European Thought About the Mind, the Body, the World, Time, and Fate.* Cambridge: University Press, 1951.

Ordine, Nuccio. *La cabala dell'asino: Asinità e conoscenza in Giordano Bruno.* Naples: Liguori Editore, 1987.

Parker, A. A. *Literature and the Delinquent: The Picaresque Novel in Spain and Europe, 1599–1753*. Edinburgh: Edinburgh University Press, 1967.

Peiresc, Nicolas-Claude Fabri de. *Lettres.* Vol. 4, *1626–1637.* Paris: Imprimerie Nationale, 1893.

Pfeiffer, Heinrich. *Zur Ikonographie von Raffaels Disputa.* Rome: Pontificia Universitas Gregoriana, 1975.

Pino, Giovanni Battista. *Ragionamento sovra del asino.* Edited by Olga Casale. Rome: Salerno Editrice, 1982.

Provvidera, Tiziana. "On the Printer of Giordano Bruno's London Works." *Bruniana & Campanelliana* 2 (1996), pp. 361–68.

Ricci, Saverio. *Giordano Bruno nell'Europa del Cinquecento.* Rome: Salerno, 2000.

———. "Giovinezza di un inquisitore: Giulio Antonio Santori, Giordano Bruno, e il Santo Uffizio a Napoli." *Bruniana & Campanelliana* 1 (1995), pp. 249–72.

Rossi, Paolo. *Clavis universalis: Arti della memoria e logica combinatoria da Lullo a Leibniz.* Bologna: Il Mulino, 1984.

Rowland, Ingrid D. "Abacus and Humanism." *Renaissance Quarterly* 48 (1995), pp. 695–727.

———. "A Contemporary Account of the Ensisheim Meteorite." *Meteoritics* 25, no. 1 (March 1990), pp. 19–22.

———. "Giordano Bruno and Neapolitan Neoplatonism." In Hilary Gatti, ed., *Giordano Bruno, Philosopher of the Renaissance*, pp. 97–120. Aldershot: Ashgate, 2002.

———. "The Intellectual Background of the *School of Athens*: Tracking Divine Wisdom in the Rome of Julius II." In Marcia Hall, ed., *Raphael's "School of Athens*," pp. 131–70. Cambridge, U.K.: Cambridge University Press, 1997.

———. "What Communion Hath Light with Darkness?" In Lydia Goehr and Daniel Herwitz, eds., *The Don Giovanni Moment*, pp. 1–14. New York: Columbia University Press, 2006.

Rubino, Ciro. *Tansilliana: La vita, la poesia, e le opere di Luigi Tansillo.* Naples: Istituto Grafico Editoriale Italiano, 1996.

Secret, François. *Hermétisme et Kabbale.* Naples: Bibliopolis, 1992.

Spampanato, Vincenzo. *Vita di Giordano Bruno*, with an afterword by Nuccio Ordine. Messina: Giuseppe Principato, 1922; Rome: Gela Editrice, 1988.

Spruit, Leen. "Telesio's Reform of the Philosophy of Mind." *Bruniana & Campanelliana* 3, no. 1 (1997), pp. 123–44.

Stephens, Walter E. *Demon Lovers: Witchcraft, Sex, and the Crisis of Belief.* Chicago: University of Chicago Press, 2002.

Sturlese, Rita. *Giordano Bruno. De umbris idearum.* Florence: Olschki, 1991.

Tansillo, Luigi. *Il canzoniere: Edito ed inenedito.* Edited by Erasmo Pércopo. Naples: Tipografia degli Artigianelli, 1926. Reprint annotated by Tobia Toscano. Naples: Liguori, 1996.

Teofilo da Vairano. *De gratia Novi Testamenti.* Biblioteca Apostolica Vaticana, MS Vat. Lat. 12056.

van Winden, J. C. M. *Calcidius on Matter: His Doctrine and Sources: A Chapter in the History of Platonism.* Leiden: Brill, 1959.

Vetere, Benedetto, and Alessandro Ippoliti. *Il Collegio romano: Storia della costruzione.* Rome: Gangemi Editore, 2005.

Woolley, Benjamin. *The Queen's Conjuror: The Science and Magic of Dr. John Dee, Adviser to Queen Elizabeth I*. New York: Henry Holt, 2001.

Wyatt, Michael. *The Italian Encounter with Tudor England: A Cultural Politics of Translation*. New York: Cambridge University Press, 2005.

Yates, Frances. *The Art of Memory*. London: Routledge and Kegan Paul, 1961.

———. *Giordano Bruno and the Hermetic Tradition*. London: Routledge and Kegan Paul, 1964.

Acknowledgments

My thanks to the extraordinary patience of my editor, Paul Elie, to whom this book owes its existence, and to Paul Richard Blum, Lina Bolzoni, Eugenio Canone, Donald Carroll, Thomas Cerbu, Maria Ann Conelli, Jon Cooper, Brian Copenhaver, Karen de León-Jones, Germana Ernst, Mordechai Feingold, Jonathan Galassi, Anthony Grafton, Dario Ianneci, James Kalsbeek, Eugenio Lo Sardo, John Marino, Peter Mazur, Mario Pereira, Dana Prescott, Pasquale Siciliani, Robert Silvers, Frank and Margaret Snowden, Joanne Spurza, Daniel Stein-Kokin, Haris Vlavianos, and the Libreria ASEQ in Rome, where Edoardo and Luca have kept me supplied with books on or by Giordano Bruno for nearly three decades. Thanks also to the Biblioteca Apostolica Vaticana; the Biblioteca Casanatense, Rome; the Biblioteca Angelica, Rome; the Biblioteca Nazionale Centrale, Rome; the Biblioteca Nazionale, Naples; the Archivio di Stato, Venice; the Herzog August Bibliothek, Wolfenbüttel; the University Library, Cambridge; the Bodleian Library, Oxford; and the British Library. Fellowships from the John Simon Guggenheim Foundation, the Rockefeller Foundation Study Center at Bellagio, and the Getty Research Institute facilitated research and writing at various stages; at Bellagio, my particular thanks to Gianna Celli, now director emerita; at the Getty Research Institute, to Michael Roth (now president of Wesleyan University), Charles Salas, Susan Allen, Wim DeWit, and the entire

Department of Special Collections. The library of the great Bruno scholar Frances Yates, now owned by the Getty Research Institute, provided extraordinary tangible inspiration. Thanks to my superb copy editor, Ingrid Sterner, for saving me from an infinite universe of *lapsus calami*. I owe thanks of a different kind to my parents: to my father for his broad view of science and to both of my parents for their example of unflagging integrity. The late Father Athanasius Kircher, S.J., read Giordano Bruno faithfully when it was still dangerous to do so, and despite the centuries that divide us, he had, like the other people and institutions here enumerated, more than a minor role in the shaping of this book. Above all, my thanks to the two people to whom it is dedicated: Hilary Gatti, infallible guide to the intricacies of Bruno's thought, and Avvocato Dario Guidi Federzoni, who revealed the legal thriller latent in a tragedy.

Index

Abarbanel, Leone, 60, 235
Abbot, George, 145–47
Abraham, 51, 56, 116, 131
Academia Julia, 209, 211, 212
Accademia degli Oziosi, 29
Acteon, 51–52
Aegidius (Pontano), 40
Aeneas, 50
Aeneid, The (Virgil), 215
Agatha, Saint, 266
Agnes, Saint, 266
Agostino da Montalcino, Fra, 71–73, 78
Agrippa, Cornelius, 82
Albania, 231
Albigensians, 73
alchemy, 201, 202, 206
Aldobrandini, Cardinal, *see* Clement VIII, Pope
Alexander the Great, 79, 108, 255
Alexander VI, Pope, 3
Alexandria, 66, 68, 161, 162, 216
Alfonso of Aragon, 38
algebra, 106, 112, 193
Altomonte, Agostino, 231
Amphitrite, 218
analogies, magic based on, 119
Anaxagoras, 181
Andria, Dominican college at, 34
Angevin kings, 38

Anglican Church, 140, 144, 192, 202, 250, 265; Thirty-nine Articles of Religion of, 273, 276
Angoulême, Henri d', 133
anima (soul), 111, 125, 127
Anthony, Saint, 97
anti-Semitism, 40, 59, 83–85, 223, 294n
Antonius, Bishop of Florence, 30
Antony and Cleopatra (Shakespeare), 283
Antwerp, 193, 238
Apis bull, 123, 124
Apollo, 135, 166
Aquilecchia, Giovanni, 5–6
Aquinas, Thomas, 43, 71, 93, 133, 191, 228, 254; Aristotle as inspiration for, 36; at College of San Domenico, 34–35, 79; Jesuits as followers of, 89; memory and mental discipline of, 62, 64, 236; in Paris, 34, 79, 121; Scholasticism of, 36, 37; transubstantiation questioned by, 273
Arabic numerals, 106, 112
Arabs, 84, 108, 109; as astronomers, 68, 69
Arcadia (Sannazaro), 40, 51
architecture, 99; Gothic, 21–22, 65, 94, 124, 141, 198, 205, 225, 229; mental, in artificial memory, 64, 123, 124
Arcimboldo, Giuseppe, 203, 205

Aristarchus, 109, 216

Aristophanes, 150

Aristotle, 69, 79, 87, 105, 107–108, 121, 133, 200, 201, 215; ancient philosophers preceding, 160; Beza's strict adherence to, 100; Bruno's refutation of, 197; cosmic system of, 90, 112, 255; Jesuits as followers of, 89, 114, 192; on memory, 125; metaphysics of, 105; misogyny of, 158; Scholasticism rooted in, 71

arithmetic, 112, 173, 193

Arius, 72, 73

Armenians, 252

Armeno, Zorzi, 231

Arrigone, Pompeo Cardinal, 287, 289

Arrigoni da Verona, Fra Celestino, 233, 236, 246–49, 268, 275

Ars Magna (Llull), 64, 73

art, 94; in Prague, 203; religious, 30, 65; of Spanish Court, 140; Venetian Inquisition and, 95

artificial memory, 62–65, 92, 110, 123–25, 174, 191

Art of Deformations, The (Bruno), 224

Ascoli, Hieronymo Bernerio Cardinal d', 287, 289

Ash Wednesday, 101

Ash Wednesday Supper, The (Bruno), 108, 149–57, 159–61, 192, 300n

asinità, 79–82, 84, 85

Assayer, The (Galileo), 107, 282

astrology, 46, 65–67, 88, 90–91, 106, 202

astronomy, 12, 65–69, 87–93; Arab, 109; instruments for, 113, 206, 281; mathematics and, 106, 107, 113, 173, 282; poetic texts on, 214; see also universe

Astrophel and Stella (Sidney), 176–77

Athens, ancient, 23, 36, 165

atomic theory, 125, 214, 216–18, 220

Augustine, Saint, 37, 42, 47, 58, 72, 73, 109, 136, 173, 294n

Augustinians, 10, 31–33, 39–43, 46, 134, 169, 191, 277, 294n

Augustus I, Duke of Wittenberg, 202, 203

Austria, 93, 202, 203

Avalos, Maria d', 293n

Aylen, Leo, 298n

Azzolini, Decio Cardinal, 261

Bagga, Demetrio Lecca, 231

Baglioni, Lucrezia, 230

Balbani, Niccolo, 98, 99

Banquet in the House of Levi (Veronese), 95

Barbadico, Sebastiano, 235

Barberini, Francesco Cardinal, 280

Beccaria, Ipolito Maria, 288

Bell, Adam Schall von, 254

Bellarmine, Robert Cardinal, 11–13, 252–62, 265, 269, 272, 273, 275–76, 281, 282, 287, 289, 305n

Bellini, Giovanni, 225

Benedict XVI, Pope, 44

Benedictines, 31

Bennett, Alan, 298n

Benzon, Antonio, 231

Bergamo, 96, 188

Berjon, Jean, 100, 101

Bernardino of Siena, Saint, 39

Bernini, Gian Lorenzo, 283–84

Besler, Hieronymus, 201, 209, 211, 213, 223–24

Beza, Theodor, 100

Bible, 54, 55, 59, 92, 93, 98–99, 180, 192, 220, 234, 235, 255; Ecclesiastes, 58, 93, 294n; Genesis, 168; Gospels, 37, 38, 43, 56, 98, 190, 192, 234, 242, 273, 276; Jeremiah, 270; Job, 190; Lamentations, 35; Psalms, 55, 58, 63, 101, 190, 270; Revelation, 164; Song of Songs, 36, 51, 52, 58, 110, 179, 180, 184; Wisdom of Solomon, 204

Blackfriars, 141

blasphemy, 240; punishment for, 26

Blindness (Epicurio), 46, 183

Boccaccio, Giovanni, 21

Bohemia, 202–203, 205, 206

Bologna, University of, 223

Bonaparte, Napoleon, 229, 248, 304n
Book of Martyrs (Foxe), 265, 306n
Book on Games of Chance (Cardano), 112
Borghese, Camillo Cardinal, 287, 289
Borgias, 3
Bossy, John, 299n
Botero, Giovanni, 195
Bourges, massacre of Protestants in, 105
Brahe, Sophie, 203
Brahe, Tycho, 68–69, 88, 89, 91, 107, 113, 203, 205, 206, 211
Brant, Sebastian, 90
Braunschweig, 202, 209, 212, 213, 221, 245
Brezula, Battista, 232
Brictano, Giacomo, 238–29
Bruniana & Campanelliana (journal), 6
Bruno, Giordano: Aristotle rejected by, 107–109, 197, 215; arraignment by Inquisition of, 75–76; arrest of, 229, 231, 237, 244; arrival in Naples of, 21, 23–26; asinità concept of, 79–81; astronomical studies of, 65–69; Bellarmine's propositions against, 255–62; birth of, 15; childhood of, 15–16, 18, 84; continued influence of, 280–83; cosmology of, see infinite universe; defiance of Inquisition by, 261–62, 266–71; defrocking of, 114, 225; degradation of, 276–77; desire to return to Church of, 114–15, 188–90, 225; divinity of Jesus doubted by, 33, 57–58, 72–73, 220, 241, 259, 263; extradition to Rome of, 244–45; excommunications of, 101, 114, 132, 213, 225, 268; execution of, 6, 7, 9–13, 270, 277–79, 284; family background of, 14; final vows of, 33; forbidden books read by, 75; forest imagery of, 46, 51, 52; in Frankfurt, 213, 217, 222; as fugitive from Inquisition, 75, 78–79, 85–86, 92, 97, 117; in Geneva, 96–101; in Genoa, 77–78, 86; in Helmstedt, 209, 212–13; imprisonment of, 6, 10, 44, 60, 233, 235, 236, 241–43, 245–46, 250, 264–65, 268; intellectual versatility of,

107; interrogations of, 236–37, 239–41, 251, 257, 259, 268; on Jews, 59–60; John Paul II's refusal to pardon, 7, 13; journey from Nola to Naples of, 19–21; in London, 139–43, 148–53, 157–59, 170, 171, 186–87; magic of, 117–20, 209–12; mathematics of, 193–97; memory techniques of, see memory, art of; Mocenigo's accusations against, 75–76, 226–29, 232, 237–38, 240, 257–60; Nola described by, 17–18; in Noli, 87, 88, 90, 92; novitiate of, 29–33, 42, 99; in Order of Preachers, 33, 35, 64; ordination of, 70; at Oxford, 143–47, 149, 151, 159, 191; in Padua, 96, 223–24; in Paris, 117, 120–23, 132–33, 137, 187–93, 197–98, 215; in Prague, 205–209; poetry writing of, 214–15; repentance of, 242–43; sentencing of, 7, 258–59, 272–76; "solitary sparrow" image of, 101–103; statue in Campo de' Fiori of, 3–7; teaching methods of, 88–89, 93, 132–33; Teofilo's influence on, 41–45, 56, 57, 79; theological education of, 34–37, 55, 70–73; in Toulouse, 104–106, 113–15; variety of writings of, 173–74; in Venice, 90, 93–95, 224–26; vernacular writing of, 42, 65, 90, 147–49, 171–72, 177, 180, 214; Vita's investigation of, 71–73, 75; Wheel of Fortune image of, 84; witnesses against, 238–39, 246–49; in Wittenberg, 199–205, 209, 226; works of, see titles of specific works; in Zurich, 221–22
Bruno, Giovanni (Giordano's father), 14–18, 84–85, 102, 105, 178, 184, 192, 194, 287
bubonic plague, see plague
Bucer, Martin, 43

Cairo, 163; observatory at, 68, 109; population of, 21, 292n
Cajetan, Thomas Cardinal, 192
Calcidius, 47

calculus, 113, 193–95
Caligula, obelisk of, 245
Calleir, Raoul, 197
Callippus, 108
Calvin, John, 43, 74, 93, 97, 100, 140, 202
Calvinists, 78, 97, 98, 101, 168, 192, 202, 203, 213, 222, 268
Cambrai, Collège de, 122, 131, 191, 197
Cambridge University, 144
Camorra, 15
Campagna, 70
Campanella, Fra Tommaso, 29, 35, 68
Campo de' Fiori ("Field of Flowers," Rome), 78; execution of heretics in, 9–12; statue of Bruno in, 3–7
Candelaio, Il, see Candlemaker, The
Candlemaker, The (Bruno), 23–28, 84, 85, 128–33, 153, 155, 174, 229, 299n
Canone, Eugenio, 67, 88
Cantus Circaeus (Bruno), 122, 132–36
Canzoniere (Petrarch), 178, 183
Capitoline Museum, 4
Capuchins, 231, 236, 246, 247
Caracciolo, Gian Galeazzo, Marchese di Vico, 97, 98
Caracciolo, Fra Teofilo, 30
Carafa, Alfonso, Duke of Nocera, 67, 295n
Carafa, Antonio Cardinal, 43, 44
Carafa, Fabrizio, 293n
Carafa, Giovanni Pietro Cardinal, 32
Carafa da Sanseverino, Galeotto, 65
Cardano, Gerolamo, 90–91, 112
Carmelites, 141
Casaubon, Isaac, 162
Castelnau, Catherine-Marie de, 159
Castelnau, Madame de, 158
Castelnau, Michel de, Lord of Mauvissière, 140–43, 149, 186–88
Castel Sant'Angelo (Rome), 249
Castor, 22
Catherine of Alexandria, Saint, 266
Catherine of Siena, Saint, 30
Catholic Church, 4, 13, 57, 110, 212, 225, 237, 255, 257; accusations of blasphemies against, 227–28; ancient Fathers of, 72; Anglican objections to, 250; Bruno's attempted reconciliations with, 114, 188–90; Cardano's prognostications on, 91; careers for second sons in, 253; converts to, 12, 53–55, 234, 274; dissidents in, 78; Elizabethan England and, 156, 170; escaped slaves received into, 231; excommunication from, 114–15, 138, 189, 225, 268; exorcists of, 118; freethinkers in, 59; independence of modern Rome from, 5; institutional, Jesus as symbol of, 263; jubilees of, 6, 10, 60, 274, 275, 283; and massacres of Protestants, 105, 137, 188; obedience of priests in, 251, 254–55; policy of persuasion in, 283; in Prague, 203; Protestant skepticism about, 260–61; reformers versus traditionalists within, 32, 41, 43, 55; ritual separation from, 276–77, 279; sacraments of, 234–25; strict interpretation of Bible by, 220; topics contested by Protestants and, 44, 192; view of divine justice of, 270; wealth and corruption of, 234; see also Inquisition
Cause, Principle, and Unity (Bruno), 157–59, 160, 166–67, 170, 176, 194, 217, 280
Cavallini, Pietro, 65
Cecaria (Epicuro), 46, 183
Cecilia, Saint, 266
Celeste, Girolamo, 235, 236
Cellini, Benvenuto, 153
Cenci family, 274–75
Ceres, 166
Cerriglio tavern (Naples), 30
Cervini, Marcello, 253
Cesi, Count Federico, 255
Chambéry, 96, 101
Charing Cross (London), 141
Charles V, Holy Roman Emperor, 82, 91, 98
Charles IX, King of France, 105
Charlewood, John, 149, 157
China, 89, 199, 254; trade routes to, 170
Christian I, Duke of Wittenberg, 202

Christian theology: Aquinas's systematic account of, 35; and divinity of Jesus, 57, 72–73; education in, 33; Hermetic texts and, 162, 163; *Imprimatur* of works of, 74; Kabbalah and, 40, 54, 56; orthodox Dominican resistance to challenges to, 73; political action linked to, 28; reconciliation of Platonic philosophy and, 46–50; of Teofilo, 44
Cicala, Odoardo, 15–16, 178, 182
Cicero, 63, 137
Ciotti, Giovanni Battista, 238
Circe, 132–37, 176, 183
City Council of Rome, 3
Clavis magna (Bruno), 110, 122, 123
Clavius, Christoph, 67–68, 88, 89, 114, 240, 253–55
Clement VIII, Pope, 6, 11, 44, 217, 226, 240, 252, 269, 274, 275, 291n
Cobham, Henry, 137, 139
Colleoni, Bartolomeo, 94
colonialism, European, 153–54, 207
Colonna, Prince Ascanio, 41
Colonna, Vittoria, 32
Columbus, Christopher, 92, 199
commedia dell'arte, 84
Commentaries (Erasmus), 75
Commentariolus (Copernicus), 66
Commentary on the Sphere of Sacrobosco (Clavius), 68, 89
Communion, 115, 192, 234
Confraternity of Saint John the Beheaded, 10
Consolatory Oration (Bruno), 212
Constantinople, 74, 140, 163; population of, 21, 292n; trade routes through, 170
Contarini, Gasparo Cardinal, 32
Copernicus, Nicolaus, 7, 107, 108, 112, 113, 152, 155, 159, 180, 200, 300n; Clavius's criticism of, 89; mathematics of, 91, 106; sun-centered universe of, 66, 68, 90, 109, 136, 146
Coptic Christians, 283
Corbinelli, Jacopo, 191, 197, 224
Corpo di Napoli, 161, 162

Cotin, Guillaume, 191–92
Council of Trent, 31–32, 41, 55, 56, 98–99, 137, 238
Cranmer, Thomas, 98, 273
Crispo, Fra Giordano, 33
Critias (Plato), 165
Crusius, Martin, 209
Cusanus, Nicolaus, 61, 109–10, 113, 173, 200, 215–16
Cyllenian Ass, The (Bruno), 169

dactylic hexameter, 214, 218
Dalmatia, 93
Dante, 65, 106, 129, 169
Da Ponte, Lorenzo, 84
De compendiosa architectura et complemnto artis Lullii (Bruno), 122
Dee, John, 205–206, 211, 217
Defense in Favor of the Reply to Eight Propositions Against Which the Most Illustrious and Reverend Lord Cardinal Bellarmine Has Written (Marsilio), 256–57
De gli heroici furori, see *Heroic Frenzies, The*
Del Bene, Piero, 191, 193
Democritus of Abdera, 216, 217
demons, 117
De partu Virginis (Sannazaro), 40
De rerum natura (Lucretius), 93, 214
De revolutionibus orbium coelestium (Copernicus), 66, 68, 91
De sphaera, see *On the Sphere*
De umbris idearum (Bruno), 121–30, 134, 136
Devereux, Penelope, 176, 183
Devereux, Walter, first Earl of Essex, 176
De vita coelitus comparanda, see *On Living the Heavenly Life*
Dezza, Pietro Cardinal, 287, 289
Dialoghi d'amore (Abarbanel), 60
Dialogue Concerning the Two Chief World Systems (Galileo), 6, 155, 283
Dialogues on Love (Abarbanel), 60
Dialogues on Love (Ebreo), 235

Diana, as huntress, 48–50, 166
Dicson, Alexander, 157, 158
Dies Irae (Day of Wrath), 80
Digression in Praise of the Ass (Agrippa), 82
Dionysius the Areopagite, 42
Discourse on the Ass (Pino), 82
Disputations (Bellarmine), 255, 261
Divine Comedy, The (Dante), 106
Doctor Faustus (Marlowe), 251
Domenico da Nocera, Fra, 225
Dominic, Saint, 229
Dominicans, 6, 10, 11, 39, 75, 97, 101, 169, 189, 191, 247, 273, 277, 287; challenges to Christian orthodoxy battled by, 73; colleges of, 34; in England, 141; in Genoa, 77; habit of, abandoned by Bruno, 6, 76, 86, 239; Inquisition served by, 30, 74, 118, 229, 252, 255, 256, 304n; martyrdom of, 266; memory training of, 62; movement from city to city of, 79; in Naples, 29, 114, 201 (*see also* San Domenico Maggiore); in Padua, 96; in Paris, 121; philosophical rigor of, 128; rise of, 234; rivalry of Jesuits and, 114; in Salerno, 70; Scholasticism of, 36, 37, 41, 71–72, 256; Spanish cruelty in Mexico denounced by, 153; standard theological textbook of, 48, 49; transubstantiation practiced by, 221; in Venice, 93, 94, 225, 232–33, 240
Donatus, 43
Don Giovanni (Mozart), 27, 84
"Donkey's Testament, The" (song), 80
Drake, Francis, 170
Drinking Party, The (Aylen), 298n
Dudley, Robert, first Earl of Leicester, 143, 200
Dürer, Albrecht, 203

Earth-centered universe, 66, 109, 136, 146
Ebreo, Leone, 60, 235
Eclogues (Sannazaro), 40
ecumenism, 56

Egidio Antonini da Viterbo, Fra, *see* Giles of Viterbo
Eglin, Raphael, 132–33, 222, 224
Egyptians, 59, 123, 161–67, 169, 180, 184, 189, 216, 301n; Christian, 283
Einstein, Albert, 7
Elizabeth I, Queen of England, 137, 139, 140, 177, 200, 275; culture and tolerance of, 138; proficiency in foreign languages of, 144, 170, 301n; Spanish aggression toward England of, 170, 207; tributes in Bruno's writings to, 156, 158, 183, 185, 218
Endymion, 50–51
England, 11, 137–40, 142, 160, 165, 183, 187, 188, 191, 192, 213–15, 217, 248, 288; burning of martyrs in, 265; Church of, *see* Anglican Church; colonialism of, 153; Dee's journey to Prague from, 205; Jesuits in, 137; Latin as language of education in, 99; parliamentary system in, 156; Punch-and-Judy shows in, 84; rudeness in, 143–45, 152, 156, 201; Spanish aggression toward, 170, 207; *see also* London; Oxford University
Ensisheim meteorite, 90
Epicurean philosophy, 214
Epicuro, Marcantonio, 46, 183
Erasmus, Desiderius, 43, 63, 74, 75, 93, 146, 152
Etruscans, 84, 252
Eucharist, 95, 191
Eudoxus, 108
excommunication, 114–15, 132, 138, 189, 225, 268; from Calvinism, 101; for reading indexed books, 43
exorcists, 118
Expulsion of the Triumphant Beast, The (Bruno), 59–60, 67, 164–72, 184, 185, 212

Favaro, Anton, 18
Felix, Saint, 191
Ferdinand, King of Aragon, 74
Ferrara, Jews in, 54

Ferrari, Ettore, 4–6
Fiammetta, 21
Fibonacci, Leonardo, 106
Ficino, Marsilio, 45–46, 51, 60, 146,
    147, 159, 162, 169; divine light
    of, 127, 136; homoerotic desires
    of, 110–11; natural magic regimen of,
    119; translations by, 47, 150, 164,
    175
Fiorentino, Mauro, 88
Flanders, 170
Florence, 45, 90, 93, 162, 241, 280; art
    in, 203; power struggles between
    Rome and, 252; University of, 42
Florio, John, 141, 142, 144, 147, 151,
    177, 187, 194
Fontana, Domenico, 245
Forest of Matter, 47–52, 126–28, 155
Fortune, John, 298n
Fountain of the Four Rivers, The
    (Bernini), 283–84
Foxe, John, 265, 306n
France, 101, 117, 140, 165, 192, 217;
    Latin as language of education in, 99;
    Naples ruled by, 22, 38, 84; Protes-
    tants in, see Huguenots; see also
    specific cities and towns
Franciscans, 10, 31, 39, 231, 234, 277
Frankfurt, 213, 215, 217, 224, 226–27,
    238; book fairs in, 95, 105, 213, 217,
    222, 233, 236
Franzino, Father, 17
Frezzaria, 90
Frischlin, Nicodemus, 202, 205, 208

Gagliardo, Fra Eugenio, 31–33
Galileo Galilei, 4, 66, 69, 155, 156, 192,
    193, 255, 280–83; on mathematics,
    107, 173, 282; prosecution by Inquisi-
    tion of, 13, 280, 281; rehabilitation by
    Catholic Church of, 6–7; telescopic
    discoveries of, 68, 113, 280, 281; at
    University of Padua, 224
Galleria dell'Accademia (Venice), 95
Garibaldi, Giuseppe, 229
Geneva, 11, 96–101, 104, 115, 140,

196, 222, 236; Consistory of, 100–
    101; University of, 100
Genoa, 76–80, 86, 90
Gentile, Giovanni, 294n
Gentili, Alberico, 199–200, 202
geometry, 106, 107, 112, 164, 173, 174,
    208; of Mordente, 193, 195, 197;
    spherical, 66
Georgics (Virgil), 214
Germany, 11, 18, 78, 101, 109, 140, 190,
    197–204, 215, 248; landscape of, 199;
    Latin as language of education in, 99;
    proximity of Venice to, 93, 245; see
    also specific cities and towns
Gesner, Conrad, 136
Gesualdo, Don Carlo, Prince of Venosa,
    35, 293n
Gibbons, Orlando, 283
Giles of Rome, 43
Giles of Viterbo, 32, 39–40, 46–47, 63,
    134, 183; divine light imagery of, 127,
    136; Forest of Matter imagery of, 47–
    52, 126; Kabbalah studies of, 56, 61,
    169; Platonic philosophy of, 56, 71,
    110–11; Seripando mentored by,
    40–41
Gillespie, Robert, 298n
Giovanni da Gara, 235
Giuliano da Salò, Fra, 249
Gonzaga of Mantua, 140
Gothic architecture, 21–22, 65, 94, 124,
    141, 198, 205, 225, 229
Gough, Michael, 298n
Gourbin, Gilles, 123
Granada, Miguel Angel, 182
Grassi, Orazio, 107
Graziani, Francesco, 264–65, 270
Graziano, Lame, 242
"Great Art" (Llull), 64, 73
Great Key, The (Bruno), 110, 122, 123
Greca, Virgina, 230
Greece, 231
Greek Orthodoxy, 55, 73
Greeks, ancient, 59, 94, 107, 167, 169,
    203, 216; astronomy of, 109; Egypt
    and, 161, 162; geometry of, 193; mag-
    ical operations of, 118, 120; mathe-

Greeks (continued)
matics as underpinning of philosophy of, 282; memory enhancement technique of, 62, 63; Naples founded by, 21, 75, 84; orgiastic cult of, 205; poetic meters used by, 214
Gregorian calendar, 68, 89, 240
Gregory XIII, Pope, 30, 68, 189, 240
Greville, Fulke, 150–51
Grifanius, Hubertus, 93
Gwinne, Matthew, 151, 177

Habsburgs, 140, 170, 202
Hadrian, Emperor, 246
Hannover, 193
Heinrich Julius, Duke of Braunschweig and Lüneburg, 213, 221
Helianus, Victor, 67
Helmstedt, 209, 211, 213, 224, 226
Hennequin, Jean, 197
Henri, duc de Guise, 105, 188, 197
Henri III, King of France, 117, 120–22, 126, 131, 135, 137, 143, 191, 275; ambassador to Court of St. James's of, 140, 186–87; Huguenots and, 115, 188; works by Bruno dedicated to, 122–23, 197; Spanish ambassador to, 189
Henri VI, King of Navarre, 115, 137, 275
heresy, cases before Venetian Inquisition of, 232–36
Hermes Trismegistus, 162–64, 166, 173
Hermits of Saint Augustine, 38, 42
Hernandez, Luigi, 231
Herod, King, 168
Heroic Frenzies, The (Bruno), 46, 60, 170, 174–86, 204, 210, 221, 235
Hieroglyphic Monad, The (Dee), 217
Hindu-Arabic numerals, 106, 112
Hipparchus, 108
Hochmah, 169
Hohenheim, Theophrastus Aureolus Bombastus von, see Paracelsus
Holy Office, 43, 97, 233; in Naples, 31, 55, 59, 75; in Rome, 74, 230, 244–46,

248–50, 254, 265, 269, 279, 281; in Venice, 93, 227, 229, 232, 238, 260, 287; see also Inquisition
Homer, 48, 134, 135
Horace, 215, 217
Host, 99; consecration of, 10; see also transubstantiation
Huguenots, 78, 105, 115, 122, 137, 188, 189, 232
Hungary, 202

Ignatius of Loyola, 190, 253–55
Iliad (Homer), 282
Index of Forbidden Books, 43, 93, 230, 238, 255, 261, 279–80, 289
infinite universe, 12–13, 18, 20, 60–61, 90, 109–12, 158, 160, 165, 215–21, 280; atomic theory and, 216–18, 220; concept of God in, 121, 155; Kepler's views on, 280; language for description of, 169–70; mathematics of, 112–13, 170, 208; transformation of imagery of, 164; in twentieth-century cosmology, 192
Innocent X, Pope, 283
Inns of Court (London), 141
Inquisition, 4, 13, 35, 55, 73–74, 100, 110, 118, 189, 223; books banned by, 146, 233 (see also Index of Forbidden Books); in France, rumors of, 137, 138; locally established protocols of, 74; in Naples, 32, 74–76, 97, 239, 242; see also Roman Inquisition; Spanish Inquisition; Venetian Inquisition
Isis, 166–69, 265; cult of, 4, 161
Islam, 66, 231; see also Muslims
Italian Association of Free Thinkers, 5
Italy, 46, 97, 99, 117, 144, 222; art in, 203; banqueting in, 151; censorship in, 232; decline of printing industry in, 241; effusive speech in, 39; fortune-telling in, 118; Gentili exiled from, 200; Hindu-Arabic numerals in, 106; Jews in, 53, 54; plague in, 78, 90; presses in, 90; Protestants in, 31; re-

gional standards for blasphemy in, 240; Turkish marauders in, 23, 163; *see also specific cities and towns*

Jacob of Flanders, 232
Jebb, Julian, 298n
Jerome, Saint, 55
Jesuits, 12, 89, 107, 192, 203, 252–55, 261; in China, 199; in England, 137; French, 114–15, 188–89; German, 215, 282–83; Roman College of, 67, 68, 253, 255, 280
Jesus, 51, 92, 190, 263; casting out of spirits by, 118; doubts about divinity of, 33, 57–58, 72–73, 220, 241, 259, 263; in Garden of Gethsemane, 241–42, 264, 270; in Gospels, 43, 242; in infinite universe, 110
Jews, 40, 53–57, 59–61, 82, 181, 260, 263, 294n; ancient, 101; conversion of, 54–55; donkey as stereotype of, 81; expulsion of, 53–54, 75, 83–84; ghettos for, 32, 54; Moors and, 73–74; mysticism of, 110, 162, 261 (*see also* Kabbalah); in Padua, 223; in Prague, 203; scholarship of, 254; Teofilo on passage into Promised Land of, 44; in Venice, 95, 225, 232, 235
John, Gospel of, 37, 136
John of Sacrobosco, 66, 67, 87–89, 92, 93, 105, 106, 114
John Paul II, Pope, 6, 7, 13
Johnson, Samuel, 142
John the Baptist, Saint, 229
Judaism, *see* Jews
Judgment of Paris, 203–204
Julius, Duke of Braunschweig and Lüneburg, 209, 212
Julius II, Pope, 295n
Jupiter, 135, 164–65, 167; planet, 66, 113, 280
Justice, Barry, 298n

Kabbalah, 40, 54, 57, 59–61, 169, 210; Christian, 56, 60

Kabbalah of the Horse Pegasus, The (Bruno), 169
Kelley, Edward, 205–206
Kepler, Johannes, 4, 193, 195, 203, 205, 215, 240, 280–82
King James Bible, 101
Kircher, Athanasius, 54, 89, 215, 220, 282–83
Knights of Saint John, 163
Kristeller, Paul Oskar, 294n

Lacrima Christi (wine), 20
Ladislas II, King of Naples, 38
La Faye, Antoine de, 100–101
Lamp of Thirty Statues, The (Bruno), 201–202
Lange, Erik, 203
Las Casas, Bartolomé de, 153
Laski, Prince Albert, 143, 205–206
Last Judgment, 80
Last Supper, 99; painting by Veronese of, 95
Latimer, Hugh, 265, 305n
Latin Bible, *see* Vulgate Bible
Lazarus, 116, 131
Leibniz, Gottfried Wilhelm von, 113, 193, 215
Leo X, Pope, 249
Leonardo da Vinci, 106–107, 173
Lepanto, Battle of, 232, 244
Levantine Jews, 225
Leyser, Polycarp, 202
Linnaeus, Carolus, 136
Lipsius, Justus, 254
Little Commentary (Copernicus), 66
Lives of the Holy Fathers, 31
Livorno, 76
Llull, Ramon, 64, 73, 112, 121, 124, 206
Llullian Combinatory Lamp, The (Bruno), 201
logic, 35, 121, 122
Lombard, Peter, 48, 49, 71, 73, 133
London, 18, 138, 147–53, 156, 170, 186–87, 236, 245, 275; bear-baiting in, 144; Castelnau's household in, 140–43, 186; hatred of foreigners in,

London (*continued*)
151–52; market for Italian books in,
158; streets of, 141, 151, 157
Lorraine, cardinal of, 105
"Love's Beautiful Hunt" (Giles of
Viterbo), 40, 46, 51–52, 183
Lucretius, 93, 214, 215–18, 220
Lucrezia, Madama (statue), 4
Lucy, Saint, 266
Luigi, Abbot (statue), 3–4
Luke, Gospel of, 38, 43, 116
Luther, Martin, 43, 74, 93, 140, 198,
202, 234
Lutherans, 12, 78, 198, 202, 203, 209,
213, 268
Lyon, 93, 96, 101, 104–105, 113; mas-
sacre of Protestants in, 105

Machiavelli, Niccolò, 170, 209
Madonna, *see* Virgin Mary
Madrid, 31
Madruzzi, Lodovico Cardinal, 11, 287,
289
Mafia, 15
Magdeburg, 213
Magi, 117, 168
magic, 117–20, 136, 168, 202, 209–11
Magris, Serafino de, 235
Mahomet of Arak, 108
Mainz, 197–99
Malaperti, Father, 89
Malta, 163
Mantua, Jews in, 54
Manuzio, Aldo, the Younger, 93
Marangon, Francesco, 249
Marburg, University of, 198
Marforio (statue), 4
Margaret, Saint, 266
Mariano da Genazzano, Fra, 39, 40
Mark, Gospel of, 263
marranos (converted Jews), 81, 84
Mars, 167; planet, 66
Marsilio, Giovanni, 256–57, 261–62
Mary I, Queen of England, 170
Mass, 70, 114, 115; Latin, 99; Protestant
disruptions of, 10, 268, 275

mathematics, 111, 112, 193–97, 203,
207, 224; astronomy and, 106, 107,
113, 173, 282
Matthew, Gospel of, 87, 190, 273
Matthias, Holy Roman Emperor, 206
Maude-Roxby, Roddy, 298n
Maximilian II, Holy Roman Emperor,
193
Maxwell, James Clerk, 7
McKern, Leo, 298n
Medici, 252
Médicis, Catherine de, 105, 122
Melanchthon, Philip, 43
memory, art of, 26, 35, 61, 120–30,
133–34, 137–38; magic and, 211–12;
mathematics and, 112; performance
before pope of, 55, 62–63; rhetoric
and, 200, 201; *see also* artificial
memory
Mendoza, Don Bernardin de, 188–90
Menelaus Romanus, 108
Mercati, Angelo, 248
Mercury, planet, 66
Merse, Walter, 250, 268, 275, 291n
metaphysics, 35, 41, 121, 122
Metaphysics (Aristotle), 121
Mexico, Spanish in, 153
Michelangelo, 32, 40, 122
Milan, 91, 245
Milky Way, 109
Miller, Jonathan, 298n
Minerva, 50, 204
Mirandola, Paolo Isaresio della, 288
Mithridates, Flavius, 53
mnemonology, *see* memory, art of
Mocenigo, Giovanni, 75–76, 224, 226–
29, 231, 232, 237–38, 240–41, 246,
257, 259, 260, 264
Momus, 165
Monforte, Laura, 178
Mons Politicus, 252
Montaigne, Michel Eyquem de, 194
Monte, Andrea de, 55
Monte Cicala (Nola), 14, 16, 17, 19, 20,
46, 84, 128
Monterentii, Giulio, 288
Moon, 50–51

Moors, 73–74, 249
Mordente (Bruno), 194–96
Mordente, Fabrizio, 192–97
Moretta, Caterina, 230
"Morgana B., Signora," 128–31
Morosini, Andrea, 224, 232
Moscow, National Library of, 209
Moses, 56, 116, 162
motion, mathematics of, 112–13, 193–94
Mozart, Wolfgang Amadeus, 27, 84
music, 35
Muslims, 73, 91, 118, 225
Mussolini, Benito, 294n
mythology, classical, 48–51, 107, 203–204

Nannini, Fra Remigio, 90, 93–95
Naples, 18, 21–23, 29, 70, 98, 102, 115, 128–29, 151, 169, 183, 206, 265; art of recall in, 62; astronomy in, 88; cisterns of, 75, 295n; climate of, 90, 141; comedy set in, 23–28; devotion to Virgin Mary in, 31; excommunication in absentia of Bruno in, 114; Giles of Viterbo in, 39, 40; Gothic architecture in, 21–22; Holy Office of, 230; influenza epidemic in, 23; Jews of, 53–54, 84; Inquisition in, 29, 32, 74–76, 97, 239, 242; journey from Nola to, 19–20; landscape around, 199, 20–21; mysterious places in, 134; National Library of, 41, 48; opponents of Paul IV in, 32; population of, 21, 292n; religious art in, 30; rhetoric in, 155, 201; riots in, 82; Royal University of, 29, 34, 102; Santori in, 251; Scholastic education in, 37; skies of, 141; Spanish rule of, 14–15, 21–23, 26, 28, 29, 31, 53, 59, 82–83, 138, 189, 240; Teofilo in, 41–42, 149; Turkish invasion of, 163; vernacular of, 171; see also San Domenico Maggiore; San Giovanni a Carbonara
Napolitano, Francesco, 242
Natalino da Perasto, Ser, 231

natural philosophy, 7, 87–89, 155–56, 201, 283; classification schemes in, 136; magic and, 210–11; mathematics and, 193; metaphysics and, 121; see also astronomy
Neapolis, ancient Greek city of, 21
Neoplatonism, 46, 61
Neptune, 166
Netherlands, 170
Newton, Isaac, 7, 113, 193
Nicholas, Saint, 72
Nigidius, Petrus, 198
Ninety-five Theses of Luther, 234
Nola, 11, 14–19, 102, 107, 128, 169, 189, 193; Bruno's boyhood in, 15–16, 62, 79, 117, 215; cathedral of, 191; dialogue set in, 178; fruit trees in, 20
Noli, 86–88, 90, 92
Noner, Antoine, 232
Normans, 84
Nostitz, Johann von, 121, 122
Notes on Reading Sacrobosco (Fiorentino), 88
numerology, 106
Nuremberg, 11, 206

Odyssey (Homer), 134
On Bonds in General (Bruno), 120, 211, 222
On the Compendious Architecture and Complement to the Art of Ramon Llull (Bruno), 122
On the Composition of Images (Bruno), 222
One Hundred and Twenty Articles Against Mathematicians and Philosophers (Bruno), 207–209
One Hundred and Twenty Articles on Nature and the World Against the Aristotelians (Bruno), 197
On the Grace of the New Testament (Teofilo), 41–44, 56, 294n
On the Immense and the Numberless (Bruno), 18–20, 117–18, 187, 215–21, 278

On the Infinite Universe and Worlds (Bruno), 159, 160, 170
On the Interpretation of Dreams (Bruno), 197
On Learned Ignorance (Cusanus), 61, 109, 113
On Living the Heavenly Life (Ficino), 46, 119, 146, 164
On Mathematical Magic (Bruno), 210, 212
On the Monad (Bruno), 217
On Mordente's Compass (Bruno), 194–97
On the Nature of Things (Lucretius), 93, 214
On the Nature of Things (Telesio), 67
On the None Other (Cusanus), 109
On the One God (Aquinas), 121
On the Progress and Hunter's Lamp of the Logicians (Bruno), 201
On the Revolution of the Heavenly Spheres (Copernicus), 66, 68, 91
On the Scrutiny of Species and the Combinatory Lamp of Ramon Llull (Bruno), 206
On the Seven Liberal Arts (Bruno), 226
On the Shadows of Ideas (Bruno), 121–30, 134, 136
On the Signs of the Times (Bruno), 90, 92–93, 95
On the Soul (Aristotle), 105
On the Sphere (John of Sacrobosco), 66, 67, 87–89, 93, 104, 105, 114, 143
On the Triple Medium (Bruno), 216, 217
On the Virgin's Childbirth (Sannazaro), 40
Orlando Furioso (Ariosto), 282
Orléans, massacre of Protestants in, 105
Ortega, Juan de, 88
Oscans, 84
"O Thou, the Central Orb" (Gibbons), 283
Ottoman Empire, 73–74, 95, 163, 274
Oxford, University of, 138, 139, 143–47, 149–51, 153, 191, 265; Bruno's letter to vice-chancellor of, 145–46, 159; Dee at, 205; Gentili at, 200, 202;

Newton's invention of calculus at, 193

Padua, 76, 96, 229; University of, 95, 223–24
painting, *see* art
Palermo, 44
Palladio, Andrea, 264
Panormita, Antonio, 161
Paracelsus, 136, 153, 201, 211
Paris, 18, 120–22, 131–35, 137–38, 151, 190–92, 215, 224, 245, 275; books printed in, 93; Bruno's arrival in, 117; Castelnau's return to, 186–88; English ambassador to, 139; massacre of Protestants in, 105; Medoza in, 189; Mordente in, 192–97; under Napoleon, 248; population of, 21, 292n; University of, 34, 66, 79 (*see also* Sorbonne)
Pasquino, Mastro (statue), 3
patria lux (light of the homeland), 127
Paul, Saint, 37, 98, 186, 191, 266, 271
Paul III, Pope, 74, 253
Paul IV, Pope, 32, 43, 54, 98
Paul V, Pope, 44
Pelagius, 43
Perseids meteor shower, 24
Persians, 162
Pesaro, Jews in, 54
Pestalozzi, Marcantonio, 234, 236, 260, 261
Peter, Saint, 190, 191, 266, 276
Peter Martyr, Saint, 229, 266
Petrarch, 21–22, 65, 171, 177, 178, 180, 181, 183
Petrucci, Alfonso Cardinal, 249
Phaedrus (Plato), 180
Pharfacon, 124
Philip II, King of Spain, 15, 122, 170, 189, 203, 207
Physics (Aristotle), 158
picaresque genre, 83–84
Pico della Mirandola, Giovanni, 54, 60, 169, 192
Pinelli, Giovanni Vincenzo, 224

Pinello, Domenico Cardinal, 287, 289

Pino, Giovanni Battista, 82

Pisa, 76, 106, 224

Piscopia, Elena Lucrezia Cornaro, 223

Pius V, Pope, 55, 62, 143, 240, 275

plague, 76, 78, 86, 90, 283

Plantin, Christophe, 193

plate tectonics, 283

Plato, 37, 55, 66, 69, 79, 107, 126–28, 149–50, 155, 165, 180, 182–84, 186, 298n; analogy between human love and love of wisdom of, 174–75; ancient philosophers preceding, 160; erotic language of, 110–11; Giles of Viterbo's study of, 40–41, 47–48; imagery of, 46–47, 136; as mathematician, 282; myths invented by, 67; parallels of Hermetic writings with, 162; revival of interest in, 36, 45–46; tragedy written by, 23, 130; in understanding of transit between God and the world, 210

Platonic philosophy, 37, 42, 56, 88, 146, 149, 155; reconciliation of Christianity and, 46, 48, 110; Scholasticism and, 41, 46, 71, 93, 126; soul in, 102, 127

Platonic Theology (Ficino), 46, 146

Pleiades, 113, 281

Podocathara, Florentia, 231

Poland, 206

Pollux, 22

Polo, Marco, 199

Pompeii, 19

Pontano, Giovanni Gioviano, 40, 161–62

Porsenna, Lars, 252

Portugal: colonialism of, 153; Jews of, 53, 54, 84, 232

Possevino, Antonio, 254

Poupard, Paul Cardinal, 7

Prague, 202, 203, 205–207, 245, 275, 280

Preachers, Order of, 33, 35, 64, 71

Prince, The (Machiavelli), 209

Priuli, Lorenzo, 237

Prognostication (Cardano), 91

Protestants, 11, 30–31, 97, 147, 162, 170, 204, 226, 254, 260–61, 273, 274; concessions to local customs of, 257, 258; at Council of Trent, 32, 55; economic power of, 240; English, 137, 140, 141, 156, 207; French, see Huguenots; in Geneva, 97, 100; German, 18, 95, 198, 200–201, 225, 244; in Index of Forbidden Books, 43; Italian, 31, 78, 95, 142, 199; Masses disrupted by, 10, 268, 275; in printing industry, 233; strict interpretation of Bible by, 220; topics contested by Catholics and, 44, 192; in Venice, 232, 234–36; vernacular liturgy of, 98, 99; see also Anglican Church; Calvinists; Lutherans; Reformation

Ptolemy, 66, 68, 112

Ptolemys, 162

Puccio, Luisa, 178

Punch-and-Judy shows, 84

Pythagoras, 181, 190, 217, 220, 282

Ragazzoni, Girolamo, 189, 190

Raleigh, Walter, 170

Raphael, 40, 122

Readings on Geometry (Bruno), 224

Rebiba, Scipione Cardinal, 62

reduction compass, 193–96

Reformation, 32, 74, 100, 140, 192, 234; see also Protestants

Regnault, Jean, 133, 136

relics, cult of, 78, 99

Renaissance, 163, 234; architecture of, 22; paintings of, 65; scholarly tradition of, 55

Response . . . in Which, with the Word of God, It Is Shown That the Sacrifice of the Mass Is a Human Invention and a Horrible Idolatry (Balbani), 99

Reuchlin, Johannes, 54, 56

rhetoric, 200–201, 209; ancient, 39; artificial memory and, 63; vernacular, 23

Ricci, Matteo, 199, 254

Ricci, Saverio, 71, 299n

Rich, Robert, second Earl of Warwick, 176
Richards, Darroll, 298n
Ridley, Nicholas, 265, 305n
Ritterhausen, Conrad, 12
Roman College, 67, 89
Roman Inquisition, 12, 79, 97, 239, 243–50, 255–62, 267–70; archives of, 73; Bellarmine's propositions against Bruno in, 256–62; Bruno's defiance of, 261–62, 268–70; Celestino's accusations against, 246–48; corroborating witnesses in, 249, 264–65; dossier sent from San Domenico to, 76; establishment of, 74; extradition of Venetian prisoners by, 239, 244–45; impact on publishing houses of, 241; prisons of, 6, 10, 245–46, 264; protocols of, 74–75, 251–52; sentencing of Bruno by, 7, 269, 258–59, 272–76; torture practiced by, 246, 268; two accusations required for arrests by, 23, 246
Romans, ancient, 101, 137, 162, 169, 199, 214, 216, 217, 246; brutality of punishments of, 264; and eruption of Vesuvius, 19; forests dreaded by, 46; Isis worshipped by, 161; Jesus and, 221; Jews and, 53; Latin spoken by, 144; Magi and, 168; magical operations of, 120; Mainz founded by, 197–98; mathematics as underpinning of philosophy of, 282; memory enhancement technique of, 62, 63; Naples settled by, 84; obscene gestures of, 305n; paterfamilias of, 140; victims of games of, 279
Rome, 31, 34, 43, 62–63, 69, 71, 134, 191, 240; and adoption of Latin Bible, 55; astronomical studies in, 67–68; beautification of, 283; executions in, 9–12, 274–75, 278; Holy Office of, see Holy Office, Roman; Jesuit College in, 253, 255, 280; Jews in, 53; power struggles between Florence and, 252; punishment of criminals in, 249; statue of Bruno in, 3–7; University of, 41, 55; vagabonds in, 78; Valla in, 162
Ronconi, Luca, 299n
Rota, Bernardino, 65
Rouen, massacre of Protestants in, 105
Rudolf II, King of Bohemia, 193, 202–203, 205–209, 271, 275

Saint Bartholomew's Day Massacre, 105, 188
Saint Peter's Basilica (Rome), 245
Salerno, 70, 192, 195; Medical School of, 34
Salonica, 203
Samnites, 84
San Bartolomeo (Campagna), 70
Sánchez, Francisco, 113
San Clemente, Don Guillén de Haro de, 206
San Domenico di Castello (Venice), 94, 220, 230, 233, 248, 304n
San Domenico Maggiore (Naples), 22, 29–37, 61, 69, 76, 88, 90, 190; aristocracy at, 29, 94, 117, 239; Bruno's novitiate at, 29–33, 42, 99; College of, 33–36, 62, 78, 79, 225; Gothic architecture of, 65, 124; Hebrew taught at, 55; Holy Office in, 75; imagery in painting and sculpture in, 65, 67; library of, 41; music at, 35; resistance to Spanish rule at, 28, 29, 82, 240, 251; royal burials at, 38; Scholastic education at, 37
San Felice Circeo (Naples), 134
San Giorgio Maggiore (Venice), 264
San Giovanni a Carbonara (Naples), 32, 33, 37–42, 45, 48, 56
San Lorenzo (Naples), 21
San Marco (Venice), 94
Sannazaro, Jacopo, 40, 51
San Paolo Maggiore (Naples), 22
Santa Chiara (Naples), 22
Sant'Agostino (Naples), 38, 41
Santa Maria de Castello (Genoa), 77
Santa Maria Novella (Florence), 93

Santa Maria Sopra Minerva (Rome), 68, 71, 75, 76
Santori, Giulio Antonio Cardinal, 251–52, 287, 289
Santo Stefano (Venice), 225
San Zanipolo (Venice), 93–95, 225, 232, 233
Sarpi, Paolo, 238
Sasso, Lutio Cardinal, 287, 289
Saturn, 167; planet, 66
Savolino, Albenzio, 17
Savolino, Fraulissa, 14, 15, 102
Savolino, Giulia, 18
Savolino, Laudomia, 18
Savolino, Don Sabatino, 169
Savona, 87, 90
Saxony, 199, 205, 209, 213
Scholasticism, 36, 71, 72, 158, 191; Inquisition rooted in, 256; Platonism and, 41, 46, 71, 93, 126; at San Domenico Maggiore, 37; at Sorbonne, 197
Schoppe, Gaspar, 12, 270, 274
sculpture, see art
Scuola Grande di San Marco (Venice), 94
Sebastian, Saint, 265–66
Seggio di Nilo (Naples), 22
semina rerum (seeds of things), 217
Sentences (Lombard), 48, 49, 71, 73
"Sentences" According to the Mind of Plato, The (Giles of Viterbo), 48–51
Sentis, Giovanni Gabriele de, 237
Sephardim, 53
Seripando, Antonio, 41
Seripando, Girolamo, 32, 33, 40–41, 45, 46, 48, 56, 183
Serveto, Miguel, 97
Servites, 88, 238
Seven Joys of the Virgin, The (devotional poem), 31, 75
Sforza, Francesco, Duke of Milan, 91
Shakespeare, William, 142, 171, 283
Shekinah, 169
Sibyl of Cumae, 134
Sicily, Spanish rule of, 15

Sidney, Philip, 143, 144, 151, 165, 174–77, 179, 181, 184–85
Siena, 142
Silk Road, 170
silva (forest), 47, 48
Silvestri, Matteo, 242, 265
Sixtus IV, Pope, 74, 295n
Sixtus V, Pope, 189, 190, 212–13, 217, 255, 261
Society of Jesus, see Jesuits
Socrates, 36, 79, 111, 182–83, 298n
Sodano, Angelo Cardinal, 7
Solomon, 190; Song of, see Bible, Song of Songs
Solon, 165
Songbook (Petrarch), 178, 183
Song of Circe, The (Bruno), 122, 133–36
"Sonnet in Praise of the Ass" (Bruno), 81, 169
Sophia, 59–60, 167–69, 294n
Sorbonne, 115, 117, 122, 197
sorcery, 118–19, 230–31
Spaccio della bestia tronfante, see Expulsion of the Triumphant Beast, The
Spain, 43, 54, 122, 144, 245; Armada of, 170, 189, 207; colonialism of, 153–54; Columbus's voyages for, 92; court of, dwarfs at, 140; misprint in Index of Forbidden Books in, 279–80; Moorish power in, 73; Naples ruled by, 14–15, 21–23, 26, 28, 29, 31, 53, 59, 82–83
Spanish Inquisition, 29, 31, 53, 82, 251, 295n; arrests and convictions on basis of single accusation by, 23, 75; converted Jews charged by, 74
Speridando, Girolamo, 294n
Spiritual Exercises (Ignatius of Loyola), 253
Spranger, Bartolomäus, 203
squaring the circle, 193, 194, 196
Starry Messenger (Galileo), 113, 280
Stephen, Saint, 266
Stoicism, 21, 103
Summa Against the Gentiles (Aquinas), 71
Summary of Metaphysical Terms (Eglin), 222

Summa theologiae (Aquinas), 121
sun-centered universe, 66, 68, 90, 109, 136, 146, 173
Switzerland, 99, 142, 147, 222
syllogisms, 36, 71
Symposium (Plato), 130, 149–50, 155, 174, 175, 180, 182–84, 298n

Tabriz, 21
Tansillo, Luigi, 15–16, 18, 178–82
Taverna, Ludovico, 237
telescope, invention of, 113, 281
Telesio, Bernardino, 67, 88, 107, 111, 218
Teofilo da Vairano, Fra, 41–46, 56, 57, 65, 79, 149, 191, 270, 277, 294n
theology, 58, 71, 143; *see also* Christian theology
Thirty Years' War, 283
thought problems, 7, 281
Thucydides, 170
Timaeus (Plato), 47, 165
Titian, 94
Toledo, Don Pedro de, 22, 82
"To the Malcontent" (Bruno), 147–48
Tor di Nona prison (Rome), 9–10, 246, 275, 277
Torquemada, Tomás de, 74
torture, juridical, 246
Toulouse, 11, 89, 105–15, 121, 138; massacre of Protestants in, 105; University of, 105, 110, 113, 115, 143
transubstantiation, 221, 257, 259, 260, 272, 273
Trinity, 58, 72–73, 240–41, 259
Triumphant Idiot, The (Bruno), 196–97
Tübingen, University of, 209
Tudor, Mary, 170
Turin, 87, 90
Turks, 23, 224–25, 232, 244; *see also* Ottoman Empire
Two Little Books (Cardano), 91

Ulysses, 50
Underhill, John, 143, 205

universe, 88, 173–74, 190, 214; biography of, 215; Dante's view of, 106; infinite, *see* infinite universe; microstructure of, 207; models of, 68–69, 173; sun-centered, 66, 68, 90, 109, 136, 146, 173
Uraniborg, observatory at, 68
Urban VIII, Pope, 280
Urbino, Duke of, 11
Urey, Harold, 192
Ursula, Saint, 266
Utrecht, 6

Vaio, Francesco, 236
Valedictory Oration (Bruno), 203
Valla, Lorenzo, 161, 162
Vatican, 3–5, 248; Library of, 41, 44; Secret Archive of, 248
Velázquez, Diego, 140
Venetian Inquisition, 73, 94–95, 99, 138, 225–43, 247–49, 264, 270; archives of, 230, 232, 260; arrest of Bruno by, 229, 239; Bruno's confession to, 242–43; Bruno's testimony to, 33, 57–58, 71–72, 87, 90, 94, 96–98, 104–105, 120–21, 225–27, 240–41; corroborating witnesses before, 237–39; extradition to Rome of prisoners of, 239, 244–45; heresy cases of, 232–34; Mocenigo's accusations to, 75–76, 226–29, 232, 237–38, 240, 257–60; prisons of, 44, 60, 229–31, 236, 237, 241–42; procedures of, 230; Protestants and Jews brought before, 234–36, 261
Venice, 32, 75, 79, 91, 93–95, 149, 223–26; Arsenal of, 94, 229, 233, 246; availability of indexed books in, 93; Ducal Palace of, 236–37; extradition of prisoners to Rome from, 244–45; Jews in, 54; New Prisons of, 229–30, 237; plague in, 76; State Archive of, 230, 232, 242; trade routes through, 170; Turks in, 224–25, 232
Venus, 50, 66
vernacular, 23, 42; dialogues in, 147–72,

174, 214; general books on technical subjects in, 88, 90–91; Protestant liturgy and Bible in, 98, 99, 234, 235; sonnets in, 65, 177
Vernacular Sphere, The (Fiorentino), 88
Veronese, Paolo, 95, 225
Verrocchio, Andrea del, 94
Vespucci, Amerigo, 199
vestigia (footprints), 48, 49
Vesuvius, Mount, 18–20
Vikings, 95
Virgil, 48, 126, 169, 214, 215
Virgin Mary, 31, 161; banishment of pictures of, 30, 31
Visconti, Maximiliano, 231
Vita, Fra Domenico, 71, 73, 75, 114
Vitruvius, 282
Vitus, Saint, 205
Voët, Gilbert, 213
Vulgate Bible, 55, 99, 101

Waldensians, 78, 234
Walker, D. P., 5
Walsingham, Frances, 177

Walsingham, Francis, 137, 139–40, 177, 189, 200
Warburg Institute, 5
Waterloo, Battle of, 248
Wheel of Fortune, 84
Whitefriars, 141
Why Is Nothing Known (Sánchez), 113
Wiesbaden, 198, 199
witchcraft, 74, 118, 230
Wittenberg, 199–20, 206, 209, 236; University of, 198, 200–202, 204–205, 226
Wolfenbüttel, 211, 213
Worlde of Wordes, A (Florio), 142, 144
World War II, 75

Yates, Frances, 5–6, 301n
Yunus, Ibn, 68, 109

Zaratan, Zuane, 231
Zaratine, Cathe, 230
Zick, Peter, 206
Zurich, 121, 221–22, 224

24123406R00220

Made in the USA
San Bernardino, CA
12 September 2015